THE SOVIET UNION AND THE STRUGGLE FOR COLLECTIVE SECURITY IN EUROPE, 1933–39

Jonathan Haslam
Lecturer in Soviet Diplomatic History
University of Birmingham

MACMILLAN

in association with the
Centre for Russian and
East European Studies
University of Birmingham

First published 1984 by
THE MACMILLAN PRESS LTD
London and Basingstoke
Companies and representatives throughout the world

Typeset by
Wessex Typesetters Ltd
Frome, Somerset

Printed in Hong Kong

British Library Cataloguing in Publication Data
Haslam, Jonathan
The Soviet Union and the struggle for collective security in Europe, 1933–39.—(Studies in Soviet history and society)
1. Soviet Union—Foreign relations—1917–1945
I. Title II. Series
327.4 DK266.A3
ISBN 0–333–30050–5

BI 0567403 4

THE SOVIET UNION AND THE STRUGGLE FOR COLLECTIVE SECURITY IN EUROPE, 1933–39

STUDIES IN SOVIET HISTORY AND SOCIETY
General Editor: R. W. Davies

The series consists of works by members or associates of the inter-disciplinary Centre for Russian and East European Studies of the University of Birmingham, England. Special interests of the Centre include Soviet economic and social history, contemporary Soviet economics and planning, science and technology, sociology and education.

Gregory D. Andrusz
HOUSING AND URBAN DEVELOPMENT IN THE USSR

John Barber
SOVIET HISTORIANS IN CRISIS, 1928–1932

Philip Hanson
TRADE AND TECHNOLOGY IN SOVIET–WESTERN RELATIONS

Jonathan Haslam
SOVIET FOREIGN POLICY, 1930–33

THE SOVIET UNION AND THE STRUGGLE FOR COLLECTIVE SECURITY IN EUROPE, 1933–39

Peter Kneen
SOVIET SCIENTISTS AND THE STATE

Nicholas Lampert
THE TECHNICAL INTELLIGENTSIA AND THE SOVIET STATE

Robert Lewis
SCIENCE AND INDUSTRIALISATION IN THE USSR

Neil Malcolm
SOVIET POLITICAL SCIENTISTS AND AMERICAN POLITICS

David Mandel
THE PETROGRAD WORKERS AND THE FALL OF THE OLD REGIME

THE PETROGRAD WORKERS AND THE SOVIET SEIZURE OF POWER

Roger Skurski
SOVIET MARKETING AND ECONOMIC DEVELOPMENT

J. N. Westwood
SOVIET LOCOMOTIVE TECHNOLOGY DURING INDUSTRIALISATION, 1928–1952

In memory of E. H. Carr

Contents

Preface

This is the second of four volumes outlining the course of Soviet foreign policy from 1930 to 1941. The first volume, *Soviet Foreign Policy, 1930–33: the Impact of the Depression* (London, 1983), dealt with Soviet foreign relations East and West. This, the second, volume covers the struggle for collective security in Europe from 1933 to 1939. Both Turkey and the United States have been relegated to volume three: *The Soviet Union and the Threat from the East, 1933–41*. The final volume will deal with Europe alone: *Soviet Foreign Policy, 1939–41: Isolation and Expansion*.

As in the previous work, no attempt has been made to deal with the history of the Comintern in any depth. E. H. Carr's *The Twilight of Comintern, 1930–1935* (London, 1982) has made any such effort unnecessary for the first half of the period; his history of the Comintern's involvement in the Spanish civil war should go some way to filling the rest of the gap. The Comintern has nonetheless intermittently crept into the story as an additional arm of Soviet foreign policy.

Wherever possible, primary sources have provided the raw material for my work, much of it thankfully published by the various Powers. The Russians themselves still shrug their shoulders when the word "archives" is mentioned – "*vse opublikovano*" ("everything has been published") the deputy head of the archive at the Soviet Foreign Ministry assured me! – but few secrets remain when one can consult the archives of the other major Powers, and the Soviet Government has itself published considerable quantities of diplomatic correspondence which are of inestimable value, though one should always use the material in conjunction with an analysis of the Soviet press.

Any reader familiar with the history of international relations will be aware that no work of this kind can be produced without digesting the rich fruits of other people's labour; but to acknowledge every item consumed in the course of many years would make little sense. I have therefore limited the bibliography to those items which were vital to the genesis of this work.

A number of people and institutions have helped me. A debt of gratitude is thus owed to the following: the British Academy for funds which financed research in Italy and the French Government which financed research in Paris; Jenny Brine (librarian at CREES, Birmingham University) for endless assistance; Angela Raspin (British Library of Political and Economic Sciences, LSE); the staffs of the British Library (including Colindale), the BDIC (Nanterre), Cambridge University Library, the Marx Memorial Library, the Modern Records Centre (Warwick University), the Institute of the History of the USSR Library in the Soviet Academy of Sciences (Moscow), the Italian Foreign Ministry archive (Rome), the Public Record Office (Kew), Dr Ben Benedikz (Birmingham University Library), Inter-Library Loans (Birmingham University Library), Mr Symington (Foreign Office Library and Records) and Ms G. Porter (Library, GEC Turbine Generators Ltd) for access to material in their care; to Dr S. Tupper, and Professor D. C. Watt (LSE), for advice on reading matter; to Dr V. Sipols (head of the Sector of the History of Soviet Foreign Policy, Institute of History of the USSR, Academy of Sciences, Moscow), K. Shirinya (history of the Comintern project, Institute of Marxism-Leninism, Moscow), and Z. Sheinis (Progress Publishers) for discussing various issues with me; and, finally, a great deal is owed to Professor R. W. Davies at the University of Birmingham for so conscientiously fulfilling his role as editor and for providing the kind of constant moral support one needs in this field of study.

University of Birmingham JONATHAN HASLAM

List of Abbreviations and Acronyms

AA	*Auswärtiges Amt* (German Foreign Ministry)
ASD	*Archivio Storico Diplomatico* (Diplomatic History Archives)
Burobin Byuro po obsluzhovaniyu inostrantsev NKID SSSR	(Service Bureau for Foreigners, NKID, USSR)
CC	Central Committee of the All-Union Communist Party (Bolshevik)
CNT	*Confederación Nacional del Trabajo* (National Confederation of Labour)
CPC	Czech Communist Party
DBFP	*Documents on British Foreign Policy*
DDF	*Documents Diplomatiques Français* (French Diplomatic Documents)
DDI	*Documenti Diplomatici Italiani* (Italian Diplomatic Documents)
DGFP	*Documents on German Foreign Policy*
DVP SSSR	*Dokumenty Vneshnei Politiki SSSR* (Documents on the Foreign Policy of the USSR)
FAI	*Federación Anarquista Ibérica* (Iberian Anarchist Federation)
FO	*Foreign Office*
FRUS	*Foreign Relations of the United States*
INO	*Inostrannyi Otdel* (Foreign Department)
INOTASS	*Inostrannyi Otdel Telegrafnogo Agentstva Sovetskogo Soyuza* (Foreign Department of the Telegraphic Agency of the Soviet Union)
KPD	*Kommunistische Partei Deutschlands* (German Communist Party)

MOPR	*Mezhdunarodnaya Organizatsiya Pomoshchi Bor'tsam Revolyutsii* (International Organisation for Aid to Revolutionary Fighters)
NKID/ Narkomindel	*Narodnyi Komissariat Inostrannykh Del* (People's Commissariat of Foreign Affairs)
NC	Neville Chamberlain
NKVD	*Narodnyi Komissariat Vnutrennykh Del* (People's Commissariat of Internal Affairs)
NSDAP	*National Sozialistische Deutsche Arbeiter Partei* (National Socialist German Workers' Party)
OGPU	*Ob''edinennoe Gosudarstvennoe Politicheskoe Upravleniye* (Unified State Political Administration)
PCE	*Partido Comunista de España* (Spanish Communist Party)
PCF	*Parti Communiste Français* (French Communist Party)
PCI	*Partito Comunista Italiano* (Italian Communist Party)
Polpred	*Polnomochnyi Predstavitel'* (Plenipotentiary)
POUM	*Partido Obrero de Unificación Marxista* (Marxist Unity Workers' Party)
PSUC	*Partit Socialista Unificat de Catalunya*
RSFSR	*Rossiskaya Sovetskaya Federativnaya Sotsialisticheskaya Respublika* (Russian Soviet Federative Socialist Republic)
SFIO	*Section Française de l'Internationale Ouvrière* (French Section of the Labour International)
TASS	*Telegrafnoe Agentstvo Sovetskogo Soyuza* (Telegraphic Agency of the Soviet Union)

1 The Struggle for Collective Security, 1933–39

Hitler's unexpected accession to power in Germany at the beginning of 1933 had by the end of that eventful year brought about a dramatic volte-face in the direction of Soviet foreign policy, ushering in the most pro-Western period Moscow has ever seen; this was the Litvinov era of Soviet diplomacy.

The new German Government threatened the peace of Europe and thereby the security of the USSR. Peace was a vital precondition to industrialisation under Stalin. The first five-year plan had nominally been completed in four years (1929–32), the USSR had made enormous strides towards catching up with the West. But there was still a long way to go; not until 1934 did the progress made in industrialisation begin to show results in terms of military power and, even then, troubles with transportation continued to bedevil the ability of the Russians to mobilise for war from 1935 to 1938. The USSR was therefore growing in stature but still needed time for further development. The Soviet response to the threat of war was understandable. From vociferous opposition to the post-war territorial status quo, tempered only by native caution – *quieta non movere* – the Russians abruptly shifted to dynamic support for the much despised Versailles settlement. They were desperate for stability and security in an uncertain and now volatile world – an irony for a regime whose initial *raison d'être* had been international revolution. The search for peace found form in the pursuit of collective security. Its inspiration and its most resolute and indefatigable advocate was People's Commissar of Foreign Affairs Maxim Litvinov, a bull of a man who had long held Stalin's confidence.[1]

Litvinov argued with great vigour that the USSR could not successfully isolate itself from the conflicts which arose within the capitalist camp. "One can scarcely doubt that, given current international relations, no war, on any continent whatever . . .

can be localised, and that practically no country can be assured that it will not be drawn into a war which it has not started. The Soviet Union," he concluded, "is therefore interested not only in preserving its own peaceful relations with other states, but also in the preservation of universal peace."[2] Convinced that further pursuit of disarmament would be futile,[3] and that non-aggression pacts – valuable as a means of testing intent – were insufficient protection in the face of states that resolutely refused to sign them, Litvinov pressed for "wider measures for the maintenance of universal peace".[4] The USSR thus sought to enmesh expansionist Germany in a web of multilateral guarantees and, failing this, the creation of an alliance system to contain Hitler's wild ambitions; entry into the League of Nations was accordingly accepted as a means to this end. Aggression by Germany would hopefully result in collective sanctions by the world community. Litvinov believed that only by committing the USSR to the defence of others, could the Russians assure themselves of allies in the event of attack; the USSR thus had to step out into the world. The story of Soviet foreign policy in these years of crisis is essentially the story of struggle for collective security, epitomised in the person of Litvinov.

The policy he evolved was a novel response to novel circumstances. It necessarily cut across the grain of foreign policy since Lenin; as a result it splintered opinion within the regime, it aroused strong misgivings, and it fed existing animosity towards Litvinov the man. "Litvinov does not possess Chicherin's brilliance", some said; "he is always the dull realist", others opined.[5] Traditionally the Soviet regime had sought security through the exploitation of frictions and antagonisms within the capitalist camp, a policy which presupposed freedom of manoeuvre *vis-à-vis* the other Powers, and which certainly precluded membership of any entangling alliance. This undifferentiated approach to the capitalist world was based on established Marxist theory reinforced by traditional Leninist practice. Aside from an idiosyncratic and half-hearted flirtation with the Allies early in 1918 when negotiations at Brest-Litovsk had run aground, the Soviet regime had steadfastly held firm against any military commitment to one group of capitalist Powers rivalled by others. Capitalism bred wars; alliances precipitated them – this was the thinking which underlay the repeated rejection of external security obligations. The alignment with Weimar Germany established at Rapallo in 1922 was no exception to the rule; it was viewed purely as a means of driving a wedge between the capitalist Great Powers: the perfect example of applying the tactic of exploiting inter-imperialist contradictions to Soviet advantage, without incurring all the disadvantages that an open alliance would entail. The German orientation was nonetheless something of a tradition in Soviet foreign policy. It was, after all, Lenin's creation. And, as so often happens, individuals who have invested their efforts to further policies which originated in pure expediency, with time come to see these policies as fixed and immutable rather than as tactics initially devised to meet particular circumstances.

The attachment to Rapallo ran deep, even after Hitler had felled its trunk and uprooted it from the earth. During a trip to the Ukraine in the late spring of 1935, counsellor Gustav Hilger of the German embassy in Moscow was surprised at the Germanophile views expressed openly by local officials:

> While I was staying in Kiev, the German consul there gave a reception in my honor, and a number of high Soviet functionaries accepted the invitation. Among them was Bredenko, a local liaison officer from the Foreign Commissariat; Vasilenko, the chairman of the Kiev Regional Executive Committee; Kattel, the Ukrainian people's Commissar for foreign trade; Pevzner, the president of the Ukrainian state bank; Palladin, the secretary of the Ukrainian Academy of Sciences; and Grushevsky, the vice commissar of agriculture. During a conversation I had with Vasilenko and Pevzner, both officials called the state of German–Soviet relations highly unnatural. Did not Germany realize that Russia had no evil intentions against her? And, on the other hand, did not Germany enjoy the highest esteem among all sections of the Soviet population? Vasilenko told me that some workers had come to him not long ago to tell him that they could not understand the current party line concerning Germany. After all, Germany was only trying to liberate herself from the oppressive fetters of Versailles. But instead of aiding her to do so, the Soviet government was making a pact with Germany's oppressors. In short, said Vasilenko, Litvinov's policy does not convince the masses, and history will soon pass over Litvinov.[6]

Opposition to Litvinov and to alliances with the more pacific Powers came also from the fundamentalist element within the Soviet Communist Party, those who also opposed the Comintern's counterpart to collective security: the Popular Front.[7] But Stalin, like Litvinov, was indifferent to the regime's international revolutionary heritage. Turning disdainfully from the hopes of successful revolution abroad to which others still clung, Stalin made domestic economic construction the alfa and omega of the regime's aims. He was only too willing to deny any interest in the goal which arch-rival Trotsky held so dear. In reply to insistent questioning from the US newspaper magnate, Howard, in March 1936, Stalin dismissed assertions that the USSR sought world revolution, as "the fruit of a misunderstanding".[8] Under Stalin the Russians failed to respond even to Hitler's ruthless suppression of the aspirant German Communist Party. The argument deployed to justify such callous neglect draped crude realpolitik in the finery of revolutionary optimism:

> The more successes – even including successes bought with sacrifices – Soviet diplomacy achieves, the more quickly will it be possible to hand over Hitler's and Mussolini's frock coats and silk hats to the revolutionary museum, to the Revolutionary Tribunal.[9]

But revolutionary sentiment still sent up the occasional flame from the smouldering ashes. It was a factor Stalin had to contend with and which, despite the terror of 1937–39, he never entirely succeeded in liquidating. A reminder that this was so would spring up in the most unexpected circumstances. In July 1935 US ambassador Bullitt wrote to Secretary of State Hull from Moscow:

> a few evenings ago I said to Karl Radek that I hoped his communist friends at the meeting of the Third International [the Comintern's seventh congress] would not behave in such a way as to break Litvinov's pledge to the President and make the continuance of diplomatic relations between our countries impossible. Radek leaped to his feet with the most violent anger and shouted. "We have lived without the United States in the past and we can continue to live without the United States in the future and we shall never permit you or anyone else to dictate to us what we shall do in Moscow."[10]

As the quotation suggests, the remnants of revolutionary fervour found a natural home in intimate and unholy alliance with traditional nationalist sentiment. Litvinov's policy flattered national pride in one sense; the arrival of French Premier Laval in Moscow after the signature a treaty of alliance in 1935 enhanced the USSR's prestige, as did the Commissar's celebrated speeches at the League of Nations. But then Litvinov's policy also led to innumerable humiliations, and the commitments incurred were viewed with deep suspicion by the less cosmopolitan, the more isolationist element. And this was an element resurgent. With the inexorable progress of Soviet industrialisation, the small islands of cosmopolitan influence were inundated by the more ignorant and isolationist masses from Russia's vast hinterland.

The reassertion of old-style nationalism – the reintroduction of the term *rodina* (motherland) was a telling symbol of this reversion to the past – reinforced a tendency already latent in Bolshevik thought, to see the rest of the world as an undifferentiated and uniformly hostile mass. An age-old xenophobia resulting from the precariousness of Russia's position on an open plain besieged on all sides, and later aggravated by a chronic sense of backwardness *vis-à-vis* the West, fostered Soviet consciousness of being a world apart. This was the natural constituency of men such as Zhdanov or Molotov, rather than Litvinov or Maisky. Litvinov was also a Jew. Much of the Narkomindel, his Commissariat, was staffed by Jews. The Jews were the most cosmopolitan element in old Russia; and cosmopolitanism of any kind sat uneasily with the cult of the motherland which sanctified Socialism in One Country. The antagonism Litvinov encountered was thus a curious amalgam of Bolshevik fundamentalism of the type expressed by Radek, and Great Russian nationalism – a potent concoction which only a common dread of Hitler could dilute, though by no means counteract, through the greater part of the thirties.

While the drama was in progress, Stalin sat at the back of the stalls engaged in other, more congenial as well as more pressing preoccupations, occasionally stirring himself to direct action on stage or, at a whim, have most of the cast removed and replaced when the moment seemed appropriate; Litvinov was acting director, but only on Stalin's sufferance. The struggle for collective security had to be fought at home as well as abroad.

2 The End of Rapallo, 1933

News of Hitler's appointment as Chancellor of Germany on the 30 January 1933 came as an unpleasant surprise to the Russians as to almost everyone else in Europe.[1] The widespread assumption in Moscow and abroad that the Nazis were a spent force had proved unfounded.[2] This false assumption – apparently borne out by the fall in the Nazi vote at the elections in the autumn of 1932 – had hitherto silenced a fundamental division of opinion as to whether Hitler's accession to power would present a serious threat to Soviet interests. These differences resurfaced. After the initial shock, registered by the German embassy in Moscow, only a minority in the Soviet capital saw what Hitler really portended.

There could be no dispute about Hitler's views on the Soviet Union. In *Mein Kampf*, he had insisted that Germany obtain living-space in the East, above all at the expense of the USSR.[3] But it was not easy to see how he could possibly implement such wild ambitions. Furthermore, as a former member of the German embassy in Moscow recalls: "For many weeks in the spring of 1933 the actual policy of the Hitler regime toward the Soviet Union was vague, hesitating and quite ambiguous. . . . Several times during the spring of 1933 Hitler made public declarations in which he affirmed that German policy toward the Soviet Union remained unchallenged. In Nazi party circles, and in the party press, such statements were rationalised by the argument that healthy political relations between Germany and the Soviet state had become possible only . . . after the complete elimination of the Communist movement from German politics. The actual reason for Hitler's attempt to soothe the Kremlin's mind was that a clear line toward Soviet Russia had not yet been developed."[4]

Ironically it was von Papen who initially worried the Russians most. As Chancellor in the summer of 1932 he had proposed to France an entente directed against the USSR.[5] Just as his downfall later that year elicited an audible sigh of relief in Moscow, so his unexpected return to power as Vice-Chancellor (and Premier of Prussia) in January 1933 naturally fed Soviet fears; it was a common assumption at the time that Hitler was the horse and Papen the rider. It was no accident that in conversation with ambassador Dirksen in Moscow towards the end of February 1933, Deputy Commissar of Foreign Affairs Nikolai Krestinsky, a known advocate of Rapallo, expressed anxiety at the prospect of a Franco-German alliance.[6] Such worries were also expressed by Commissar of Foreign Affairs Litvinov, himself no enthusiast for Rapallo and a man more aware than most of the dangers Hitler really represented. At the world disarmament conference – still leading a twilight existence at Geneva – on the 6 February the Commissar had risked German hostility in showing some sympathy for French insistence on the achievement of security guarantees prior to the implementation of disarmament measures,[7] a move justified by the haste with which the French ratified their non-aggression pact with the USSR; notes were exchanged on the 15 February. Litvinov's speech represented a reversal of existing policy, and he defended this when challenged by Neurath on the 1 March.

It was at this encounter with the German Foreign Minister that Litvinov reiterated the same anxieties expressed by Krestinsky with respect to the possibility of a Franco-German *entente*, adding his concern that the suppression of Communists within Germany was being paralleled by an anti-Soviet foreign policy. "Naturally," Litvinov warned Neurath, "we have no intention of altering our relations with Germany, but we certainly cannot look kindly upon the prospect of an anti-Soviet bloc involving Germany and France. Until now it appeared possible to forestall such a bloc by exerting pressure on Berlin, but if this, however, turns out to be insufficient, we will of course not hesitate to exert pressure on Paris."[8] This represented the first unequivocal warning to Germany that the Soviet Union might swop partners and ditch the Rapallo relationship for the next best alternative. The difference in tone and emphasis between Litvinov and Krestinsky reflected more than personal prejudice; the Soviet leadership and the apparatus at its command were divided as to how to proceed. Stalin, cautious as ever and preoccupied with the disaster of famine and its unsettling effect on his own supremacy, perched awkwardly on top of the fence.

Doubts as to the true direction German foreign policy would take under Hitler were reflected in the circumspect treatment of

German affairs in the Soviet press; the Narkomindel's German language weekly, *Moskauer Rundschau* – a relic of the Rapallo era – actually observed total silence on the drama unfolding in Germany until finally Hitler's anti-Soviet outbursts at the Berlin Sportpalast early in March 1933 provoked a vigorous response in the Russian press, which also found expression in the *Rundschau*.[9] Doubts about Hitler's foreign policy were not matched by doubts about his domestic policies. "The new Fascist Government", the Comintern journal *Kommunisticheskii Internatsional* warned, "*is a government of civil war against the toiling masses* to save capitalist Germany from the coming revolution. *The destruction of German Bolshevism and the struggle against world Bolshevism – this is the fundamental task which the leaders of this government are formulating for themselves*". It is significant, however, that in referring to Hitler's foreign policy, the journal stressed the dangers Hitler represented to the Versailles Powers who banked on the maintenance of the territorial status quo, rather than the USSR, originally excluded from and thus hostile to the Paris peace settlement (1919). The new regime was thus described as "*a government for the preparation of a revanchist war by German imperialism against Poland and France and of provocations against the USSR*".[10] Hitler talked vaguely of protecting the German nation's "vital rights" and of seeking "the reconquest of their freedom", but he also promised that the country "must not and will not sink into anarchistic Communism".[11] On the 2 February 1933 the KPD (German Communist Party) was henceforth forbidden the right to open-air demonstrations, and the Party headquarters, Liebknecht House, was occupied and systematically ransacked by police; the Reichstag fire on the 27 February then set the stage for the final suppression of the KPD.[12] As a consequence an unsigned article appeared on the front page of *Pravda* acidly referring to the Hitler regime as "Jesters on the Throne", but this reflected little more than an outburst of hurt indignation. There had been no plans for a KPD uprising – everyone was anxiously awaiting the elections scheduled for early March – and there was no question of attacking Rapallo. "*It is no secret to anyone that the only state with no hostile feelings towards Germany is the USSR. Everyone knows this*", the article emphasised; but, it added, the "*anti-Soviet outbursts*" of the Nazis were an attempt to ruin relations with the only friend of the German nation.[13]

Soviet indifference to the suppression of the KPD, the second largest Communist Party in Europe and hitherto the sole repository of any realistic hope of revolution on the continent, was at the very least a source of considerable embarrassment. It was made easier to accept only when swallowed with a strong dose of self-deception about the supposed weakness of the Nazis in comparison with the organised working-class – a belief difficult to dispel even after the near total suppression of the KPD. "Hitler isn't Mussolini; Germany isn't Italy; regardless of German apathy and the flabbiness of the workers' parties, the German proletariat possesses a strength which cannot but manifest itself", were the words of one diplomat at the Soviet embassy in Berlin, an opinion reportedly also expressed by Stalin.[14] Even Litvinov – a man not usually given to outbursts of revolutionary fervour – reacted to Hitler's "ruthless reckoning"[15] by "smiling" and remarking that "Hitler isn't Mussolini";[16] furthermore, even those on the receiving end of Hitler's repression, former members of the Rot-Front-Kämpferbund said: "Tell the comrades in Moscow: Germany is not Bulgaria."[17]

This was purely wishful thinking. Soviet aloofness was hard to sustain indefinitely. When the Italian ambassador, an informed observer of the Soviet scene, encountered a representative (unnamed) of the Soviet Communist Party, he remembered Russian sang-froid with respect to Mussolini's persecution of the PCI (Italian Communist Party) and was therefore most surprised by the response he elicited when reassuring his interlocutor about Hitler's good intentions towards the USSR:

> You are indubitably right ... but even if the German Government avoids actions which are too overtly anti-Soviet, how are we to remain impassive while millions of German Communists are being persecuted?
>
> We have, of course, been well aware that world revolution was no longer an immediate possibility, but it doesn't mean that there can be no reaction to the extermination of the strongest Communist Party which exists in the world outside Russia.
>
> If things continue in this way even after the elections, it is impossible to believe that it will not leave its mark on political relations between the two countries.[18]

Yet even the Comintern made little effort to mobilise solidarity with the persecuted KPD. A conference of Socialist parties meeting in Paris on the 4–5 February 1933[19] sent telegrams to the Socialist and Communist Internationals urging a conference to plan common action to resist Hitler and Fascism in general: "Our divisions enfeeble us; our forces are spent in mutual struggle instead of being directed at the common enemy; we are driven further apart although as class-conscious workers our interests are the same", they pleaded – a plea that was to remain tragically timely for many months.[20] On the 13 February French, German and Polish Communist leaders issued a joint communiqué to the socialists offering a united front against Fascism.[21] Five days later the Second International offered the Comintern a kind of non-aggression agreement, and not until the 5 March did the Comintern finally appear with a directive to all sections "to establish a united fighting front with the Social Democratic working masses through the Social Democratic parties".[22] Yet when the Second International responded with the suggestion of talks at executive committee level, Moscow failed to pursue it, despite the fact that the Czech, French and British Communist leaders urged acceptance of the offer.[23] Soviet reticence appears to have been due to a number of factors which converged: the sectarian spirit deeply embedded since the disillusionment of the twenties and the sixth Comintern congress of 1928, the support given Hitler's foreign policy by socialist deputies in the Reichstag, continued concern on the part of the French socialists to improve relations with Germany, and, last but not least, traces of the same caution *vis-à-vis* Berlin which had hitherto overshadowed Soviet diplomacy.

Moscow's hesitancy was closely related to two interconnected factors which promised to paralyse Soviet foreign policy completely. The famine that struck the USSR in 1932 threatened to bring the country to its knees; the consequent turmoil distracted and weakened already overburdened armed forces. Their defences seriously undermined, the Russians faced a growing danger of war in the Far East from aggressive Japan. The more pessimistic and anti-Western element in Moscow believed that the Western Powers, in particular the Anglo-Saxon countries, were working to bring such a war about. In a letter to the Politburo on the 3 March 1933, Deputy Commissar of Foreign Affairs for the East Leo Karakhan warned: "It seems to me that there can be no two ways about it: the most ideal way out of the crisis and of the situation created in the Far East for the USA and for the other [sic] European Powers, would be a war between the USSR and Japan. They will draw and push us into one." He went on to argue that not only was war possible, but the USA, Britain, France and others would use the League of Nations to mobilise world opinion against the USSR. He then drew this bleak conclusion: "In the event of war all existing resolutions, combinations of Powers, the anti-Japanese front – all this will go to the devil and one problem alone will remain: how to make use of the war that has arisen to extricate themselves from the crisis and from the contradictions in the capitalist world at our expense."[24] This was certainly not the language Litvinov used; the whole thrust of his policy was in the direction of greater involvement with the Anglo-Saxon Powers, as the events of the next few years so clearly demonstrated. Karakhan represented a strand of opinion which the Commissar had increasingly displaced since Chicherin's *de facto* retirement in 1928. It is probable that Karakhan was arguing against those like Litvinov who considered Rapallo a lost cause.

Ultimately, and despite the opposition aroused in Moscow at the mention of any dramatic change, it was growing German hostility that drove the USSR in a direction that many mistrusted. It was not merely the KPD that was under attack in Germany, so was every Soviet institution in the country, official and semi-official, including business premises (Germany was the USSR's main trading partner), trade missions and consulates. During the course of 1933 the Soviet Government issued no less than 217 notes of protest in response to over 39 arrests of Soviet citizens, 69 raids on Soviet property and other such provocative acts.[25] "Where is Germany Going?" asked a bewildered Karl Radek, in an article in *Izvestiya* on the 22 March 1933.[26] And the Russians now increasingly threatened the Germans with retaliatory action. It was military co-operation that had bound the two countries together for so long. It was therefore logical that the Russians should react to growing German hostility by threatening to end such collaboration. On the 3 April Krestinsky met Hartmann, the German military attaché, enumerated acts of hostility on the part of the German regime, and stated that if the German Government wanted to maintain friendly relations with the USSR, it would have to "immediately put an end to all these excesses with an iron hand. The government has sufficient strength to do this; all that is required is sufficient will to do so. If the government does not intervene and the outrages in relation to the USSR continue, then I think Mr Hartmann will understand that his work here would be seriously hindered. Through his Minister he must point out to the government the difficulties arising from the current situation and create in Germany a favourable rear for his work in Moscow".[27] Then on the 28 April polpred Leo Khinchuk finally obtained an audience with Hitler. He read out to him a statement prepared beforehand, acknowledging the reassurances given repeatedly by Neurath, and by the Chancellor himself in his speech to the Reichstag on the 23 March, but pointed out that "the belief of my Government in the future of our mutual relations has often in recent times been subjected to severe trials as a consequence of the nature of the activities of official and unofficial government organs throughout Germany in relation to the interests of the USSR". Khinchuk demanded an end to such incidents, and, in a circumlocutious phrase, warned that their repetition would leave "people" incapable of believing that "former relations have been maintained" between Germany and the USSR. Amongst other measures, he called for the ratification of the protocol extending the life of the Berlin treaty[28] "without delay".[29]

Having delivered the statement verbally, Khinchuk then had to listen poker-faced to Hitler's disparaging dismissal of the Nazis' enemies as "extremely weak". "He had", Khinchuk recorded, "overestimated the strength and significance of the Communist Party and Social-Democracy. They had turned out not to be men. Had he, for instance, headed the Communist Party or Social-Democracy, then things would have been very different." Hitler then turned to foreign policy matters. "He said that independently of the differences in the Weltanschauung of the two countries, they are tied by mutual interests and this bond is of a long-term nature. This is true both in the economic and political field, because they have one and the same difficulties and enemies. The Soviets, for example, have to worry about their western frontier, Germany has to worry about its eastern frontier [a transparent reference to their common interest *vis-à-vis* Poland]. Germany has a serious economic situation, but that of the Soviets is also problematic." Hitler also said that the Berlin protocol would be ratified in the near future; but this was as far as he would go in granting concessions listed by Khinchuk in his statement.[30] The démarche brought one concrete result: on the 5 May the Germans finally ratified the Berlin protocol.[31]

The ratification of the protocol was too little and came too late. The Soviet leadership was not about to risk everything on such an uncertain guarantee. The incidents Khinchuk complained of continued with monotonous regularity. There were good reasons to build bridges with Germany's natural enemies, particularly Poland, the best endowed heir of the Versailles settlement, the Power with most to lose from its revision. Having mended fences with the USSR in August 1932 by signing a non-aggression pact,[32] the Poles were reluctant to choose between close association with revolutionary Russia or revanchist Germany, and some still hoped to profit by the weakening of Soviet defences in a Russo-Japanese war. Just as many in Moscow clung to illusions about Hitler's chances of success, so there were also large numbers in Poland who thought that "Hitler will not be able to dominate the aspirations he has evoked, that he will have to grapple with immense difficulties, that the struggle against Communism will absorb him." The improbable hope was that these two forces – Fascism and Communism – would exhaust one another in combat. As the French ambassador in Warsaw reported: "Of course no one denies that the danger subsists and that the future remains bleak, above all should Hitler succeed in reorganising Germany, but those I talk to think the danger is not immediate, that time is working as much on Poland's side . . . as on that of its powerful neighbour. This opinion", Laroche added, "corresponds totally to that of Marshal Pilsudski [Poland's head of state] who, as your Excellency knows, does not believe in an immediate danger from Hitler."[33] The precautionary measures taken by the Polish military – on the 6 March 1933 the garrison at Westerplatte was dramatically reinforced[34] – were largely designed to meet the fears of the opposition; General Sikorski, formerly President of the Council and War Minister, was worried, but more about Hugenberg, the leader of the German National Party and Minister of the Economy, than about Hitler himself, whom he considered a mere demagogue.[35] When Poland's Foreign Minister, Colonel Beck, addressed the Sejm's foreign affairs committee in mid-February, he did so, on Pilsudski's advice, in such a way as to play down the German menace.[36] Initially, therefore, there was little prospect of a Russo-Polish entente at German expense. But the Italian proposal of a Four Power Pact, involving only Britain, France, Germany and Italy, not merely threw the Russians into near panic – more of this below – it also intensified feelings in Warsaw that the French were deserting their allies, thereby opening the door to German expansionism eastwards. This had a double effect on Polish policy. It drove the Poles to seek further reassurance from Moscow, and it prompted Pilsudski to seek a modus vivendi with Hitler which would release him from dependence on so unreliable an ally. But whereas the rapprochement with the Russians was to take place in a blaze of publicity – to impress Berlin – negotiations with Hitler were conducted in the strictest secrecy.[37] In this elaborate game, the USSR played the unknowing and ultimately humiliating role of pawn, subsequent awareness of which did nothing but harm to Polish–Soviet relations.

Ignorant of Polish moves towards Berlin which began in early April 1933, the Russians debated the feasibility of a rapprochement with Poland.[38] The anxieties which did arise, particularly concerning longstanding Polish ambitions *vis-à-vis* the Baltic states, were hastily suppressed while Moscow feared war from Japan and the danger of a Polish–German axis simultaneously. The path towards an understanding between Poland and the USSR was paved by the timely arrival of Colonel Miedziński, chief editor of the semi-official *Gazeta Polska*, on a visit to Moscow from the 30 April to the 3 May 1933, as Pilsudski's personal envoy. The task assigned him was merely "to assure the Bolsheviks that there was no way Poland would ally with the Germans in any kind of aggressive action against the Soviet Union".[39] He was certainly well-received, particularly by fellow Pole Karl Radek, a figure familiar to Polish diplomats in Moscow.[40] At around this time, after several years' atonement for associating with Trotsky in opposition, Radek was taken under Stalin's wing and put in charge of foreign affairs in his personal secretariat;[41] it was characteristic of Stalin to keep open as many channels as possible, not merely to diffuse the responsibilities he delegated, but also to ensure that sources of information were not constricted by bureaucratic procedure, or malign influences.[42] Radek had undertaken unofficial missions abroad for Lenin, though Lenin had grave doubts about Radek's ability as a diplomat.[43] Radek often indulged in intrigue for its own sake; the pre-revolutionary conspirator by necessity, he became the post-revolutionary conspirator through force of habit. Eventually Stalin, too, tired of his ways, but more of that later.

Hitherto the Soviet leadership had resisted any moves which could be interpreted as contributing to the destruction of Rapallo; anti-Fascist sympathies had been sternly checked. Miedziński's visit shifted that delicate balance in favour of action. Ironically, only five days after Hitler finally conceded ratification of the Berlin protocol, *Pravda* appeared on the 10 May with an article by Radek entitled "The Revision of the Versailles Treaty"; this was a *ballon d'essai*. The fact that it was signed rather than unsigned, and that it appeared in *Pravda*, the party newspaper, rather than *Izvestiya*, the governmental organ, showed that the opinions expressed were not yet official policy, with the implication that they would become so if the Germans did not pull themselves sharply into line.[44] But this did not make it any the less provocative. The Russians had embarked on this new trail because they were desperate for peace. By seeking to revise the Versailles settlement, the Germans threatened to drag Europe, and ultimately the USSR, into a disastrous war; few in Moscow, if any, still believed a war would herald new revolutions, none with any responsibility was prepared to take that risk:

> *The very fact that the revision of the Versailles treaties is tied up with the victory of Fascism demonstrates the extent to which this revision could be considered as in the national interests* of nations recognised by the Fascists as 'inferior'.
>
> The road towards the revision of the predatory and agonising Versailles peace goes by way of *a new world war* . . .
>
> . . . As a consequence of its attitude towards imperialism, towards the self-determination of nations and imperialist wars, *the international proletariat – the enemy of the Versailles peace – cannot be on the side of those imperialist forces which seek to bring about a new division of the world in the conflagration of a new imperialist war.*[45]

The manner of its publication indicated that all hope had not been lost of reviving Rapallo, but that the initiative was now up to the Germans. Litvinov pressed on with the rapprochement he favoured, with France and its allies, and although he continued as ever to talk about this as merely a means of hindering a Franco-German entente "at Soviet expense",[46] there was evidently more to it than that; as Radek's article indicated, the

Russians were as much worried by Hitler's threat to unleash war in Europe to revise the postwar status quo as the danger of an anti-Soviet bloc. Although Litvinov had yet to proclaim his famous slogan that peace was indivisible, his mind had by now almost certainly moved to this position. Furthermore, the virulent anti-semitism which took to the streets of Nazi Germany had undoubtedly combined with the suppression of the KPD to create a groundswell of opinion favourable to the policies Litvinov himself discreetly advocated.

* * *

Litvinov was notoriously Anglophile, yet he made no overt attempt to draw Britain in as a counter-balance to Germany, though it undoubtedly made sense even to the most Anglophobe to exploit whatever tensions existed in Anglo-German relations to Soviet advantage. But relations with MacDonald's National Government and its Foreign Secretary, Sir John Simon, were at one of their periodic low-points, largely due to Soviet neglect; by securing the appointment of fellow Anglophile Ivan Maisky as polpred in London, Litvinov undoubtedly hoped to reverse that trend,[47] but Litvinov's superiors were still too captivated by apparent French strength and relative British weakness. France had hitherto – though not for long – escaped the worst of the Depression, whereas Britain had succumbed to an ignominious moral and material blow in the Invergordon mutiny, itself a reflection of the rapid economic decline which forced the abandonment of the gold standard in the fateful September of 1931.[48] Britain's clumsy denunciation of the Anglo-Soviet trade agreement of 1930 in October 1932 thus met with little more than contempt in Moscow,[49] and by early March 1933 the subsequent trade negotiations had reached impasse.[50]

On the 12 March 1933, apparently after no prior consultation with the Narkomindel, the OGPU arrested several British employees of Metro-Vickers Ltd in the USSR – Monkhouse, Thornton, MacDonald, Cushny, Nordwall and Gregory – and charged them with espionage and sabotage. Whereas the charge of sabotage was almost certainly baseless – some convenient scapegoat had to be found for setbacks in industrial production then embarrassing the regime – the charge of espionage appears justified. According to Soviet sources, which seem reliable in the light of other evidence, as early as the 16 October 1930 – soon after the French introduced trade restrictions on imports from the USSR, and with talk of an international blockade in the air[51] – the major companies supplying vital electrical equipment to the Russians, including Siemens (Germany), General Electric (USA) and Metro-Vickers (Britain), reached an agreement together with the major Western Intelligence services – the British amongst their number – to exchange information gathered in the USSR on Soviet industrial and defence capabilities.[52] The forum chosen for co-ordinating these efforts was the international price arrangements committee which met in Berlin.[53] In Britain it was the Committee of Imperial Defence Sub-Committee on Industrial Intelligence in Foreign Countries which handled such matters;[54] a specialist unit, the Industrial Intelligence Centre was set up in 1931[55] under Major Morton,[56] evidently to put the gathering of such Intelligence – including that on the USSR's war potential and organisation for industrial mobilisation[57] – onto a more professional level. Although private companies officially played no formal role, they were undoubtedly a vital source of such Intelligence, especially in the USSR, where Britain had no military attaché and where foreign companies played a crucial role in the more advanced and defence-related sectors of the economy during the first five-year plan (1929–32). Progress towards the implementation of the international agreement of 1930 was then made at a further meeting, this time in Zurich, from the 5 to the 6 June 1931. Unfortunately for those involved, the OGPU's foreign department (INO) obtained an account of the proceedings and a decision was taken to penetrate Metro-Vickers' Intelligence-gathering operations in Leningrad. There, OGPU agents successfully laid their hands on photocopies of company documents, including branch manager Thornton's diary.[58] During Monkhouse's interrogation, the Russians "proudly produced copies acquired in Berlin of the minutes of all secret meetings of the International Price Arrangements Committee on which Richards [London manager of Metro-Vickers and formerly a military Intelligence agent in Russia] sits".[59] They also produced "a copy of minutes" in which Richards reported on conditions in the USSR after his visit there during the autumn of 1932.[60] Evidently ignorant of all this, the outraged British ambassador Sir Esmond Ovey, formerly quite amiable towards his hosts, responded melodramatically in a Palmerstonian manner, demanding the immediate release of those arrested.[61] To the bewilderment of officials at the Foreign Office, unaware of such spying activities, Richards made the "somewhat startling suggestion that if a trial was held, it would be a good thing if a Foreign Office Legal adviser were to proceed to Moscow for the purpose of assisting with the defence".[62]

Foreign observers were not entirely taken in by the outburst of righteous indignation that swept Britain,[63] and a professional journal, *Aeroplane*, put the whole matter into a more sober perspective. Its editor commented drily: "I have in this office practically a complete list of all the Russian aircraft factories and aero-engine factories, with a fairly reliable description of what each makes, and the amount of its output, and the number of people it employs . . . those figures were got by some form of enquiry for which the persons responsible might reasonably be shot if they were caught, just as I would be liable to be shot, and should certainly be imprisoned, if I were caught asking questions about exactly what is being made at Woolwich Arsenal, or Devonport Dockyard, or let us say, at Porton, or even at Farnborough."[64] Nonetheless the arrest, imprisonment and arraignment of the British engineers were a disaster for Litvinov. Surely with Stalin's assent, the OGPU had unwittingly and irresponsibly ignited yet another anti-Soviet campaign in Britain at the very time that Moscow desperately needed more friends, not more enemies. Given the spurious nature of the evidence at two previous such trials – the Shakhty trial (1928)[65] and the Promparty trial (1930)[66] – as well as the absurdities in much of the material supposedly incriminating the engineers, the British Government had little difficulty in whipping up public opinion in defence of the accused and in vociferous denunciation of Soviet actions. A trade embargo was announced on Soviet goods in order to force the Russians into submission. The trial duly opened on the 12 April, ending six days later with the sentencing of only MacDonald and Thornton to two and three years imprisonment respectively. Eventually the Russians conceded. Soviet isolation in these dangerous times was too high a price to pay. After protracted negotiations the sentences were commuted on the 1 July and the two men were subsequently deported. The whole episode underlined the precariousness of Litvinov's hold over Soviet diplomacy, when his superiors were prepared to jeopardise relations with potential allies unthinkingly at a time of great international uncertainty. Soviet foreign policy more than once fell victim to domestic political demands, a malpractice which reached its apogee during the years of the terror (1937–39).

Exploding against the background of a proposed Four Power Pact, the Metro-Vickers affair, dramatically reinforced Moscow's deep mistrust of the Entente. On the 2 April the Soviet military newspaper *Krasnaya Zvezda* appeared with an editorial arguing against revision of the Versailles treaty – apparently favoured by Britain – and attacking British foreign policy under Ramsay MacDonald. It concluded on an isolationist note which jarred with the softer tones of Litvinovian internationalism: "We have not interfered and will not interfere in the scuffles between competing imperialist groups."[67] This was a refrain which found constant resonance in a country isolated in a hostile world and only too vulnerable to attack from without; in this atmosphere the most that could be permitted was a policy of exploiting the contradictions within the capitalist camp which stopped short at any commitment to the defence of one country against another. In these terms peace was divisible. But one should be wary of seeking too much consistency in Soviet foreign policy. Under Stalin any kind of fundamentalism took second place to the needs of the moment; the settlement of the Metro-Vickers affair to Britain's advantage indicated that an error had been recognised, albeit tacitly. Increasingly the underlying trend of events was working in Litvinov's favour.

* * *

The greatest blow to those in Moscow still looking to revive Rapallo came when, on the 14 June at the world economic conference in London, Hugenberg delivered a statement on the need to extend Germany's living-space and called for an end to existing conditions in the USSR – a reference to the famine – in one and the same breath.[68] This not only lent a further sense of urgency to Soviet proposals unveiled by Litvinov at the conference, for an economic non-aggression pact – an echo of Moscow's fears of a blockade resonant since October 1930 and reverberated by the Metro-Vickers affair;[69] it also precipitated a crisis in Soviet–German relations. Krestinsky called on Dirksen to deliver a protest and "begun his remarks by saying that during the 12 years that he had been occupied with German-Russian affairs he had never had such a serious and unpleasant question to discuss".[70] *Izvestiya* followed this by demanding "complete clarity" from Berlin,[71] and a formal note of protest was despatched to the German Government.[72] Hitherto the Soviet leadership had carefully avoided public identification with their fallen comrades in the KPD; the appearance of the Hugenberg memorandum removed all restraint. On the 22 June 1933 Stalin and Molotov (chairman of the Council of People's Commissars) led the way in carrying the funeral bier of Klara Zetkin, veteran of the KPD leadership and only recently chairman of the Reichstag – she died of old age – to her burial on Red Square. A photograph of the scene appeared prominently in the centre of *Izvestiya*'s front page on the 23 June, celebrating, in Molotov's words, the inspiration she gave "to revolutionary workers all over the world". Three days later an astonished German military attaché at the Moscow embassy was coolly informed that all agreements on military collaboration between the two Powers were henceforth rescinded.[73]

It was with Soviet-German relations at their nadir that Radek returned Miedziński's visit with his own tour of Poland from the 6 to the 22 July. He was there not merely to see his mother, but also as an unofficial envoy easily disowned but armed with bold proposals to pre-empt a Polish–German understanding – at the very least; for while he was still in Poland, Khinchuk reported from Berlin on "an array of information concerning the determination of the German Government to reach a rapprochement with France and Poland at the expense of the USSR".[74] In addition, the signature of the Four Power Pact on the 15 July underlined Moscow's need to find common cause with those similarly excluded from the club; Litvinov had told the Germans that "the original purpose of the pact might be a limited one. But in political arrangements of this kind one never knew where they would ultimately lead".[75] The bogey of a united anti-Soviet front in Western and Central Europe haunted the Soviet leadership. "Anything done without us . . . can only be something done against us", Litvinov told the French, neatly encapsulating Moscow's dread of the outside world and its ceaseless machinations.[76] The Poles, also excluded from the Four Power Pact, thus appeared more attractive as potential partners than ever before.

Stalin had shown the greatest interest in Radek's report of his conversations with Miedziński and had authorised their continuation, the Poles were told. Radek went on to outline the likely course of events. Faced with an ultimatum from Germany, Poland would be forced to choose between joining forces in a move eastwards or of becoming the first victim of the *Drang nach Osten* as the Reichswehr drove through en route to the USSR. The alternative might be that Berlin would propose a treaty transferring the Polish corridor to East Prussia into German hands either in full or in part, thus guaranteeing a powerful base for operations against the USSR. But the Poles resolutely refused to see things in such terms and, faced with their obduracy, Radek played his last card: offering Poland a free hand vis-à-vis Lithuania. Lithuania was still technically at war with Poland, a thorn in Warsaw's side since Polish annexation of its capital, Vilnius, in 1920. "*Róbcie sobie z nimi co chcecie*" ("do what you want with them"), Radek told Miedziński in Polish, adding later, in Russian: "*Puskai penyayut sami na sebya*" ("they will only have themselves to blame").[77] Soviet diplomacy had become that simple; more was to follow. In an article signed "Duo", which appeared in the Soviet Communist Party journal *Bol'shevik* at the end of August 1933, Deputy Commissar of War Tukhachevsky[78] openly speculated on the launching of "a preventive war to join Danzig and East Prussia to Poland" – a curiously reckless suggestion, only partly mitigated by the afterthought that, of course, "an attempt to liquidate the [Polish] corridor in the current political situation would amount to an attempt to liquidate Versailles outright, and the outbreak of a new war";[79] the public rehearsal of such drastic solutions reflected Soviet despair at their encroaching isolation and increasing vulnerability now that Rapallo was effectively at an end, while war still loomed menacingly on the Far Eastern horizon.

But the Poles were making headway in secret negotiations with the Germans, and, in his eagerness to obtain a modus vivendi with Germany, Pilsudski did not want these hopes dashed by an entente with the USSR; a public flirtation was one thing, a serious commitment to the Russians, quite another. This left Moscow in some disarray. Distracted by their growing isolation, the Russians flew off in all directions, hovering to suck pollen from every flower. They now proposed to the French a verbal and secret understanding which provided for joint consultation on general issues and on all agreements envisaged with other Powers. This met with puzzlement and suspicion in Paris, largely due to the tactless Russian assurance that such arrangements had worked well with Germany in the past; this admission raised more embarrassing questions than it answered, though it vividly illustrates the naked pragmatism of Soviet thinking in the summer of 1933.[80] The Russians also endeavoured to obtain a hitherto elusive non-aggression pact from the Italians[81] – eventually signed on the 2 September[82] – and on or around the 17 July a close associate of Stalin's, chairman of the central executive committee Yenukidze, arrived in Germany, of all places, on holiday.[83] Soviet officials had long taken to visiting spas in Germany – Chicherin at one time spent more time there than in Moscow – but to have gone with Soviet–German relations in a state of dissolution had some political significance. Then, on the 4 August, "an opportunity . . . arose", in Molotov's evasive terminology, for him to meet Dirksen. Allowing for the new customary exchange of recriminations which were by now the norm, the conversation was remarkably amicable, as Molotov stressed his government's wish for good relations. Indeed, at times he sounded almost apologetic. More particularly, he placed concern at the violent overthrow of the Versailles treaty a poor second to improved Soviet–German relations. The crucial passage in Molotov's record is worth quoting in full:

> Our attitude towards the Versailles treaty is determined by the aim of preserving universal peace. This aim . . . and also the principle of the free national development of all peoples were and are the bases of Soviet policy throughout its existence. Our attitude towards the Versailles treaty is determined by these principles. I further stated that I can assure the ambassador that our position on this question has not changed, our future relations with Germany will therefore depend exclusively on the position Germany adopts in relation to the USSR. If it follows its former policy, then we will have no bases for altering our line.[84]

Molotov never firmly held to any opinion Stalin might disagree with; but he was not totally devoid of his own ideas, and he and Litvinov never had good personal relations. For the greater part of the thirties Molotov took every opportunity to trip up the Commissar of Foreign Affairs and this inevitably made him a more outspoken opponent of any real opening to the Entente than otherwise he might have been. History is replete with instances of personal antipathy elevated to issues of principle.

At this stage, in the late summer of 1933, there was still no clear guideline from Stalin as to the direction the USSR should take. The Russians lurched uneasily between reassuring the Germans and threatening them, uncertain whether German hostility was merely an abnormal phase of short duration and equally unsure whether any feasible alternative to Rapallo really existed. Just a few days after Molotov's mollification of Dirksen, Radek issued another broadside at Berlin:

> The Fascist foreign policy programme is for the moment a matter of propaganda. . . . Should this programme begin to be implemented . . . then the Soviet Government would find the necessary means to rebuff it, and then it would be a matter not of non-aggression pacts but of defence pacts.[85]

Yet little more than a week later Yenukidze, now returned from his cure at Bad Königstein, invited the Dirksens to dine at his dacha on the outskirts of Moscow. Krestinsky and Karakhan were also present, though Yenukidze dominated the discussion. He denied "rumours" of a volte-face in Soviet policy, and insisted that Stalin himself had no desire to alter Moscow's German orientation. He then quoted Lenin on Soviet opposition to the Versailles treaty and its untenability, arguing that the leadership was very understanding of recent events in Germany; after assuming power, radical elements within the Nazi party would gradually give way to those inclined towards realpolitik.

This was precisely the kind of language Dirksen understood. He expressed the hope that it would be possible to stabilise relations between the two countries; whereupon Krestinsky pitched in with the remark that an opportunity for such talks might arise in October. For he intended to take a cure at Kissingen and hoped to stop en route in Berlin for two or three days, during which he might speak with Hitler or Göring.[86] If Litvinov knew of this meeting, evidently sanctioned from above, he would certainly not have approved. He himself remained "convinced, and this conviction could be changed only by deeds and no longer by words, not even in official speeches, that Germany had entered onto an anti-Soviet course".[87] As a consequence he was working the French connexion for all it was worth. Chairman of the foreign affairs committee of the French Chamber of Deputies, Edouard Herriot, had arrived in the USSR for a fortnight's stay on the 26 August. At the Moscow municipal banquet held in his honour, chairman of the regional Soviet Kaminsky concluded his speech with an indiscretion, the reaction to which cast a shaft of light onto disagreements within the Soviet hierarchy over the desirability of an alliance with France. He remarked that Soviet desires and efforts for peace would, if necessary, be channelled towards defence. "I hope very much", he said, "that we will guarantee this defence together." But this passage was not translated by Konstantin Umansky, head of the Narkomindel's Press Department.[88]

The bottom line of Soviet foreign policy was to exploit the differences between the capitalist Powers to forestall the development of any united front against the USSR; after Hitler's accession to power the top line of Soviet foreign policy was soon to become the pursuit of an alliance with those Powers also scared by Nazi Germany's wild ambitions. But Litvinov's efforts towards "a far-reaching rapprochement with France" were frustrated by French reserve. Paris was reluctant to accept Russian proposals for the definition of aggression and a gentleman's agreement binding each party to exchange confidential information on relations with the other Powers.[89] Litvinov expressed his "bewilderment" at the French Government's "indecisiveness". He pointed out to Alphand, the French ambassador, that forging new friendships "sometimes results in the loss or, at least, the weakening of old ones", adding that the Russians could not be sure of current French policy continuing should men like Tardieu return to power.[90] The unreliability of the French only weakened Litvinov's position. Once again, however, it was Nazi intransigence which came to his rescue. While Stalin was away on his customary holiday in the Caucasus in the early autumn of 1933 a publication appeared in Berlin, said to be based on official sources, and claiming direct Soviet involvement in the plotting of an armed uprising by the KPD. This and other incidents threw the Narkomindel's Second Western Department, responsible for relations with Germany, into complete despair.[91] At the same time the Comintern was campaigning for the release of Dimitrov, head of its West European Bureau, now arraigned on trial for the Reichstag fire. Soviet-employed journalists Keith (a German national working for *Izvestiya*) and Bespalov (a Russian working for TASS), were banned from attending the trial by the German authorities, and when they defied the order by travelling to Leipzig, they were arrested.[92] The Soviet Government then retaliated by recalling them and demanding that the German Government recall its own nationals working as journalists in the USSR.[93] Only now, with relations teetering on the brink, did Hitler recognise the need for a tactical retreat.[94] Khinchuk had informed the Germans of Krestinsky's impending arrival and asked that the Reich Chancellor receive him.[95] On the 27 September state secretary Bülow told the Russians that this was possible.[96] Krestinsky was, however, already ensconced at his spa, having passed through Berlin, stopping off merely to borrow the embassy car (and chauffeur).[97] The issue was therefore whether he would return to Moscow via Berlin. But no sooner had the Germans granted the concession of an audience with Hitler, than they began to shorten sail, making it clear that any meeting would have to be unofficial and could in no circumstances be represented as a German initiative.

This last-minute reservation was conveyed to the Russians during a conversation arranged at Soviet request between a "friend" – probably the Kremlin's unofficial emissary Boris Steiger – and chargé d'affaires Twardowski, on the 2 October, possibly the result of pressure from Khinchuk on the Narkomindel to forestall a breach of relations with Berlin.[98] The Soviet emissary stressed that although an improvement in the atmosphere could not be expected before the end of the Leipzig trial, "the conflict about the journalists should not be permitted to run its course, because here as perhaps also in Germany forces were at work to deepen this conflict". He went on to suggest the outlines of a communiqué which might be issued after Krestinsky had talks in Berlin, announcing an end to the dispute.[99] But German reluctance to reciprocate by making such a meeting official scuttled the whole project. On the 27 September Khinchuk had, on Krestinsky's behalf, requested a transit visa to Austria,[100] and, with the Germans now disinclined to show any genuine interest in improving relations, Krestinsky left Kissingen early in October, returning home via Vienna instead of Berlin.[101]

This did not mean that Moscow was uninterested in improving relations. The growing menace from Japan and continuing uncertainties in France militated in favour of at least some sort of *detente* with Berlin. The dramatic departure of Germany from the disarmament conference and the League of Nations in mid-October had unsettled the Russians considerably. The assumption being made in Moscow was that "the collapse of its internal policy" and its "international isolation" were driving Germany towards "extremely dangerous adventures", and *Izvestiya* gave notice that "Germany's exit from the League of Nations is, for the supporters of peace, an alarming warning of the need to be on guard".[102] But until there was a decisive shift in French policy or a more effective means of leverage on German politics than the outlawed and defunct KPD, the Russians had little or no freedom for manoeuvre. Merely two days after the appearance of the *Izvestiya* editorial, Litvinov astonished Twardowski with his conciliatory manner, which the Germans rightly attributed to "the ghost of German–Japanese collaboration".[103] For their part, the Germans, too, had become hesitant about risking a breach with Moscow. Thus for the next two months both sides toned down the mutual recriminations that had poisoned press comment for most of the year.[104] Clearly the Russians were grateful for any, however temporary, release from the existing tension. What Radek graphically referred to as "The Dynamite in the Far East"[105] appeared about to explode at any moment, as the Russians moved gratefully towards a long-awaited reconciliation with the United States.[106] Some of the sense of urgency had been taken out of Soviet–German relations by the lull in the press war; the Soviet military attempted to lure their German counterparts back to the Rapallo tradition,[107] in a rather transparent attempt to split the Reichswehr from the Nazis over foreign policy. But Litvinov was still intent on some sort of security guarantee involving France; and now that the Far Eastern threat had returned to prominence, he also attempted to obtain from the French a commitment to aid the USSR in the event of a conflict with Japan.

3 The Origins of the Franco-Soviet Pact, 1933–35

Germany's departure from the League of Nations, announced on the 14 October 1933, had a traumatic effect on the French. After wavering for so long between the alternatives of conciliation or confrontation, the French Government was finally propelled into action. On the 20 October Paul-Boncour, the French Foreign Minister, approached polpred Dovgalevsky with the suggestion of a "mutual assistance pact", should the situation in Germany continue.[1] But the French were not prepared to pay too high a price. As Léger, the Quai d'Orsay's secretary-general, made clear barely a week later, there could be no question of France acting in concert with the Russians in the Far East, for fear of provoking a Japanese attack on Indochina, let alone a French commitment to support the USSR in the event of war with Japan.[2] This was something the Russians had long dreamed of, and a prize for which they were apparently willing to trade revolutionary nationalism in Asia.[3]

More immediately concerned at the dangers threatening them from the East, the Russians were also temporarily the beneficiary of a detente with Germany, so they wrongly believed that by biding their time, they could force the French into conceding assistance against Japan, particularly as Paul-Boncour appeared to be in a desperate hurry to conclude a pact.[4] But the French were, in fact, as much divided on policy as the Russians; Paul-Boncour had limited room for manoeuvre. In a speech to the Chamber of Deputies on the 14 November he left the door open to the option of bilateral talks with Berlin, a tendency which von Papen, for one, was notoriously eager to encourage.[5] The Quai naturally sought to use this fact as a bargaining counter with the Russians. On the 25 November – one day after Hitler received ambassador François-Poncet[6] – Paul-Boncour warned Dovgalevsky that there were "influential political and commercial-industrial circles striving for an agreement with Germany"; in the same breath he argued that "if French public opinion knew and was convinced that France could carry out a positive policy through the creation of a firm barrier against the onslaught of Hitler's Germany, then this would calm public opinion and disarm those who are insisting on a deal with Germany". Paul-Boncour added that "the time has come and the matter brooks no delay".[7]

The spectre of a Franco-German rapprochement could always be counted on as a means of rousing Moscow into action. By the 29 November 1933 the Politburo had discussed Paul-Boncour's offer of talks, as well as his suggestion that the USSR join the League of Nations; it was agreed that Dovgalevsky should open negotiations with the French to see precisely what they had in mind.[8] Rumours that Franco-German talks amounted to more than merely an exchange of opinions between François-Poncet and Hitler undoubtedly ensured continued Soviet interest in what Paris had to offer;[9] "as usual, they think they are being discussed", the French ambassador to Moscow noted wearily.[10]

Dovgalevsky indicated to Paul-Boncour that the USSR would be prepared to consider an agreement "aimed at organising . . . mutual assistance between Russia, France and, by extension, Poland and the Little Entente".[11] Paul-Boncour insisted that the Russians first had to join the League of Nations; otherwise the projected pact would not harmonise with the Covenant. He also believed that this would deprive the Poles of an excuse for refusing to join in the arrangement.[12] Soviet doubts had to be suppressed. On the 6 December Ybarnegaray, a member of the French Chamber of Deputies, caused something of a sensation when he suggested to the foreign affairs committee, that, faced with the alternatives of a *rapprochement* with Germany or with the USSR, he favoured Germany. He then proposed that France abandon the League for a time to facilitate direct negotiations with the German Government.[13]

Dovgalevsky was recalled to Moscow.[14] Litvinov had already arrived from the United States on the morning of the 9 December, in a blaze of publicity following on US recognition, though the attempt to interest Roosevelt in joint action against Japan had proved unsuccessful.[15] Fears of a Franco-German *entente* were now joined by growing concern at the renewed deterioration in relations with Berlin, which had resulted from Soviet condemnation of German rearmament,[16] and which was exacerbated by German speculation on the likelihood of a Russo-Japanese war in the near future. An acrimonious conversation took place between Litvinov and Nadolny, Dirksen's unhappy successor, on the 11 December, only a few weeks after Nadolny's arrival in the Soviet capital. Trying to make an impression, Nadolny said he did not like the look of the situation in the Far East. Litvinov replied that he did not like it either, but that "it seems that someone in Germany does"; at which point Nadolny remarked that this would depend on the Russians.[17]

For the best part of a year the Russians had tried to give the Germans the benefit of the doubt; now Stalin finally decided the time had come for a decision. On the 12 December, the day after the Litvinov–Nadolny confrontation, the Politburo passed a resolution in favour of collective security – a turning point in Soviet foreign policy. The Narkomindel was duly instructed to formulate concrete proposals for action.[18] These proposals were then submitted to and approved by the Politburo on the 19 December.[19] Litvinov had won, with the unwitting aid of the Germans. The proposals envisaged a multilateral assistance pact encompassing not only the USSR, France and Poland – as originally envisaged by the Russians – but also countries such as Belgium, Czechoslovakia, Lithuania, Latvia, Estonia and Finland. Accepting the French insistence that such a pact be limited to Europe alone, the Russians nonetheless argued that "independently of the obligations agreed upon for mutual defence, the parties to the agreement are also under an obligation to render one another diplomatic, moral and as far as possible, material aid in cases of military attack not provided for in the agreement itself, and also to exert appropriate pressure on the national press". For its part, the USSR would join the League under certain conditions – essentially limitations on the type of cases open to international arbitration.

The current obsession with the danger of war in the Far East was also reflected in Soviet reluctance to appear the initiator of the struggle to contain Nazi Germany through collective security measures; there was always the danger that publicised Soviet proposals directed against Berlin would fail to find form in an international agreement, thereby leaving the USSR more isolated and vulnerable than before. Stalin was a man given to acute suspicion, and the remainder of the Soviet leadership had no reason to trust the Western Powers to any greater extent. A section of the leadership, whose names are still only a matter of surmise – Molotov and Kaganovich emerge in the subsequent pages as the most likely candidates at this early stage – had serious doubts about the wisdom of committing the USSR to the maintenance of the post-war territorial status quo, which entry into the League inevitably entailed; this was yet one more reason for the Russians to move only cautiously and discreetly in attempting to fetter Hitler's foreign ambitions. The Politburo resolution thus stressed that France would be responsible for summoning a conference to discuss the proposals, "being the initiator of the entire affair". This was also an image Litvinov industriously conveyed to foreign observers. He told Bullitt, the US ambassador designate, that "the French had asked the Soviet Government to make a 'regional agreement' for defense against attack by Germany" – not entirely untrue, neither was it entirely accurate.[20]

Hitherto the Soviet regime had steadfastly opposed alliances with any capitalist Powers – not that many had been on offer – for fear of being drawn into war for the interests of others. Commitment to one set of capitalist states against another would require a distinction to be drawn between the nature of one group as against the other, a doctrinal innovation unacceptable to the more fundamentalist element in the Soviet leadership and Party apparatus. These doubts were totally suppressed in public, but it did not take long for them to emerge in veiled form. Initially the Politburo's decision on collective security led to a revival in the anti-German campaign that had fallen silent in recent weeks. The speeches by Molotov – who now saw the way the wind was blowing, and who buried his opinions until Stalin once again seemed ready for them – and Litvinov, to the central executive committee on the 28 and 29 December 1933, were unusually frank where Germany was concerned. No longer were the capitalist Powers to be viewed as an undifferentiated mass. Litvinov led the way in distinguishing between the "deeply pacificist" and the more militaristic imperialist Powers.[21] But the fact that not everyone in the Soviet leadership was entirely happy about breaking the mould soon became evident: it is significant that although Molotov was prepared to refer to the "reactionary

Fascist camp" in his speech, he was not prepared, then or later, to talk of "pacific" Powers in the capitalist world.

An editorial in *Izvestiya* on the 30 December 1933 entitled "Clarity and Definition" congratulated Molotov and Litvinov on their "Bolshevik candour" and reiterated Soviet fears concerning Germany and Japan. Yet amidst uncompromising remarks one finds a curious passage, ringing with ambiguity, where the odd word-spacing indicates hurried last-minute changes to the text – silent testimony to lingering doubts:

> It goes without saying that the Soviet
> Union is incapable of enmity
> towards the German or Japanese
> people, with which our
> national masses are tied
> by a community of interests.[22]

Having taken a bold step forwards, the Soviet leadership was beginning to look around nervously for a possible line of retreat. Litvinov's outspoken condemnation of Germany's foreign policy provoked indignant protests from Nadolny, who expressed his astonishment at this new departure, given the agreement to tone down mutual recrimination. It placed him in an extremely difficult position *vis-à-vis* his superiors. But Litvinov was unrepentant. The result was a row, during which Nadolny accused the Russians of conducting "a dishonourable policy (*unherliche Politik*)".[23] Litvinov appears to have overreached himself. An editorial in *Pravda* only four days later, on the 7 January 1934, though not uncritical of both Germany and Japan, struck a much less strident note.[24]

It was sometime in early January that Radek, who revelled in intrigue, spoke to some German journalists in Moscow. He emphasised that the USSR's hard line *was* Stalin's own; he "does not know where he stands with Germany. He is uncertain", Radek stressed. He did, however, offer some words of reassurance:

> Do not believe that something has already been decided. When Alphand says that Paul-Boncour is coming here you must know, after all, that diplomats do not always tell the truth. . . . We shall do nothing that could commit us for a long term.

> Nothing will happen that will permanently block our way to a common policy with Germany. The dangers in the Far East are very great. But as soon as it is evident that war can be avoided there, which I myself believe, then new possibilities will develop for us with Germany in Europe.[25]

Of course, journalists do not always tell the truth, either.

Negotiations with France were slow in making progress. When Dovgalevsky presented the Soviet proposals to Léger on the 4 January 1934, the reference to assistance beyond that envisaged in the case of German aggression proved totally unacceptable. Léger emphasised that aid by France to the USSR in a Russo-Japanese conflict "might serve eventually as a pretext for Japan's seizure of harbours and bays in French Asiatic possessions, which France will be in no conditions to defend and which Japan has its eye on". They debated this for nearly an hour to no result, though to placate Dovgalevsky Léger did agree to study the proposals and present them to Paul-Boncour.[26] Thus by the time Politburo member Kaganovich, Stalin's hammer, came to deliver his speech to the Moscow Party conference on the 17 January 1934, Litvinov's line had yet to show substantial results. The signature of a Franco-Soviet trade agreement six days before – lauded in *Izvestiya* as "an important stage in the rapprochement between France and the Soviet Union"[27] – was still poor consolation for the absence of the promise of assistance against Japan. Kaganovich's speech therefore echoed the crude realism of Soviet isolationist sentiment rather than the softer tones of Litvinovian internationalism. In a rare reference to "rightist" attitudes to international politics, Kaganovich condemned their "line of compromise" and was unusually frank in resurrecting a traditional Leninist maxim as the guide for future policy: "*to make use in every possible way of the contradictions between capitalist countries and to deny them the opportunity of resolving their own contradictions at the expense of the USSR*" – scarcely an argument for allying with France.[28]

In direct contrast, Leningrad Party Secretary Sergei Kirov, speaking at a conference that same day, referred to people in the bourgeois camp who sought a way out of the capitalist crisis through the dismemberment of the USSR. He continued:

> The most striking and straightforward exponents of this policy

are the two representatives of militaristic imperialism: on the one hand Araki and, on the other, Hitler. The one dreams of reaching Chita, the other, "modestly" seizing the Ukraine together with the Black Sea and the Baltic.

I repeat, these are the most straightforward and undisguised of our enemies.[29]

This section of Kirov's speech was not reproduced in the account given by *Pravda* on the 24 January.[30] Kirov and Kaganovich appear to have been on opposing sides within the Politburo; Kirov's speech was evidently tailored by the censor to match the prevailing scepticism about French intentions.

The news from France brought little hope before the opening of the XVII Party congress on the 26 January 1934. The last report from Paris was that Paul-Boncour had still not replied to the Soviet proposals. Dovgalevsky ascribed this to "the struggle within France, and even within the Cabinet itself, of two doctrines: pro-Soviet and pro-German". In addition, there was direct pressure from London for a Franco-German agreement and for Germany's return to the world disarmament conference – still limping along – and the League. Dovgalevsky also thought it possible that Paul-Boncour was holding up negotiations until the situation with regard to Germany had been clarified.[31] Thus by the time the congress convened, it was by no means certain which direction Soviet policy would take, despite the Politburo's resolution to pursue collective security. Not surprisingly Stalin's speech reflected the USSR's sense of uncertainty, caught awkwardly at the junction of two eras, unsure as to whether it was yet possible to go further forwards, and not totally convinced that it was now impossible to retreat.

In Stalin's view, the world was unquestionably heading for another war. But he was tantalisingly non-committal as to Moscow's chosen path. On the one hand, he ruled out preventive war – evidently with Germany in mind as the prospective victim; on the other hand, he threatened the German Government, albeit in the veiled form of a reference to the unification of barbarian resistance to ancient Rome. Progress had been achieved in Franco-Soviet relations towards "an incipient process of rapprochement", "a factor in the advancement of the cause of peace". But Stalin cautioned against unreasoning optimism. Welcome though this process was, he could not regard it as "sufficiently stable and guaranteed of ultimate success". With regard to Soviet–German relations, Stalin did little more than repeat what the Russians had been saying throughout 1933: the USSR's objections to the course Germany had taken were not a matter of anti-Fascism, but of concern at German determination to use force to break the fetters of Versailles and above all at their " 'new' policy, which is largely reminiscent of the former German Kaiser's policy, a man who at one time occupied the Ukraine and marched on Leningrad, after converting the Baltic countries into a springboard for this campaign". The supporters of this policy were gaining the upper hand over the advocates of the Rapallo line. But Stalin, cautious as ever, stressed Soviet disinterest in a manner reminiscent of Palmerston:

> We never had any orientation towards Germany, nor have we any orientation towards Germany, nor have we any orientation towards Poland and France. Our orientation in the past and our orientation at present is towards the USSR and only towards the USSR.[32]

Another significant feature of the XVII Party congress with implications for the struggle for collective security in Europe was Litvinov's elevation to membership of the Central Committee; Soviet policy was advancing only somewhat unsteadily along the road he had mapped out, but Stalin was evidently sufficiently confident of Litvinov's judgement to follow in the general direction he had advised.

* * *

Soviet lack of confidence in the French was well justified. Officials at the Quai, long prejudiced against the USSR,[33] temporarily acquired greater influence over foreign policy as a result of the chronic instability of government under the Third Republic. On the very day of Stalin's speech, they disowned Paul-Boncour's Russian initiative. "The statement that Mr Paul-Boncour had envisaged an agreement on mutual assistance including France is doubtless the result of error" – so spoke the Quai's *Direction politique*, as it lowered the coffin of collective security into the ground.[34] Had his own position been more secure, Paul-Boncour may well have contested the claim that a mutual assistance pact with the USSR would jeopardise the commitment to the Locarno treaty (1925). As matters stood, however, he was one of the many implicated in the Stavisky scandal. Thus he had neither the time nor the motivation to defend his policy, and when he met Dovgalevsky on the 28 January 1934, he avoided all mention of the Quai's objections, merely reiterating the familiar reservations concerning commitments in the Far East.[35] Two days later, France had a new government – Daladier became both Foreign and Prime Minister – but it lasted barely more than a week.

France was in turmoil. The Stavisky scandal prompted Fascist elements into threatening the overthrow of the left of centre government.[36] A mass demonstration was organised by the Fascists on the 6 February. The PCF sent its members onto the streets to oppose both the Fascists and the government; as a consequence they soon collided with the police.[37] The Socialist SFIO called for a general strike on the 12 February as a means of preventing the Fascists from gaining the upper hand. In Moscow it was evidently decided that an exception had to be made to the still dominant sectarian policy of non-co-operation with so-called "social-Fascists" (Socialists); the Communists joined the strike.[38] This dramatic episode, paralleled in Vienna on the 12 February by an uprising on the part of the Socialist militia against the installation of the Dollfuss clerical–Fascist dictatorship, was to pave the way towards a fundamental change in Comintern strategy, forged by the Bulgarian Communist, Dimitrov, after his celebrated return to the Soviet Union at the end of February 1934.[39]

The appearance of the Doumergue cabinet on the 9 February 1934 scarcely reassured the Russians. Both Tardieu and Barthou, the latter now Minister of Foreign Affairs, were known for their dislike of the Soviet Union. They liked the Germans even less, however, and Alphand correctly predicted that Germanophobia would ultimately win out against anti-Soviet sentiment.[40] Although accurate, this assessment took some time before it was borne out by events. It was not until the 20 April that Barthou informed the Russians of his government's intention to continue where Paul-Boncour left off.[41] In the interim the Germans moved to mend fences with Moscow. Nadolny dangled before the Russians the prospect of greater economic co-operation leading to improved political relations. Member of the Narkomindel's collegium, Stomonyakov, gave the unconsidered response that "in the existing situation it is not the development of economic relations which must be the precondition to an improvement in political relations, rather than the reverse".[42] But this was by no means Moscow's last word. Only three days later, on the 20 March the Russians signed a credit agreement with Germany.[43] This proved less significant than might at first appear, for when the Germans revalued the Mark, a quarrel ensued which festered for the rest of the year.[44] Nevertheless, such flexibility on the part of the Soviet Government was a natural response to doubts about French intentions. Litvinov himself was in no position to ignore Nadolny's suggestions that relations be improved, however bogus he believed them to be.

The French were not the only focus of mistrust; their allies the Poles were a source of even greater concern to the Russians. Early in December 1933 the Poles – still uncertain as to whether negotiations with the Germans would yield results – had proposed close co-operation to protect the Baltic from German expansionism.[45] Yet when Litvinov suggested a joint declaration guaranteeing the independence and territorial integrity of the Baltic states, the Polish Government hesitated,[46] reminded that signature would jeopardise secret negotiations in Berlin. When the Poles at last obtained a non-aggression declaration from the Germans on the 26 January 1934, they then shied away from the Soviet offer for fear of wrecking the new modus vivendi with Berlin.[47] The Polish–German agreement, set against the refusal of the Poles to guarantee the Baltic with Moscow, left a gaping hole through which German armies might reach the USSR, as Stalin indicated in his speech to the XVII Party congress. Polish hostility inevitably weakened Litvinov's position and played into the hands of his opponents. On the 28 March, and evidently with considerable misgivings, Litvinov offered the Germans a bilateral protocol assuring the independence of the Baltic states.[48] Behind this move lay more than a hint of condominium. When Krestinsky and Voroshilov came to enlarge on the proposals in conversation with Nadolny later that same day, they made it clear that the very Baltic territory most coveted by Berlin – the Memel in Lithuania – would be excluded from the agreement.[49] This desperate gesture of appeasement – an omen for the future – was, however, ably transformed by Litvinov into more of a nettle than an olive branch. A German refusal – almost certain – would present sure proof that Germany held predatory designs on the Baltic.

The Germans did, indeed, reject the Soviet offer. Their decision was based on the belief that acceptance would "rob" their "Eastern policy . . . of all freedom of action".[50] But they concealed this reason behind a smokescreen of excuses.[51] While Krestinsky vainly pressed Khinchuk to ascertain the "fundamental reason" for this negative attitude,[52] Litvinov moved onto the offensive. Having informed the French of what had happened,[53] he secured publication in the Soviet press of both the German reply and his own response. "What is important", Litvinov emphasised, "is the very fact that the offer was rejected."[54] This was a point further underlined in an editorial entitled "Germany and the Baltic", which appeared in *Izvestiya* on the following day, the 28 April:

> THE WHOLE WORLD KNOWS AND THE WHOLE WORLD WILL REMEMBER THAT THE USSR PUT FORWARD A CONCRETE METHOD FOR CLEANSING THE ATMOSPHERE IN EASTERN EUROPE AND THAT GERMANY HAS REJECTED THIS METHOD.[55]

Having once more tested the water to see whether Rapallo could be resurrected in some form, the Russians recoiled from Berlin, aware that the French option was all that was now open to them. By the time the editorial on Germany and the Baltic appeared, the Russians had finally heard some good news from Paris. On the 20 April 1934 they were informed that the French Government had at last consented to negotiations on a pact.[56] A symptom of the new spirit of optimism as regards French policy was the appearance – evidently hitherto delayed – on the 25 April of *Le Journal de Moscou*, a fortnightly, and later a weekly, replacing the now defunct *Moskauer Rundschau* as the mouthpiece of the Narkomindel under Litvinov.

On the 28 April Litvinov responded positively to the French decision. He instructed chargé d'affaires Rozenberg that "in conversation with Barthou you must, even in the event of the Boncour offer being withdrawn as a result of Poland's position, reassure him that we will not alter in our striving for a rapprochement and co-operation with France in the cause of preserving peace".[57] New difficulties now arose, however. The

Russians were preoccupied with the problem of defending the Baltic, an obsession drummed home during the Allied war of intervention in 1918–19, reinforced by fears of British action in the late twenties, and now reawakened by the declared ambitions of Rosenberg, Hitler's party specialist on foreign affairs. The Russians therefore pressed the French for a commitment to defend the whole of Eastern Europe. But the French, for their part, sought to limit commitments to the minimum. At the outset they had agreed to include the Baltic states within a projected multilateral pact to supplement a separate Franco-Soviet treaty of mutual assistance;[58] but on the 18 May the Russians were informed that this was no longer possible, due to objections from France's allies – an obvious reference to Poland. Once again Poland came between the USSR and a Baltic guarantee. The French would accept only an arrangement which encompassed their East European allies, the USSR and – to appease the disgruntled British – Germany.[59] London was naturally concerned lest this multilateral pact displace Locarno, which the British still treated as the sine qua non of security in Western and Central Europe. For the moment, however, the Russians could afford to talk in terms of Germany's inclusion within the proposed collective security arrangements, knowing full well that Hitler would resist to the last, in the hope that the arrangements could be effected even after a German refusal to participate. The Russians were more preoccupied with the exclusion of the Baltic states. Throughout the ensuing year, until the signature of the Franco-Soviet pact in May 1935, Moscow persistently pressed the French for their inclusion.

An early fruit of Litvinov's policy was the securing of de jure recognition of the USSR from France's allies Romania[60] and Czechoslovakia[61] in exchanges of notes on the 9 June 1934: and whereas the continued occupation of Bessarabia – annexed from the Russians in 1919 – continued to bedevil any further advances in Soviet–Romanian relations, the Czech Government was now prepared to follow France in obtaining a mutual assistance pact with the USSR. The French were naturally pleased at the Soviet *rapprochement* with at least two of its allies in Eastern Europe, though both Yugoslavia and Poland still stood aloof. It was out of concern to prevent any conflict between an alliance with the USSR and alliances in Eastern Europe that the French were so insistent that the Russians join the League of Nations. Although the Politburo had agreed in principle that the USSR might join, and Stalin had publicly stated that he would "not exclude" the "possibility" that Moscow might "support" the League,[62] there was more than residual opposition to the idea within the Kremlin. Dislike of the organisation went hand in hand with a traditional attachment to the memory of Rapallo, a deep mistrust of the West, and a tendency to see all capitalist Powers as indistinguishable one from another. In an informal conversation with the League secretary-general Avenol, on the 11 June 1934, Litvinov stressed that in Moscow the issue of membership was still being "freely debated" and that no decision had yet been taken. "Public opinion is still unfavourable to the League of Nations", Litvinov informed him.[63]

* * *

The issue of entry into the League was, of course, the other side to the coin of relations with Germany. The Soviet attitude to entry thus tended to reflect the degree of optimism or pessimism with which events in Germany were viewed. On the 30 June 1934 prospects seemed brighter than ever. Hitler had finally been cornered into sanctioning the brutal liquidation of the more radical forces within the NSDAP. Although not entirely unexpected,[64] the coup appeared the answer to a dream in Moscow. Far from seeing it as the final confirmation of Hitler's supremacy,[65] the Russians viewed it as the "explosion" of the tensions within this amorphous regime. Although the massacre enveloped only the upper echelons of the Nazi Party, Radek nonetheless hailed it as "a crisis of Fascism" and claimed that it represented a decisive step in "the transformation of Germany's Fascist Government into a Government of Germany monopoly capital and landed gentry, relying primarily upon the Reichswehr which, at present, are the true masters of the situation".[66] The Russians had long been waiting for their old allies in the German army to assert themselves and now that time appeared to have come at last. Radek was not alone in this. Stalin, too, had long portrayed Fascism as an ephemeral phenomenon, a sign of capitalism's weakness, albeit a force capable of provoking war.[67] Even Litvinov incautiously accepted this interpretation. He told Attolico, the Italian ambassador, on the 12 July, that the situation in Germany was still not yet stable, that the events of the 30 June had delivered "a mortal blow" to Hitler's regime, that Hitler could remain in power only as an instrument in the hands of the Reichswehr and big business, and that in the event of President Hindenburg dying, one could expect a new crisis which would probably result either in a restoration of the monarchy or the replacement of Hitler by Göring. And Krestinsky, when asked whether Hitler would be able to remain in power, replied: "Yes, but becoming a sort of MacDonald".[68] The Comintern now moved in, eager to secure the resuscitation of the KPD, stressing the importance of "the struggle to win the deceived and betrayed members of Brown Storm Detatchments".[69]

These extravagant hopes burned brightly for only a brief moment, though their embers could still be seen to glow on occasion in the future when the lights dimmed and co-operation with France seemed lost. The spirit of unalloyed optimism about Germany lasted only into the second half of July; it was evident in Litvinov's insistence that the USSR had to be assured of its pact with France prior to entering the League.[70] French talk of the Russians joining before the League Assembly convened on the 10 September thus appeared hopelessly unrealistic,[71] but not for long. The event which more than anything dashed hopes that Hitler was in decline was the Nazi attempt to overthrow the Austrian Government on the 25 July.[72] Although abortive, the attempted coup, which resulted in the bloody assassination of Chancellor Dollfuss, immediately shook the Russians from their indifference to French entreaties. On the day after the putsch Litvinov informed Rozenberg that the USSR was prepared to join the League on condition that it received the appropriate invitation and the guarantee of a permanent seat on the Council.[73]

The pendulum had once again swung away from Rapallo, as Jacob Surits, a Jew, designated Khinchuk's successor in Berlin, discovered on returning to Moscow from his former post in Ankara. He discussed the situation with Stalin, Kaganovich, Voroshilov and others, and found very little if anything to encourage him in his new mission. Speaking to Twardowski, political counsellor at the German embassy, on the 17 August, he emphasised that "mistrust" of Germany was both "universal" and "deeply rooted". "The Soviet Union must have security and will take it where she finds it", he said, justifying the turn towards France. It was not, he stressed, a question of Litvinov's hostility towards Germany, though the Commissar was undoubtedly "a temperamental man". There were also domestic as well as foreign political reasons for the course currently being pursued by the USSR, Surits added.[74] Another polpred, the charming Alexandra Kollontai, was received by Stalin later that month. On returning to her post in Stockholm early in September, she related the substance of the conversation to the Italian ambassador – with the appropriate omissions and embellishments, of course. Stalin reportedly had little hope of a multilateral pact succeeding. Instead he envisaged a more restrictive arrangement which would create a balance of forces "necessary to cajole the reluctant to acquiesce, even unwillingly, in a real policy of European pacification which Europe, but above all Russia needs, in anticipation of a conflict with Japan".[75]

The shift of emphasis to Japan reflected the sudden deterioration in relations which had been dormant since the spring.[76] Litvinov's task was undoubtedly facilitated by the argument that even if France provided no direct guarantees for the USSR in the Far East, League membership might conceivably afford the Russians some assistance in the event of war in the Pacific. *Le Journal de Moscou* argued:

> it is impossible to desire peace for oneself and war for others. The idea that it would be possible to precipitate a war between the Soviet Union and Japan, while other countries enjoyed complete contentment and sold arms, is an absurd idea, a stupid utopia. A collision between the two Great Powers in the Far East would be the prelude to world war.

Litvinov had to impress upon others in the Soviet Union that peace was necessarily indivisible, and he saw League entry as a logical extension of that assumption:

> equally illusory would be the idea of a war setting the capitalist Powers at one another's throats without touching the Soviet Union.[77]

The Comintern journal was even more explicit about the interrelationship between the League and guarantees in the Far East:

> Given the current world situation, with Japan, having turned Manchuria into a springboard for war against the Soviet Union, day after day provoking the outbreak of war, and with a German-Japanese rapprochement on the subject of war a fact, one does not have to rack one's brains for an answer to the question as to what prompted the Soviet Union to accept the invitation to enter the League of Nations.[78]

The dangers in the Far East acted as a spur, but as difficulties emerged concerning Soviet membership of the League, Litvinov's opponents made the most of them. With Litvinov on the other side of Europe battling for Soviet entry – the Poles, in particular, were making difficulties – *Le Journal de Moscou*, evidently under the influence of others, appeared on the 8 September with an extraordinarily misleading editorial on the Nuremberg congress of the NSDAP, which had opened four days earlier. Eulogisation of the army by the Nazi leadership was recklessly taken to mean that "in Germany, the Reichswehr is increasingly the master of the situation".[79] For the opponents of collective security in Moscow even Germany's refusal to join the mutual guarantee provisions of the proposed multilateral pact – the so-called Eastern Locarno – had a silver lining: the Germans were apparently prepared to consider a commitment to non-aggression and consultation in the event of aggression.[80] These were anxious moments for Litvinov, who had staked his future on obtaining a place for the USSR at the League. Finally on the 15 September Moscow received the requisite invitation, and three days later the USSR took its permanent seat on the League Council.[81] Traces of Moscow's lingering misgivings were apparent in *Izvestiya*'s comment that the USSR had "taken part in all the conferences on peace convened by the League of Nations, despite its hostile attitude to the land of Soviets". And, referring to the fact that there were a number of Powers whose "hostility" to the USSR "might be stronger than the fear of war" – Polish obstructionism underlined that fact – *Izvestiya* stressed that this was why "public opinion in the Soviet Union", while welcoming membership, "must not forget for one moment that the cause of peace depends first and foremost on two factors: on the desire for peace of the masses of the people all over the world and on the strength of the Soviet Union".[82] Furthermore, no sooner had the USSR taken the irrevocable step into the League than Moscow's restraining hand touched Litvinov on the shoulder. On the 24 September, after receiving instructions from the Politburo, Krestinsky warned Litvinov: "do not hasten with the initiative for a pact without Germany and Poland"; any decision would have to await the Commissar's return to the Soviet capital.[83]

Litvinov arrived back in Moscow at the beginning of October to battle for the conclusion of a mutual assistance pact with or without German participation. The US ambassador, who saw him on the 5 October "found him rather pulverized". Bullitt suspected that this was due not merely to his experiences at Geneva, but also that "he had been thoroughly kicked around the Kremlin" on the 4 October; Bullitt had the impression "that the fight had gone out of him". The French, having got the Russians into the League, now appeared to be cooling off.[84] As a result Moscow was in a state of some confusion over foreign policy. Apart from a minor indiscretion from the Soviet President, Kalinin, German diplomats met with silence when they tried to elicit expressions of opinion on the current state of relations.[85] On the one hand there were signs that in Germany the pro-Soviet lobby was at long last asserting itself; ambassador Schulenburg, Nadolny's genial successor, had suggested a new trade agreement which would facilitate "a significant improvement" in political as well as economic relations.[86] Yet when Surits presented his credentials to Hitler on the 26 October, it proved to be the briefest audience in recent memory – scarcely an encouraging sign.[87]

Although prevailing opinion in Moscow could in no sense be termed Germanophile, and the prospects for an improvement in relations with Germany were too bleak for all but the incurable optimist, dislike of the policy pursued by Litvinov still ran deep. The tragic assassination of Barthou in Marseilles on the 9 October 1934 brought further complications for the Commissar. France had already shown signs of dragging its feet over the conclusion of a pact which excluded the Germans.[88] Barthou's untimely death now meant the loss of an invaluable ally, praised for his "breadth of vision, his courage and his capacity to understand the realities of the international situation", in the fulsome words of *Le Journal de Moscou*.[89] It meant his replacement by a man whose motives the Russians already had good reason to mistrust: Pierre Laval.[90] Laval said he would continue the policy of his predecessor. But, as Rozenberg noted in a telegram to Moscow, "he does not conceal the fact that he is aiming at an agreement with Germany", on the grounds that "peace in Europe is impossible without a Franco-German agreement". He was also surrounded by people pressing him in that direction and he talked openly to the Soviet chargé d'affaires of using an agreement with Moscow as a means of achieving this end.[91] It was extremely difficult for Litvinov or, indeed, anyone, to interpret this in anything other than the most uncharitable light.[92] And, as events were shortly to reveal, the Kremlin's suspicions of Laval were amply justified. This did not, however, altogether ruin Litvinov's argument for a pact excluding Germany; at least this might forestall a Franco-German agreement. It was also apparent that Berlin was playing fast and loose with both the Russians and the French, in an attempt to halt progress towards a Moscow–Paris axis;[93] faced once again with the spectre of a Franco-German rapprochement, the Soviet leadership had good reason to allow Litvinov to continue along his path. The only condition laid down was that the French vessel should be swiftly and firmly anchored within sight of Russian waters, so that it could not drift out to sea and into German hands. An agreement was required, binding both parties not to conclude any political agreements with Germany without prior notification, and to exchange information on any political discussions held with the Germans. Having stipulated this reservation, on the 2 November the Politburo agreed to accept the prospect of a pact excluding Germany and Poland, in the event of only French – or, better still, French and Czech – consent.[94]

Everything now depended on the attitude of France, whom the Russians warned of German duplicity.[95] However, in his haste to secure a coalition against Germany, Litvinov had taken insufficient care to leave the door ajar behind him. As the likelihood of an agreement with Paris began to fade once more, rumours of his impending disgrace became increasingly widespread in Moscow.[96] Laval's equivocations only made matters worse. When Litvinov met him at Geneva on the 21 November and suggested a mutual obligation to refrain from political agreements with Germany without the approval of the other party, Laval initially welcomed the proposal but, as the conversation proceeded, he began to wriggle away from the idea, delaying any decision indefinitely on the grounds that the appropriate formula had to be elaborated.[97] Litvinov therefore left Geneva on the 26 November 1934 "disappointed and worried", as Attolico discovered: "disappointed at the resistance he encountered from Laval" and "worried by the position this placed him in vis-à-vis his superiors". On his arrival in Moscow three days later, he was scarcely to be seen, not setting foot in the Narkomindel and, in rare and brief encounters with his closest collaborators, he showed himself irritable and in extremely low spirits.[98] To his great relief, what *Le Journal de Moscou* mischievously nicknamed Germany's "diplomatic dumping" failed to convince the French.[99] On the 5 December a Franco-Soviet protocol – along the lines suggested by the Politburo – was finally concluded, and was triumphantly brandished by Litvinov in a statement to the press.[100] This, *Le Journal de Moscou* jubilantly and somewhat prematurely proclaimed, would put an end to rumours that Barthou's policy was being abandoned and that French foreign policy was on the retreat.[101]

The protocol was undoubtedly a prize, but it was still a long way from the pact which the Russians sought. A salutary reminder came with Laval's visit to Rome on the 4 January 1935 and the agreement which resulted three days later, suggesting collective non-aggression pacts to maintain the independence of Austria.[102] Ultimately less significant than Laval's redefinition of Franco-Italian spheres of influence in East Africa, the agreement caused consternation in Moscow. It lessened interest in the projected Eastern pact in Western Europe, while providing no effective substitute; Germany obviously preferred to obtain sanction for rearmament by accepting the Rome proposals rather than the Eastern pact; it created a precedent for consultation and non-aggression pacts deprived of provisions for mutual assistance; "adherence to the agreement by England, Turkey, Greece and other countries might give the impression of an anti-Soviet bloc"; and lastly, "in the event of England's adherence, Mussolini might, under the cloak of a new agreement, attempt to resurrect the Four Power Pact".[103] A further blow fell with Germany's victory in the Saar plebiscite in mid-January 1935. Hitler had scored an unexpected triumph, which would undoubtedly weaken French resolve.[104] Its outcome, Litvinov wrote gloomily from Geneva, "has completely eclipsed the Rome agreements".[105]

* * *

In these circumstances the Soviet pendulum began to veer once more towards Berlin. At the seventh congress of Soviets on the 28 January Molotov proved exceptionally effusive *vis-à-vis* Germany. He emphasised that the USSR wanted nothing better than good relations with Berlin, gratuitously adding that "we make no attempt to conceal our deep respect for the German nation, as one of the great nations of our times".[106] As Schulenburg noted in a telegram to the Ausamt five days later, on the 2 February: the speech "makes clear that the Soviet Government does not want to demolish the bridges to an understanding with Germany".[107] Soviet concern to keep open the road to Berlin was a logical response not merely to Laval's Germanophile proclivities, but also to the trend of British policy, which acted as a constant source of pressure on Paris to come to terms with the Germans.

When proposals for an Eastern pact first came to light, the Foreign Office – in the words of one prominent official – "agreed . . . to give the scheme . . . their support (a) because, and on condition that, the pact would enable disarmament negotiations to be resumed; and (b) because they hoped in this way to prevent a Franco-Russian alliance".[108] By 1935 it was clear that neither of these hopes had any prospect of being realised. A reconsideration was in order. Some in London were preoccupied that pre-war alliances might re-emerge – this stemmed from the widespread Liberal–Socialist assumption that alliances had precipitated the First World War. They also grossly underestimated the scope for an *entente* between Berlin and Moscow – understandable, given Hitler's obvious hatred of the USSR, but a complacent assumption which later cost them dear. For them the solution was obvious: sabotage the Franco-Soviet negotiations, secure in the thought that the Russians could not then turn to Berlin, for "the need of expansion will force Germany towards the East as being the only field open to her, and as long as the Bolshevist régime exists in Russia it is impossible for this expansion to take merely the form of peaceful penetration".[109] The Russians had reason to be wary. Although Lord Privy Seal Eden and Permanent Under-Secretary at the Foreign Office Vansittart found this kind of reasoning distasteful and short-sighted,[110] they were overruled by the determination of Foreign Secretary Simon and Prime Minister MacDonald – themselves veterans of battles with the Soviet Union in 1932–3 – to reintegrate Germany into the European Concert.[111]

The British were, as the Narkomindel noted, attempting "to drown the Eastern pact in some general agreement";[112] Laval was accordingly invited for talks in London at the beginning of February 1935. A communiqué was subsequently issued placing the Eastern pact within the framework of a general settlement with Germany, which essentially amounted to the postponement of the pact until other issues – such as disarmament – had been settled. The Russians were right to worry, because if the British had had their way entirely, there would have been no mention of the pact at all.[113] The proposals focused on the conclusion of an arms limitation agreement replacing Part V of the Versailles treaty – which had imposed restrictions on German armaments alone, the return of Germany to the League, and the signature of an air convention by the Locarno Powers (Belgium, Britain, France, Germany and Italy), providing for automatic mutual assistance in the event of air attack.[114] The British had inevitably strengthened Germany's international position, one result of which was Berlin's procrastination in negotiating trade credits with the USSR.[115] The Russians were thus weakened on both fronts simultaneously – in their alliance politics and their trading relations with Berlin – and, as Collier, head of the Foreign Office Northern Department, wrily noted: "those in power in Moscow are beginning to wonder whether they did not after all back the wrong horse".[116] In the circumstances the Soviet reaction was unusually self-restrained. Official comment was only cautiously critical.[117] There was little left for them to do except wring their hands and alert the West allegorically to the fate of the lamb which spoke so patiently and politely to the wolf, only to become its meal.[118]

Hitler once more came to their aid. On the 16 March 1935 he announced the introduction of compulsory military service. Although this measure greatly alarmed the Russians – it led directly to the hasty removal of doubtful elements from the Western border regions of the USSR,[119] – "Hitler's bombshell" was in fact welcomed in the Narkomindel at Kuznetsky Most for its likely impact on British and French illusions.[120] The Russians also benefited from Germany's decision to complete the trade credit negotiations with the USSR, a decision prompted not only by Berlin's growing economic difficulties,[121] but also by a desire to intimidate the French.[122] All this came as a great relief to Soviet diplomats, as is evident from an editorial in *Le Journal de Moscou*, which appeared on the 30 March 1935:

> The Soviet Union is certainly conscious of the dangers that threaten it; it is ready to rebuff them. It is perhaps for this reason that Soviet politicians, who base their activities on the real power of the Soviet Union, show no symptoms of an "inferiority complex" and are a long way from believing that the entire world must come to the aid of the USSR. Nor do they think that the defence of the Soviet Union in the face of the German threat must be the central question in European peace policy. No, we do not think it is Soviet frontiers as such which constitute the most vulnerable line on the map of Europe.[123]

The Russians thus felt their bargaining position had been immeasurably strengthened by Hitler's insensitivity to Western concerns, and this was evident when Eden visited Moscow on the 28 March, Simon having decided that Berlin alone merited his presence. Although certainly piqued by this snub from the Foreign Secretary, the Russians were pleased to see Eden; Maisky, for one, was actually "glad" that it was "Eden and not Simon" whom he had to chaperone to Moscow.[124] On the 29 March, in his first encounter with a Western statesman, Stalin impressed upon Eden the importance of collective security, and the Eastern pact in particular. "What, in actual fact, is the essence of the pact?", Stalin asked. "Here we are, six people, in the room. Imagine that there is a mutual assistance pact between us and imagine, for instance, that comrade Maisky would like to attack one of us, what would happen? Joining all our forces we would beat comrade Maisky", he quipped, to Maisky's evident discomfort. He also had a little surprise for Eden. Having asked about his and Simon's conversations in Berlin on the 25–6 March,[125] he went on to reveal news of German offers to sell arms to the USSR on credit – much to Eden's astonishment.[126] But convincing Eden of something was easier than convincing the Foreign Office as a whole; Simon's absence from Moscow, rather than Eden's presence, reflected the true nature of British policy.

For the next month, with some prospects for improved Soviet–German relations on the horizon, the Russians battled hard in Paris for the conclusion of the long-desired pact, while Laval and his advisers – egged on from the sidelines by London – attempted to evade any far-reaching commitments to defend the USSR.[127] Laval's attendance at the Stresa conference, a gathering of the Italians, British and the French, from the 11 to the 14 April, annoyed the Russians. Before Laval left Italy, polpred Potemkin, in his best schoolmasterly manner, warned him "that the slightest indiscretion . . . might lead to the decomposition of the front of states interested in peace in Europe".[128] Nothing concrete resulted from Stresa. Ironically, however, it was the very prospect of a common front excluding the USSR which engendered so much Russian suspicion, yet it was this that made the Germans more interested in improving relations with Moscow.[129]

On the 9 April 1935 the German Government concluded a five-year agreement with the USSR for a DM200 million credit.[130] The Russians greeted this as a sign that "the interests of *German industrial exporters* have predominated over the interests of Fascist demagogy" and the Fascists had, they concluded, been forced to enhance their "political" as well as economic credit by toning down their anti-Sovietism.[131] It was not long before the welcome improvement in relations with Berlin began to circumscribe Litvinov's freedom of manoeuvre *vis-à-vis* the French. In one sense it bolstered his bargaining position; the French were asked firmly for "immediate military assistance in cases of obvious aggression before the League Council takes a decision", a clear definition of aggression and an agreed interpretation of the Covenant's article 16.[132] In another sense, it threatened Litvinov's whole policy. No sooner had he arrived in Geneva than on the 14 April strict instructions came from the Politburo, via Krestinsky, not to vote with the French in condemning Germany's breach of the Versailles treaty (the introduction of conscription).[133]

Litvinov held his ground, arguing that there was no way he could abstain on the motion in view of the fact that it also supported the idea of regional mutual assistance pacts.[134] At this the Politburo gave way.[135] But further difficulties soon arose. After the Stresa conference Laval appeared alarmingly indifferent to the whole idea of a pact. He rejected Litvinov's proposals for immediate assistance prior to a decision by the League Council on the grounds that it infringed the Locarno treaty. This would, he argued, provide the German Government with an excuse to denounce Locarno, thus throwing aside the security system that had enveloped Western Europe since the end of 1925. He did, however, agree to assistance being obligatory even in the absence of a League decision, though he refused to initial the proposed text until he had obtained his government's consent. This was scarcely the fully-fledged alliance the Russians had originally sought. Litvinov nonetheless saw it as still of considerable value to the Soviet Union:

> although real assistance in the projected pact is problematic on the French side – as a result of its subordination to Locarno and the decisions of the League Council, and from our side – as a result of the absence of frontiers [with Germany], the pact will have great political significance as a factor diminishing the temptation on the part of Germany, Poland and Japan to attack, and hindering the establishment of close ties between France and Germany. One also has to take into account the negative effect of rejecting the pact after all these months of negotiations.[136]

Worse was to follow before success could be assured. On returning to Paris, Potemkin discovered that Léger had introduced changes into the text, further diluting the automaticity of mutual assistance by obliging both parties to await the League Council's recommendations before acting. Potemkin telephoned Litvinov, who insisted that the French hold to the original text. Laval then rang Potemkin, informing him that the *conseil d'état* approved the new wording and had empowered him to sign; he brusquely dismissed the changes made in the protocol as purely formal. On hearing this, Litvinov instructed Potemkin to inform Laval of his astonishment at this method of conducting negotiations, that making additional changes to the agreed text was inadmissible, and that given the Soviet Government's dissatisfaction even with the original text, there could certainly be no question of further weakening it. Litvinov decided to return to Moscow immediately. Any directives for the finalisation of the text would be given from there by telephone.[137]

The whole affair was fast becoming a fiasco. But this was more the concern of the Russians than the French. Litvinov's failure to arrive in Paris – he had been expected on the 21 April – caused a certain amount of embarrassment to the French;[138] but Laval was quite capable of living with that. He still refused to concede on the issue of automaticity.[139] Finally a compromise was reached. Mutual assistance was explicitly subordinated to the decision of the League Council in the event of aggression, but both parties were under an obligation to hasten this process, and in the event of no decision, assistance would nonetheless have to be rendered.[140] The Franco-Soviet pact was finally signed on the 2 May. It was duly followed by the signature of a Czechoslovakian–Soviet pact on the 16 May, indistinguishable from the Franco-Soviet pact except in the provision that aid to Czechoslovakia or the USSR by the other signatory would be conditional upon France taking action first.[141] This was a condition the Czechs were keen to see introduced with respect to their obligations to the USSR – essentially subordinating their obligations to the Russians to their obligations to the French; the Soviet side naturally insisted on reciprocity.[142]

The sense of achievement in Moscow was counter-balanced by accumulated disappointment and frustration at the tortuous course of the negotiations with Laval, well reflected in Soviet press comment.[143] The reserve which Soviet officials displayed when questioned about the pact indicated continuing disagreements at the top.[144] Litvinov's "friendly conversation" with the German ambassador barely a week after signature, and not long before Laval was expected in Moscow – on the 13 May – also indicated that Litvinov was not altogether in control.[145] Instead of removing Soviet anxieties, the signature of the pact only whetted the Soviet appetite for further guarantees; thus the pact did not substitute for attempts to revive Rapallo. Instead it became a bargaining counter held in reserve for future negotiations with Berlin. Laval may have thought he had scored a *coup de grâce* by inserting within the communiqué at the end of his visit a statement to the effect that Stalin expressed his "complete understanding and approval of state defence, carried out by France with the aim of maintaining its armed forces at a level commensurate with the needs of its security",[146] but he had gravely underestimated his negotiating partners. At this stage it was not so easy for Stalin alone to reverse Comintern practice, and he had no reason to trust the French anyway. Auvergne peasant cunning had carried Laval a long way, but the Russians tossed this scrap of paper into the wastepaper basket, along with any illusions about complete co-operation with the French – under Laval, at least.

4 The Seventh Congress of the Comintern, 1935

There was never a clear and complete concord in outlook or tactics between the Narkomindel and the Comintern despite the self-evident fact that both institutions were ultimately answerable to the Politburo under Stalin. Foreign policy was not his métier. He had never lived abroad. He knew no foreign languages. He cared little for the world outside. It was merely an ever-present menace to the revolution he had appropriated and sought to transform. Not until 1939, with the centralisation of Party and state as complete as it would ever become, did Stalin consider himself sufficiently confident to jettison the pilot, Litvinov.

During the greater part of the thirties Stalin took only a sporadic interest in the detailed working of both the Narkomindel and the Comintern. Aside from the occasional and potentially disruptive use of unofficial emissaries to run idiosyncratic errands – Radek in Poland (1933), Kandelaki in Germany (1935 and 1937) – on the whole Stalin abstained from direct intervention and contented himself with merely reviewing and approving, underlining or revising policy guidelines at intermittent intervals; a practice which occasionally caused chaos. Even the process of review was occasionally delegated to others. "In the apparatus", recalls one former senior Soviet diplomat, "it was known that a Politburo committee with a changing membership existed on foreign policy."[1] The Politburo committee was serviced by Stalin's personal secretariat, where Radek initially handled foreign policy matters (until the summer of 1936) and reportedly also "edited 'the Central Committee Secret Bulletin' (a review of international press coverage of the USSR for members of the Central Committee)".[2] Yet formal structures – the Soviet constitution was a prime example – counted for little under Stalin. What counted was who could obtain direct access. At the Narkomindel only Litvinov had Stalin's ear and was of sufficient stature to address Stalin's immediate subordinates – technically the Commissar's own superiors – as something approaching an equal; the likes of Krestinsky, Stomonyakov and, later, the wily Potemkin, had to tiptoe barefoot across broken glass. In this respect both Litvinov at the Narkomindel and Dimitrov at the Comintern were exceptionally privileged. It meant that the two institutions had a fair degree of latitude; and, given Stalin's distractions, it also meant that they were ill-coordinated one with the other in their daily business. The Comintern and the Narkomindel followed different paths, parallel only in the loosest sense.

The origins and development of the Comintern's Popular Front strategy were a prime example of the ramshackled nature of foreign policy decision-making under Stalin. Prior to Hitler's accession to power, there was a curious mismatch between the sectarian strategy of class against class heralded at the notorious sixth Comintern congress in 1928, and the policy of the Narkomindel under Litvinov, who appeared in pacifist fancy-dress at Geneva, pleading for general and complete disarmament; the Comintern was always terrified this pacifist rhetoric would infect the minds of its cherished class warriors.[3] To some extent this curious contradiction was merely a reflection of the innate ambivalence of Soviet power: a revolutionary state, the USSR had to exist and grow in a non-revolutionary environment; forced into co-existence, it also drew strength from the forces of revolution in the hostile world outside. This was a situation Stalin inherited. He could do nothing to alter it; even abolishing the Comintern in 1943 did no good whatever. He made statements disowning world revolution. He dismissed the Comintern as a petty clique (*lavochka*). He spoke out in favour of the French war effort in 1935, only for the world to discover that the PCF was still free to act on totally contradictory assumptions. In one sense this could be put down to tactics. Stalin certainly acted at times as though he were operating in a gigantic oriental bazaar. But he was also a prisoner of the revolution, and such acts of deception were often merely a screen for his own impotence and indecision in the face of historical forces he could never control.

The breakthrough in Comintern policy did not come about until after the crises in France and Austria – see p. 35 – in February 1934, when Dimitrov arrived back in the USSR as the conquering hero of the Leipzig trial. This was a full two months after the Politburo had made the fateful decision to embark on the hard but promising path of collective security. On the 27 February 1934 the offices of *Pravda* in Moscow received a telegram announcing that Dimitrov was en route to the Soviet Union. The Comintern executive committee rushed to the airport to greet him. Dimitrov was showered with congratulations, and Manuilsky, Soviet representative on the committee, pointed to the outstanding example given to Communists the world over. As a consequence Dimitrov had "drawn towards the Comintern over a million new workers".[4]

The combination of the rising in Austria and events in France convinced Dimitrov that the current Comintern hostility towards Social Democracy was mistaken. Until early April 1934, however, he was confined to hospital and unable to act. But his global reputation made him a prized object in the USSR, and on the 4 April he was summoned before the Soviet Politburo to air his views on the needs of the international Communist movement. There he argued for a new strategy based on co-operation with Social Democracy against Fascism. Stalin was sceptical; however, the Politburo as a whole appears to have been impressed by Dimitrov's arguments. After further discussion Stalin suggested that Dimitrov take charge of the Comintern, and promised him the continuing support of the Politburo.[5]

The immediate consequence of this meeting was that Dimitrov became a member of the Comintern's political secretariat, replacing the notorious sectarian Knorin as head of the Central European Department. This was a crucial change, for this office had been the stronghold of class against class, the folly of the sixth congress. Dimitrov had some reason for believing that Social Democracy was ripe for co-operation now that the menace of Hitler was alarmingly obvious. At Toulouse the French Socialist Party congress revealed as much. A resolution called for an appeal to the Comintern for joint action on a revolutionary basis. It was suggested that the congress send a delegation to Moscow for discussion as soon as practicable. The resolution was rejected by 2324 votes to 1301, but it was significant that at least one-third of the Socialists were in favour of a united front with the Communists.[6] The Communists then took the initiative. On the 31 May *l'Humanité* published an appeal for a "united front of anti-Fascist struggle to save Thälmann", the leader of the KPD imprisoned by the Nazis. The declaration also added that "a united front will stem the growth of Fascism in France".[7]

By the 11 June the French Socialist leaders were negotiating with their counterparts in the PCF. Led by Léon Blum, the Socialists demanded that Communist criticism should cease as a precondition to any agreement. This demand had formed the basis of the Second International's offer of a non-aggression pact soon after Hitler came to power early in 1933. The Communist reply was evasive, claiming that the broader the co-operation, the less basis there would be for criticism.[8] Reluctance to concede on this issue reflected the belief that sooner or later the rank and file of the Socialist Party would force its leadership to come to terms with the Communists.[9] That prediction was fulfilled. After assurances from the Communists that they would support and fight for "democratic freedoms", the two Parties signed an agreement on the 27 July 1934.[10] This agreement on joint action against Fascism allowed both parties to maintain their independence, though not to the detriment of the common enemy. Thus criticism was permissible only against those who failed to comply loyally with the terms of the agreement. The breach in the French Left had at last been healed. The new strategy was now coming into effect, though the results were still open to debate.[11]

Meanwhile, in Moscow preparations were under way to open the seventh congress of the Comintern. At the thirteenth plenum it had been decided that the congress should meet some time in the second half of 1934, and that the Comintern executive committee should publish the agenda not later than the 1 June 1934.[12] But the sudden decision to allow Dimitrov to experiment with a change of strategy complicated this task. Worse still, Dimitrov's poor health promised to slow proceedings even further.

Two commissions were set up to prepare the programme for the congress. The first had to draw up the plan for the first point on the agenda: the executive's report to the congress. It was headed by Otto Kuusinen, the Finn, a longstanding secretary of the Comintern. It included Dimitrov, Knorin, Manuilsky, Pyatnitsky and Pieck, amongst others. Although not members of the commission, the German, Heckert, and the leader of the PCI, Palmiro Togliatti – Gramsci, formally its leader, was dying in an Italian prison and Soviet attempts to secure his release were proving totally ineffective[13] – also participated; Togliatti was soon to become Dimitrov's right-hand man. The most important task of all was to be carried out by the second commission, headed by

Dimitrov himself. This was to deal with the tactics of the Communist movement in the struggle against Fascism. It included Pytanitsky, Heckert and Šmeral from Czechoslovakia, amongst others.[14]

The deadline for completion was exceeded. Not until the 1 July did Dimitrov send his proposed outline plan from the second commission to the Politburo. In it he advocated all the heresies of the preceding period: an end to the stigmatisation of Social Democracy as social-Fascism, the need for a united front from above with the Socialists, and for democratisation of the Comintern in its relations with member sections.[15] These proposals amounted to a complete rejection of both the letter and spirit of the sixth congress strategy, a tacit admission that the Comintern had inadvertently facilitated the rise of Hitler to power by splitting the labour movement at a time when united action could have forestalled the tragedy. In retrospect Dimitrov's proposals might seem common-sense to many, but at the time of their introduction they excited considerable animosity largely from those who had firmly believed in and ruthlessly imposed the previous, sectarian strategy, and those who believed that revolution was still a practicable proposition in Western and Central Europe.[16]

Dimitrov's proposals were therefore taken on board only conditionally; Stalin and the Politburo were still undecided by the autumn of 1934 as to whether the new tactics would work.[17] After the February events in France, the PCF now played a crucial role; if the new strategy could succeed, it was more likely to win out here than elsewhere. With Soviet moves towards an alliance with Paris, much was at stake, even though the Socialists had no immediate prospect of gaining power. Thus from Moscow Dimitrov and Manuilsky urged the PCF to press ahead with their united front tactics. But Thorez, its leader, decided to introduce his own innovation into the strategy, a heresy of heresies: an alliance with the Radicals, a petty bourgeois party. Lenin had never allowed any such notion to dilute the revolutionary life-blood. A delegation was hurriedly despatched from Moscow to warn Thorez to back down. It consisted of Togliatti, Gottwald and Stepanov. When the group arrived at the French Party headquarters, they received an icy welcome. Togliatti explained the detrimental effects that would result from an alliance with the Radicals, both in terms of the need to avoid helping the Socialists out of their difficulties and of the instability of the Radicals as an ally – they represented a loose coalition of Left and Right. Thorez reportedly gave Togliatti barely enough time to deliver this message, before he informed him that it was too late. That evening, on the eve of the Radical Party conference, he was going to put forward the slogan of the Popular Front of work, freedom and peace. Togliatti and Gottwald, realising that nothing was left to be said, returned to their lodgings empty-handed, and Thorez delivered his famous speech, which truly marked the birth of the Popular Front, on the 24 October 1934 at Nantes.[18]

This extraordinary reversal of orthodoxy was not accepted without a murmur. Stalin himself had no vested interest in the substance of the Leninist heritage, whether in domestic or foreign policy, as long as the outward forms were duly preserved – and even these were gradually being supplanted. But this challenge to orthodoxy fed existing dissatisfaction within Soviet Communist ranks over the general direction taken by the regime's foreign policy in recent years. Since 1933 the Soviets had reneged on their stalwart opposition to the Versailles settlement; the regime had in fact become the leading proponent of the post-war territorial status quo. An echo of the resultant discontent aroused in certain quarters can be heard in the comment on Soviet proposals for the Eastern pact which appeared in *Kommunisticheskaya Revolyutsiya* in August 1934:

> The Soviet Union backs the Eastern pact, in so far as it might lead to a strengthening of peace and security, and this is the most important issue for the mass of the people. One can find and there exist critics who say: "How come? The Soviet Union stands for the immutability of frontiers; does this mean it is in favour of the Versailles peace?". Such an assertion does not stand up to scrutiny. The Soviet Union has not changed its attitude towards Versailles. But the fact is that the capitalist opponents of Versailles are merely aiming at establishing their own Versailles. German Fascism is aiming to redraw the Versailles map in its own favour through force, and this means war. The Soviet Union is unflinching in its determination and resolution to fight for peace.
>
> In signing non-aggression pacts, conventions on the definition of aggression . . . with bourgeois states, in fighting alongside bourgeois states for the realisation of the Eastern

> pact, the Soviet Union entertains no illusions about the class nature of its partners and is perfectly well aware that should a range of bourgeois states support the USSR's peace initiatives, it is not from a love of peace in principle, but from their own class interests, which require the preservation of peace for the time being.[19]

Communists repeatedly claimed that Litvinov conducted a policy which was "too *pacifist* and not revolutionary".[20] The shift in Comintern strategy towards the controversial Popular Front further fuelled this discontent. Yevdokimov, arraigned alongside Zinoviev and Kamenev for attacking the regime's policies, told the court on the 15 January 1935 that in addition to dissatisfaction with Stalin's domestic policies:

> We accused the Party leadership of not taking measures to activate the international Communist movement, falsely claiming that the Central Committee [the Politburo] was putting the brakes on the development of this movement. As an example I will cite my conversation with Zinoviev at the end of 1934. Zinoviev accused the CC [the Politburo] of handing over the initiative in the leadership of the labour movement in France to the Second International.[21]

Such dissatisfaction was to re-emerge with some force in the summer of 1936, with the Comintern's negative approach to the revolt of French workers in June and the regime's neglect of the Spanish revolution from July to September, becoming a decisive factor in triggering Stalin's decision to purge the Party of malcontents once and for all.

On the 16 January 1935 the Comintern's political secretariat, evidently on instructions from above, finally approved the Popular Front strategy as practised in France.[22] Then on the 1 May Stalin placed his personal seal of approval on the theses to be presented at the seventh congress of the Comintern, which duly convened from the 25 July to the 21 August 1935.[23] Discontent with the new course was stifled. From total sectarian rigidity, the international movement was launched onto a path of complete extemporisation. Old shibboleths and sacred principles were unceremoniously smashed as archaic icons representing times long past, swept away from the floor of the congress in an atmosphere of desperation induced by the overriding threat from Nazi Germany. World revolution was put off for better times. The international Communist movement had to be mobilised in its entirety for war in alliance with erstwhile and future enemies. Both the Narkomindel and the Comintern's strategy were a response to the same threat; collective security and Popular Front were twins. But they were difficult and by no means identical twins, always pulling youthfully in different directions; and Stalin was not always there with a firm hold on the harness. Speaking of the identity of aims shared by the USSR and the Comintern, Togliatti told the seventh congress:

> this identity of purpose does not in fact mean that there must be a coincidence in every action, at every moment and on every question, between the tactics of the proletariat and the Communist parties which are still fighting for power and the concrete tactical positions of the Soviet proletariat and Bolshevik party, which now exercise power in the Soviet Union.[24]

The very governments which Litvinov was so persistently attempting to win over in an alliance against Germany were the governments which looked with alarm at the Popular Front as a threat to their survival. As well as facilitating and complementing the policy of collective security, by precipitating the expansion of Communist ranks to an unprecedented extent, the Popular Front unfortunately also complicated and undermined the fulfilment of an already impossible task.

5 The Abyssinian Crisis, 1935–36

Given the priority of containing Nazi German expansionism, there was no incentive in Moscow to exacerbate relations with Italy. On the contrary, despite fundamental ideological differences, Italo-Soviet relations had rarely been anything less than amicable. Indeed, the relationship was frequently cited by the Russians as a prime example of peaceful co-existence between states with different social systems. Furthermore, Hitler's extensive foreign ambitions threatened Italian and Soviet security alike. The Italians were worried about the fate of Austria; the Russians, about the territorial integrity of Eastern Europe. This gave added reason for the development of active collaboration against a common enemy. At the same time, however, the primacy of Soviet worries about Germany also made Moscow determined to uphold the League of Nations. The problem was that Mussolini's foreign ambitions drove him into direct conflict with the Covenant. The Soviet Government was therefore faced with an acute dilemma when the Italian Government made clear its intention to conquer Abyssinia.

Towards the end of 1934 Mussolini decided upon "the destruction of the Abyssinian armed forces and the total conquest of Ethiopia" [Abyssinia].[1] He believed that "no one will raise difficulties in Europe, provided the conduct of military operations rapidly produces a fait accompli. It will suffice to let England and France know that their interests will be safeguarded",[2] as a Power with no interests in the region, the USSR did not even warrant a passing reference. With the conquest of Abyssinia in mind, Suvich, the Palazzo Chigi's secretary-general, emphasised the importance of seeking "an agreement with Great Britain as well as with France to obtain, as far as possible, a free hand".[3] In fact the evidence available indicates that the Italian Government was reluctant to be too explicit about its overseas ambitions.

Private conversations took place between Mussolini and Laval in Rome on the 5–6 January 1935. But a fatal combination of Italian reticence and Laval's instinctive preference for ambiguous statements of policy left both sides with a different idea of what precisely had been agreed, an ambiguity both sides were happy to leave untouched. The French Government believed it had merely sanctioned Italian hegemony over the Abyssinian economy – as the written agreement that resulted had made clear. The Italians, on the other hand, were convinced that they had obtained carte blanche with respect to the fate of Abyssinia as a whole.[4] Italian incommunicativeness was equally evident *vis-à-vis* the British Government. The subsequent overture to London on the 29 January was made unofficially and in extremely vague terms.[5] The scene was thus set for a gross misunderstanding with tragic consequences for all concerned, and serious implications for Soviet foreign policy.

Relations between Rome and Moscow were complicated by the strategies each conceived independently to contain German expansionism. Soviet leaders sought a mutual security system in Eastern Europe. But this was stymied by Polish opposition. On the other side of the continent, the Italians were not only attempting to forge a Danubian grouping to protect Austria against Germany, they were also aiming to win Polish friendship as a means of counterbalancing Germany. The problem for the USSR was that in pursuit of Polish amity, the Italian Government was prepared to back the Poles in their hostility to Soviet proposals for collective security.[6] Throughout the spring of 1935, the Russians tried hard to dissuade the Italians from their Polonophile activities. This gave them further incentive to avoid alienating Rome. When the Abyssinian Government warned Moscow that Italy was likely to attack, in collusion with France, in October 1935,[7] the Soviet press campaigned vigorously on behalf of the Abyssinians, a campaign which precipitated protests from Suvich at the Palazzo Chigi, in conversation with polpred Boris Shtein on the 16 May 1935. Evidently without explicit authorisation from Moscow, and being one of those Soviet diplomats confident to act independently, Shtein immediately replied to these protests by saying that this was "a matter which does not concern Russia and in which it does not want to get involved".[8]

Whichever way they approached this awkward issue – whether

by exerting pressure on the Italians or through delicate persuasion – the Russians had a vested interest in forestalling any Italian adventure in distant East Africa. It was unfortunate that in attempting to correct any impression of outright hostility to the Italian Government, Shtein unwittingly conveyed the illusion that the USSR was indifferent. Italian hostilities against Abyssinia could only weaken Rome's capacity to act effectively in Europe as a potential ally against Berlin; Moscow was well aware of Italy's existing economic problems, which could only worsen in the event of war.[9] Italian aggression would also pose a threat to the principles of collective security, thereby weakening the chances of containing German expansionism through the League of Nations, a factor Shtein appeared inclined to play down in his anxiety to appease the restless Italians.

These principles were hitherto zealously upheld by the Soviet Government, even where its own interests were not directly involved. The outbreak of the Chaco war between Bolivia and Paraguay in early 1935 prompted Litvinov to insist on action under the Covenant, because failure to take the necessary measures in this particular case would create the risk that one of the fundamental clauses of the Covenant would lose all significance. Thus Litvinov argued that "although we have no special interest whatever in this South American territorial conflict . . . should it be suggested that private palliative measures be taken in the spirit of article 16, such as, for example, an embargo on arms and so forth, then it must be stated that we consider more decisive action is required".[10] But it was always easier to take such a forthright position on Latin American issues than on issues affecting a major European Power.

The Russians were initially determined to prevent Italy's dispute with Abyssinia from erupting into military conflict, even at the expense of the spirit, though not the letter, of the Covenant. This delicate task required some agile diplomacy, the hope being that by facilitating a pacific settlement of the dispute outside the League, they could leave the Covenant in pristine condition – though after the Manchurian crisis it was only notionally still a virgin. Litvinov's job was greatly eased by his fortuitous presidency of the 86 session of the League Council. This gave him the opportunity to press for a peaceful settlement behind closed doors. When told that Britain – a natural opponent of Italian expansionism in East Africa – insisted upon a Council meeting for the 29 July to discuss the Italo-Abyssinian dispute, Litvinov instructed Shtein to warn the Palazzo Chigi, advising the Italians to make a formal request for a delay, a proposal he would then officially support.[11] The last thing Litvinov wanted was a confrontation between the British and the Italians which would paralyse all efforts to form a united front against Germany. The Russians were therefore prepared to go to considerable lengths to delay discussion at Geneva. On the afternoon of the 31 July Litvinov had a conversation with Eden, Britain's Secretary of State for League Affairs, and "said he thought it would be difficult for the Council to decide here and now to discuss broader aspects of the dispute . . . since Italy would demand an adjournment to prepare her case and that would be difficult to refuse. On the other hand he thought it essential to fix during the present session of the Council [a] date for [a] public session at which all aspects of the dispute would come under review. He suggested [the] beginning of September for this".[12] Only too aware that quiet diplomacy might not succeed where Italy was concerned, and conscious also of the British interest in deterring the Italians from any rash action, the Commissar for Foreign Affairs had to consider other measures as well. Eden noted: "Litvinov maintained that [the] present dispute was one which might have a decisive effect upon the League's future. He thought [the] Council should consider whether there was not some declaration that it could make before September which might induce Italy to realise the serious crisis for which she was heading. He thought it would be helpful if the Council could declare as a body that in this dispute it was prepared to carry out its obligations under the Covenant. There was the memory of Manchuria and this no doubt had encouraged Italy. If the Council could show clearly that Manchuria would not be repeated [the] effect might be salutary. I asked M. Litvinov whether he was prepared to take part in such [a] declaration; he stated that he was, though he had not of course as yet consulted his government and had made [the] proposal to me in the first instance."[13]

At this stage, although he had managed to obtain for the Italians a breathing-space within which they could solve the dispute peacefully, Litvinov's attitude towards the Italian Government was hardening rather more than that of his superiors. Comment on the dispute in Moscow seized on Germany's apparent attempts to prevent a peaceful settlement,[14] but this was the opinion expressed by Litvinov's mouthpiece, *Le Journal de Moscou*; the same organ also emphasised the need to assert League principles even with respect to a conflict "on a secondary front in world politics", because "warmongers in Europe" were counting on "the certainty that no collective action whatever" could possibly foil their plans.[15] But elsewhere in the Soviet press a blanket of silence descended on the whole matter, especially noticeable when talks between Britain, France and Italy broke down on the 18 August.[16] Litvinov was out on a limb in defence of the League Covenant.

Stalin and the Politburo were clearly most reluctant to take up a firm position; the attitude of the Comintern mirrored this reserve. When border conflicts between Italian Somalia and Abyssinia broke out with increasing severity from December 1934, the Italian Communist Party (PCI) was somewhat slow to react. All the West European Communist Parties were usually loath to touch the delicate issue of colonialism. Not until early February 1935 did the Italian Communists campaign under the slogan "Hands Off Abyssinia!",[17] and even then, with no great enthusiasm. The leader of the PCI, Togliatti, wrote to his confrères on the 23 March stressing the importance of "the danger of a European war, whether in connexion with the Abyssinian war, whether in connexion with the measures recently taken by German Fascism [the introduction of compulsory military service]. In speaking of these measures one has to concentrate one's fire on Fascism (in general, and German, in particular) and denounce Italian Fascism and Mussolini because his foreign policy has become one of the principal factors in the current situation".[18] Yet Togliatti's views were not reflected in Comintern activity. Italian diplomats noted its "relative silence" on the issue.[19] A compromise was obtained whereby the Italian Party could agitate on Abyssinia and the French Party could attempt to mobilise the leading European Socialist Parties into solidarity with the unfortunate Abyssinians, but the Comintern proper would remain mute. At the seventh Comintern congress in August 1935 Togliatti alone raised the Abyssinian issue at any length. He assured the assembly that should the Negus – the Emperor Haile Selassie – foil Fascism's plans for conquest, he would thereby help the Italian proletariat "to deliver a blow between the head and the tail of the regime of the blackshirts" and "no one" would reproach Abyssinia "for being 'backward', and proletarians throughout Europe will hail it as a progressive force. The Abyssinian people", he continued, "is an ally of the Italian proletariat against Fascism and from this platform we express to them our sympathy, best wishes for their victory, the aid that it is up to us to give them. . . . The revolutionary traditions of the Italian people, the traditions of the legions of the Garibaldi volunteers . . . drive the Italian workers to take their place at the side of the Abyssinian people against the Fascist bourgeoisie".[20] But Togliatti was careful to talk only in the name of the Italian proletariat, though such subtleties scarcely appeased the Fascist regime.[21] It was the French Communist Party that took on the role of turning to the British Labour Party – the key obstacle to co-operation with the Second International – with proposals for an international conference against war in Africa, in defence of Abyssinia. The aim of the conference, wrote PCF secretary Jacques Duclos, "consists of . . . preparing concrete measures directed at the organisation of a mass struggle against war and Fascism, in defence of the Abyssinian people".[22] The conference took place hurriedly two days later in Paris. Someone from the Labour Party was there. A resolution was passed calling on the League of Nations to take energetic measures in defence of Abyssinian independence.[23] But the Second International was simply not interested, and the continued discretion with which the Comintern handled the issue testified to hopes in Moscow that all was not yet lost. Italy had still to embark on war.

After Baron Aloisi spoke for Italy at the League the prospects for peace looked dim. *Le Journal de Moscou* commented, on the 4 September 1935, that the speech left "little hope" for "peaceful resolution" of the conflict.[24] Litvinov then pressed the issue more vigorously at an open forum of the League Council on the following day. The task, he declared, was "all the more unpleasant", because "one of the parties to the dispute is a state with which the Soviet Union . . . has, for more than a decade, maintained consistently friendly relations, with which it would like to further maintain these relations, which it would least of all like to damage, with which we highly value co-operation both within and outside the League for the maintenance of peace in Europe and . . . a nation which commands the deepest respect and sympathy in my country". Having expressed his regrets, Litvinov went on to disagree openly with Aloisi that the League should disinterest itself in the dispute. The conflict,

Litvinov stressed, had to be seen in terms of the "indivisibility of peace".[25] Although not more explicit, Litvinov's remarks implied that the USSR would have to support sanctions against Italy in the event of aggression. The speech was then buttressed by an editorial in *Izvestiya*, though the apologetic tone of the message it relayed indicated continuing misgivings about maintaining the sanctity of the Covenant regardless of the consequences.[26]

Moscow's doubts were reinforced by the same kind of reservations that leading Communists held with respect to the conclusion of the Franco-Soviet alliance: was not the USSR aligning itself with one set of imperialists against another? Prior to Litvinov's speech, the Soviet press tended to portray the Italo-Abyssinian dispute largely in terms of British versus Italian imperialism, the implication being that Moscow should stand aloof.[27] Then in a speech to Party activists, unreported in the Soviet press until mid-October, head of the Soviet delegation to the Comintern, Dimitri Manuilsky, expressed his antipathy towards "British imperialism". London, he argued, was "displaying an extremely suspicious concern for the 'independence' of Abyssinia". He went on to emphasise that "Communists do not want to follow in the wake of Italian Fascist policy, nor do they want to be taken in tow by British imperialism".[28] The same philosophy which underlay opposition to Litvinov's anti-German line – that there was no fundamental difference between the Fascist states and the bourgeois democracies, that the USSR should therefore treat them even-handedly – reappeared as the rationale for inaction over Abyssinia. In direct contrast, *Le Journal de Moscou* was by mid-September arguing that British imperialist, as against moral and legal motivations for taking an anti-Italian position only enhanced the weight of Britain's intervention in the dispute.[29] The argument turned on whether, by aligning with one imperialism against another, the USSR was exploiting the ambitions of one imperialist Power to its own advantage, or whether it was in fact being exploited by an imperialist Power to Soviet disadvantage.

Doubts were certainly reinforced by the apparent reluctance of Britain and France to fulfil their obligations under the Covenant. As an editorial in *Le Journal de Moscou* had emphasised on the 9 August: "in the Italo-Ethiopian conflict, the maintenance of peace does not depend uniquely on the Soviet Union and its initiatives". Thus the speeches of Foreign Secretary Sir Samuel

Hoare – on the 11 September – and Pierre Laval – on the 13[30] – in support of the Covenant, both of which were cautiously welcomed in the Soviet capital,[31] undoubtedly made Litvinov's position easier. Yet they did not entirely allay the suspicions of everyone.

It was undoubtedly to convince his sceptical superiors of the need for concerted action with Britain and France – and following a conversation with Hoare on the 12 September[32] – that Litvinov sent a telegram to Moscow insisting: "the very fact of implementing serious sanctions against Italy by the League will be a formidable warning for Germany as well".[33] The reference to Germany was crucial. Soviet hopes for an accommodation with Berlin through the exploitation of Germany's economic difficulties – discussed in the next chapter – were abruptly, though only temporarily, eclipsed by the Nuremberg rally of the NSDAP on the 10 September 1935. There, as *Izvestiya* noted, "in contrast to past rallies the current one has not seen anything on foreign policy. The only exception is the USSR, to which Hitler referred to in an extremely unfriendly way several times in the course of his speech".[34] And although the Russians continued, as ever, to assume that "Herr Hitler's power is fragile", they also acknowledged that "there is the risk that he will ignite a world war before his final collapse";[35] speculation on the final collapse of the Nazi regime had begun to sound as ritualistic as talk of the collapse of capitalism. The argument that, by taking firm action against Italy, the Russians would drive it into the German camp was not seriously considered. The Italo-German dispute over the fate of Austria was viewed as too intractable to allow for an entente between Rome and Berlin. From the German capital Surits continually advised that "Germany will never decide to choose in favour of Italy";[36] incredible as it may seem, the Narkomindel was later extremely surprised by the extent of the Italo-German rapprochement.[37]

Litvinov's plea for sanctions did not elicit a positive response from Moscow soon enough to allow for a more vigorous defence of the Covenant at Geneva. The speech he delivered to the League Assembly on the 14 September with, as *Izvestiya* emphasised, "all the restraint which the situation demands",[38] indicated continuing hesitations in Moscow. Not until the end of a lengthy and dull discourse on general principles, did he finally touch upon rather than grasp the nettle. "I could at this point end my statement, but I know that many will be puzzled and wonder why I don't speak on the most topical question and the one most worrying the League plenum – namely the Italo-Abyssinian conflict", he declared, adding a thinly veiled comment with regard to Germany: "I preferred to go no further than general questions because the current conflict does not, as far as I am concerned, push into the background the entire international horizon and other, more menacing dangers looming on it." He went on to reiterate Soviet loyalty to League principles. The only novel element in his concluding statement was an uncharacteristic reference to the Soviet Government's opposition to colonialism "and to everything that relates to imperialist aims".[39] Without further instructions, he could not be more forthcoming and, as matters stood, his fundamentalist reassertion of Bolshevik doctrine fell far short of a concrete commitment to action in the event of Italian aggression.

Yet within twenty-four hours opinion in Moscow had swung in his favour. Litvinov's terse reference to colonialism had struck a chord. *Pravda* appeared with an emotive editorial boldly entitled "For a Policy of Peace, Against the Seizure of Colonies!." It stressed the damaging effect of the war on the Italian economy and in encouraging German ambitions. It also underlined the Abyssinian issue as a "deep matter of principle". Concern was expressed at the possibility of an "imperialist deal" at Abyssinia's expense.[40] *Izvestiya* also appeared with a similar editorial, though more restrained than that in *Pravda*. It came out resolutely against "those who, attempting to avoid war for a time, betray weak and backward nations to be savaged by powerful states possessing the most up-to-date means of destroying and exterminating people".[41] Emphasis had shifted sharply from the need to secure a peaceful settlement of the dispute – with the implication that Abyssinia would have to make concessions to Italy – to confrontation with the aggressor. This change of line must have been prompted by news concerning secret Anglo-French conversations aimed at appeasing Italy.[42] A deal involving the Stresa Powers to the exclusion of others would set a dangerous precedent for the future means of coping with German aggression. Faced with this alarming prospect, the Russians were now obliged to take a more forthright position against Italian ambitions.

As one might expect, the hardening of Moscow's attitude was apparent in Comintern activity. On the 25 September the Comintern's executive committee approached the Socialist

International for co-operation in the face of a threat of war in Abyssinia, which, they believed, might give Germany an opportunity to attack "weak Lithuania and seize Memel".[43] In its directives to the Comintern delegation which was to conduct these negotiations, it was emphasised that the proposals "must be looked upon not as *a pretext* for possible talks, but as *the starting-point* for discussions for the successful establishment of a united front on an international scale on the basis of the decisions of the seventh world congress". The Comintern proposed the following measures:

(a) *Mass campaigns in the undermentioned forms*:
1. Mass demonstrations against war and Fascism.
2. The despatch of delegations to Fascist embassies and consulates (Italian and German).
3. The banning of any transportation of weapons and war material whatever, needed by Italy and Germany for war (tie this question in with the question of sanctions).
4. The election of workers' control committees at enterprises engaged in the production of war material.

(b) *The mobilisation of public opinion and the exertion of pressure on governments with the aim of taking the following measures*:
1. The closing of the Suez canal to freight destined to meet the needs of Italian Fascism;
2. no lending, no financial aid to Italian and German Fascism;
3. call a halt to the supply and transportation of war material destined for Italian and German Fascism;
4. compliance by all governments with the League of Nations Covenant in relation to the Fascist aggressor, in particular the immediate implementation of economic sanctions;
5. support for the Soviet policy of peace.

(c) The setting up of a permanent committee composed of representatives of the Communist International and Socialist Labour International to lead and organise the campaigns and, in case of need, to take every measure which would be required in connexion with the future development of the situation.

In addition: a) Systematically integrate the campaign against Italian Fascism with the campaign against *German Fascism* (taking particular account, in relation to the latter, of the Memel issue).

> b) With respect to Abyssinia, give prominence to the slogans: bring the Italian soldiers back to Italy; freedom for the Italian people.
>
> c) In the event of the Socialist Labour International suggesting that the USSR immediately and in the event of need independently introduce an economic boycott, reply:
>
> 1. The CI is in favour of immediate economic sanctions and will support all action aimed at making these sanctions effective.
> 2. If the representatives of the parties in the Socialist Labour International cannot guarantee that the bourgeois governments of their countries will introduce sanctions, then the measures taken by the USSR alone will only be turned against it.[44]

The remainder of the text contains little of interest. As it was, co-operation with the Socialist International never materialised; hostility to the Comintern was longstanding and had been reinforced by the class against class strategy inaugurated at the sixth congress in 1928. Hitler's accession to power had underlined the costs of mutual enmity within the international movement, but only the Communists under Dimitrov had drawn the obvious lesson. The Socialist International was little different from the bourgeois governments of the West in that it mistrusted the Russians as much as the Fascist Powers.

The Italians launched their attack on Abyssinia on the 2 October. On the following day, with Litvinov back from Geneva and reports of hostilities in the Soviet press, the Politburo instructed the Narkomindel to treat the Italian attack as an act of aggression.[45] Accordingly, with the League Council due to meet on the 5 October, Potemkin – now polpred in Paris and Litvinov's substitute at Geneva – was instructed to oppose measures based on proposals to appease Italy.[46] These instructions were then echoed in a *Pravda* editorial on the 5 October, expressing concern at the possibility of "an attempt to patch up the colonial conflict between the imperialist Powers at the expense of the Abyssinian people".[47] Should France and Britain nonetheless press ahead with such proposals, Potemkin was advised not to vote against them, but merely to abstain, in order not to appear opposed to a peaceful settlement.[48] The Russians were in the awkward position of trying to prevent a peaceful settlement without alienating the

Entente Powers – a typical dilemma Litvinov faced in pursuit of collective security. Luckily it never came to a vote. Potemkin duly registered objections to the idea of concessions to Italy,[49] and the dispute was passed on to the League Council in plenary session.

At this stage Potemkin was also armed with instructions to accept economic sanctions against Italy "on condition that the other members of the League implement them".[50] The Russians were thus committed to action against Italy. But the cumbersome League machinery made only faltering progress. Not until the 7 October did a sub-committee of the Council conclude that Italy was indeed an aggressor,[51] and it took a further three days before the Assembly created a Co-ordination Committee to manage sanctions. This met on the 11 October and recommended an embargo on the exportation of "arms, ammunition and implements of war" to Italy.[52]

The Russians could scarcely now retreat from the position they had adopted. But the doubts which Litvinov's opponents had expressed about aligning with one set of imperialists against another were now working in a direction similar to Litvinov's own concern not to step too far out of line with France, the USSR's only ally in the West. The French, in their overriding anxiety about Germany, were still inclined to bury the Abyssinian dispute. In conversation with Surits in Berlin, ambassador François-Poncet stressed that Germany was the "main enemy" and that "all French policy, in particular in the Abyssinian conflict, must be subordinated to the struggle against this enemy; France must win over Italy as an ally against Germany, and not contribute to its weakening and push it towards Germany".[53]

In these circumstances, and against a background of grave misgivings within certain quarters about siding with one imperialism against another, news of British moves to appease the Germans whilst simultaneously making bellicose noises at the Italians inevitably fed growing Anglophobia in Moscow. The dislike of Britain was evident in the Comintern executive's declaration on the Italo-Abyssinian war of the 7 October. "The imperialist struggle of the capitalist Great Powers, first and foremost England and Italy, over Abyssinia, has led to Italian Fascism's attack on the Abyssinian people", it began, adding no less unjustly: "English imperialism under the guise of a suspect concern about the 'independence' of Abyssinia is preparing for war with Italy for the possession of Abyssinia."[54] This simplistic equation of Italian and British policy undoubtedly complicated the task of foreign Communist Parties in opposing Italian aggression in East Africa, a campaign which proved noticeably ineffective.[55] Articles in the Soviet press took on a less explicitly Anglophobe appearance,[56] but nevertheless sufficiently irritated London to elicit angry protests from the Foreign Office.[57] In response to such criticism, Krestinsky – no lover of the Entente Powers – disingenuously replied that he was "quite unaware that Great Britain was being particularly harshly treated", and suggested that the French had no less to complain about. Far more revealing was his remark that "Soviet writers naturally looked at events from a different angle from others and that any news which made them think that England was pandering to Germany, a country which was openly preaching war against this country, aroused their wrath".[58]

Against such a background, it could only be expected that the USSR would fulfil its obligations under the Covenant to the letter, but with evident reluctance and continued misgivings. On the 13 October 1935, Litvinov arrived back in Geneva, and two days later received word from Moscow of the Politburo's decision: "The Government of the USSR, like other members of the League of Nations, will be implementing the resolution passed by the Co-ordination Committee."[59] A decree banning the export of war material to Italy was duly passed by the Council of People's Commissars on the 17 October.[60] However, other states, for differing and varying reasons, were not only loath to contemplate sanctions, but were also only too ready to jeopardise the future effectiveness of the League in order to escape their obligations. This was altogether too much for Moscow to swallow in dignified silence. Faced with such special pleading, and with sanctions now extended beyond purely military items,[61] Litvinov warned the Co-ordination Committee on the 19 October that if these states threatened the effectiveness of sanctions, then he reserved the right of his government "to reconsider its attitude to the measures recommended by the Co-ordination Committee".[62]

Not much could be expected from sanctions.[63] But Litvinov drew some hope from the bellicose attitude of many British Conservatives, including Eden, towards the Italian Government's aggression. By early November, it appeared to many who were not privy to the hesitations and doubts within the British Cabinet, that London would pursue the Italians to the end.[64]

Thus news of the Hoare-Laval plan – which the Russians always referred to as the Laval-Hoare plan – came as a great blow. Not only did it threaten to wreck the League sanctions and thereby discredit the Covenant. It also left the Russians in complete disarray. Only one week prior to the revelations, Radek had publicly dismissed the likelihood of an Anglo-Italian compromise.[65] News of the plan therefore reawakened fears of collusion between the imperialist Powers at the expense of "weak nations, and also at the expense of the USSR".[66] Concern lest this set a precedent was reinforced by news from London and Berlin. On the 9 November a worried Maisky scurried to the Foreign Office for reassurance that rumours of an Anglo-Franco-German agreement "at the expense of Russia" were not true.[67]

News of the Hoare-Laval plan thus hit Moscow like "an exploding bomb". In an article on the subject Radek stressed the "great resentment and indignation" it had caused. He was puzzled: "what drove Great Britain to make such a move which, if it were put into effect, would compromise the League of Nations to an unprecedented extent and which even only in draft form is already greatly damaging the authority of the English Government?".[68] Hoare's resignation as Foreign Secretary – amidst public uproar in Britain – was therefore greeted with undisguised relief in the Soviet capital as a sign that, however belatedly and half-heartedly, the British were mending their ways. Heartened by this change of line, Radek could now sound a more sympathetic note, expressing the wish that "*the turmoil which England is experiencing will end in England's consciousness of its responsibility for the cause of peace and the decision to pursue a firm policy in defence of the collective peace*". Evidently all had been forgiven. In fact the Russians now showed considerable sympathy for Britain's plight, for it mirrored the Russians' own. Radek acknowledged that a policy in defence of peace "may meet with great difficulties" and "may demand both temporary retreats and complicated manoeuvres", but such a policy, he added, ultimately should "not sacrifice what is fundamental – the cause of peace, the cause of the security of all nations, regardless of the colour of their skin and social systems".[69]

As the tenor of Radek's comments indicate, the Russians were not totally inflexible over Abyssinia. What they hoped for was to preserve the outward appearance of conformity to the Covenant as a realistic second-best. This much is clear from Litvinov's instructions to Potemkin at Geneva, contained in two consecutive telegrams. The first of these outlined the objections to approving the Franco-British plan – still on the table – at the League:

> The Laval-Hoare proposals mean the partition of Abyssinia and the violation of its territorial integrity. This contradicts the Covenant of the League, guaranteeing all League members the inviolability and integrity of their territory, in the name of which the League of Nations has both intervened in the conflict and begun to apply sanctions. The League of Nations therefore cannot approve such proposals. Should Abyssinia, for whatever reason, itself consider it possible to accept the Paris proposals and Geneva be so informed, then the League of Nations must not prompt them to continue the war, but merely register the agreement existing between the warring sides. Until Abyssinia declares its acceptance of the Laval-Hoare proposals, the League of Nations can in no way approve them.

Litvinov also instructed Potemkin: "Acquaint yourself with the article in *Le Journal de Moscou* which will appear on the 17th";[70] the editorial referred to launched a fierce attack on Italy, comparing its foreign policy with that of Germany and that of Japan – a theme which was to be repeated in the New Year. A further telegram – sent on the 16 December – sheds more light on Soviet policy. Here Litvinov instructed Potemkin to hold firm "even at the risk of arousing Laval's displeasure", but "in private tell him that we will by no means raise objections to mediation by anybody and the elaboration of any conditions for ending the war, provided it is not done in the name of the League. It is quite natural", Litvinov continued, "that France and England, as neighbours of Italy and Abyssinia [via their colonial possessions], should have shown a special interest not only in their capacity as members of the League. If they succeed in persuading the Negus to accept these or other conditions, we will not raise objections to the League Council registering the agreement of the parties, [but] we will not enter into a discussion of the conditions. However, in so far as they attempt [to obtain] the approval of the League for the partition of Abyssinia, we will resolutely oppose it".[71]

The Council met in closed session on the 19 December, and was set for a surprise: Hoare had resigned on the previous day; his deputy, Eden, was now Foreign Secretary. "This time", Potemkin wrote to Moscow, "Eden took every opportunity to express his wish to co-ordinate his line with ours. It is apparent to everyone that he is exultant at the collapse of the Laval-Hoare plan."[72] Britain's new Foreign Secretary had turned undertaker. He pointed out that "if indeed it was a question of burying the corpse, it was necessary to work out the formalities of the burial".[73] When asked for Soviet support in the continuation of sanctions, Potemkin replied that there was no reason for removing them "while the aggressor has not ceased military action".[74]

Pleased though they undoubtedly were, that Britain appeared to be returning to a firm line *vis-à-vis* Italy, the Russians had suffered a nasty jolt with the Hoare-Laval plan revelations. Henceforth Soviet policy was, at least in private, extremely cautious in relation to sanctions, tempered by the sustained anxiety lest the other Great Powers renege on their obligations and leave the USSR isolated and dangerously over-exposed. They had good reason to be suspicious. Whereas Italo-Soviet trade was grinding to a halt with the combined effect of sanctions and Rome's retaliatory measures, the other Powers appeared to be profiting by continued commercial and financial transactions. Shtein, undoubtedly prone to exaggerate in such matters, reported the following to Moscow on the 24 December 1935: "At a time when, after the publication of the retaliatory decree, Italy has renewed trade agreements with Belgium, Spain, Switzerland, is conducting talks with the Germans and French, and is reaching agreement on long-term clearing settlements with England etc., we face unilateral denunciation of a trade agreement."[75]

Soviet fears of losing out to others culminated in moves towards the revival of Italo-Soviet trade. When the idea of oil sanctions was considered by the Committee of Eighteen at Geneva towards the end of November, the Russians announced that they would be willing to participate if all others followed suit, and when Eden raised the issue again on the 22 January 1936, "Litvinov stated that his government's attitude was unchanged."[76] Yet that very month Soviet oil exports to Italy, though considerably below the level of the previous year, rose by a third and, with discussions on oil sanctions continuing, rose again in February, though by a lesser amount. The Russians simultaneously also increased their exports of other items not covered by League sanctions.[77] However, too much should not be made of this; it has to be seen against the background of what the other Powers were doing. The

Russians loyally fulfilled their obligations on items specified for sanctions, and as a result the existing downward trend in trade with Italy slumped even further and never entirely recovered. The revival of oil and other exports was significant only as a telling symptom of continuing fears of being left in the lurch by fickle associates. These fears sprang not merely from known French hopes to retain amity with Italy and wavering British resolve, but also from the knowledge that for all the differences which set the Italians apart from Britain and France, there was nonetheless more to unite them than to divide them. The same feeling of alienation affected Soviet reactions to the German problem. By the end of January 1936, Litvinov was warning Eden that "many in Russia" were "beginning to doubt whether the policy of collective security was in truth the correct one",[78] and he was certainly not bluffing.

The Russians attempted to remain aloof, in so far as this was possible. While rebuffing Italian hints that an Italo-German rapprochement was imminent,[79] they simultaneously showed no willingness to take any initiative with respect to oil sanctions.[80] Leaving this to the British, they consoled themselves that Italy was unlikely to achieve victory prior to the onset of the rainy season in Abyssinia during the coming spring.[81] Even after Hitler's troops marched into the Rhineland on the 7 March 1936, the Russians held firm, despite Italian efforts to use the crisis to press the USSR for an end to sanctions.[82] This balancing act could not continue indefinitely, however. An Italian victory over Abyssinian forces at Amba Alagi on the 31 March and the 1 April 1936 raised the prospect of "a complete collapse" of the Haile Selassie's cause.[83] This hastened French attempts to secure a compromise with Italy at any price. Sanctions had clearly proved a wretched failure. Rome was urgently needed as an ally against Germany. As a result, the Russians found themselves in an awkward position. The Franco-Soviet pact had at long last been ratified by the French senate – on the 12 March – so the Russians were extremely reluctant to offend a hard-won ally. On the other hand, Litvinov did not want a breach of the Covenant through which Hitler could drive his armoured columns. Moscow's instructions to Potemkin at Geneva were therefore an elaborate attempt to combine defence of the Covenant – at least in form – with the need to maintain a common line with France. Potemkin was told to accept the idea of peace proposals provided they were dealt with outside the confines of the League.[84] Litvinov then informed Valentino, the Italian ambassador to Moscow, that the Russians could not initiate or even actively support any initiative to end sanctions, and warned the Italophile Shtein in Rome that the instructions to Potemkin did not imply the removal or unilateral renunciation of sanctions. "We want to remain loyal members of the League", Litvinov emphasised. "We will always be pleased to improve relations with Italy, but the predetermining factor will be Italy's attitude towards aggression. If Italy recognises that Hitlerism is a massive military danger for the whole of Europe, and in particular for Italian policy, then the ground will be laid for co-operation".[85]

Yet no sooner had Litvinov moved to maintain the sanctity of the Covenant, than the British Government cut the ground from under his feet. The reason for ensuring observation of the Covenant was ultimately to deter Germany. But British policy went in the opposite direction. While attempting to maintain sanctions against Italy, London simultaneously sought a rapprochement with Hitler. Soviet and British priorities were completely at odds with one another – not for the first or the last time – and the argument, raised by Manuilsky and others during the previous autumn, to the effect that British imperialism might take the USSR in tow to further its own interests, now looked more convincing than ever.

The Russians reacted vigorously to what they saw as British perfidy. On the 14 April 1936 *Le Journal de Moscou* appeared with an editorial entitled "Two Fronts". It attacked "certain English politicians" who well understood that Hitler "was ready to promise security in the West, with the aim of obtaining his freedom of action in the East", yet who persisted in their attempts to reach an accommodation with him. Peace was indivisible, the editorial stressed, but "if the means are insufficient for fighting on both fronts, the question inevitably arises of establishing which front presents the greater danger". In an obvious reference to the position of the USSR, *Le Journal de Moscou* continued: "what enthusiasm can a man have in putting out a small fire far away if, beforehand, he has to count on the indifference of others towards the fate of his own house which, he is convinced, will from tomorrow fall prey to fire, when today even precautionary measures are not being taken". Preparations were being made for a European conflagration by "a zombie of a state", "a danger incomparably greater than the Italo-Ethiopian conflict".[86] Similar sentiments were also expressed by Maisky in conversation with Eden a fortnight later.[87]

In these circumstances Emperor Haile Selassie's departure for exile on the 4 May 1936 came as a great relief to the Russians. "The liquidation of the Italo-Ethiopian conflict . . . simplifies the task of the League of Nations Council, in reducing it to one major problem: the defence of Europe against the danger which is advancing on it and the obvious symptom of which is the violation of Locarno – which is on the Council's agenda", *Le Journal de Moscou* commented candidly.[88] Now that Abyssinia had fallen, Litvinov saw a possibility of using the removal of sanctions as a lever on Italian policy. "In exchange for calling a halt to sanctions", he told Eden on the 13 May, "we must . . . obtain from Italy firm obligations with respect to the strengthening of peace in Europe, in support of the principle of collective security and the League of Nations."[89] But this opportunity was lost. Once again the British took their own road, leaving Litvinov bedraggled in the dust.

In London the Cabinet was divided as to which course of action to pursue. Eden's "strong inclination . . . was not to raise sanctions".[90] Others disagreed. But time was running out. Not until the 17 June 1936 did the Cabinet finally agree to withdraw sanctions and this was not translated in a League Assembly resolution until the 4 July.[91] Litvinov's suggestion was completely ignored. Furthermore the lifting of sanctions came too late. By then Hitler had prepared the ground for a rapprochement with Austria and on the 11 July signed an agreement which amounted to the subordination of Austrian domestic and foreign policies to German influence. The Russians now realised the full cost of sanctions: "Italy, tied up with Abyssinia and in the unresolved conflict with England, could not permit itself the luxury of rendering armed resistance to Germany and was forced not to protest against the German-Austrian agreement." In this the USSR was bound to suffer: "Italy will not hinder Germany from strengthening its anti-Czech policy and . . . Germany, even without a formal Anschluss, may, without opposition from Italy, extend its influence into the Balkans in order to carry out an attack on us through the Balkans."[92]

The true cost of the whole futile exercise became apparent on the eve of the civil war in Spain. Barely had one drama ended than another had begun. The speed with which these crises succeeded one another left the Entente Powers confused and fatigued. A sense of impotence, engulfing Britain since the onset of the Depression, was now also eating its way into the vitals of French society. Both Powers were increasingly debilitated in spirit, conscious only of the process of their own decay and unable to judge the true measure of their strength and the true vulnerability of their adversary. To them Litvinov's staunch defence of the Covenant was an irritant rather than an aid, a complication rather than a solution to their difficulties. Here lay the flaw in Litvinov's strategy. It ultimately depended for its success on the support of those deeply mistrustful of Moscow's motives, and while Hitler was successfully exploiting the antagonisms between the other Powers, the rigidity of Soviet policy left the USSR frequently the loser. It was therefore inevitable that the arguments of Litvinov's rivals, that alternative courses of action had still to be fully explored, once again found a sympathetic ear.

6 The Limits to Co-operation with France, 1935–36

The signature of the Franco-Soviet pact unquestionably placed the USSR in a stronger international position, but not to such an extent that it decisively resolved the conflict of opinion in Moscow as to whether separate negotiations with Berlin were feasible and worthwhile, counterproductive or impracticable. For the manner in which Laval treated his negotiating partners, the severe limitations imposed by him on the provisions of the pact, and his stated determination to make use of the pact in bargaining with Germany, only reinforced the argument that the pact should be seen by the Russians as the prelude to negotiations with Berlin, and not as an alternative to a Soviet–German settlement. Still facing the bleak prospect of enforced isolation which Laval's policies would almost certainly produce, the Russians flirted once again with Berlin, using Germany's economic difficulties as a means of leverage over German policy towards the Soviet Union.

The German economy was distinctive in its dependence on the importation of industrial raw materials and in the passive balance of trade it incurred with its suppliers. The expansion of industrial output from 1932, although insufficient to solve the chronic problem of mass unemployment, was nonetheless sufficient to raise the demand for raw material imports. This increased demand unfortunately coincided with a decline in exports as a result of the high prices set on German goods. The weakness of the Mark in foreign exchanges only worsened the situation by further raising the demand for imports, since it was obviously cheaper to buy at the existing rate of exchange than at some future and more disadvantageous rate. One solution was to block repayments of reparations and Allied debts. The German Government announced that from the 1 July 1934 it would pay no interest on foreign debts for six months an action which simply prompted retaliation from France and Britain. Other means had therefore to be found. In search of a solution, the Nazi leadership secured the appointment of Schacht, the Reichsbank president, as head of the Reich and Prussian Economy Ministries in August 1934. A few weeks later, he unveiled his solution at Leipzig. What it amounted to was an attempt to find substitutes for the raw materials hitherto imported. The establishment of a system of licensing imports was to be accompanied by the use of cheaper surrogates, the attempt to produce raw materials within Germany and the use of bartering in foreign trade to obtain these items.[1] However, during the following year – 1935 – these new measures proved inadequate. Rearmament placed a heavy burden on the development of industry, and this coincided with a crisis in agricultural production. Between 1934 and 1935 Germany paid even more for raw materials imported from abroad: in 1934, 217 million DM, and in only the first eight months of 1935, 215 millions. At the same time, exports continued to decline. The average monthly exports in 1933 amounted to 406 million DM, in 1934, 347 millions, and in 1935, only 336 millions (averaged over the first eight months). By the end of October 1935, payments for raw material imports were being delayed by German banks due to so-called "transfer difficulties".[2] The country's agricultural problems placed even greater pressure on the management of foreign trade. Consumers suffered acute food shortages in the autumn of 1935. It was impossible to buy butter, lard, margarine, pork or bacon; food queues appeared outside the shops.[3] But the shortage could not be relieved through extensive food imports due to the precarious balance of payments situation, and food shortages, like inflation, threatened the stability of the Nazi regime.

The crisis in Germany thus opened up interesting possibilities for the Russians. By the end of November 1935, a "significant section of the German business world" was looking to the USSR as a way out of its difficulties – at least, according to *Izvestiya*'s Berlin correspondent.[4] And the Soviet Union was by no means an unlikely solution. In 1931–2 the USSR had been one of the most important purchasers of Germany's manufactured exports. However, Soviet–German trade had declined as industrialisation made the USSR more self-sufficient in manufactures, and as the scourge of famine put an end to already falling food exports. Hitler's accession to power and the consequent harassment of Soviet trade officials further hastened the decline in trade. Yet by the beginning of 1934 the Germans appeared to have realised the error of their ways. In March of that year ambassador Nadolny had suggested to the Russians that improved economic relations might improve political realtions.[5] But whereas they were willing to see trade continue – a trade and payments agreement was signed on the 20 March 1934[6] and this was followed on the 14 April by an agreement extending part of the credit afforded the USSR by Germany in February 1933[7] – the Russians were nonetheless reluctant to take on any obligations to purchase German goods.[8] And once Soviet negotiations for an Eastern Pact were under way, Moscow viewed any German proposals as a devious means of sabotaging progress towards collective security. Not until the Franco-Soviet pact had been concluded were the Russians disposed to seek a response from Berlin.

The ink was barely dry on the Franco-Soviet pact when Litvinov suggested to Schulenburg, Nadolny's patient and agreeable successor, that the signature of a Soviet–German non-aggression pact would help to "lessen the significance of the Franco-Soviet pact" and lead to improved relations between the two Powers.[9] Not surprisingly, given Hitler's unabated hostility towards the USSR, the offer went unanswered. But the fact that it was made at all was revealing; Litvinov evidently hoped that Berlin's rejection of the offer would confirm to his superiors that the Germans were still of aggressive intent. To that extent, he appears to have succeeded. However, the persistence of the Entente Powers, with Britain now leading the way, in pursuit of a separate settlement with Berlin scarcely strengthened Litvinov's position.

The Russians had reason to worry. On the 21 May 1935, some two months after announcing compulsory military service, Hitler delivered a speech to the Reichstag assuring the various Powers – with the notable exception of the Soviet Union – of his peaceful intentions. With an eye to Britain, he also suggested the conclusion of an agreement on the limitation of naval armaments. Moscow naturally attacked the speech[10] and, nervous lest it encourage the Western Powers to seek an accommodation with Berlin, once more reminded them that "the East is not the only possible and inevitable direction which German aggression might take".[11] The fears underlying this warning were then confirmed by the unexpected conclusion of the Anglo-German naval arms limitation agreement on the 18 June.[12] The convention was sarcastically referred to in *Pravda* as "The Anglo-German Agreement for the Expansion of Naval Armaments", since it provided for German naval construction up to 35 per cent of the British level,[13] thereby breaching the provisions of the Versailles settlement. "The fact that it is an agreement which no one believes will last, even in England, does not diminish but on the contrary enhances the importance of this event, pregnant as it is with incalculable consequences", *Le Journal de Moscou* pointed out with some vehemence.[14] The agreement also came as a grave blow to France. Although initially Laval "did not quarrel . . . with His Majesty's Government for catching the German ball as it bounced", he was much concerned that the issue of naval armaments had been treated apart from the issue of land and air armaments.[15] In addition: "It was the French view, derived from the London and Stresa conversations and the subsequent events at Geneva, that none of the Powers whose solidarity was confirmed at these meetings would be in a position to enter into an agreement with Germany on its own which would involve revision of the Versailles Treaty."[16] Indeed, the conclusion of the agreement severely shook French opinion.

"Comment, whether from the Right or the Left, is almost without exception hostile both to the principle and to the matter of the agreement", the British ambassador to France noted disconsolately.[17] Hostile comment from the French press was given wide publicity in the Soviet press;[18] the agreement and the reaction to it prompted an article by Radek entitled "The Anglo-German Naval Agreement and a Breach in the Anglo-French Front".[19] Soviet concern stemmed less from the fact of the agreement itself – though Moscow was anxious at the prospect of a renewed German naval presence in the Baltic[20] – than its unfortunate impact on the direction of French policy. As the British themselves noted, Laval was "a man whose instinct is to reach an agreement whenever and wherever he can get it" and had "only been brought round with some difficulty to [the] collective policy of the Quai d'Orsay".[21] The Russians were already disturbed at the French Foreign Minister's attempts to reassure the Germans about the Franco-Soviet pact by arguing its subordination to the Locarno treaty, and at the lack of movement towards ratification, despite assurances from Léger on the 6 June 1935 that Laval was determined to secure ratification as soon as possible. The news from Paris was, indeed, uniformly bad. In a letter to Litvinov dated the 26 June polpred Potemkin remarked on "the noticeable increase in the activity of elements hostile to us" as a result of domestic developments within France. "The French press of a bourgeois persuasion is howling about the successes threatening from the united front", he pointed out, adding that: "In the political salons there is talk about the growth of our influence over the internal life of France after Laval's Moscow visit. The Ministry of Internal Affairs and the War Department are presenting the Council of Ministers with data supposedly testifying to preparations for revolutionary activity by the united front and to work by the Communist Party to secure the disintegration of the French army."[22]

Stalin's statement in support of the French armed forces had indeed come to nothing. On the 18 May 1935, only two days after the Stalin-Laval communiqué appeared in the Soviet press, the Comintern's *International Press Correspondence* began to smudge the issue of support for the French war effort. It appeared with the following editorial:

> Our struggle must be conducted not *against* the weapons, but rather for the control of the weapons . . . the struggle for peace thus simultaneously passes into *the struggle for power*, for only a people which has shaken off the rule of the bourgeoisie and of the big landlords, will represent the invincible power which is necessary in the present stage of tremendously developed war technique, in order to secure its national independence.

The paper also quoted *l'Humanité* to the effect that:

> The French toilers cannot have any confidence in the leaders of the bourgeois army.
> . . . We shall mobilise all forces in order to defend peace and its bulwark, the Soviet Union. For this reason we shall continue to exert all our forces in order to fight against the inner enemies of peace and of the Soviet Union as well as the chauvinistic incitement which opposes the defence of peace and drives to war.[23]

It is scarcely surprising that the difference in tone between the Stalin-Laval communiqué and the opinions expressed above, left the French Communists bewildered. As PCF notable André Marty remarked at the Comintern's seventh congress on the 14

August 1935: "it is impossible to deny that for a short time confusion was caused in the ranks of the French party". Indeed, PCF leaders had to call a meeting of 5000 Party activists in Paris in order to clarify the position, a position which Marty then outlined in no uncertain terms to the Comintern congress:

> The reactionary bourgeoisie, certain leaders of . . . social democracy and . . . Communist renegades declare that since the conclusion of the Pact for mutual assistance between France and the Soviet Union there has been a contradiction between the policy of the Communist Party of the Soviet Union and the policy of the Communist Party of France, which votes against the granting of military credits, the lengthening of the terms of military service, and the militarisation of . . . youth and of the whole civilian population under the pretext of defensive measures against gas attacks . . . we French Communists cannot trust the bourgeoisie to fulfil its obligations under this pact . . . the French Communists are not prepared to give up the political independence of the working class, and . . . will never lead the workers into a block of civil truce. . . . What guarantees have we that the French army will not be used tomorrow against workers and peasants, as was done in Belgium, in Geneva and in Asturias? None at all . . . therefore we vote against the enormous credits which are being demanded at a time when the impoverishment of the French people is greater than it has been for 35 years . . . our Party sets itself the urgent and important task of winning the army for the people in order to prevent its use against the people and to guarantee the fulfilment of the Franco-Soviet peace pact.[24]

The Russians did not trust Laval sufficiently; the failure to mobilise the PCF in support of his government's defence expenditure, and thus to enforce the Stalin-Laval communiqué in turn fuelled fears of Bolshevism amongst anti-Communist diehards in France. A vicious circle of mutual suspicion thus undermined the residual effectiveness of the Franco-Soviet pact. Unilateral overtures to the Germans were the inevitable result.

When the Germans contacted torgpred Kandelaki in Berlin in late June 1935, offering the Russians a one billion Deutsche Mark credit for a ten-year period – Moscow would repay in minerals – he argued in favour of acceptance and suggested that the Soviet

Government obtain confirmation of the offer in writing.[25] The political significance of these proposals was hard to hide and Litvinov would appear to have successfully pressed the argument that this was merely a "German manoeuvre" designed to sabotage Franco-Soviet relations. Kandelaki was overruled.[26] Yet Litvinov's position was dangerously undermined by Laval's continued equivocation over ratification of the pact; the Soviet leadership therefore changed its mind. By mid-July Stalin had evidently decided to bounce the ball back into the German court. In the company of Friedrichson, his deputy, Kandelaki visited Schacht on the 15 July. Here he reiterated much of what he had said some weeks earlier concerning the desirability of expanding trade. Schacht sensed that this could not be the true purpose of the visit, and indicated as much. Then, "after some embarrassment . . . Kandelaki expressed the hope that it might also be possible to improve German-Russian political relations". But Schacht wanted none of this. He suggested Surits contact the Foreign Ministry. Whereupon Kandelaki insisted that Schacht could be of some help. "I asked him what kind of help he expected me to give", Schacht recorded; "Kandelaki then stammered something about the Eastern Pact." When called upon to clarify exactly what he meant, Kandelaki was vague and unforthcoming.[27] Evidently he had instructions to go no further than generalities It certainly appears that neither Litvinov nor Surits were privy to this odd initiative – at least, prior to the event. In straddling two beams, the one of Soviet insecurity in the face of a hostile Germany, the other that of Western indifference to the fate of the USSR, Litvinov found it increasingly difficult to balance as his supports slowly edged away in opposite directions.

The ensuring months saw an intensification of the German economic crisis and renewed disputes within the Nazi regime over policy towards Russia. At the same time, Laval redoubled his efforts to secure an understanding with Berlin and delayed ratification of the Franco-Soviet pact indefinitely – a combination of opportunities and uncertainties which worked to the advantage of Litvinov's rivals. Yet those in Moscow still banking on a change in Berlin as a result of Germany's economic problems were deluding themselves. Such solid information as there was about the true state of opinion within the population and the prospects for unrest only fostered a misconceived optimism. What will happen when the hour of trials arrives in Germany? asked Radek.

"These trials", he wrote, "will inevitably come and perhaps sooner than the observer who has no possibility of following these processes in their internal evolution can today predict. The crucial point in the whole situation is Germany's economic condition, which certainly constitutes a serious menace to the Fascist regime, for it risks aborting its military and economic plan."[28] In one sense Radek's musings were no more than wishful thinking; on the other hand, they had some foundation in fact. Whereas knowledge of daily life in Germany was minimal because of the destruction of the KPD and the liquidation of its network of worker correspondents (*Betriebsberichtserstattung*) reporting on conditions at the work-place, Soviet Intelligence had gained direct access to top-level information on the economy. At the end of 1934 Dr Arvid Harnak, a German economist hostile to Fascism and sympathetic to the USSR, entered service in the Reich Economy Ministry, and from 1935 began passing on "important information" to Soviet Intelligence.[29] All the evidence indicates that the Russians had no other reliable source available to them in Germany for the greater part of the thirties. Thus sound and encouraging data on the German economic crisis combined with a grave lack of reliable reports on the political consciousness of the population left the Russians free to indulge in extravagent illusions about the fragility of the Nazi regime.

In the meantime, relations with France proved as frustrating as ever. Visiting Red Army commanders were well received in early September 1935, but General Gamelin and his colleagues evaded all general and political issues.[30] In these conditions the Russians had no incentive to alter Comintern/PCF intransigence on the issue of support for the defence effort. In September Manuilsky, head of the Soviet delegation to the Comintern, outlined his position to Soviet Party activists:

> The French proletariat is deeply interested in the strictest observance of the Franco-Soviet agreement, which serves the interests of universal peace against the Fascist warmongers. But the French proletariat and French Communists have not concluded any agreements with "their" bourgeoisie. The French bourgeoisie may at any moment attempt to set its army on the working class. This army serves not only the aim of defending France against German Fascism, but also the imperialist aim of suppressing colonial peoples. Amongst

> French officers there are many Fascist elements, dreaming about a Fascist coup in the country and aiming at an agreement with German Fascism at the expense of the French people. Therefore French Communists declare that they will vote against military credits, against all measures of a military character by the French bourgeoisie. Simultaneously they will expose and will relentlessly expose before the broad masses of the people the zig-zags and vacillation of the bourgeois politicians of a Fascist and semi-Fascist character, attempting to come to an agreement with German Fascism.[31]

The Czechs, too, had signed, though unlike their French allies, they had also ratified, a pact of mutual assistance with the USSR. However this did not prompt the Russians to look more benevolently on their defence effort. The Czechs were too dependent on the French and too irresolute in the face of dangers from the extreme Right at home, for the Russians to treat them any differently. This became apparent when, towards the end of 1935, the Czech Communists moved out of line with Comintern policy. Confronted with the need to support Beneš' candidacy for the presidency, because the alternative was backed by the Right and pro-Fascist parties, the Czech Communist Party (CPC) began to drift from the position dictated by the Comintern. The Czech Communists not only voted in favour of the new administration's foreign policy, they also supported the national defence effort in *Rudé Právo*, the Party daily. This act of heresy prompted a warning from Dimitrov in November 1935; but this was never followed up by more decisive action, evidently because he was not as concerned about the consequences of this deviation as some of his colleagues. Not until the 9 January 1936, some three weeks after Beneš' election, did an extensive discussion of the matter take place in the Comintern secretariat. With the caveat that the CPC should not then lurch into the opposite direction and adopt a sectarian position – there were those in Prague, and in Moscow as well, only too eager to sabotage the Popular Front strategy – it was instructed to return to orthodoxy.[32]

The point was that Moscow mistrusted Beneš no less than Laval or Flandin. Referring to the dubiety of Prague's anti-German stance, in a subsequent attempt to rectify his errors, the CPC leader Gottwald wrote:

> What does it mean to vote for the military budget of the existing government in such circumstances? It means to trust it, to refrain from class struggle and, in the end, to hand the fate of the national independence of the country to people patently unfit for it . . . *it is precisely because* we really want to defend the republic from internal and foreign Fascism that we will not vote for the allocation of military credits to the existing government and the ruling bourgeoisie, since we know that in *the hands of the bourgeoisie* these means can always be used not only against the class but also against the national interests of the toiling people.[33]

* * *

By the autumn of 1935 the Russians were increasingly exasperated and dispirited at the growing frequency with which the French ambassador to Berlin was meeting Nazi leaders. In late October Ribbentrop's secretary mentioned to Surits that the head of the NSDAP foreign bureau attributed "great significance" to his meetings with François-Poncet, and considered that "the current direction of French policy opens up perspectives for an agreement". "Laval's policy", Surits reported to Moscow, "is evaluated by them as a gradual retreat from Barthou's constructive plan and as a shift in the centre of gravity of French foreign policy from the plane of collective security to the plane of defending the direct interests of French prestige."[34] News of these conversations – apparently kept secret even from Neurath at the Ausamt – aroused deep suspicion in Moscow. On their receipt Litvinov immediately informed Potemkin in Paris by telegram, advising him to pass on the information to Herriot[35] – then still regarded as the USSR's best friend in the *conseil d'état* – and on the following day he instructed Potemkin to draw Laval's attention to the fact that these conversations breached the Franco-Soviet protocol agreed on the 5 December 1934.[36]

The Russians naturally turned once more to Germany in an attempt to penetrate and widen the fissures appearing in the Nazi monolith. Deputy Commissar of Military Affairs Mikhail Tukhachevsky had already spoken in friendly terms to General Köstring, newly appointed military attaché at the German embassy in Moscow, on the 26 October 1935. Emphasising that "the Red Army still felt great sympathy for the Reichswehr", Tukhachevsky also "remarked several times that he was sorry that Germany and the Soviet Union were not working together. The two countries", he observed, "could very well complement each other economically and they had no territorial issues in dispute; he then added: 'If Germany and the Soviet Union still had the same friendly political relations they used to have, they would now be in a position to dictate peace to the world' ". But the Germans were rightly disinclined to take all this at face value, given Tukhachevsky's reputation as a Francophile.[37] They were similarly suspicious of anything Litvinov uttered in a like manner. The Commissar was, by early November 1935, convinced that "Laval has decided, in so far as it depends on him, that whatever happens he will wreck Franco-Soviet co-operation and join a German anti-Soviet bloc."[38] At the festivities on the 7 November Litvinov, sitting at the same table as Schulenburg, "suddenly raised his glass and said in a loud voice: 'I drink to the rebirth of our friendship' ".[39]

Litvinov's gesture could easily be dismissed as a rather crude attempt to offend the French, which it undoubtedly was, but it also indicated the gloomy state of mind in the Kremlin. Kandelaki had left Berlin for Moscow at the end of October 1935, evidently still arguing for co-operation with the Germans. Surits, a sceptic on this matter, followed later. The subsequent discussions in the Soviet capital then led to a decision that Surits activate contacts in Berlin.[40] Further news of Laval's latest moves must have played some role in this decision. On Laval's instructions François-Poncet briefed Surits along with other ambassadors on the results of a meeting with Hitler which took place on the 21 November.[41] Such candour might have been appreciated by some; it merely scared the Russians. Furthermore, in Paris Laval told Potemkin that Germany saw the Franco-Soviet pact as an "obstacle" to any improvement in Franco-German relations – the Russians certainly hoped so – and, much less believably, that Hitler said he had no intention of attacking the USSR. From this Potemkin concluded that Laval was making ready a retreat from the alliance to a mere non-aggression pact with Germany, "or even a mere declaration from Germany obliging it not to attack the USSR". Laval explained his "Germanophile attitude" (*germanofil'stvo*) in terms of French pacifism – "without an improvement in relations between France and Germany peace cannot be achieved. Should I have to commit a crime for peace, I would", he stated disarmingly. "I am conveying these words literally", wrote Potemkin, "because I see in them Laval's attempt to legitimate in advance any act of disloyalty he may commit." What also emerged from the conversation was Laval's disquiet at continuing sabotage of the French defence effort by the PCF. He linked the delay in ratifying the Franco-Soviet pact with the failure of the Comintern to act in line with the Stalin-Laval communiqué – a linkage already in Soviet minds, but from the opposite point of view – by warning that "the work of the Comintern within France is producing complications in our relations and is weakening his arguments in defence of the pact. Enlarging on this", Potemkin continued, "Laval went so far as to complain that he was 'tricked in Moscow' ". He also justified his intention to exclude the USSR from future negotiations with Germany by saying that the discussions might concern "special" French interests which did not relate to the USSR.[42]

Against a background of deep suspicion concerning France, the Soviet embassy in Berlin set to work sounding German opinion. In a letter to Litvinov on the 28 November, Surits reported on the results of his efforts:

> In accordance with the objectives I was given, immediately on returning to Berlin I set about activating contacts with the Germans. For this I made use of every occasion that presented itself and had time in this comparatively brief period to see a fair amount of people . . . and at a number of receptions . . . to meet a number of prominent "Nazis", including Goebbels and Rosenberg. I arranged a number of receptions of my own, to which I invited Schacht and Blomberg, amongst others. All my contacts with the Germans merely reinforced the conviction I already held that the course against us taken by Hitler remains unchanged and that one cannot expect any serious changes whatever in the immediate future. Everyone I spoke to was unanimous in this. For instance I was told that Hitler has three "obsessions" [*punktika pomeshatel'stva*]: hostility towards the USSR (towards Communism), the Jewish question and the Anschluss; hostility towards the USSR stems not only from his ideological position vis-à-vis Communism, but [also] forms the basis for his tactical line in the field of foreign policy.
>
> Hitler and his immediate entourage are firm in the convic-

> tion that only by means of maintaining an anti-Soviet course to the end can the Third Reich succeed in its tasks and acquire allies and friends. They are counting on the fact that the future development of the world crisis must inevitably lead to a deepening of contradictions between Moscow and the whole of the rest of the world. They consider that the only means of pressure which we now possess for alleviating this anti-Soviet course is Germany's interest in establishing normal economic relations with us; more precisely, in receiving our raw materials.

"Hitler and his entourage" would "not willingly change their course" *vis-à-vis* the USSR, Surits emphasised repeatedly, arguing in harmony with Litvinov that: "They might be pressed into this either by some sort of dramatic event within this country (by all accounts one cannot count on this in the immediate future) or by a strengthening of the international front against Germany." His advice was as follows for the short-term:

> In the meantime apparently nothing else remains for us in fact except to wait patiently and continue to build up our strength and expand our work on the economic front. The strengthening of our economic ties on the basis of Schacht's latest suggestions is profitable to both sides (this and only this explains the blessing Schacht has been given by Hitler). The implementation of the new agreements [of April 1935] will bring interested commercial circles into motion; it will draw them closer to us; it will undoubtedly reinforce our "base" in Germany and significantly ease the way to a change in political course when those now ruling Germany are brought to this point in real earnest by subsequent events.[43]

Embassy officials in Berlin thus continued to lobby their various German counterparts, but with no substantial success.[44] The only progress Surits could report by mid-December 1935 was that the issue of Russo-German relations was being discussed "in circles close to the leadership" and that the "official anti-Soviet course" was giving rise to criticism even within the NSDAP.[45] Yet, as he readily acknowledged, "there is no doubt that Hitler and his immediate entourage stand firmly by their primitive anti-Soviet positions".[46] In Moscow Litvinov was very pessimistic about the prospects for a rapprochement with Germany. He was more struck by information recently received about negotiations towards a German–Japanese alliance.[47]

The year 1935 thus ended on a note of acute disappointment. Franco-Soviet relations had at first seemingly progressed – with the signature of the alliance – but then slid back into former uncertainties as Laval endlessly obstructed ratification. The disturbing zig-zags in British policy over Abyssinia, accompanied by British moves towards an understanding with Germany – the Anglo-German naval agreement of June 1935 being the beginning rather than the end of the process – also came as a blow to the Russians. The sense of disillusionment was ably characterised by Radek: "Everything which they [the Entente] achieved in the field of strengthening peace . . . in the first half of 1935, they themselves to a significant extent upset and destroyed in the second half of the same year."[48] "Certain states", *Le Journal de Moscou* pointed out in reproach, would have to decide whether to advance more steadfastly "along the road to organising collective security" or "to submit to pressure from Mr Hitler and follow his recipe for bilateral pacts and the localisation of war."[49]

The West was turning its back on the USSR, and at a time when the risk of war was as pressing as ever. This inevitably favoured the re-emergence of isolationism in Moscow, a belief that the USSR had to rely exclusively on its own resources, a conviction underpinning a further expansion in the national defence budget, announced to a session of the central executive committee in January 1936. The key words of Molotov's address on the 10 January were that: "we toilers of the Soviet Union must count on our own efforts in defending our affairs, and above all on our Red Army in the defence of our country".[50] As Schulenburg noted, "a marked increase in arrogant boastfulness is noticeable, and this is backed up by the announcement of substantial increases in the military estimates".[51] The emphasis on going it alone was even more pronounced in accompanying comment in the Soviet press. A special column on the subject appeared in *Pravda* with the following message:

> One must . . . fully take into account the fact that the foreign policy of the capitalist countries supporting the system of collective security is subject to those same contradictions which are characteristic of the capitalist world as a whole. These

> contradictions predetermine the vacillation and inconsistency and at times blatant if temporary retreat from the principles of collective security and the indivisibility of peace. And this situation has played its role in enhancing the threat of war, in so far as it has facilitated an activisation of the forces of the aggressors.
>
> The Soviet Union has therefore had to pay particular and incessant attention to the reinforcement of its defences. Our country is drawing a very definite conclusion from the current international situation and from the fact that the danger of war is growing: if you want peace – prepare for defence; if you want life to become even better, even happier – strengthen the country's defence capability; if you want to defend the achievements of socialism's new world, the happiness of people, the joy of liberated labour – strengthen the Red Army, prepare to repel the Fascist birds of prey, the last hope of the old world![52]

Le Journal de Moscou was unusually blunt: "Such is the state of affairs, it is no surprise that in the USSR the conviction is growing that in its struggle for peace and its security, the Soviet Union ultimately can hope to count only on its own strength."[53] The arms increase was clearly linked to the fears of a Japanese–German alliance. On the 15 January 1936 Tukhachevsky not only underlined much of what had already been said, but also referred to "enhancing preparedness for mobilisation in order to repel a surprise attack" – a telling indication of the seriousness with which news of an impending alliance between Berlin and Tokyo was being taken.[54] Flanking the text of Tukhachevsky's speech was an editorial in *Pravda* suitably entitled "The Frontiers of Our Motherland are Impregnable", which built upon the theme of fortress Russia and followed Molotov in brusquely dismissing German assertions that the absence of a common frontier precluded the possibility of war as "an argument for simpletons".[55]

The resurgence of Soviet patriotism was accompanied by an implicit rejection of dependence upon the West and carried with it the notion that all capitalist states, whether Fascist or democratic, were little different from one another. In an *Izvestiya* article on the 12 January 1936 Radek described Soviet policy as "aiming at improving relations even with those countries whose ruling strata are preparing for war".[56] Significantly Molotov's speech also omitted the theme of collective security, except for a perfunctory and distinctly unenthusiastic summary of Soviet involvement in sanctions against Italy.[57] Clearly all was not well with Litvinov's policy. In case Western Governments failed to read the signs correctly, the Commissar pointed them out. Prior to departing for Geneva he directed Alphand, the French ambassador, to Molotov's speech and in particular the emphasis therein on increasing armaments to ensure the defence of the USSR. "The People's Commissar told me that he had had to struggle against certain of his colleagues who desired that the Soviet Government should demonstrate more clearly its desire for autarchy and take the initiative in renouncing the Franco-Soviet pact whose ratification has been awaited for nine months", Alphand reported to Paris.[58] These isolationist tendencies were also inextricably associated with the belief that prospects for improving relations with Germany had not vanished. Whereas Molotov's speech was intended as a warning to the Entente, it was also designed – however clumsily – as a means of eliciting a positive response from Berlin. Although Schulenburg considered its tone to be "sharper" than on a similar occasion in the previous year,[59] the Russians themselves thought it "softer".[60] The mystery is what precisely impelled Molotov – clearly with Stalin's acquiescence, if not encouragement – into tossing an olive branch into the German camp when even Krestinsky – in the past certainly no enemy of Rapallo – readily acknowledged that there were "no signs whatever" of any change in Berlin's attitude towards Moscow. "On the contrary", the Deputy Commissar noted, "there are growing signs of a consolidation of German-Japanese relations, with an obviously anti-Soviet bent."[61] Clearly disillusionment with the Entente ran deep; Stalin evidently believed a gesture of co-operation towards the German Government would in some way weaken Hitler's resolve to come to terms with Japan. This conviction also no doubt stemmed from the suspicion that Litvinov and his men were allowing their anti-Nazi sentiments to cloud their better judgement.

Molotov not only reiterated the customary Soviet call for "better relations with Germany", he also remarked on the evident contradiction between "the impudent anti-Soviet foreign policy of certain ruling circles in Germany" and German moves to expand trade with the USSR. Not merely had a DM200 million credit agreement been signed on the 9 April 1935, but "in recent months representatives of the German Government raised with us the question of a new and larger credit – for as long as ten years". This was, in fact, the very offer that had summarily been dismissed as a "German manoeuvre", but which Molotov now said "we have not refused and will not refuse to discuss". He justified this approach in terms of a Soviet policy to expand trade with other countries "independently of [their] temporary domination by this or that political force" – itself a revealing indication that Soviet leaders continued to see Hitler's regime as a bird of passage. "We think", he added, "that this also corresponds to the interests of the German people. But drawing practical conclusions from this is, however, the job of the Government of Germany."[62]

It proved a futile gesture. Molotov's outstretched hand hung limply in the void. The Germans themselves were concerned at the political consequences of expanding trade. In Moscow Pyatakov, responsible for heavy industry, waited impatiently for news from Kandelaki of German readiness to continue talks on a 500 million Deutsche Mark credit,[63] but Schacht regarded Molotov's speech as offensive and refused to meet him.[64] The Soviets then hardened their position by issuing a decree on the 16 January 1936 – evidently hitherto held in abeyance – limiting exports to "certain countries".[65] In fact it was directed against Germany in retaliation for the restrictions on the use of foreign currency to pay for raw material imports, introduced in December 1935. Evidently this aroused some concern in Schacht's ministry and talks with Kandelaki eventually resumed. But despite fairly optimistic reports from Surits, Soviet–German relations remained as atrophied as ever.[66] Meanwhile, Litvinov continued his battery of warnings to the West. Attendance at the funeral of King George V towards the end of January 1936 afforded an opportunity to give a personal warning to Eden – now Foreign Secretary – that "many in Russia" were "beginning to doubt whether the policy of collective security was in truth the correct one".[67] Similarly, en route back to Moscow in early February 1936 Litvinov delivered the same message to the French. Any further delay in ratifying the Franco-Soviet pact would, he argued, lead to "a growth of isolationist tendencies in the USSR".[68] The future of the pact was a vital and sensitive issue. What the Russians referred to as "unfair and groundless attacks" in debates on the pact in the Chamber of Deputies aroused their wrath. "It is absolutely pointless to present matters as if the fate of the Soviet Union could be determined in the French parliament", *Le Journal de Moscou* opined, in an outburst of indignation.[69] Potemkin was instructed to warn Flandin – Laval's successor at the Quai – that "the continuation of the debates and the speeches of some deputies is producing an extremely distressing impression on public opinion in the USSR. The character of the debates is completely unprecedented in the history of relations between two states striving for a rapprochement and towards mutual aid in the interests of peace".[70]

These remonstrations finally had some impact, now that Laval had fallen from power. On the 27 February the Chamber of Deputies passed a motion on ratification by 353 votes to 164. But the matter had yet to go before the Senate; a margin of doubt therefore remained. Interviewed by the US newspaper proprietor Howard on the 1 March Stalin welcomed the resolution passed by the Chamber as "one of the most recent successes" for the "friends of peace". Furthermore he uncharacteristically went out of his way to attack Hitler personally. The German Chancellor had delivered a "pacific" speech in response to news that the Chamber of Deputies had voted for ratification, but it was also laden with threats against France and the USSR. "As you can see", Stalin remarked, "even when Hitler wants to talk of peace, he cannot get by without threats. This is symptomatic."[71]

Yet only two days after Stalin's interview, Potemkin reported moves within the French Senate to have the pact submitted to the international court at the Hague for judgement as to whether it breached the Locarno treaty.[72] This was some measure of the continued strength of anti-Soviet and Germanophile sentiment at high levels in France; Laval was not an isolated figure in this respect. The reaction in Moscow was predictable. When the Germans occupied the Rhineland on the 7 March, Flandin began pressing Potemkin for assurances of Soviet support at Geneva during the forthcoming discussions; Flandin hoped to initiate economic and financial sanctions against Germany. But Potemkin received such suggestions with indifference.[73] It was symptomatic that no editorial on the crisis appeared in either *Izvestiya* or *Pravda* for a week, and such comment as there was reflected a sense of cool detachment from the whole affair. In an *Izvestiya* article on the 8 March entitled "Yet Another 'Scrap of Paper' Torn Up", Radek treated the problem as an entirely Western matter, with no serious implications for the USSR – a clear echo of the isolationism still current in Moscow:

> Threatening the East, German imperialism has already moved westwards – this is a fact. All the rest is idle chatter. What France, England and Belgium do in the future will depend on how they react to these actions by German imperialism. If the Western Powers find the strength in themselves for the speedy preparation of defensive counter-measures, then Mr Hitler will have to think long and hard before playing with his head as a football. If the Western Powers display confusion, lack of unity in will and thought, then sooner or later – more likely sooner than later – there will be war in the West.

"Tell Flandin today", Litvinov wrote to Potemkin on the 9 March, "that in response to his enquiry . . . about our position . . . he can count on my full support at Geneva. However, in view of the fact that our public opinion is still agitated by what has happened to the pact, I would feel more free at Geneva if by then complete clarity had been brought into our relations by means of final ratification of the pact."[74] Thus far the Russians had done nothing more against Germany since the occupation of the Rhineland than suspend negotiations on the 500 million Deutsche Mark credit proposals, then reportedly near completion.[75]

The Russians had made their point; the Germans had foolishly underlined it. On the 12 March – the eve of the League Council meeting in London – the French Senate hurriedly voted for ratification by an overwhelming 231 votes to 52; even outspoken opponents of the Soviet alliance evidently now thought it wiser to seek reassurance in the East, a fact which did not pass unnoticed in Moscow.[76] Two days later, *Izvestiya* at last responded with an editorial attacking Hitler's breach of Locarno:

> The Soviet Union, which has been against every attempt to deny self-determination to the German people . . . declares itself opposed to Germany's breach of the Locarno treaty, against a breach which will only enhance the danger of war.[77]

Unfortunately for the French, and the Russians as well, the British were in no mood to punish the Germans. Litvinov arrived for the meeting on the evening of the 12 March. Flandin's call for sanctions was drowned in a chorus of British protests; faced with a reassertion of the British guarantee, the French succumbed to British pressure.[78] This in turn weakened the position of those who had so precipitiously rallied to ratify the Franco-Soviet pact; if the choice lay between Britain and the USSR, no French politician outside the PCF was about to hesitate in choosing Britain. Litvinov, of course, tried his best to stiffen Anglo-French resolve. He spoke out on the 17 March in the name of the maintenance of the "integrity of international obligations, especially those which directly concern the maintenance of existing frontiers" and stressed that the issue was one of German hegemony over the whole continent of Europe.[79] The British were not merely irresolute when confronted with Hitler, they were also determined to win over the Germans as a means of stabilising the situation in Europe. Once again the fragile structure of collective security began to wobble precariously as the British drilled away at its foundations.

In Britain there was little sympathy for the Soviet case. In reply to protestations from Maisky, Under-Secretary of State for Foreign Affairs Lord Cranborne insisted that: "His Majesty's Government must . . . consider what action at this moment was most likely to secure the peace of Western Europe."[80] The omission of Eastern Europe was revealing. A fierce debate was under way within the Foreign Office over policy towards Germany. Underlying the whole discussion was the assumption that Germany would have to expand in one direction or another. Those arguing for a rapprochement with Hitler insisted that all ties with Eastern Europe be severed – an echo of the British position at the time of the Locarno pact negotiations in 1925.[81] This was the view expressed by "Moley" Sargent, head of the Central Department, and it was supported by Cranborne. Cranborne wrote: "our main object must be to stabilise the situation in Western Europe, and give Germany a free hand, in so far as her and our League obligations permit, further East".[82] The ritualistic reference to the League made the whole idea of giving Germany a free hand more palatable; the true significance of this policy became clear when Britain acquired a Prime Minister who regarded the League as an unnecessary burden on the freedom of British foreign policy. The Marquis of Lothian was more explicit than Cranborne: "provided our complete disinterestedness in Eastern Europe is combined with the Locarno guarantee against unprovoked aggression against the frontiers and soil of France and Belgium, the German General Staff, in the event of another war, will probably reverse the Schlieffen plan and strike Eastwards first whilst remaining on the defensive in the West. It may be difficult to keep out of another European war to the end, but there is all the difference between automatic commitment to go to war on one side when somebody else presses the button and a free hand. If we are not committed nobody will try to bring us in against them".[83]

This was a mirror-image of views held by the isolationist element in Moscow. Litvinov was thus being squeezed from both sides. If the British were trying to redirect Hitler eastwards, why should the USSR not try to drive him westwards? The difference, of course, was that whereas Hitler was willing to negotiate with Britain, he resolutely refused to do so with the Soviet Union. The most that Moscow could manage was to give the British the impression that the Germans were not to be trusted, that they were already negotiating with the Russians. In Litvinov's absence, Molotov used the opportunity of an interview with Chastenet, editor of *Le Temps*, to emphasise that the main threat from Hitler was directed at the West rather than the East. Then, in a frank but calculated admission of differences between Soviet policy makers, Molotov pointed out that: "Among a certain section of the Soviet people there is a trend with an extremely hostile attitude towards those currently ruling Germany, particularly in connexion with constantly repeated hostile outbursts by German leaders against the Soviet Union. However, the chief trend determining the policy of the Soviet authorities considers it possible to improve relations between Germany and the USSR."[84] No one could say the West had not been warned. But such warnings sounded distinctly hollow, given the tenor of German policy. Inevitably the Russians made more belligerent noises in a vain attempt to intimidate the British into being more accommodating. They threatened to disrupt British attempts to conclude an arms limitation agreement with Germany by arguing that if the USSR were excluded from such arrangements, then it would "have to embark on the path of future increases in its army and air force" – an echo of the speeches by Molotov and Tukhachevsky. Yet the Russians were not optimistic of success. They reverted to the half-way house of renewing pressure for an Eastern pact in the hope that "England, France or Germany would themselves be obliged to offer a pact of non-aggression between the USSR and Germany as a compromise."[85]

Soviet impotence was all the more frustrating now that British constraints on French freedom of action against Germany precipitated a volte face in French foreign policy. At Herriot's bidding, the French Government once again began to talk of submitting the Franco-Soviet pact for judgement at the Hague as to whether it breached the Locarno treaty. This was a desperate attempt to appease the Germans, following on the failure of Flandin to secure sanctions against Berlin.[86] The French had lurched from a tough stand against Hitler to a position of undignified appeasement. Henceforth French foreign policy became little more than a pale reflection of British foreign policy; momentary reassertions of French independence were quickly counteracted from London. The Russians were left with an alliance which was essentially inoperable without British goodwill, and since the British did not trust the Russians, Soviet isolationists did not have to look far to find support for their views.

Only after further persistent pressure were the instruments of ratification finally exchanged between France and the USSR on the 27 March 1936. But, as Potemkin noted with his usual cool objectivity, Herriot – a one-time ally turned opponent – was not alone in his readiness to sacrifice everything for peace. French resolve was weakened not merely by the British but also by the attitude of allies in Eastern Europe – with Poland leading the way. Furthermore:

> Hopes of our support in the event of armed conflict with Germany are manifestly weak in France. This must be stated with complete objectivity. Here it is repeatedly said that the USSR is too far away. It has no common frontier with Germany. The Red Army is insufficiently prepared for an offensive war. Conditions of transport in the USSR are such that the transfer of the Soviet armed forces faces extreme difficulties. The speed of Soviet planes is significantly below that of the Germans and so on and so forth. If you add to this the insinuation that the USSR is consciously pushing the states of Europe towards war, that it continues to work for world revolution, that it will have to beat off Japan, then one obtains quite a clear idea of the atmosphere of doubts, fears, mistrust

> and hesitations, in which the French Government must act at the present critical moment.[87]

French hesitancy and the persistence of British moves to appease Hitler thus left the Russians as insecure as before. "Generally, political perspectives in Western Central Europe are very, very unclear", wrote a despondent Krestinsky towards the end of March 1936. "It is difficult to think that the French Government will have sufficient firmness over a long period to maintain a policy of refusing direct negotiations with Germany".[88]

* * *

This pessimism about the French Government meant that Soviet leaders were even more reluctant than before to countenance PCF compliance with the national defence effort. The Communists continued to undermine the fighting power of the armed forces – though their effectiveness in so doing is open to doubt – since these forces were presumed to threaten domestic social change. Even the entry of German troops into the Rhineland and the subsequent ratification of the Franco-Soviet pact left the position unchanged. Hostility towards the French defence effort was thus a direct reflection of Moscow's continued mistrust of the intentions of the French Government. What appears to have been an attempt within the Comintern's executive committee, meeting from the 23 to the 25 March 1936, to alter this line, failed completely. The resulting resolution, not published at the time, contained the following passage:

> In so far as power today is in the hands of bourgeois governments which do not represent a guarantee for the genuine defence of the country and which employ the armed forces of the state against toilers, Communists cannot bear any responsibility for the defensive measures of these governments, and therefore oppose the military policy of the government and the military budget as a whole.[89]

Those advocating a different line managed only a minor, though useful victory, in obtaining explicit acceptance of the notion that a future world war would be fundamentally different from the previous war. It would be something more than an imperialist war. An unsigned article in *Kommunisticheskii Internatsional* stressed: "Lenin precisely at the time of the last world war, which he branded in the severest manner as *an imperialist war of plunder*, simultaneously underlined that in an imperialist epoch *national-liberation wars* are possible. This is all the more true for the current period of the face of *Fascist aggressors*."[90] The door had not been opened for Comintern sections to support the national defence effort in their respective countries; but it had at least been unbolted.

The Russians once more turned to Berlin. Since breaking off talks on a 500 million Deutsche Mark credit in early March in retaliation for the occupation of the Rhineland, they had made no further moves in Germany's direction. And with Litvinov earnestly pressing for economic and financial sanctions at the League, no progress was likely.[91] But the failure of the French to obtain sanctions caused the Russians to re-open contact with Berlin. On the 29 April a new Soviet-German trade and payments agreement was concluded, renewing the 200 millions in credit obtained in 1935 and largely unused.[92] Simultaneously the Russians revived suggestions that better political relations would improve trading prospects.[93] This message appears to have struck a chord in the Reich Economy Ministry. There, Herbert Göring attempted to persuade his powerful cousin Hermann, that Hitler should alter his policy towards the USSR from hostility to friendship, on the grounds that Germany badly needed Russian resources.[94] But German restrictions on Soviet goods remained in force, political negotiations were still out of the question, the Russians themselves had no interest in 500 millions credit without any prospect of earning the Deutsche Marks to pay back the debt, and with the election of the Popular Front Government in France, finalised on the 3 May 1936, hopes naturally rose in Moscow that the Franco-Soviet pact might yet be made to work.

The French elections had left the Communists with 72 seats, the Socialists with 146, and the Radical-Socialists with 115. Together with the lesser parties, they combined to form an overwhelming majority of 378 deputies as against some 236 in opposition. This left the PCF and the Comintern in a dilemma: how should they now behave with regard to the national defence effort? Interviewed by journalists soon after the election victory, PCF notable Jacques Duclos issued the following evasive statement:

> . . . we have been asked whether we have decided to vote for military credits.
>
> We have already said in the agreement on unity we elaborated more than a year ago, that we will refuse to vote for military credits for imperialist ends.
>
> Hitherto to have asked for these credits would have unquestionably meant supporting imperialist ends.
>
> We do not know whether, tomorrow, a situation will not arise in such a way that the vote for military credits might have a different significance.

What he then added indicated that the PCF might vote for war credits if domestic reforms were adopted, including a purge of the armed forces and the suppression of Fascist elements – worries which the PCF shared with Moscow. The PCF, he declared, had fought "the Hitlerites at home" and could not disinterest itself from "the dangers that the Hitlerites abroad" presented to France, "but", he continued, "it is clear that the problem of security presupposes a certain number of political measures at home";[95] "if the changes enumerated by us come into effect, the Communists could be persuaded to vote for the budget", Thorez added.[96] With the election of the Popular Front in France, the unbolted door to support for the national defence effort could now be opened. On the 25 May the PCF Central Committee declared the Party's "complete and unfailing support" for the new regime.[97]

But there were other problems to contend with and not everyone in Moscow regarded the victory of the Popular Front and the high Communist vote in France as entirely a good thing, particularly when it sparked off the sort of social unrest one associates with revolutions. The wave of radical discontent that swept the Popular Front to power was not satiated by electoral victory. The consequent upsurge in unrest, the widespread strikes and factory occupations, were welcomed by those on the left in the PCF as a demonstration of "how the government will be supported tomorrow . . . and how it can and must carry out its tasks".[98] It ripped the tattered fabric of the Third Republic and in so doing laid bare not merely the profound class conflicts in French society, but also half-concealed antagonisms within the governing coalition. By the 11 June PCF leader Maurice Thorez was calling on Party members for restraint:

> Though it is important to lead well the struggle for better conditions, it is also important to end it at the right moment. We must even accept a compromise in order to preserve all our forces and especially in order to counteract the panic campaigns carried on by the reactionaries.[99]

The call for restraint was more than merely a product of Thorez's own unease. It was also an echo of Moscow's preoccupations. At the Narkomindel the victory of the Popular Front met with misgivings. Soviet diplomats rightly feared that Communist successes at the polls would alarm the Centre as well as the Right in France and thereby further complicate the search for a united front against Germany.

One Soviet diplomat expressed his apprehensions to Luciani, Moscow correspondent of *Le Temps* (also believed to have been on the payroll of the Quai d'Orsay): "We would like the Franco-Soviet entente kept above party controversy not complicated by domestic political polemic. In our opinion what counts is that our relations with France are treated as a necessity admitted by all, by Right as well as Left. There are seventy-two Communists in the Chamber, but the circles of the Right continue to hold the real levers of power." "We do not want any internal trouble facilitating the designs of the Reich", the diplomat added.[100] Stalin himself had an instinctive aversion towards anything approaching revolution in Western Europe, being ever pessimistic of its prospects for success, and ever fearful of the consequences of failure. These anxieties coincided with the overriding concern of the more fundamentalist elements within the Comintern to prevent participation of the PCF in the Popular Front Government. There had always been a vociferous element within the PCF opposed to joining a governing coalition including bourgeois parties. As early as the 6 February 1936 the PCF Politburo authorised its secretariat "to reassure Party organisations which, following certain declarations on ministerial participation, have asked to be told our Party's position".[101] But the leadership itself favoured participation and applied to Moscow for the requisite permission.[102] They were to be disappointed. "Our position of principle has been and remains correct", Dimitrov told the Comintern's executive committee secretariat on the 2 May; "the Communist Party will not participate in a coalition government with the bourgeoisie." The "greatest danger" for the French proletariat, the world proletariat, for peace (the USSR) "would be the discrediting and the defeat of the Popular Front. That would mean the isolation of our party and revenge by reactionary forces as well as the downfall of the revolutionary movement of France".[103] The ghost of the KPD and the events of 1933 still haunted the corridors of the Comintern. Moscow was in no mood to take risks, though caution, too, had its price; the decision on non-participation had unfortunate repercussions which only became evident as the summer drew on. It left the *conseil d'état* with no effective counterbalance to the hesitations of the Socialists under Blum and to the reluctance of the Radicals under Delbos to contemplate a confrontation with Germany.

That summer no detailed discussion on relations with Germany took place in Moscow. As Krestinsky noted in early August: "The Germans, of course, are not renouncing their offers of credit and are prepared even now to sign a credit agreement with us for half a billion and even a billion Marks. But, as you know, they will do this not from political but exclusively from economic motives . . . They have become candid to such an extent that even their official representatives are unashamed to add that the conclusion of a credit agreement will not improve existing political relations to the slightest extent."[104] The Russians were thus left with no choice but to continue Litvinov's policy. His sixtieth birthday on the 17 July gave rise to unusual acclamation in the Soviet press and the beginnings of a personality cult on a small scale.[105] Clearly events were, however imperfectly, redeeming Litvinov's approach to the maze of complications confronting Soviet foreign policy. Nothing more was heard of winning over the Germans for some time to come. But the uninterrupted succession of crises was still in progress. Events in distant Spain now cast a lighted match into the international munitions dump.

7 The Outbreak of the Spanish Civil War, 1936–37

On the 17–18 July 1936 leading generals with Fascist sympathies launched a rebellion against the Spanish Popular Front Government. Elected that February and headed by the moderate Republican Giral, the new regime was thereafter unable to contain the widespread social unrest resulting from years of immiseration and repression.[1] On the 19 July the Giral Government appealed to its counterpart in France for considerable quantities of arms and munitions. The initial response was favourable, but news of the request was leaked to the press by pro-Franco diplomats at the Spanish embassy in Paris. Before long the issue had become a major source of conflict within France, dividing opinion and threatening the survival of the ruling Popular Front. The Radicals, a major part of the coalition, were disturbed at the revolutionary excesses perpetrated in Spain under the Republic and were anxious lest the supply of arms precipitate a conflict with Germany, which was loudly voicing its support for the rebels. This was the view strongly pressed at the *conseil d'état* on the 25 July by Foreign Minister Delbos, leading the Radical opposition to arms supplies. Blum and his colleagues in the SFIO, unnerved by the danger of confrontation with Berlin and fearful at the prospect of breaking with the Radicals, gave way. The supply of arms to Spain very soon evaporated.[2] By then, however, the Italians were already arming the rebels and on the 26 July Germany followed suit.[3] By early August Germans and their weapons were disembarking at Cádiz.[4]

From the outset the civil war had become an international issue, with France playing a pivotal role. This inevitably meant that the Soviet Union could not long remain aloof. A victory for the rebels backed by the Fascist Powers would leave France, the

USSR's only ally in the West, cornered on land by three hostile neighbours; and the collapse of the Popular Front in Madrid would set a dangerous precedent for its sister coalition in Paris. The threat to France and the evident reluctance of the Blum Government to intervene threw the USSR into a dilemma. On the one hand intervention was required to save France from near encirclement by the Fascist Powers. On the other hand any attempt to intervene would threaten the already fragile cohesion of the Franco-Soviet alliance.

Initially, however, the Soviets showed little immediate concern at the breaking of the storm in Spain. At its headquarters in the calle de Piamonte, Madrid, the Spanish Communist Party (PCE) itself at first believed the revolt could easily be overcome,[5] and the Russians lacked any other source of direct information on events. The first Soviet newspaper correspondent to enter the country after the 18 July was Mikhail Kol'tsov, a popular editor of *Pravda*, who had visited the Republic in its early days; he arrived no sooner than the 8 August.[6] *Izvestiya*'s editors were loath to grant Ehrenburg's wish to follow suit.[7] His fiery anti-Fascism was evidently seen as an unwelcome complication at a time when Moscow had little inclination to intervene. But, tired of waiting, Ehrenburg left Paris of his own accord and arrived in Spain later that month: the first in a rash of independent initiatives which the Spanish drama inspired among Russians who now identified with the Republican cause. Coming when Stalin was extraordinarily jealous of his supreme authority, this sort of wayward behaviour could, in certain conditions, easily be interpreted as insubordination or worse; many were to discover this to their cost in the coming months, though Ehrenburg curiously remained one who survived.

As to diplomatic representation – there was none. The newly born Spanish Republic of 1931 had established diplomatic relations with an exchange of notes on the 27–28 July 1933.[8] The ailing former Commissar of Enlightenment, Lunacharsky, was briefed on his mission as polpred by Litvinov in Paris towards the end of November, but he died on the 26 December 1933 before he could proceed further.[9] By this time the Spanish were no longer interested. The new regime in Spain under Lerroux that had taken power for the Right in September 1933 presented a series of obstacles to hinder "the immediate exchange of ambassadors", provided for in the original agreement.[10] Finally, at the end of

January 1936, before the elections, Madariaga, Spain's delegate to the League of Nations, showed a reawakened interest in its implementation. For his part Litvinov saw no objections – they had all been on the Spanish side – but neither was he in any haste:[11] a minor Power tucked away behind the Pyrenees and cut off from the maelstrom of Great Power politics to the north and east, Spain had little to offer the USSR. Even after the outbreak of the civil war, the Russians took an extraordinary length of time – given the circumstances – to exchange ambassadors. This was due not merely to the Narkomindel's patent lack of interest, but also to a deep-seated concern on the Spanish side, certainly amongst the bourgeois politicians, lest an official Soviet presence exert an unwelcome influence on internal political developments and stain the Popular Front's credentials as a non-revolutionary regime. Only when it was clear that France had deserted the Republic, and that the USSR remained the sole source of military assistance on any scale, was an exchange of diplomatic missions unavoidable. Indeed, Spanish fears found an echo in the speech delivered by polpred Rozenberg, who arrived in Madrid after a hair-raising flight from Paris on the 28 August – the very day his appointment was hurriedly announced in Moscow.[12] As with everything else connected with the civil war in Spain, this decision bore all the signs of hasty improvisation. Hitherto senior political counsellor at the Paris embassy and formerly assistant secretary-general at the League of Nations, Rozenberg handed his credentials to President Azaña on the 29 August, emphasising: "I am perfectly aware that the government of the Spanish Republic does not wish to impose its own political and social conceptions on others, and this completely accords with the views of my government."[13] However, force of circumstances before long belied the USSR's soothing assurances. Rozenberg arrived in Madrid along with military attaché Gorev and a military delegation headed by Berzin; naval attaché Kuznetsov and air attaché Sveshnikov were already en route.[14] The trickle of Soviet military personnel soon swelled into a purposeful stream. Involvement blended into intervention; intervention inexorably became interference. But it would be wrong to believe that the USSR leapt into this new commitment. Quite apart from doubts about the feasibility of rendering any aid, the Russians for long remained hopelessly optimistic that the Republic would easily win. Azaña was much alarmed by the fact that: "In

Moscow they appeared to have imprecise or, rather, mistaken information about the Republic's situation, perhaps from having believed the optimists too much. I had only two conversations with the Soviet ambassador. From them I learnt that in Moscow they believed in the immediate and easy triumph of the Republic."[15]

Soviet diplomats were at the outset mostly preoccupied with the fact that the Italians and Germans were using supposed Soviet aid – this was as early as the end of July 1936, well before any had yet materialised – as a "smokescreen" for their own activities. Non-intervention thus made sense as a means of exposing the unjustified interference of the Fascist Powers in Spanish affairs, confident in the assumption that the Giral Government was capable of victory even in the face of Italo-German backing for the rebels – which at this stage was of only modest proportions. "The Spanish Government has never asked for aid from our Union [the USSR] and we are convinced that it will find sufficient strength within the country to stifle and liquidate the revolt of the Fascist generals who are carrying out the orders of foreign countries in Spain", *Le Journal de Moscou* stated confidently on the 28 July.[16] However, on the following day Dolores Ibárruri, a leading figure in the PCE – the voice of defiance against the Fascists: "¡No pasarán!" (they shall not pass) – called on all countries to prevent the destruction of democracy in Spain.[17] This plea struck a sympathetic chord outside the Narkomindel and before long opinion in Moscow was beginning to swing against the policy of caution favoured at Kuznetsky Most and, as we shall see, reportedly also by Stalin.

Pressure came from the international Communist movement, though the Comintern proper initially remained curiously mute, evidently in deference to Kremlin fears of provoking the other Powers; the June events in France had once again touched off a latent anti-Communism in Western capitals. At the same time, however, it was difficult for the Russians to put the lid back on the saucepan once its contents had begun to boil. On the 21 July the World Committee Against War and Fascism, a Communist front organisation, sent a telegram of solidarity to the Spanish Government.[18] On the 23 July International Workers' Aid (MOPR) in France, Belgium, Switzerland and Italy called on workers to express their solidarity with their brothers in Spain.[19] This was followed by a declaration "For the Spanish People's

Struggle Against Fascism!" by the World Committee Against War and Fascism, on the 25 July.[20] There were also declarations from the US,[21] Polish,[22] and British Communist Parties,[23] plus an appeal by International Red Aid to its Second International equivalent for joint action to raise funds for medical aid to Spain.[24] The Comintern proper still stood cautiously in the wings, awaiting a sign from Stalin to come on stage. The main source of pressure for action came from the PCF. On the 27 July the Communist writer Péri told readers of *l'Humanité*: "It is not a matter of indifference to us that France should tomorrow have a frontier to defend in the South-West."[25] Finally, on the 1 August, an entire issue of *Inprecorr* appeared devoted to the events in Spain. The Comintern press had come on stage. Furthermore, sometime early in August Polish Intelligence intercepted Comintern directives to the Portuguese Communist Party concerning Spain.[26] But the Soviet leadership still appeared reluctant to commit the Comintern body and soul to the Spanish cause; instead it used the device of mobilising the trade union movement to aid Spain, a somewhat transparent fig leaf supposedly concealing the Soviet regime's overt involvement in a potentially embarrassing and perilous enterprise – a method made use of later, from 1943, after the dissolution of the Comintern.

The first public sign of a Soviet commitment to the Republican cause came unexpectedly at 5.00 pm on the 3 August 1936, with a massive demonstration in Red Square, summoned in aid of the Spanish Republic. "The demonstration had not been prepared," noted Kol′tsov in his diary, "the decision to hold it was taken only this morning."[27] But this was only one face of Soviet policy. That same evening "a responsible Soviet official" told the US chargé d'affaires in Moscow that "a number of Soviet officials charged with the conduct of Soviet foreign relations were opposed to sending funds to Spain since they felt that such action would be used by Germany and Italy to justify the aid given by themselves. These objections were overruled, however, by the Soviet leaders who take the view that if the Soviet Union is to continue to maintain hegemony over the international revolutionary movement it must not hesitate in periods of crisis to assume the leadership of that movement".[28] This new line grudgingly accepted at Kuznetsky Most was reflected in an editorial on "Foreign Intervention in Spain", which appeared in *Le Journal de Moscou* on the 4 August. Ridiculing calls for neutrality by the

Fascist Powers as pure hypocrisy, the leader concluded that "the workers of Spain must obtain moral and material support in their struggle". Similarly, *Pravda* appeared that day with an editorial "In Defence of the Spanish People, Against the Fascist Murderers and Interventionists". "In supporting the Spanish reactionaries", the leader asserted, "the German and Italian Fascists intend to establish in Europe and North Africa a new hotbed of war. This is why the fight of the Spanish workers and peasants for a democratic republic, for a free, indivisible Spain is at the same time a fight for peace." But *Pravda* spoke only in the name of "the multi-million toiling masses of the Soviet Union". There was no mention of the Soviet Communist Party, the Comintern or the Soviet Government. The governmental newspaper, *Izvestiya*, appeared with no editorial on the subject of Spain, but the photo of the demonstration in Red Square was even more impressive than that in *Pravda*, and the whole of the front page was devoted to verbatim accounts of the speeches delivered at that occasion by Shvernik, the trade union leader, and others. Inside the paper, Karl Radek published an article warning that "The Warmongers Are Preparing Intervention Against the Spanish Revolution". The Soviet response to events was thus somewhat ambiguous and confused, a curious mixture of formal reserve and outspoken "unofficial" support for the Republic, accompanied by vituperation against the Fascist Powers. Stalin was clearly still uncertain, and the state of confusion only increased as the summer drew on.

Litvinov was away on holiday and Krestinsky out of town when, on the 5 August 1936 French chargé d'affaires Payart appeared at Kuznetsky Most with his government's proposals for non-intervention in Spain.[29] The Italian ambassador reported that "the French proposal for a non-intervention agreement with regard to Spain was received with the greatest relief",[30] but this was not an opinion widely held throughout the Soviet apparatus. On his return to the capital that evening Krestinsky summoned Payart to inform him that the USSR would participate, provided Portugal was involved and on condition that all governments effectively ceased providing aid.[31] The reasoning behind this decision was that:

> Although the distance separating us from Spain makes the question of our rendering any form of military aid very difficult, we have nonetheless hastened to give an unambiguously

> positive reply, because we understand that Italy and Germany will continue to aid the rebels and will also justify their activities by the fact that we are supposedly interfering in Spanish affairs and are giving aid to the other side in the struggle.

In fact the Russians did "not expect . . . any official understanding on this question", and Krestinsky himself did "not doubt for one minute that Germany and Italy will provide aid in the most active way until the final defeat of the rebels".[32] They therefore continued to gather funds to aid the Republic.

By the 5 August the total amount of money deducted from the wages of Soviet workers had reached over 12 million roubles, and on the following day the trade unions' executive committee formally requested the State Bank to place this at the disposal of the Spanish Republic.[33] But complications were already in sight. Contrary to every expectation, French proposals for a non-intervention agreement made significant, though slow, progress. The Russians hastened to stress their lack of control over aid to the Republic. On the 7 August Krestinsky instructed the Soviet embassy in London that should the Foreign Secretary – now pressing for non-intervention – point to the collection of money from Soviet workers as interference in Spanish affairs, this had to be vigorously denied,[34] a protestation belied on the following day by the appearance of an editorial in *Inprecorr* provocatively entitled "Not Passive Sympathy but Active Help for the People of Spain".

By the time Litvinov had returned from his vacation in mid-August, an agreement among the Powers was almost certain. This put the Russians in an awkward position. They had to decide whether to sign, which they were loath to do, or risk isolation. *Le Journal de Moscou* now argued "For an Effective Neutrality" – either non-intervention must be completely effective, or the Spanish Government should "be placed at least on an equal footing with the rebels."[35] Yet the Germans acceded to the agreement on the 17 August, the Italians on the 21, and on the 22 the Russians, fearing ostracism, followed suit, evidently after heated debate – "even Litvinov . . . often found it necessary to refer certain points to his government", the US embassy noted with some surprise.[36] The discontent this caused within the Soviet Communist Party had yet to make itself felt. Officially the Soviet

Government had agreed "to refrain strictly from any direct or covert interference in the internal affairs" of Spain.[37] In accordance with this, the export of arms to the Republic was formally banned on the 28 August.[38] But the misgivings aroused in Moscow were evident from comment in the Soviet press. On the 25 August *Le Journal de Moscou* attacked Britain and France for not giving aid to Spain at the outset, criticised the pro-Fascist sympathisers of these countries, and concluded that a firm line needed to be taken with the Fascist Powers, who kept blackmailing the rest of the world with the threat of war.[39] On the following day *Izvestiya* was even more outspoken, voicing the opinion that had a leftist rising taken place against a Fascist dictatorship, those now clamouring for neutrality would be taking a rather different view. "For this reason", the paper added, "one must not close one's eyes to the fact that in the current concrete example of Spain the theory of neutrality is in fact a general retreat in the face of the Fascist governments and their supporters in various countries."[40]

By the time the Russians had agreed to participate in the non-intervention agreement they were also making moves to support the Republic beyond merely the despatch of money. The Spanish Government had, along with the bulk of its generals, lost its naval high command as well. Nikolai Kuznetsov was at sea on the 19 August when he received a signal summoning him to Moscow immediately and bearing the name Fleet Commander Kozhanov. Only in Voroshilov's offices did he discover the purpose of the summons. He was to be posted to Spain as naval attaché, but because the posting carried with it certain "special conditions", the greatest secrecy had to be observed, and his agreement was required. He soon discovered that this amounted to an active role in command of the Republican fleet.[41] The decision to send Kuznetsov was one in a series of moves towards the commitment of Soviet military advisers. No arms were yet on their way, but the pressure to send them was mounting. On the 9 September – the very day that the non-intervention committee held its first meeting in London – polpred Shtein reported from Rome that one hundred officers of the Fascist militia were on their way to Spain and in Spanish Morocco ten Italian heavy bombers were being handed over to the rebels.[42] Having already despatched a team of military advisers, the Soviet leadership now decided to allow volunteer officers to follow suit. On the 12 September Alexander Rodimtsev, a junior officer who had repeatedly requested enlistment in Spain, was at last informed that his wish had been granted. Removed from his post without a word to his colleagues, he became one of the many who now made their way across Europe to Spain on forged documents, including passports provided by the Czechoslovakian authorities.[43]

The loss of San Sebastián to the rebels on the 13 September underlined the gravity of the Republic's position. The issue of arms to Spain could no longer be evaded, and Litvinov found himself in direct line of fire from revolutionary internationalists in the Comintern and outside. Later he insisted to French diplomats that "we too have difficulties, and . . . 'neither myself, nor my colleagues, nor Mr. Stalin do all that we want, contrary to what is believed in Paris' ";[44] and Litvinov never used Stalin's name lightly. Rumour had it that Thorez, prominent in the campaign to save the Republic, "tried to move Moscow to take action".[45] Some, like Radek, who had argued vigorously for intervention "in the name of the interests of the revolution"[46] were now under investigation by the NKVD for Trotskyism, having been named at the trial which resulted in former oppositionists Zinoviev and Kamenev receiving the death sentence on the 23 August.[47] Radek might thereby have been discredited, but the same arguments continued to appear, fuelled by the precariousness of the Republic's position, and Stalin sooner or later had to adjust to them. Rumour had it that while Stalin was on holiday in the Caucasus – from late August to late September – a move was made within the Politburo to unseat Litvinov as a result of his insistence on non-intervention.[48] True or not, there certainly appears to have been a threat to Litvinov's policy position. On the 17 September Dimitrov told a meeting of the Comintern executive committee that the secretariat should immediately prepare "concrete measures for the maximum increase in aid to the Spanish Popular Front".[49] On the following day the first load of arms left the Black Sea coast for Spain, containing cases of rifles and ammunition labelled "pressed meat". Arriving at Alicante on the 26 September, the cargo was unloaded at night directly into lorries, while the port was closed to access.[50] Small arms were, of course, relatively easy to conceal. Nonetheless, this represented a new stage of escalation, a defeat for Litvinov which was mitigated only by a Politburo resolution on the 20 September reaffirming the need to continue to pursue collective security.[51] Policy towards Spain thus evolved from a series of awkward compromises between conflicting demands and conflicting views, patched together when Stalin diverted his attention from the more absorbing task of eliminating all dissent from the Party and state. On the 25 September he and Zhdanov – now Leningrad Party secretary and candidate member of the Politburo after the death of Kirov in December 1934 – sent a telegram from Sochi to other Politburo members with this ominous message:

> We deem it absolutely necessary and urgent that Comrade Yezhov be nominated to the post of People's Commissar for Internal Affairs. Yagoda has definitely proved himself to be incapable of unmasking the Trotskyite-Zinovievite bloc. The OGPU is four years behind in this matter. This is noted by all party workers and by the majority of the representatives of the NKVD.[52]

The tragedy was that Soviet aid to Spain included the arrival of NKVD agents as advisers on internal security – the problem of the "fifth column" plagued the leaders of the Republic – with ominous implications for those labelled Trotskyists. "Whatever happens", the Comintern executive committee instructed the PCE on the 27 December, "the final destruction of the Trotskyists must be achieved, exposing them to the masses as a Fascist secret service carrying out provocations in the interests of Hitler and General Franco, attempting to split the Popular Front, conducting a slanderous campaign against the Soviet Union, a secret service actively aiding Fascism in Spain."[53] By then the process of eliminating these so-called Trotskyists was already under way.

The "Trotskyists" referred to were the POUM. This was a breakaway Communist grouping led by Andreu Nin, formerly a close collaborator of Trotsky in Moscow during the twenties. All formal links with Trotsky had been broken when the POUM temporarily came out in favour of the Popular Front early in 1936.[54] But the organisation's outspoken condemnation of the Zinoviev-Kamenev trial and of Moscow's neglect of its international revolutionary duties placed it directly in line of fire from both the Soviet regime and its allies in Spain within the PCE.[55] Insignificant as a political force in the country as a whole, the POUM nonetheless had a foothold in Barcelona and thereby found a place in the Generalitat, the Catalan Government. There they resisted every attempt by the PSUC – the recently formed united

Communist and Socialist Party – to centralise power in the hands of the authorities and at the expense of autonomous paramilitary groups run by the POUM and the anarchists of the CNT and FAI.[56] From the outset of the rebellion against the Republic, the CNT had commandeered weapons and assumed *de facto* control over areas of the Catalan capital formerly held by the rebels. It was in recognition of this and in deference to prickly Catalan nationalism that the Soviet leadership was persuaded into installing a consulate in Barcelona.

The initiative apparently came from Ehrenburg, whose pro-anarchist sympathies at first elicited only indulgent smiles from both Kol'tsov and Rozenberg.[57] But the anarchist issue was hard to avoid. Anarchism had deeper roots in the Spanish working-class than either socialism or communism (Russian style) and the anarchists still refused – up to the end of October – to participate in the central government of the Republic. The formation of a new administration on the 4 September under the demagogic left-wing Socialist Largo Caballero resulted in the granting of two ministries to the Communists, but the anarchists still stood self-consciously to one side. And not only was the working-class movement dangerously disunited, the Spanish state itself hung together uneasily as Basque and Catalan nationalism continued to press for equality with Castilian-dominated Madrid. In mid-September, with relations between Madrid and Barcelona strained by the former's failure to supply arms, Companys, at the head of the Generalitat, impressed upon Ehrenburg the need "for Catalonia to have some sign of recognition from the Soviet Union".[58]

Relations between the PSUC and the anarchists in Barcelona were also deteriorating. Ehrenburg did his best to win over leading anarchists, such as García Oliver, to the Soviet cause, and pressed Rozenberg for the establishment of a consulate in Barcelona as a means of accomplishing two goals – that of appeasing Catalan pride and that of winning over the anarchists – vital to the successful conduct of the war. Rozenberg passed these recommendations on to Moscow and, returning to Paris towards the end of September 1936, Ehrenburg received an unexpected visit from Antonov-Ovseenko; a leading figure in the October revolution, caught up in Trotsky's feud with Stalin, he had since been exiled to ambassadorial posts abroad, more recently he had become Procurator of the RSFSR and was now covering his flanks with vicious denunciations of Trotsky, Zinoviev and Kamenev – a bitter price many were paying for their survival. He told Ehrenburg that Moscow had appointed him consul-general in Barcelona, with the aim of facilitating a rapprochement between Madrid and the Catalans and of making the anarchists "see reason".[59] Arriving in Barcelona on the 1 October,[60] he paid his first official visit to Companys two days later.[61] The Russians were now firmly established as an integral part of the Spanish political scene.

Antonov-Ovseenko arrived to find the Republic's defences in chaos. A soldier by profession, after seeing the state of affairs in besieged Madrid, he appeared to believe that the rebels were almost certain to win.[62] In these circumstances he advised Soviet officers en route from France "to establish close contact with the Spanish Communists and to rely above all on them", while also taking care to act loyally towards the Republic as a whole and making no "official" distinction between the various political parties.[63] The Communists had themselves taken the initiative to recreate a regular army and their "fifth regiment" became the nucleus for its reorganisation, buttressed by the arrival of foreign volunteers, which formed the famous international brigades. Yet Largo Caballero resisted moves to depart from the militia system – a product of hasty improvisation after the revolt by the military – which accorded with his idea of what the Spanish revolution required. He had attempted to neutralise the PCE by insisting on two Communists as Ministers in his administration – a demand the Communists accepted only with great reluctance; they had no love of Caballero and participation in a coalition government with bourgeois parties was as yet unknown in Comintern history.[64] This manoeuvre ultimately failed, and in fact backfired, not merely because the PCE Ministers could take advantage of their new status to further Party interests, but also because the arrival of Soviet military advisers – and from mid-October vast quantities of armaments and munitions from the USSR – inevitably tilted the precarious balance of power in their direction, a process Caballero soon began to resist, until the crisis that resulted from these efforts ended in his enforced resignation early in 1937. "Their main task", a Soviet officer recalls with respect to the role of these military advisers, "consisted in helping the Republican army with their recommendations. But life itself expanded their functions."[65] Inevitably this engendered tension between the

PCE, Rozenberg and Soviet advisers on the one hand, and Largo Caballero, who occupied the post of War Minister as well as that of Premier, on the other.

The Spanish leadership had little choice but to lean on the Russians regardless of the cost. On the Soviet side, aid to the Republic was seen as the only means of forestalling its collapse and inevitable capitulation. The fall of Toledo to the rebels on the 28 September meant that the path to Madrid was open. The Russians now accepted the Republican view that the priority should be one of removing obstacles to arms purchases rather than of restricting supplies to the rebels. "Given the current situation in Spain", Krestinsky wrote to Kagan, at the embassy in London, on the 4 October – Maisky was still on holiday – "the signature of the Soviet Union to any new limitations whatever on aid to the Spanish Government would produce a very serious impression on the forces standing behind the Government and would weaken their firmness and ability to fight."[66] With preparations for large-scale shipments of aid under way, the Russians now moved perilously close to breaking with the non-intervention committee. While Litvinov was in Geneva pressing the Entente for collective pressure on Germany,[67] on the 7 October Kagan presented the non-intervention committee with an ultimatum: "The Soviet Government has no alternative . . . but to declare that should breaches of the non-intervention agreement not cease immediately, it will consider itself free from the obligations arising out of the agreement."[68]

For a moment it appeared that Moscow contemplated breaking with the committee. Probably as a result of sharp words from Litvinov at Geneva, the Soviet leadership drew back from the precipice. Nevertheless the decision to send such quantities of arms as to make a Soviet breach of the non-intervention agreement patently obvious had already been taken, evidently on the 7 October – the very day Marcelino Pascua, appointed Spain's ambassador to Moscow on the 22 September,[69] arrived in the Soviet capital to take up his post. There he immediately gave an interview to the press pleading above all for assistance to reinforce the Republican air force, vital to the defence of Madrid.[70] Although Molotov was characteristically evasive on the subject, that same day – the 10 October – Kaganovich told Pascua of Stalin's personal concern for the fate of the Republic.[71] In fact, although the Russians were still wary of saying so openly, the first shipload of heavy armaments must have left Odessa on or around the 7 October, for the *Komsomol* arrived in Cartagena on the 15, and the trip usually took eight days.[72] But, having taken this momentous decision, the Soviet Government could scarcely afford to alienate the Entente any further and thereby risk total ostracism at a time when Surits was warning from Berlin that "open aid" to the Republic might precipitate "open conflicts" with Germany.[73] The Russians therefore fell in line with the official hypocrisy of taking their place on the non-intervention committee, but maintaining their dignity by using it as a platform from which to expose the extent of Italo-German and Portuguese intervention.

On the 15 October the *Komsomol* finally arrived at Cartagena – Spain's main naval base – laden with arms for the Republic. Kuznetsov was instructed from Moscow to meet the vessel on arrival.[74] That same day an exchange of telegrams took place between Spanish and Soviet Communist Party leaders. Their publication in *Izvestiya* ended all ambiguity about Moscow's position, and in Spain the Soviet telegram came as welcome relief from the desperate feeling of isolation that had descended upon the besieged Republic.[75] In his telegram to PCE leader José Díaz, Stalin was uncompromising in his stated commitment to their cause: "The toilers of the Soviet Union are only doing their duty in rendering all possible aid to the revolutionary masses of Spain. They are well aware that the liberation of Spain from the yoke of Fascist reactionaries is not the private concern of the Spanish, but the general concern of all advanced and progressive humanity."[76] But Soviet assistance was bought at a price. In payment the Spanish Government had no choice but to hand over gold reserves and, evidently conscious of the USSR as the main, if not the sole, arms supplier, it also decided to transfer the bulk of these reserves to Moscow for safe-keeping. The first shipment arrived in the Soviet capital in the early hours of the 6 November 1936.[77]

* * *

Aid to Spain inevitably entailed a political cost. Although Surits' fears that it might lead to a direct conflict with the Germans never materialised, it did isolate the USSR from the Entente. They were more concerned to end the civil war – and large numbers of British

Conservatives were keen to see Franco win – in order to ease tension in relations with the Fascist Powers, than to hinder the course of German expansionism. It also reinforced the axis between Italy and Germany, consolidated by agreement on the 21 October 1936, and impelled Berlin towards a quasi-alliance with Tokyo: the anti-Comintern pact was signed on the 25 November. The Russians certainly did their best to belittle the significance of the German–Japanese agreement in public in so far as it was directed against themselves.[78] But in private they were only too aware that the agreement carried secret provisions aimed at the USSR.[79] "We have the text", senior political counsellor at the Soviet embassy in Tokyo, Raivid, told a member of the German embassy.[80]

However, it would be wrong to see Soviet policy as impotent. On the contrary, aid to Spain did save Madrid from Franco's forces, and thereby ensured the continuing survival of the Republic. But the anti-Soviet bias of the agreements concluded between the aggressor Powers underlined the fact that Moscow had adopted a far more militantly anti-Fascist position than any of its allies or potential partners. Dangerously over-exposed, the Russians soon succumbed to a growing sense of isolation; before long a reaction set in, signs of which were already apparent.

By the end of October 1936 Payart at the French embassy was warning the Quai that the Russians might well retreat from the arena and "deprive us for the time being of a diplomatic counter-weight *vis-à-vis* Germany"; it was only to be expected that such a move would be accompanied by an intensification of Comintern activity[81] – something the Blum Government was extremely nervous about and therefore a point worth stressing in any despatch.[82] When Coulondre, the new French ambassador, arrived in Moscow in mid-November he added his voice to these warnings.[83] But Paris took little notice. The crisis over Spain impelled Delbos into seeking an understanding with Berlin rather than a reinforcement of links with Moscow.[84] And inevitably Payart's prophecy came true. Initially, the signs were ambiguous. Rumours that Moscow was negotiating with Berlin began to appear in various capitals.[85] On instructions from Litvinov they were promptly denied.[86] But Litvinov's own speech to the congress of soviets on the 28 November suggested that isolationism had indeed begun taking a grip on the regime, along with the preparations for the widespread repression now under way.

Litvinov used the emotive issue of Spain – which in fact complicated rather than facilitated his larger aim of building a collective security system in Europe – as a means of emphasising the need to combat Fascism. He also spoke in more general terms. "You may ask me why we are worried about Fascism's military preparations if in actual fact they do not necessarily have an anti-Soviet significance. I will venture to answer this with a little story. When a man, who had been attacked by barking dogs was asked why he was frightened, did he not know that barking dogs do not bite, he replied that he knew this, but that he was not certain that the dogs knew it (*general laughter*). We Bolsheviks are not afraid of barking dogs, but all the same we are not about to rely on dog consciousness (*general laughter throughout the hall, applause*) and it is better to arm ourselves more strongly and effectively with a club (*general laughter, applause*)." This ironical and sarcastic defence of the USSR's forward policy against Fascism was later followed by a faint but unmistakable echo of the isolationist sentiments fast gaining currency within Party circles: "Our security does not depend on bourgeois documents and on foreign policy combinations. The Soviet Union is sufficiently strong on its own."[87] This was a message with great emotional appeal to both the xenophobic Russian nationalist – or new Soviet patriot – and the old-style Bolshevik internationalist – an endangered species in Stalin's Russia. Significantly *Pravda* later commented that: "Comrade Litvinov's speech resounded in unison with the mood of all the delegates at the extraordinary congress of soviets. Thundering ovations overwhelmed the words of the People's Commissar of Foreign Affairs when he spoke of the unprecedented power of our socialist motherland."[88] But his was not a complete victory. The new showpiece constitution unveiled at the congress and hailed in the press as "An Act of Indictment Against Fascism"[89] presented the Narkomindel with a new problem. It placed Zhdanov at the head of the forthcoming Supreme Soviet's chief commission on foreign affairs. At the congress Zhdanov used his new elevation to launch an assault on Litvinov's own domain. He undiplomatically warned the Baltic states against collaboration with Germany[90] – an ominous sign for the future of Litvinovian methods, which other Powers would have done well to have recognised. But aside from collective security, what other options remained to the Russians?

While the USSR was cautiously but irrevocably stepping into

the Spanish imbroglio an opportunity arose for action *vis-à-vis* Germany on a unilateral basis. In response to Hitler's anti-Soviet tirade at the Nuremberg rally in early September 1936 Surits recklessly advocated "the suspension of the supply of raw materials to Germany's detriment, even if this entails the payment of some of our bills of exchange in gold".[91] The German economy still faced a crisis in its trade balance and an acute shortage of raw materials. In contrast, industrialisation had succeeded in making the USSR more autarchic. An editorial in *Pravda* on the 10 January 1937 was boastfully entitled: "The USSR – the Most Solvent Country". "The Soviet Union", it concluded, "now commands strong reserves of gold and foreign currency, and this is one of the essential factors in its economic and defensive power." The Russians could therefore confidently act on the assumption that "the attack against the USSR represents not an expression of the strength of the Fascist regime, but a fundamental expression of its relative internal and foreign weakness".[92] However, the Politburo would not in any way countenance drastic and direct economic sanctions against Germany on a unilateral basis, and Surits' suggestion was firmly rebuffed.[93] The fact that rumours of talks between Kandelaki and the Germans were soon floating across Europe is significant. Those most opposed to Surits' advice, one must surmise, were not against unilateral moves to improve relations with Berlin, even at the cost of enhancing Hitler's sense of self-importance. Stalin was particularly receptive to such moves when Britain and France appeared to be playing the same game. This was precisely the situation at the beginning of 1937.

The signature of the anti-Comintern pact had the unfortunate effect not only of enhancing Moscow's sense of isolation but also of increasing its dependence on the Entente. As a consequence the Russians suffered a further humiliation in being obliged to accept Anglo-French proposals for mediation in the Spanish civil war – a most disagreeable concession which was awkwardly rationalised in the pages of the Soviet press. *Izvestiya* justified Soviet involvement in terms of the USSR's "efforts to support any initiative capable of aiding the cause of peace to any extent".[94] The end result was to weaken Litvinov's standing still further when the Russians became aware that the French and the British were once again chasing after rather than hunting the Germans. The French Government now interlaced their discussions with Berlin – on the withdrawal of foreign volunteers from Spain – with references to the need to ensure that "the Spanish affair does not become envenomed, to remove its most dangerous aspects from it as soon as possible and, with an eye to easing tension, to engage with Germany in an exchange of views from which the outline for a settlement of European problems . . . might emerge".[95] It did not take long for echoes of these conversations to reach Soviet ears. From Paris on the 8 January 1937 *Pravda* correspondent Maiorsky reported that "from Berlin they are beginning to drop hints about the desirability of opening Franco-German talks 'on economic questions' and on the settlement of Franco-German relations in general". Barely a week later he informed Moscow that the French Government was satisfied with an exchange of assurances (unspecified) between Hitler and François-Poncet; he also added that "in French official circles the conclusion has been drawn that Germany wishes to enter into talks with France".[96] This was not merely the idiosyncratic opinion of an over-anxious Soviet journalist. The Soviet embassy in Berlin reacted with even greater nervousness. Britain's ambassador to Germany noted with innocent surprise that "Suritz displays an unhealthy curiosity, and indeed panic, whenever my French colleague or I have an interview with the Chancellor. Very shortly afterwards he appears in our respective Embassies in order to bombard us with questions."[97]

The signature of the Anglo-Italian "gentleman's agreement" on the 2 January 1937[98], providing for a modus vivendi between the two Powers in the Mediterranean, only further agitated the Russians. Taken together with French moves *vis-à-vis* Berlin, it was not altogether implausible for the Russians to believe another Four Power Pact was in the offing, and at a time when, as a result of intervention in Spain, the USSR was in conflict with the Axis Powers and faced endless complications in relations with the Entente on the issue of non-intervention. The vision of both Britain and France flirting irresponsibly with Italy and Germany inevitably prompted a resurgence in isolationism. An article appeared, unusually, on *Pravda*'s front page reporting the opinions of *Week*, a London based journal under Communist control. This was an indirect but fairly transparent means of indicating what was weighing on Moscow's mind:

> The agency *Week* points out that London and Paris now find themselves face to face with the first phase of a German attack in the West of Europe and are realising that they have abandoned many important positions as a result of their policy of capitulating in the face of Germany's aggressive position. As the agency points out, England and France are beginning to ask themselves the alarming question: "How long can and will the Soviet Union act in isolation in the capacity of defender of international order in the West?"

The *Pravda* article concluded with a warning:

> Co-operation between the Soviet, French, English and Spanish Governments and the Governments of the countries of Central Europe might still guarantee peace in Europe from German attack. However, the agency points out in conclusion, there are already fears that the USSR is tired of defending Western democracy and will let it deal with its own problems itself.[99]

A further indication that opinion within the Kremlin was turning aside from collective security appeared in the "evidence" fabricated for the trial of the so-called "Anti-Soviet Trotskyist Centre", which opened on the 23 January 1937. A letter, supposedly written by Radek to Trotsky, was quoted in court. It asserted that the bloc of which Radek formed a part could only hope to seize power if the USSR were defeated in war – a resurrection of the "Clemenceau" thesis put forward by Trotsky in 1927. "To this end", the letter noted, "the bloc must make energetic preparations" and "in so far as possible a conflict must be precipitated between the USSR and Germany."[100] The message was underscored in a *Pravda* editorial on the 1 February with the assertion that: "The Trotskyist criminals have banked on forcing a war by the Fascist states against the USSR."[101] In this sort of atmosphere not merely revolutionary internationalists but also proponents of collective security came perilously close to being accused of Trotskyism. The tactical line evidently advocated by Litvinov's rivals found a place in despatches published from *Pravda*'s London correspondent, probably touched up in Moscow for the purpose, and stressing that Britain was aiming "to bide its time and manoeuvre. Should war become inevitable", he concluded, "then England would be the last to take part''[102] – a tempting philosophy for a regime convinced that war would precipitate a *coup d'état* unless the state and the army were purged clean from top to bottom. In these circumstances it made good sense to mend fences with the Germans, and the chronic deterioration in the German economy provided the opportunity for action.

On the Russian side, the first public hint that this was an option under consideration came with an article on "Soviet–German commercial relations" in *Le Journal de Moscou* on the 5 January 1937, which reviewed the decline in Soviet-German trade and pointed in explanation to the adverse impact of "abnormal political relations" upon it. This was followed nearly a month later by a further article from the same pen – that of D. Borisov (probably a pseudonym) – which pointed out that: "Today it is precisely Germany's economic weakness which is the most powerful weapon in the hands of those who could, if they wished, obtain real guarantees of peaceful intentions from National-Socialist Germany".[103] Quite apart from the disagreement over tactics in Moscow, the Russians would surely have preferred concerted action to exert joint pressure on Berlin, using the economic weapon as a means of containing German ambitions, if only because this was far more likely to be effective than any unilateral action on their part. But the British saw no value in involving the Russians in their plans – to them the Soviet intervention in the Spanish civil war was a dangerous gamble with the peace of Europe – and the Kremlin was not prepared to see an opportunity pass of gaining something, even a minimal *detente*, with Berlin. This must have rankled with Litvinov. Indeed, the arguments he presented to the US ambassador against Anglo-American moves were as relevant to and probably also deployed against Soviet initiatives towards Berlin. Early in February 1937 he "vigorously" expressed his "failure to understand why England and France were 'continually bothering' with Hitler in Germany . . . he could not understand why they should project notes and questionnaires and constantly stir up the German situation and thereby accentuate Hitler's importance and 'feed his vanity' into his self-conception that he (Hitler) is the dominating figure in Europe . . . he thought they ought to let him 'stew in his own juice'. . . . He seemed very much stirred about this and apprehensive lest there should be some composition of differences between France, England, and Germany".[104]

Concerned lest the Western Powers reach a separate agreement with Hitler which did not take full advantage of German economic difficulties to press for an end to his expansionist plans eastwards as well as westwards, Stalin was once more persuaded into sanctioning a return to the "former tactical line" of linking "the problem of improving economic relations with Germany and ourselves with the question of the real normalisation of political relations".[105] This was, however, an unpropitious moment. In mid-October 1936, despite Germany's urgent need for Soviet raw materials, such as manganese, Hermann Göring left strict instructions that all business with the Russians had to be purely non-political, so that Moscow could not play off one part of the German state apparatus against another – as the Russians had attempted in 1935.[106] But the Russians, as we have seen, were acutely conscious of Germany's economic plight and, evidently without consulting Surits in Berlin, and probably against Litvinov's advice, Stalin and Molotov sanctioned further soundings by Kandelaki and his deputy Friedrichson. Towards the end of December 1936, Kandelaki asked to see Schacht. In the course of the discussion, evidently on instructions from above, Schacht insisted that any further expansion of trade would require an unequivocal political gesture from Surits in the form of an undertaking that the USSR would refrain from "all forms of Communist agitation". On returning to Moscow, Kandelaki reported this to Stalin, Molotov and Litvinov. Then on the 29 January 1937 – with Moscow over-anxious at Western moves towards Berlin – he reappeared, acting on instructions from Stalin and Molotov (Litvinov's name was never mentioned). Kandelaki repeated the assertion that the Soviet Government had "never refused" political negotiations with the Germans and "had even made concrete political proposals" to them in the past: the non-aggression pact offer made immediately after the signature of the Franco-Soviet pact. The Soviet Government did not see its policy as aimed against German interests, Kandelaki insisted. It was willing to enter into negotiations to improve mutual relations and to further peace in general. The talks would be conducted in confidence, without any publicity. But to this Schacht reasserted his earlier insistence that any such moves had to be made to the Ausamt by Surits.[107] Hitler was simply unimpressed by anything the Russians had to offer. He was more struck by Soviet links with the Entente than their professed interest in normalisation of relations with Berlin; furthermore, any Soviet assurances with respect to ending Comintern propaganda were, on past experience, completely valueless.[108]

The Kandelaki soundings were a symptom of Litvinov's waning influence. The treatment of General Köstring, the German military attaché, implicated at the Radek trial, was also indicative of the confusion at the top and ultimately of the need to avoid an open confrontation with Berlin. On the 18 February 1937, Stern, head of the Second Western Department at the Narkomindel, informed the German embassy that Köstring would have to be recalled.[109] The Germans, however, refused to do so and also refused to recall Baum, the press attaché, also implicated at the trial, on the grounds that both were innocent;[110] the Russians eventually relented. All kinds of rumours were in circulation. On the 20 February Delbos, the French Foreign Minister, told the US ambassador to France that "Coulondre, the French Ambassador in Moscow, had been about to leave for Paris three days ago. He had refrained from coming and had sent a most secret message to say that his reason was that he believed Litvinov was in serious trouble and probably would soon be dismissed from his post and might soon be on trial. It appeared certain", he said, "that Litvinov's wife (Ivy Low of British origin) was seriously compromised having had most intimate relations with many of those who are about to be placed on trial."[111] Litvinov tactfully despatched his wife to teach English in the Urals,[112] out of harm's way, and although the story that he thereafter slept with a revolver on his bed-side table is probably apocryphal,[113] his own survival certainly appeared to be in jeopardy. The trial and execution of former Deputy Commissar of Foreign Affairs Sokol'nikov in late January opened the doors of the Narkomindel to the "neighbours", the predatory NKVD. All those associated with collective security feared something was in the wind. Stalin's terror soon enveloped the country in a macabre web of suspicion, denunciation, imprisonment, torture, confession and execution, more medieval than modern.

8 The Year of the Terror, 1937

Stalin's attempt to crush the slightest opposition to his rule had a grave impact on the Soviet Union's international standing, reinforcing the latent anti-Bolshevism in Western counsels of state and weakening the position of those in and out of government advocating an alliance with Moscow against the Axis. It threatened but did not succeed in submerging the policy of collective security.

The repression did not originate in the international predicament of the USSR, but its tenor was undoubtedly much influenced by Soviet isolation in a hostile world; a climate of acute xenophobia shrouded Russia. As early as the first show-trial Stalin sought to taint his opponents and would-be opponents with the smear of Fascist association: "Trotsky-Zinoviev-Kamenev-Gestapo" was the title of an editorial in *Pravda* on the 22 August 1936. More was to follow. After a further trial held from the 23 to the 30 January 1937 involving, inter alia, Radek and Sokol'nikov, both foreign affairs specialists, Stalin's speech to the Central Committee plenum on the 3 March set an ominously xenophobic tone for the unfolding campaign of terror, shortly to reach its peak that dreadful year:

> From the statements and discussions . . . heard at the plenum, it is evident that the issue here amounts to the following three basic facts.
>
> Firstly, the wrecking and sabotage-espionage work of the agents of foreign states, amongst whose number the Trotskyists have played a relatively active role, has affected to one degree or another all or almost all our organisations, both economic and administrative and Party.
>
> Secondly, agents of foreign states, including Trotskyists, have penetrated not only lower organisations, but also certain responsible posts.

> Thirdly, certain of our leading comrades, both in the centre and locally have not only proved unable to discern the true face of these wreckers, saboteurs, spies and murderers, but have proved careless, complacent and naive to such an extent that they themselves have frequently facilitated the advancement of agents of foreign states to some responsible post or other.[1]

In this sinister climate of insane suspicion towards anyone in contact with foreigners, the Narkomindel, long an object of mistrust in Party ranks, staffed as it was with the country's more cosmopolitan, pro-Western and liberal elements, including innumerable Jews, inevitably became a prime target for police persecution, alongside that "nest of spies" the Comintern, which was unfortunate enough to be composed largely of foreigners.

One victim at the Narkomindel was to be Rozenberg, polpred in Spain. Rozenberg was, as Litvinov himself admitted to the French ambassador to Moscow, "very active and perhaps a little hasty in taking initiatives".[2] By the time Stalin, Molotov and Voroshilov addressed a letter to Largo Caballero on the 21 December 1936, Rozenberg had already come into conflict with the Spanish Premier through his immersion in the internal politics of the host country. Not that Stalin was averse to such intervention; indeed, the letter to Caballero contained fatherly advice to "pay attention to the peasants", to "draw onto the side of the government the petty and middle urban bourgeoisie", to avoid alienating "the leaders of the party of the republicans" [sic], and to announce to the press that the Republican Government would not harm foreign interests in Spain. But Stalin had become suspicious of all independent initiatives. He asked Caballero "frankly and plainly" for his opinion of Rozenberg; should he be replaced? The Spanish Premier expressed himself content with the polpred in his reply on the 2 January 1937,[3] but that same month he exploded in extreme irritation when Rozenberg brazenly supported the PCE's demand for the dismissal of Caballero's protegé, General Asensio.[4]

Rozenberg's fate was ultimately determined by the fact that Litvinov lost his longstanding battle to keep the NKVD at bay. In February 1937 NKVD official Korzhenko was installed at the Narkomindel as director-general;[5] he was evidently placed there to direct the purge. On the 19 February Rozenberg was recalled to Moscow.[6] He was replaced by his deputy, senior political counsellor Gaikis.[7] However, Rozenberg did not disappear for several months,[8] though his spirit of independence was clearly his undoing. Not until some time after Stalin's speech to the Central Committee were the *Litvinovtsy* removed en masse. When that time came only those with a considerable international reputation, or the chosen and fortunate few Litvinov himself succeeded in protecting, remained untouched: Maisky in London, Surits – transferred to Paris from Berlin in June 1937,[9] Troyanovsky in Washington, Shtein in Rome, Kollontai in Stockholm – though her lover Dybenko was shot in 1938; Potemkin – who replaced the unfortunate Krestinsky as first Deputy Commissar on the 4 April 1937;[10] Veinshtein – appointed head of the Second Western Department in 1937,[11] who wisely befriended Korzhenko;[12] the young Gnedin – who became head of the Press Department in July 1937[13] – and a mere handful of others. The roll-call of the disappeared is like a casualty list from the First World War; it is easier to count only those who survived.

Stalin's warnings about the dangers from abroad, undoubtedly deliberately exaggerated to further his own domestic purposes, sounded familiar to many – particularly in the NKVD – and was a theme taken up by the new favourite, Zhdanov, who had already established himself publicly as an opponent of Litvinov's. "Many have forgotten about the international situation," Zhdanov declared on the 15 March 1937, "they have forgotten that Soviet power has so far triumphed on only one-sixth of the earth's surface, while on the remaining five-sixths the bourgeoisie still rules. Capitalist encirclement sends us plenty of spies, snoopers and saboteurs. . . . It must be remembered that the roots of Trotskyism are not in the USSR, but abroad. . . . International capital is galvanising the remnants of the classes in the USSR hostile to us and first and foremost makes use of Trotskyism as its weapon."[14] From being the original source of contagion at home, Trotskyism had now become the carrier of a more deadly virus from abroad. This xenophobic fanfare was duly echoed by lesser mortals. All those involved in anything foreign had now to cover their tracks. The historian Tarle wrote a suitable refrain on "Espionage and Subversion as an Instrument of Bourgeois State Policy".[15]

The arrival of the NKVD at the Narkomindel and the symptomatic substitution by Zhdanov of an undifferentiated approach to the hostile world outside for the pre-existing distinction between pacific and aggressor states, left the initiated convinced that a change of policy and Litvinov's demise were imminent. There was a clear sign of Litvinov's precarious position. In an unprecedented way, *Izvestiya* on the 23 April 1937 published a letter from "Engineer A. Khvatkov" who worked in a Moscow plant, addressed to comrade Litvinov. The newspaper published it under the title: "A question to People's Commissar of Foreign Affairs comrade Litvinov". On the 12 March the Soviet public learnt that two of their ships, the *Komsomol* and the *Smidovich*, had been sunk by Franco's forces, their crews interned by the Spanish rebels. Khvatkov wanted to know what Litvinov was doing to secure their "speediest" return.[16] The Commissar gave a prompt but indifferent reply, to the effect that since the USSR did not recognise Franco as a belligerent, there was little that could be done, though the Narkomindel was, of course, doing its best.[17] No more was heard of this curious incident, but it was an ominous reminder that Litvinov's own position was far from secure. According to one source, which in other respects confirms what we already know, when Potemkin was appointed first Deputy Commissar – this was early April 1937 – he told Willi Münzenberg that he was leaving for Moscow with a heavy heart: Litvinov's retirement appeared certain, and his departure from office would mean the end of a policy they both believed in.[18] But Litvinov kept a cool head, and does not appear to have conceded his principles to NKVD pressure. Gnedin recalls that after one trial the NKVD came to him with a request to give details about "sabotage" in the Narkomindel. Litvinov ironically replied: "So, what the papers tell you is not enough?".[19]

Although Potemkin's pessimism proved unfounded – the pressure of world events, the unremitting hostility of Nazi Germany, kept the USSR on the path of collective security – in other respects the situation worsened to an extent which even the most despondent could never have imagined. The first sign was the disappearance of Steiger, the Kremlin's unofficial emissary, generally regarded as a protegé of the now disgraced Yagoda.[20] Karakhan was recalled from Ankara on the 7 May 1937[21] though, like Krestinsky, he was not actually arrested until early June.[22] It was only then that the terror assumed mass proportions, prompted by the tensions which Stalin's demand for total conformity had created in his relations with the leadership of the Red Army.

By that time the NKVD's deadly tentacles were already reaching out abroad.

In Spain the NKVD "advisers" sought out and liquidated the counterpart to the Trotskyists in the USSR. Their mission was made easier by the foolhardy actions of their intended victims. The persistence of POUM and CNT/FAI demands for a fully-fledged revolution, and their attempts to bring one into effect wherever they held sufficient power, inevitably frustrated the war effort and consequently laid them open to damaging charges of facilitating Franco's task by undermining the Republic from within. It was not merely the PCE and PSUC (a much less significant force) which were itching to crush autonomous revolutionary elements in order to centralise control over military mobilisation and operations. "One could write a book about the spectacle which Catalonia presents, in complete dissolution", wrote the moderate President Azaña, in his diary. "There, nothing remains: Government, parties, authorities, public services, law and order; nothing exists."[23] Even the Barcelona telephone exchange lay beyond local government control; Azaña's own conversations from the Catalan capital with the central government, now in Valencia, were interrupted by recalcitrant CNT telephone operators. On the 3 May 1937 it was the exchange which was occupied by Catalan police on the instructions of Aiguader, responsible for internal security.[24] The incident sparked off a civil war within the civil war: extremists from the FAI, the POUM and others called a strike and the barricades went up. The situation was soon out of control: Azaña criticised Aiguader severely "for having given battle without preparation" and Companys, "for having talked so much about doing so, which had alarmed the anarchists".[25] On the 4 May an insurrection took place, but there was little prospect of complete success once central government forces were committed to the fight; finally, on the 8 May the CNT called a halt to hostilities.[26]

The events of May 1937 confirmed the Russians in the belief that the POUM was a Fascist fifth column, and precipitated the downfall of Largo Caballero – now seen as a cuckoo in the nest – reluctant as he was to take repressive measures against the rebels. Caballero had already come into conflict with the PCE, which blamed him for the fall of Malaga on the 8 February; he clashed with his Soviet advisers over his plans for battle in the West, and with all his colleagues by arrogating to himself sole political control over conduct of the war. His reluctance to take firm action in Barcelona thus hastened a crisis long overdue.[27] On the 13 May it finally broke after the Communists formally demanded the dissolution of the POUM and punishment of those responsible for the rebellion in Catalonia.[28] The PCE had taken on the task of challenging Caballero, while the others sat back and applauded. Thrust into prominence, the temptation was too much for some: suggestions that the PCE take the opportunity to seize power for itself alone came not only from the mercurial General Miaja, who as commander in Madrid, had come into collision with Caballero, but also from within the Party, though it is unclear precisely at what level in the hierarchy. Such a move would have not only wrecked the Popular Front in Spain, it would also have discredited it throughout Europe; Díaz firmly ruled out any such suggestion,[29] though the Communists continued to seek and win positions of power, particularly within the armed forces, and soon came into conflict with the new Minister of War in the Negrín Government, Prieto, in so doing.[30] At the November 1937 plenum of the PCE Central Committee, meeting in Barcelona, Ibárruri pointed out that "some" Communists overestimated the strength of the Party, attempted to resolve vital questions relating to the war without consulting other organisations in the Popular Front, and certain comrades had even tried to remove them from government.[31] On one issue, however, the PCE was adamantly unrepentant: the fate of the POUM and its leader, Nin.

Nin's long association with Trotsky had made him a prime target for the NKVD. Wild claims that prominent figures such as Togliatti and fellow Italian Vittorio Vidali were involved in his disappearance have been substantially disproved.[32] But there can be little doubt that the PCE's hands were not entirely clean in the matter; Ortega, a Communist who had been appointed director-general of security, was certainly implicated and as a result investigations into the affair became something of a farce – more was at stake than merely PCE intrigues.[33] Nin's disappearance before long became a cause célèbre among socialists and Trotskyists in the West. But by that time Russia's rulers were already up to their knees in blood.

* * *

The full impact of the terror made itself felt only with the assault on the Red Army which began in June 1937. At the outset the purging of the armed forces was an extension of the terror applied to the Party and state apparatus, but because of the peculiar pre-eminence of the fighting services as the most powerful element within the country, the terror applied here naturally assumed a more dramatic form. The first victims were, unsurprisingly, associated with Trotsky's Opposition in the late twenties: Putna, exiled abroad as military attaché, was arrested in September 1936, and Primakov – in November.[34] Then, on the 24 January 1937 at the second show-trial the accused Radek mentioned that Putna came to see him "with some request from Tukhachevsky".[35] Later, prosecutor Vyshinsky returned to this point in order to clarify, as Radek obligingly stated, that "Tukhachevsky had no idea either of Putna's role or of my criminal role",[36] but the damage had been done. The naming of Tukhachevsky was evidently a warning Stalin wanted delivered in no uncertain terms. The two had not got along easily, ever since their clash over strategy during the civil war. In 1930–2, with the adverse impact of forced collectivisation of agriculture on the fighting power of the armed forces, tension had grown in relations between the military and the Party leadership.[37] Stalin's deep-seated suspicion of the military had erupted in early 1930 when he rejected proposals from Tukhachevsky for greater priority to weapons production, with a contemptuous reference to "red militarism".[38] But the subsequent threat from Japan, which emerged in the autumn of 1931, saw a significant increase in Soviet defence expenditure;[39] what Stalin had been loath to grant, force of circumstance dictated. Hitler's accession to power in 1933 then resulted in a massive expansion in the USSR's armed forces; by the end of 1936 the army alone amounted to some 1 300 000 men.[40] Concessions had to be made to military pride – the restoration of some Tsarist ranks, including that of Marshal, in 1935 – and a more autonomous role naturally evolved from the indispensibility of the military as war approached: in April 1936 the Politburo conceded to the Defence Commissariat's request for an independent publishing house to answer the growing demands of military education.[41] This enormous growth in military power and influence coincided with the purging of Party ranks to remove the disaffected, the idle and the corrupt;[42] Red Army membership of the Party therefore declined along with Party membership as a whole. By the end of 1936 there were only about 150 000 Communists left in the armed forces out of a total of some 4.2 million men under arms[43] – and this was only half the membership of 1932, when the services were a third of their current size.[44] Although Stalin did not trust Party members, he trusted those who escaped Party (or police) control even less; once he had become convinced that a pre-emptive assault on every conceivable locus of actual or potential opposition was a matter of urgency, it was only a matter of time before lingering suspicions of "red militarism" clouded his heated mind.

Following Primakov's arrest in November 1936 Moscow was buzzing with rumours of further arrests among Red Army officers.[45] This apparently reflected increasing tension in Stalin's relations with the military; and the NKVD had their own scores to settle with their nearest and most powerful rivals. Although Tukhachevsky was widely held to be very ambitious,[46] no sound evidence has yet emerged that he aspired to supplant Stalin. But it was probably his obsessive professionalism that proved his undoing. It inevitably led him into the political realm, for defence was closely interrelated with the economy, foreign policy and the cohesion of society and Stalin demanded blind political conformity at any price. To attain it he was prepared to jeopardise military efficiency; for Stalin the threat of war was less immediate than the perceived threat to his own supremacy.

Stalin's notorious speech to the Central Committee plenum on the 3 March 1937 made no direct reference to problems with the Red Army. At the same time, however, he did make clear that the armed forces were not exempt from the hunt for the ubiquitous fifth column: "To win a battle in time of war", he declared, "may require several corps of Red Army men. But to lose this prize at the front would take only several spies somewhere at army headquarters or even at divisional headquarters, capable of stealing operational plans and handing them over to the enemy."[47] Molotov was more explicit in a section of his speech which went unpublished at the time, where he accused Red Army cadres of failing to fight the "enemies of the people".[48] Its leading officers certainly resented and opposed the disruption of the normal chain of command by the campaign of self-criticism imposed on them by Stalin and his minions, who exempted themselves from such humiliating practices. A vivid example of their response was that of General Kork, commandant at the

Frunze Academy. The following account subsequently appeared in *Krasnaya Zvezda* on the 27 March 1937:

> Comrades cited many examples of the inefficacy of self-criticism and evidence of its direct suppression. Student comrade Demura wrote a note to the academy newspaper *Frunzovets* about the fact that Major Nikonov gave a bad lecture on military history. That the note was correct was acknowledged even by the Professor of military history, who immediately announced that he would henceforth look over a synopsis of the lectures. However, at a public meeting of the class, head of the academy comrade Kork called comrade Demura an undisciplined student and advised him not to commit such "deeds" again.
>
> This example was also cited: a note was inserted in the newspaper *Frunzovets* by Major Krylov about the bad work of the supply department and the medical unit. The author wrote that in preparing for some occasion or other the supply department initially takes its time and then begins "storming" for several days. The note was essentially correct. Nevertheless comrade Kork summoned comrade Krylov to see him and, in the presence of senior members of staff, rebuked him for the fact that he "sticks his nose" in other people's business.[49]

This could not have been the only such conflict. As an editorial in *Krasnaya Zvezda* pointed out later, in the autumn of 1937: "After the February–March plenum of the CC VKP(b) a wave of meetings of activists took place in units and formations of the Red Army. The fresh voice of Bolshevik self-criticism resounded at these meetings. Severely and without respect for persons, army Bolsheviks criticised inadequacies in work and training; they boldly exposed the bureaucratised people who gave themselves airs and were cut off from the masses."[50]

The NKVD in the meantime set about fabricating its version of "a counter-revolutionary military Fascist organisation" within the armed forces.[51] Stalin's preoccupation with military recalcitrance found only oblique expression in the press: a *Pravda* editorial appeared entitled "The Red Army Oath", which warned of the dangers from "spies, agents of foreign Intelligence services, hirelings of the Gestapo, trotskyists".[52] He then moved onto the offensive. Early in May the Politburo held an enlarged meeting with the chiefs of staff at which the latter were confronted with a proposal to return to collective leadership in the armed forces. Then on the 8 May the Politburo decided to extend this reform – the introduction of military councils – to include the reinstitution of military commissars, a practice defunct since the days of mistrust in the civil war.[53] Accordingly, on the 10 May a Central Executive Committee and Council of People's Commissars decree was issued: "On the creation of military councils of military districts and the establishment of the institution of military commissars in the worker-peasant Red Army."[54] On the following day Tukhachevsky was relieved of his post as first Deputy Commissar of Defence and appointed to command the Volga military district; it is not known whether the Marshal's demotion was precipitated by opposition to the imposition of tight political controls over the Red Army, but the timing certainly suggests that Stalin pushed through these measures only in the face of stiff resistance from Tukhachevsky and his close associates and acolytes. He did not remain at his new post for long. On the 26 May he was dismissed and arrested.[55] An enlarged session of the Defence Commissariat Military Council was convened with the participation of the Politburo from the 1 to the 4 June. Here the plot of the fictitious "counter-revolutionary military Fascist organisation" elaborated by the NKVD and implicating Tukhachevsky, Yakir, Uborevich, Kork, Eidman, Fel'dman, Primakov and Putna, was unveiled by Voroshilov.[56] Stalin also spoke, demanding the complete liquidation of the conspiracy.[57] Then at a special session of the Supreme Court on the 11 June, the supposed conspirators were sentenced to death,[58] and were executed later that day.[59] Only Gamarnik escaped the whole process by committing suicide.[60] They had been accused of the usual crimes falsely attributed to "Trotskyists", including preparations for a coup d'état and treachery; the *Pravda* editorial on the following day was suitably entitled "For Espionage and Betraying Their Country: The Firing-Squad".

In order to make their execution more palatable to domestic and Western democratic opinion the so-called conspirators were pilloried as German agents. This was a story lent specious credibility by Beneš, the Czech leader who, sometime in January 1937, passed onto the Russians the hint from the Germans that a Soviet-German rapprochement would be possible once the Red Army seized power.[61] Although the British military attaché, a man of sound common-sense,[62] and for that matter the French military attaché as well,[63] refused to believe this story, and those at the German embassy were equally dismissive,[64] there were nonetheless some who were taken in. At the Foreign Office Vereker in the Northern Department was evidently expressing a commonly held view when he noted that "the culpability of Tukhachevsky . . . from our information seems proven";[65] and a colleague, Walker, wrote that Tukhachevsky was known to be in favour of a rapprochement with Nazi Germany.[66] But the Foreign Office was hopelessly amateur where Russia was concerned; the former generation of Russianists who had lived in the country for years and acquired Russian wives had never been replaced by men of equal devotion. In contrast to the French, Italians and the Germans, no one stayed in the Moscow embassy longer than a couple of years if possible. Their ignorance of Stalin's tentative soundings in Berlin unquestionably also led them into the dark, and their dislike of Tukhachevsky as a personality – the epithet "ruthless" contrasted him with the amiable and apparently harmless Voroshilov[67] – undoubtedly reinforced their prejudice. The German military attaché in Moscow, General Köstring stated that "all the senior Red Army officers" were well disposed towards him[68] and quite possibly such reports lulled others, in Berlin, into believing that with the Red Army in power an understanding could be achieved. Ironically, as a German diplomat who served at the embassy in Moscow at the time has recalled: "In contrast to Tukhachevsky's rumoured links with Germany, our Moscow Embassy considered him rather cooler towards Germany than many of the other Russian generals. Indeed, we were worried over his being excessively pro-French."[69]

The execution of Tukhachevsky and the greater part of the Red Army command was followed by the systematic liquidation of a significant proportion of their subordinates, a purge which hit the more experienced rather than the untried, leaving a breach gaping in the walls of fortress Russia which crippled its diplomacy for the better part of a year. It also drastically weakened the Red Army's fighting power for several years to come, but this fact was exposed only much later, in 1939–40, with the Finnish campaign;[70] until that time the leadership successfully deceived itself into believing that all was well, and in the all-pervasive terror few would dare contradict an opinion from above. Some did speak out, and perished. One Soviet officer incautiously told the French military attaché on the 16 June 1937: "I only hope there's no war, now that our frontiers are open."[71] At a session of the Military Council in November 1937, commander of the Caucasus military district N.V. Kuibyshev said the repression had bled white the cadres in his region and it was the underlying reason for the low military preparedness of his forces. For this bold indiscretion he too fell victim to the omnivorous NKVD.[72]

This bloodletting inevitably weakened the USSR's credibility as a potential partner against Nazi Germany. It served as a convenient alibi to those in Western governments who, through ideological hostility born of Russia's revolutionary proselytism, had no intention of becoming entangled in an alliance with the USSR. It undermined the position of those, like Winston Churchill in Britain, who laid aside their former enmity for fear of Germany and who pressed for a Russian alliance against German militarism.[73] It should nevertheless be noted that not all Western evaluations of the Red Army's fighting power were flattering even prior to the terror; the terror tended to confirm existing doubts rather than lead to a completely new evaluation. After attending Red Army manoeuvres in early September 1936 Major-General Wavell, a Russian speaker, judged it to be "a very formidable opponent indeed in defence" but he had doubts about its ability in attack;[74] the evaluation given by Firebrace, the military attaché, in April 1938 was little different.[75] Generals Schweisguth and Vuillemin of France also attended the September 1936 manoeuvres and returned to Paris more pessimistic about the Red Army:

> The Soviet army appears strong, equipped with abundant and modern material, prompted by a will to win, at least at officer level, but insufficiently prepared for a war against a European Great Power.[76]

For them the effects of the terror provided a convenient excuse for not pursuing contacts at staff level any further, despite Soviet entreaties. Even prior to June 1937 the French found good reason for keeping their distance from Moscow. This is clear from their "Reflections on the possible consequences of Franco-Soviet military contacts" drawn up in May 1937. The fact that by establishing such contacts the French could risk alienating

"Germany, Poland, Romania, Yugoslavia, England" caused them to scrutinise the value of Russian credentials with a greater degree of scepticism and pessimism than otherwise warranted. First and foremost they were naturally preoccupied with British reactions, for "French security rests above all on a *close entente* with England", and it was evident that "*a Franco-Soviet military agreement risks putting in jeopardy the warmth and candour of Franco-English relations*".[77]

The impact of the terror on Western evaluations should therefore not be exaggerated. There was, as with most Intelligence assessments, always a strong dose of subjective judgement involved. The British military attaché, more perceptive than most, noted wryly that in their estimates of Soviet strength his foreign counterparts were "to some extent swayed by their desires"[78] – an understatement, in fact. A prime example was the reaction of German diplomats in Moscow; a former member of the embassy recalls:

> On the one hand, we could describe the results of the purges as disastrous for the Red Army. This would indicate to many reasonable people in Berlin that the possibility for an accommodation between Germany and the USSR was growing. But at the same time we knew full well that Hitler might read such a report as an invitation to take advantage of Russia's weakness. Yet if we emphasised the extent to which the Russians were still capable of putting up a strong fight, we could be sure that Hitler would denounce us for having been hood-winked. In the end, we decided that our responsibility was to point out the continuing strength of the Soviet Union. This was the drift of innumerable reports which Köstring prepared for the Ambassador's counter-signature. We soon discovered that Hitler interpreted our reports in exactly the opposite way to what we had expected. Learning that the Russians were still strong and were likely to grow yet stronger, Hitler resolved that he had better strike immediately, lest the Russians grow to the point where they could dictate their terms to all Europe.[79]

* * *

The liquidation of the so-called military conspiracy was accompanied by the first wave of arrests at the Narkomindel; the next wave engulfed the Commissariat in the autumn. The arrests of Karakhan and Krestinsky were only the beginning. Not surprisingly this left the Narkomindel in a state of chaos and uncertainty throughout the rest of June. "Many of the activities of the Foreign Office are apparently suspended", US chargé d'affaires Henderson informed Secretary of State Hull on the 13 June. "No one there seems willing to make important decisions", he added;[80] "The Tukhachevski affair, and excess of 'vigilance' that accompanied it and has not yet subsided, have seemingly paralysed the People's Commissariat of Foreign Affairs", wrote British chargé d'affaires Mackillop on the 3 July.[81] Any such intimacy as foreign diplomats acquired with their counterparts at Kuznetsky Most was gone forever; even their Russian dentists were arrested. Only Litvinov continued to speak out openly; Potemkin and Stomonyakov were relatively forthcoming, but those below them played safe. Referring to the "minor officials" at the Commissariat, US diplomat Kennan noted from Washington: "They are largely lacking in influence and are uncommunicative on principle. The high mortality rate to which they have been subject . . . [this was written in November 1937] has done nothing to increase the cordiality and openness with which those who have survived greet the visiting diplomat. In their conversations there is apparent the fear that their rooms contain dictaphone installations".[82]

Unpleasant though this undoubtedly was, it did not spell the end to collective security as Soviet policy; yet it certainly further complicated Litvinov's difficult task in winning over the West. All that happened was a certain retrenchment from the USSR's former role in the anti-Fascist vanguard. In mid-May Litvinov "intimated" to Lord Chilston, the British ambassador, "that the Soviet Government's foreign policy had perhaps been rather too forward in furthering collective security. They would now play their part with the others, but would not take the lead".[83] Throughout that stormy month of June and for the greater part of July 1937 the Russians took shelter from the world outside. This was most apparent with respect to the new crisis that broke in China; it also gave the Spanish Republic a momentary tremor.

On the 7 July 1937 an exchange of fire occurred on the Marco Polo Bridge outside Peking between Japanese and Chinese Nationalist (Kuomintang) forces. By mid-month, when the Chinese approached the Russians for assistance, the incident had turned into full-scale war.[84] Despite the fact that General Blyukher and the Soviet Far Eastern Army were as yet untouched by the terror, the Soviet leadership was nonetheless fearful at the prospect of becoming embroiled in the conflict. Bogomolov, polpred in the Kuomintang capital Nanking, was severely reprimanded by Litvinov for intimating that the USSR would be prepared to sign an alliance with the Chinese;[85] "in forcing this question at the present moment, the Chinese are attempting to get us involved in a war with Japan", he warned.[86] Bogomolov paid for this indiscretion. In September he was recalled; he was later shot. Nothing seemed less likely at this stage than that the Russians would intervene in any way which might precipitate a conflict with Japan. Similarly, with respect to Spain: Litvinov was openly prepared to say to foreign diplomats that a Fascist regime there would be perfectly acceptable provided it was no satellite of the Germans or the Italians[87] – an echo of attitudes to Mussolini's Italy up to 1935. The Spanish Republicans themselves sensed a decline in Soviet concern for their fate. This anxiety had grown since the launching of their offensive at Brunete in early July. The effort had taken a heavy toll with little to show for it. As a result they were dangerously short of equipment, particularly aircraft;[88] thus on the 25 July, after instructions from Negrín, Pascua approached Voroshilov with an urgent request for more supplies.[89] At first the Russians appeared unresponsive but Pascua finally managed to see Stalin – at this time the only foreign diplomat who ever succeeded in doing so – and almost everything requested was agreed to.[90] The decision to increase aid to Spain came at a time when the Soviet leadership also finally decided to supply armaments and munitions to the Chinese, a decision reached at the end of the month.[91] The Russians also stood firm on the issue of recognising Franco as a belligerent in the face of strong Anglo-French pressure to secure the withdrawal of "volunteers" from Spain.[92] After momentary withdrawal the Russians had stepped back out into the world. This was signalled by an editorial in *Le Journal de Moscou*, which re-emphasised the indivisibility of peace and pointed out that: "The events which are taking place in China and Spain are closely interdependent", ridiculing the notion that the two conflicts could be "localised".[93]

The reassertion of Litvinovian values was also evident with respect to Germany; in fact the Germans left the Russians little choice. It was announced that Surits would leave Berlin for the

Paris embassy – a move effected in late June 1937.[94] He was replaced by Yurenev, who was duly transferred from Tokyo.[95] A change of guard also took place at the trade mission in Berlin; both Kandelaki and Friedrichson returned to Moscow and became Deputy Commissars of Foreign Trade[96] prior to arrest and imprisonment. In addition, the independent-minded Caucasian, Astakhov, who headed the Narkomindel Press Department, proceeded to Berlin as political counsellor prior to Yurenev's arrival.[97] He arrived at an unpropitious moment. Surits presented Astakhov and Nepomnyashchy, the new torgpred,[98] to Foreign Minister Neurath on the 3 June. But, as Surits' note on the conversation recorded: "Not a sound about our mutual relations, not a word about the perspectives for our trade relations."[99]

Although Neurath greeted Yurenev as an old acquaintance when they met on the 7 July 1937 – both had served as heads of mission in Rome during the mid-twenties – the conversation contained nothing new; Yurenev repeated the Soviet maxim that for any improvement in trade relations, there had to be political preconditions,[100] a point made with the usual futility. Without much justification Yurenev then deluded himself that his new mission was something other than fruitless (Surits had given up in despair). Hitler insisted on receiving Yurenev's credentials at Obersalzberg, near Berchtesgaden. There, on the 21 July, Yurenev expressed his hope that he could count on Hitler's co-operation in creating and maintaining normal relations between the two countries. In turn, Hitler agreed with Yurenev "that such relations between the German state and the Soviet Union will meet, now in particular more than ever, both the necessary requirements of non-interference and the interests of both countries, and may also serve the cause of universal peace".[101] In a sanguine letter to the more sober and sceptical Litvinov over a week later, the enthusiastic Yurenev made much of the fact that his visit and the speeches exchanged had created something of a sensation, particularly when considered in the light of the positive remarks made by Neurath and head of the Ausamt political section, Weizsäcker, plus the toning down of the anti-Soviet hysteria which had hitherto predominated in the German press. Yurenev tended to overlook Hitler's reference to "non-interference", which in fact appears to have reflected his continuing obsession with the subversive dangers of Bolshevism, and not merely in Spain. "Naturally", Yurenev wrote, "the question arises, what does all this mean: is Hitler not trying to improve relations with us, to blackmail such states as Frane and England, or is there something 'more genuine' here in his wish to improve relations with us albeit only so far? I do not deny the possibility that Hitler may have blackmail in his mind, but I believe all the same that this is not the meaning of his wish 'to normalise relations' with us." Following traditional assumptions Yurenev saw Germany's economic problems behind these supposed moves and recommended that "we must continue the former tactical line of linking as closely as possible the problem of improving economic relations between Germany and ourselves with the question of a real normalisation of political relations (the press, Ministers' speeches, etc.)".[102] In fact Yurenev was daydreaming. The following despatch from the French ambassador in Berlin was more accurate: "The information which I have obtained on the subject of the presentation of the letters of credence of the new ambassador from the USSR, received by Mr Hitler yesterday, at his alpine villa in Obersalzberg, modifies the initial impression which this reception gave . . . I have, in fact, learnt from an excellent German source that Mr Hitler had categorically refused to receive Mr Yurenev's letters in Berlin. He did not want it to be accompanied by a military parade and the customary ceremonial in honour of the Soviet envoy. If he has given him an audience in Obersalzberg, it is not from a concern to be courteous and to save him waiting too long; it is, on the contrary, to keep the interview protocol to a minimum. In fact, the Minister of Foreign Affairs was not there, nor the state secretary. Only Mr Meissner [head of the Reich Chancellery] assisted."[103] After returning on leave later that summer Yurenev was arrested and arraigned on trial early in 1938.

The German option still did not exist; Litvinov's pursuit of collective security continued by default, though observers continued to detect a certain reserve in Moscow on international questions. "For the USSR the Spanish question is a subsidiary issue", Pascua acknowledged in conversation with Azaña in August 1937.[104] By then the Russians had ceased sending supplies to Spain via the Black Sea because of the massive losses incurred as a result of action by Italian and Italian-supplied submarines. Nonetheless, between October 1936 and March 1937 more than 25 vessels delivered from the USSR to the Republic 333 planes,

256 tanks, 60 armoured cars, 3181 medium and 4096 light machine-guns, 189 000 rifles, 1.5 million shells, 376 million cartridges, 150 tons of gunpowder, and 2237 tons of combustibles. In addition the Russians sent 21 planes, 16 tanks, 243 heavy guns, 126 mortars, 874 machine-guns, 62 640 rifles, 441 tons of gunpowder and 11 motor vehicles purchased in France, Czechoslovakia, Switzerland and elsewhere.[105] But Russian shipments were now gravely threatened; Moscow had no navy worthy of the name. "In five years", Maisky boasted to the Spanish ambassador in London, "we will have a navy which will give England pause for thought and our programme will be a shock for her from the first year."[106] Yet this was merely wishful thinking. The Russians were certainly no match for the Italians. Between October 1936 and July 1937, 96 Soviet merchant ships were captured and 3 sunk.[107] By August the Russians were loath to risk further shipments and these were drastically cut. The increasing losses in shipping inevitably placed a strain on the continuation of the Soviet commitment to the survival of the Republic. In addition the Russians contracted a new and more urgent commitment to supply arms to the Chinese, with the outbreak of the Sino-Japanese war in July 1937. Entente efforts to curb Italian piracy in the Mediterranean made a temporary halt to shipments seem more acceptable to Russian eyes.

* * *

Alarmed at the destruction of British shipping and at information that Italian submarines had been instructed to attack oil tankers, including those under the British flag en route to Valencia,[108] the British responded positively, if guardedly, to a French proposal for a conference of various Mediterranean and Black Sea Powers – minus the Italians, but including the British – to decide on measures to protect threatened shipping.[109] As Eden noted: "our original wish was to convoke a conference of Mediterranean Powers (including Italy but excluding the Black Sea Powers) to consider measures to put an end to piracy in the Mediterranean. It was the French who insisted on Russia being invited,[110] and we argued that in that case Germany would have to be invited as well".[111] The British were, as ever, falling over themselves to avoid alienating Berlin. The Russians, along with the others, did not receive an invitation until the 6 September,[112] but they were aware something was in the wind and, evidently determined to set the record straight before the conference convened, they sent a note of protest to the Italian Government on the 5 September; chargé d'affaires Guelfand was given strict instructions on the timing of its delivery to the Italian Government. The démarche protested at "the aggressive activities of Italian naval vessels against the USSR's merchant ships", which included the sinking of the *Timiryazev* on the 30 August 1937 and of the *Blagoev* on the 1 September.[113]

"I have received the Soviet indictment", Italy's Foreign Minister, Ciano, noted in his diary on the 6 September. "The Duce has approved my plan: Russia wants to sabotage the conference", he recorded. He put the matter in these specious terms to the British ambassador, who proved most receptive. "For the moment the Bolsheviks have made a false move. It is we who will underline that point", Ciano wrote, at that time still assuming that Italy would participate in the forthcoming conference at Nyon.[114] But after further deliberation with Mussolini, and learning that the Germans would refuse to attend, the Italians also rejected the offer – citing the Soviet démarche as a convenient excuse.[115] Having lodged their protest with the Italians on the 7 September, the Russians now accepted the Anglo-French invitation to Nyon, but expressed their incomprehension at the extension of the invitation to the Germans – the German refusal had yet to be made public – yet denied the Spanish,[116] the main victims of the piracy. The Soviets naturally expected the Germans and the Italians to sabotage the conference,[117] given their complicity in the sinking of merchant shipping. Undoubtedly the issue of the protest to Rome had played into the hands of the Italians, but the Foreign Secretary could scarcely complain about Soviet behaviour with any justification; if Eden had had his way, the Russians would have been excluded altogether.[118] As in every other instance of Soviet opposition to Italo-German aggression, the Russians were pilloried as trouble-makers by the British – and Eden was as much a culprit in this as Premier Neville Chamberlain, who had taken office in May 1937 – whereas the Italians and the Germans were constantly treated as prodigal sons.

The agreement reached at Nyon on the 14 September 1937[119] was not wholly satisfactory from the Soviet point of view and proved even less satisfactory as time wore on. It did not go all the way towards enabling the speedy destruction of predatory submarines and it excluded Spanish Republican ships from protection provided by the British and French fleets. Nonetheless Litvinov pressed for acceptance. The reasons he outlined were as follows: "1. The conference was conducted without the participation of Italy and Germany, which attempted to get us excluded, 2. England and France rival Italian domination of the Mediterranean, 3. Recognition of our interests in the Mediterranean, 4. A certain mitigation of the danger from submarines."[120] However, the value of the agreement was further undermined by the British determination to draw in the recalcitrant Italians – the real villains; the other delegates supinely agreed to this extraordinary piece of hypocrisy. The Russians were indignant. Litvinov "explained that, in accusing Italy of infringing the freedom of the seas, we cannot at the same time entrust it with the defence of this freedom".[121] These proposals to include the Italians thus assumed the more limited character of an Anglo-French offer, which the Italians accepted; agreement was recorded on the 1 October.[122] The official hypocrisy of the non-intervention committee now had a twin, and shipping arms to Spain remained as hazardous as ever. As from December 1937 the Russians renewed shipments, but from Baltic and northern ports to France; the French, alarmed at the extent of Italian intervention and presumed ambitions in Spain, had re-opened their frontier with Spain in desperation.[123] Soviet supplies thus became totally dependent on French goodwill which, with the drift of French politics to the Right, gradually faded into oblivion.

The near total futility of the Nyon proceedings was more than matched in Far Eastern affairs by the ineffectual Brussels conference, convened from the 3 to the 24 November 1937 to discuss the Sino-Japanese war and its repercussions. Litvinov attended for only a few days. One reason for his early return to Moscow was his participation in the election campaign for the Supreme Soviet – an ironical accompaniment to the ever-increasing terror which had by now acquired a dynamic of its own, feeding on guilt by association, a seemingly limitless diet. Polling was due to begin on the 12 December and Litvinov had been adopted as candidate for the Petrograd district of Leningrad. But this was a lesser explanation for his departure. More importantly, the NKVD had returned in force to clean out the

Narkomindel. Antonov-Ovseenko had been recalled from Barcelona at the end of August. He waited in enforced idleness for several weeks until finally Stalin summoned him to the Kremlin. There he was reprimanded for acting with too much independence in Barcelona. He defended his record; Stalin appeared convinced. But he was appointed People's Commissar of Justice – an omen, given what happened to Krestinsky – and he was duly arrested on the night of the 11 October 1937.[124]

Four days before, on the 7 October, polpred Bogomolov returned from China, reportedly with every intention of urging direct Soviet military intervention.[125] He disappeared. Between the 2 and 6 November Viktor Kin, editor of *Le Journal de Moscou*, followed suit. The climate of terror was such that at the Turkish ambassador's celebrations on the 29 October only five Soviet officials attended, and all sat at a separate table.[126] It had become too dangerous to deal with foreigners even in an official capacity. After Kin, Arosev was reported arrested; he had had the misfortune to handle, or mishandle as the NKVD would have seen it, André Gide's visit to the USSR, and paid the price of his life for the latter's disillusionment and outspoken condemnation of conditions in the USSR.[127] Davtyan, polpred in Warsaw, was arrested; Podolsky, polpred in neighbouring Kaunas, was summoned for interrogation; Karsky, polpred in Ankara since May, and Yurenev, were also gathered into the net.[128] Within days it was also reported that Asmus, polpred in Helsinki, and Brodovsky, polpred in Riga, had also been arrested.[129] The leading Swedish-language newspaper in Finland, the *Hufvudstadsblad*, carried the news that Litvinov had protested against these arrests, arguing that they damaged Soviet prestige abroad.[130] If, indeed, he did protest, it had little effect. The arrests continued into 1938 – Stomonyakov fell to the axe – recommencing after Litvinov's dismissal in 1939. On the 19 December 1937 Karakhan, Tsukerman (formerly head of the Near Eastern Department) and Steiger were sentenced to death and executed.[131] Skvirsky failed to return to his post in Kabul. Tikhmenev failed to reappear in Copenhagen. Bekzadyan never returned to Budapest. A few refused to pack their bags for Moscow when ordered to do so – Barmine, senior political counsellor and latterly chargé d'affaires in Athens, was one of the first;[132] there was also General Yakubovich, polpred in Oslo, and Raskol'nikov, from Sofia, who fled to Paris in April 1938 to die a natural death after writing a letter of protest to the Soviet leadership in the summer of 1939. Even Litvinov's private secretary, Gershelman, was arrested in the Commissar's own office; yet Litvinov himself remained untouched. On the 12 November 1937 *Pravda* finally gave full details of his candidacy in the elections, announcing that at a factory meeting an old worker had praised Litvinov as an "experienced fighter at the post of People's Commissar for Foreign Affairs". "Through his lips", the old man is reported to have said, "our people speak in the international arena, expressing their inflexible desire for peace. Thanks to his Bolshevik firmness and ability the Soviet policy of peace is implemented unflinchingly."[133]

* * *

By December 1937, with so many struck down and in the face of continued Western indifference, Litvinov was in a bitter and gloomy mood. His longstanding rival Molotov, speaking on the 6 November, had disparagingly referred to "the governments of states which claim to pass for democratic countries"[134] – a straw in the wind. The real problem was British policy. Britain was the cornerstone of any successful collective security mechanism. The French were too hopelessly dependent upon Britain as their ultimate guarantor to exercise any real independence in foreign policy. Paralysed by fear of war in the Mediterranean, in Central Europe and in the Far East, with no expectation that rearmament could meet the threat until at least 1939, the British Government was entrusted to a man who deluded himself that without exerting real pressure on Hitler, the German leader could be talked out of aggression.

Moscow did not need spies to ascertain Chamberlain's views – though it appears that the Russians had access to British diplomatic codes and ciphers in the late thirties;[135] Maisky's conversation with Neville Chamberlain on the 29 June 1937 left no room for doubt. The only question that remained was how long the British would continue to tolerate the indignities which his policies inevitably entailed. Chamberlain told Maisky: "If we could sit with the Germans at the same table and, pencil in hand, run through all their complaints and claims, then this would to a significant extent facilitate a clearing of the atmosphere or at the very least a more precise definition of the current situation. We could then know what the Germans want, and would also know whether it is possible to satisfy German demands. If possible, we would meet Germany to the maximum, if impossible, we would take other decisions. This is, it seems to me, what is at present most required."[136] The naivete this betrayed was subjected to the rapier of Litvinov's sarcasm when he addressed the electors of Leningrad on the 27 November 1937. Litvinov still stressed the clear distinction he had always drawn between the aggressor and the pacific Powers, but with less emphasis than formerly:

> You know comrades, that imperialism, i.e. the craving to expand one's frontiers, the annexation of foreign lands, colonies, the enslavement of other nations, is to a greater or lesser extent characteristic of almost all bourgeois states. Certain of them, however, at the current stage of history, since the world war, are contented with their 'acquisitions', as though they no longer dream of new conquests. There are those who dream, but who have not for the moment decided to talk about it loudly and intelligibly. There are, however, three states which show no restraint in publicly, loudly, day in and day out proclaiming their resolve to respect no international laws, nor any international treaties, even those they themselves have signed, their resolve to annexe other people's territory, wherever they can, and therefore they reject any collective co-operation in the organisation of peace. They proclaim this aggressive policy of theirs with the utmost clarity, with the utmost cynicism even, and not only proclaim it, but in places they also put it into effect. Nonetheless there are states which do not believe their statements about their aggressive designs and devote all their diplomacy to obtaining confirmation and clarification of these completely unambiguous statements. They just turn to the aggressors with enquiries more or less like this: "They say you have stated that you do not recognise international treaties, and even actually violate them, that you have no intention of respecting the security and territorial integrity of other states and have actually deprived some of their security and territorial integrity. You have rejected co-operation with us and have actually refused to participate in international organisations, gatherings and conferences. We want to know, whether we have correctly understood you and whether you really believe

> what you say. Would you be so kind as to confirm and clarify this" (*Laughter*). The receipt of confirmation does not stop further enquiries. Not confining themselves to verbal enquiries, from time to time they send the aggressors written questionnaires to be completed: "confirm that you are an aggressor" (*General laughter in the hall*). When the aggressors scornfully throw these questionnaires into the wastepaper basket, they are sent official and unofficial envoys, Ministers and other men of state, to obtain further confirmation and clarification. Replies to these enquiries are sometimes received in an unambiguously insulting form. But even then they ask for confirmation and clarification. Unfortunately the aggressors go beyond sending verbal or written confirmation and to ensure complete clarity, they tread on the corns of all those feet in the way, and little by little carry out their programme of aggression. Thus we are left with a division of labour in the international arena, whereby some states attack, and others – make enquiries and await confirmation and clarification (*Laughter*).[137]

Litvinov's caustic caricature of British and French policy was clearly prompted by Lord President of the Council Halifax's visit to Hitler from the 17 to the 21 November 1937.[138] What the Russians saw as Chamberlain's attempts to revive the Four Power Pact approach to the European crisis certainly embittered Litvinov and made his position at home that much more precarious. The more the Russians felt betrayed by the West, the greater the xenophobia that imbued their spirit; ultimately the xenophobia worked in one direction only: it favoured a full-scale retreat into fortress Russia, and if this could be accomplished only by means of a new modus vivendi which would give Germany a free hand against the West, so be it.

The Russians looked on with deep mistrust as the British co-ordinated their appeasement of Germany with the French,[139] and eyed with grave suspicion the meeting between French Foreign Minister Delbos and Neurath on the 3 December 1937. Delbos was en route to Warsaw; Neurath wished to make a gesture of courtesy, not entirely devoid of political significance. As François-Poncet recorded: "neither Mr Barthou, in June 1934, nor Mr Laval, in May 1935, were beneficiaries of such treatment. . . . The fact that Mr Delbos did not extend his journey as far as Russia has been carefully noted in Germany. It has been interpreted as an indicator that the French Government, while remaining faithful to the Franco-Soviet pact, nevertheless made no effort to firm up its ties with Moscow any further".[140] But just as it met with approval in Berlin, it met with disfavour in Moscow: "I fear that, not without Delbos' consent, the story has spread that we invited him to Moscow, but that he refused", Potemkin wrote gloomily to Surits on the 19 December; he added that, "not satisfied with a short conversation with Neurath at the Silesian station, Delbos favours the idea of meeting with Hitler's Minister of Foreign Affairs once more in circumstances favourable to a more fruitful exchange of opinions".[141] Comparing the democracies with the Fascist Powers, whom the Russians saw as economically much the weaker, *Le Journal de Moscou* asked why Italy and Germany did not turn to the other Powers for help. "For the simple reason", it answered, "that they have steadier nerves, more control over themselves, more patience, greater political judgement and understanding of psychology than England and France. They are aware of the advantage of a situation in which it is the others who show anxiety and who send them their Halifaxes, Flandins and Cormets."[142]

On the 25 December 1937 Litvinov agreed to see Luciani, *Le Temps* correspondent in Moscow. Luciani asked Litvinov whether it would be correct to describe the Soviet position as "isolation, withdrawal into itself". His response was: "Obviously, since at the moment no one wants anything to do with us. We will carry on waiting . . . and then we'll see". The conversation then took an unforeseen path:

> "What do you mean by that, Commissar?"
> "There are other possible combinations."
> "With Germany?"
> "Why not?"
> "But is a German–Soviet rapprochement possible?"
> "Perfectly possible. On coming to power, Hitler renewed the treaty of 1926. He wished to remain on good terms with us. He changed his attitude when he realised that we were opposed to German expansionism in Central Europe, that we wanted to maintain the territorial status quo, that, by our policy of collective security, we were blocking his plans".
> "But if we gave him to understand that we have no interest in maintaining the status quo . . . ?"

> "It is you, the French, who have an interest in respect for the territorial articles of Versailles. But we undertook nothing at Versailles. We therefore have nothing to give back. . . . The USSR would not be touched by territorial revision. We could therefore disinterest ourselves. . . . Oh, it would not be a question of signing new treaties! Things would happen differently!"[143]

* * *

Outward signs that Litvinov was running into difficulties now began to appear with increasing frequency. Once again it was Zhdanov who led the way. Using his position as chairman of the chief foreign affairs commission of the Supreme Soviet as a platform for attack, he began his assault on the 17 January 1938 with polite references to "our respected Maxim Maximovich Litvinov" – most of Litvinov's colleagues used the term "much respected". Zhdanov announced that he had "some questions concerning the Narkomindel's activities". The first of these questions concerned foreign consulates, the second – Japan (this will be dealt with in a subsequent volume), and the third – France. The issue of foreign consulates had arisen in the course of 1937 with the spy fever which gripped the country soon after Stalin's speech to the Central Committee plenum in March 1937. The first sign appears to have emerged on the 16 April, when head of the First Western Department Karsky, in conversation with Janowski, political counsellor at the Polish embassy, raised the question of equalising the number of consulates each held on the other's territory.[144] Then early in May the German consul-general in Kiev reported that the Russians wished to close down German consulates in order to reduce the number to two – the USSR had only two consulates on German soil; by July the issue had been raised by the Russians with the German embassy in Moscow.[145] Next, a Japanese diplomat, Saito, failed to obtain a visa as consul to replace his predecessor in Odessa; in fact the Russians wanted the consulate closed, though the Japanese were in ignorance of that fact. Saito waited in vain for his visa from March to June 1937.[146] The diplomats at the Narkomindel were acutely embarrassed. No diplomat likes cutting back on diplomatic representation. But someone in the Soviet leadership – and clearly not

Stalin, otherwise all this would have been settled abruptly – had clearly asked why the USSR had less consulates in other countries than they possessed in the USSR. Such inequality was evidently regarded as an affront. Since it was automatically assumed that, particularly in the cases of Poland, Germany, Japan and Italy, these consulates were a cover for spies, it was felt that the issue should be pressed by the Narkomindel. On the 4 October 1937 Potemkin summoned Schulenburg to announce that the USSR wanted to open two new consulates – in Breslau and Munich. This would equalise the number on both sides only if the Germans also closed three of theirs in the USSR; each country would then host four consulates from the other side.[147] The Germans refused. They would agree to close only two consulates. At the very least the Russians wanted the Leningrad consulate closed,[148] since they – and evidently Zhdanov in particular – considered it an important Intelligence centre for the Germans.[149] The Germans then insisted on maintaining two consulates – in Kiev and Novosibirsk – but added that since Russian consulates in Germany were in ports and German consulates in the USSR were not, the Russians should move theirs inland.[150] Whereupon Litvinov warned Schulenburg that if the Germans insisted, they would find all consulates removed on both sides – this eventually happened in March 1938.[151] On the 17 November 1937 it was announced that German consulates were being closed in Leningrad, Tbilisi, Kharkov, Vladivostok, and Odessa, leaving only those at Kiev and Novosibirsk open. Four days later it was announced that the Italians would close theirs in Kiev, Leningrad, Tbilisi, Novorossisk and Batum; the Poles and the Japanese received the same treatment.[152] Prior to Zhdanov's speech on the 17 January 1938 the Soviet Government requested the British, Estonians, Latvians, Danes, Norwegians and Swedes to close their consulates in Leningrad.[153]

Despite the fact that these measures had already been decided upon, Zhdanov still insisted on stressing that there was "a very large quantity of consuls of various foreign Powers" in Leningrad. Speaking as though no action had been taken, he continued: "In Leningrad we have a consul from almost every foreign Power. Here I must say that a number of these consuls manifestly exceed their authority and obligations and act with impropriety, engaging in subversive activities against the people and the country to which they are accredited." He then raised the now defunct issue of parity: "It is also known that the USSR does not have an equal number of consuls in these countries. Why does the Narkomindel tolerate such a situation in which the number of consuls representing foreign Powers in the USSR is not equal, but greater than the number of consuls representing the USSR in foreign states. Does it not follow from the strength and the might of our great socialist power that there should be parity between our consular representatives abroad and foreign representatives here? (*Applause*)." Turning to Franco-Soviet relations he said: "I do not understand what is going on in France." "How can one understand a situation where the government of a country with which we – the USSR – are in relatively close relations and with which we have, as it were, a continuing rapprochement, allows on its territory the existence of organisations carrying out and organising terrorism against the USSR?". "They say", he continued, "that this is done on the basis of a law on the right of asylum for foreigners. It seems to me that this is not so. It seems to me that the fact of the existence on French territory, on the territory of a state with which we have normal relations, with which we have a pact of mutual assistance – the fact of the existence of an organisation of this type represents nothing less than special and notorious encouragement of actively hostile machinations by all kinds of scoundrels of Russian and non-Russian origin, on the part of a government with which we have a pact of mutual assistance." "And we must ask here and now: does this pact exist or does it not, is this pact a reality or is it not? And I would like to chairman of the Council of People's Commissars of the USSR to pay attention to these defects and take the appropriate measures to remedy them (*Applause*)."[154] In his reply Molotov updated Zhdanov on the measures taken with respect to consulates, but supported his attack on France.[155] The significance of these strictures lay not in their particulars, but in the fact that they illustrated the increasingly intemperate milieu in which Litvinov was struggling. Stalin himself had not done with collective security – continuing German hostility saw to that – but his patience was evidently wearing thin.

The bloody regression of Russia's political revolution in the form of the terror, combined with the persistent and seemingly inescapable isolation imposed upon it by ideologically hostile states in the face of the growing threat of war, East and West, was undeniably taking its toll of the pre-existing Litvinovian internationalism of Soviet foreign policy. Although the Western Powers saw what was happening and were alarmed, their continued underestimation of the USSR as a potential partner to the Germans as much as themselves, and their exaggerated sense of their own impotence but their excessive over-estimation of the power of their likely adversaries, meant that nothing was done to ensure that the precarious pendulum driving Soviet foreign policy did not swing too far in the other direction. The events of 1937 contained a lesson for the Entente; the lesson remained unlearnt, as is evident from the manner in which the Western Powers handled the Czechoslovakian crisis in 1938.

9 The Czechoslovakian Crisis, 1938

The events of 1938 reinforced Moscow's reservations about the practicability of collective security. The year began badly. After Zhdanov's attack on the Narkomindel for not asserting Soviet interests *vis-à-vis* the capitalist world in general, came the publication of Stalin's written reply to comrades Ivanov and Filippovich on the 14 February 1938. He spoke of the need to combine "the serious efforts of the international proletariat with the still more serious efforts of the whole of our Soviet people". Stalin continued: "We need to strengthen and reinforce the international proletarian links of the working-class of the USSR with the working-class of the bourgeois countries; we need to organise political aid from the working-class of the bourgeois countries to the working-class of our own country in the event of an armed attack on our own country, equally we need to organise all possible aid from the working-class of our own country to the working-class of the bourgeois countries."[1] Given the paranoia about subversion in France, the statement was extremely tactless. But it was a telling symptom: the Soviet Union was turning in on itself, folding the Comintern around its exposed form for added protection. The tragedy was that the protection it could afford was gravely diminished by the very terror which Stalin himself had initiated to assure his own security, to appease his own fevered imagination. It was a tragic and bitter irony that the spirit of isolationism in Stalin's time should find expression in the traditional language of revolutionary internationalism. This isolationism was immediately apparent in Soviet reactions to the Anschluss in the spring of 1938.

On the 11–12 March 1938 German troops marched into Austria. The route to the East, and ultimately to the USSR, was now open; Czechoslovakia was next in line. Yet there were no outspoken denunciations from the Soviet Union. Barely a week prior to the Anschluss the spirit of isolationism was made apparent in an unsigned article entitled "The Brest Peace and the Struggle of the Party of Bolsheviks Against Trotskyist-Bukharinite War Provocateurs", which appeared in *Bol'shevik* on the 5 March. It pointed out that in 1917–18 "the Anglo-French imperialists attempted by every means to draw Soviet Russia into the war with Germany".[2] The informed reader was well aware that this was a tale with a moral to it, relevant to the current situation. This was the unpropitious milieu in which the Anschluss was reported on the 12 March. *Pravda* was still spewing boiling oil over Bukharin, Krestinsky and other poor unfortunates on the eve of sentence being passed at this the latest and the last show-trial. "Death to the Fascist Spies!", the editorial ranted; the only consolation for Litvinov was that at least they were not accused of being British or French spies. The events in Austria took second, if not third place, then and on the following day when the accused were sentenced.[3] Not until the 14 March did any comment appear, and then only on the inner pages. Typically Britain took the brunt of Soviet criticism:

> Endless concessions to the aggressors are turning into – as is evident from the example of Austria – direct complicity with, and incitement of, the war-mongers. This is a fatal policy with inevitable consequences. And those who are carrying it out cannot relieve themselves of the responsibility for complicity in the growing threat of war in Europe.[4]

Izvestiya went one step further than *Pravda*. Head of the Narkomindel's Press Department Gnedin, writing under his usual pseudonym E. Alexandrov, expressed the Soviet attitude thus:

> An overt threat to peace in Europe can only meet with severe condemnation from the Soviet Union, ever ready to play its part in the cause of strengthening peace between nations. But the Soviet Union can view the events that have taken place with complete tranquillity.[5]

Similarly, *Le Journal de Moscou* stressed the dangers to Britain rather than to the USSR. "England is harvesting the fruits of Neville Chamberlain's policy", the paper emphasised, adding that it was up to London to organise collective security against

German aggression.[6] The USSR was au-delà de la mêlée, a sentiment echoed by Potemkin in conversation with the Polish ambassador on the 14 March.[7] It was evidently in a frantic attempt to shake Stalin and the others from their lofty and self-conscious indifference that Litvinov sent a letter to the Politburo that same day, pressing the argument that: "The seizure of Austria represents the most important event since the world war, fraught with the greatest dangers and not least for our Union [the USSR]".[8]

Litvinov did not succeed in rousing the kind of response he evidently hoped for, but a further crisis came to his rescue in the form of Polish belligerence. Ironically the USSR was, from 1933 to the summer of 1939, less of a revisionist Power than neighbouring Poland. The Poles always sought to dominate the Baltic; some also dreamed of an empire "from sea to sea", encompassing the Baltic states and the Soviet Ukraine. The more realistic were merely looking to take advantage of the opportunities thrown up by German expansionism to gather pickings along the perimeter of Berlin's sphere of interest; in this the Poles shared the aims of the revisionist Hungarians to the south. At five in the morning on the 11 March 1938 at Trasnykas, a Polish soldier was killed by a Lithuanian policeman; according to Lithuanian sources, the Pole had crossed the border in hot pursuit of a smuggler, and responded to warnings by opening fire.[9] The Polish press – not without prompting from the Foreign Ministry – began to threaten Lithuania with dire consequences should the Lithuanians refuse to open diplomatic relations, broken off in 1920. The Poles viewed the Baltic as their own "sphere of influence",[10] and in an article in *Slowo*, a Vilnius publication, the editor Mackiewicz wrote of his having always favoured "a policy which would give Germany the Anschluss and Lithuania to Poland".[11] Indeed, Poland was one of the first Powers to recognise the Anschluss.[12] The Russians took these threats very seriously. "The supposition that Poland had no intention of limiting itself to the establishment of diplomatic relations with Lithuania is confirmed by the position taken by the press of the Polish conservatives and of the Fascist national party", Potemkin wrote shortly after the Polish–Lithuanian incident was over.[13]

The incident bolstered Litvinov's argument that peace was, after all, indivisible. No one could deny that the lack of reaction to Germany's invasion of Austria had encouraged the Poles in their adventurism. But putting Litvinov's principles into practice, as was evident in the case of Italy and Abyssinia, was no easy matter. Contradictory impulses were at work. The Russians had not entirely given up hope of winning Poland as an ally against Hitler – it lasted into 1939 – and this idea was reflected somewhat obliquely in the assertion by Potemkin that "Hitler wants to unleash Poland against the Soviet Union."[14] In 1933 the Russians had been prepared to give carte blanche to Warsaw vis-à-vis the Lithuanians, in return for collaboration against Germany.[15] "Berlin is strongly interested in a military conflict breaking out between Warsaw and Kovno" (the Lithuanian capital), the Russians now noted nervously.[16] Moscow therefore had an interest in preventing a Polish-Lithuanian war, but at the same time the conflicting interest of avoiding an open confrontation with Poland. On the 16 March 1938 Litvinov called in the Polish ambassador and "told him that, without going into an evaluation of the Polish-Lithuanian dispute, we are interested in seeing it resolved purely by peaceful means and that the use of force may bring danger to the whole of Eastern Europe".[17] The Russians to some extent attempted to shift the burden westwards. *Izvestiya* reflected briefly on the dispute, emphasising "the need for a swift and speedy reaction from the peace-loving Powers".[18] The French certainly had an interest in preventing any untimely explosions in this part of the world. The Poles rightly interpreted Litvinov's remarks to mean that the Russians would not intervene, and chose to emphasise this rather than the Russian warning against the use of force. In their reply to the Soviet warning, the Poles stated, inter alia: "We are content to receive the Soviet Government's point of view, as an expression of a practical understanding of the desirability of peace. We particularly appreciate the statement that the Soviet Government does not wish to intervene in both the old and new disputes between ourselves and Lithuania."[19]

The policy the Soviets followed tried to marry avoidance of a confrontation with Poland with a firm reaffirmation of the need to keep the peace; this was a second-best solution, a formal respect for the principles Litvinov upheld rather than the maintenance of their spirit – a position identical to that adopted over Abyssinia. Litvinov thus advised the Lithuanians to accept the Polish ultimatum.[20] At the same time, however, he made clear to Grzybowski, the Polish ambassador, that the USSR was concerned about "the maintenance of the complete independence of the Lithuanian Government" and warned that "in the situation that has arisen, any misunderstanding may have fatal consequences".[21] As further insurance the outlawed Polish Communist Party, whose leaders were ironically under arrest in the USSR on preposterous charges of espionage,[22] launched a strident campaign against war with Lithuania.[23]

The Polish–Lithuanian dispute was soon resolved in favour of Poland. Deprived of any outside support, the Lithuanians swallowed the indignity of exchanging missions with the Poles. Looking on the bright side, the Russians could congratulate themselves on having curbed any wider ambitions the Poles may have harboured – ambitions the Narkomindel continued to take seriously[24] – but the whole affair unquestionably bruised Soviet prestige and gave the Poles a misleading impression of their true weight in the international balance. Litvinov was no longer silenced, but his voice was still muffled; a similar reserve was even more evident during the initial phase of the Czechoslovakian crisis.

The Anschluss predictably placed Czechoslovakia in the front line of German expansionism; the Czechs therefore sought reassurance that the USSR would come to their assistance under the terms of the pact signed in 1935. But since there was no common frontier between the USSR and Czechoslovakia, no assistance could conceivably be rendered without co-operation from either Poland or Romania, preferably both: "a corridor would have to be created", the Russians said.[25] Since France was allied to these states, it was originally assumed that if the French moved to rescue the Czechs, Poland and Romania would be obliged to aid the French by at the very least allowing Soviet land and air forces through to Czechoslovakia. In their turn the Russians were obliged to come to the aid of the Czechs only if the Czechs themselves resisted the Germans and only if the French also came to their assistance first. In 1935, although Poland still steadfastly refused to join in a multilateral system of mutual assistance with the USSR, it was by no means certain nothing would ever alter this policy. Although Romania was tied by a separate alliance with Poland, and was therefore unlikely to stray too far from the Polish camp, under Titulescu the Romanians very nearly concluded a mutual assistance pact with the USSR. In July 1936 Titulescu had actually initialled such a pact, but without fully consulting his colleagues, who shortly afterwards threw him out of the government; nothing therefore became of the project.[26] The stumbling block on the Romanian side was the issue of Bessarabia. The Romanians were determined to obtain de jure recognition of their possession of this territory, seized from the Russians in 1919; Moscow was prepared to sign a pact overlooking the issue and was also prepared to give an undertaking that Soviet forces would withdraw east of the Dnestr′ immediately after the end of hostilities, but would never renounce its claim to Bessarabia.[27]

By 1938 no further progress had been made with Romania, and the Polish–Lithuanian crisis underlined the continued instability in Soviet–Polish relations. The growth of social turmoil in Poland consequent on the intensification of the Depression and only selectively eased by the growth of Polish defence industries was reflected in the strike statistics: from a low point of 330 recorded industrial disputes in 1930, the number had risen to 2103 in 1937.[28] The unrest encompassed both town and country. However much Stalin's Russia subordinated the goal of world revolution to that of socialism in one country, the fact stubbornly remained that at bottom Russia was still a revolutionary Power, through force of circumstance if not through fixed belief. The Russians were the natural allies, for they were also the natural beneficiaries, of revolution in Poland. It was this, as much if not more than muted Soviet claims to Polish-occupied territory inhabited by ethnic Ukrainians and Byelorussians, which made Polish–Soviet relations so unstable. Polish Communists naturally joined and sought to lead any manifestations of social unease; they were therefore easily identified as the source of all discontent by a ruling class unable to see the true roots of the problem, and the fact that the Communists formed a section of the Comintern run from Moscow naturally meant that they were also viewed as a Soviet fifth column. The Soviet leadership certainly mobilised Polish Communists to serve their interests. A month after the signature of the anti-Comintern pact in November 1936, which the Russians feared Poland might join, Dimitrov instructed the Polish Communist leadership that the main task was to prevent their country from becoming an instrument of German Fascism. "This is the fundamental question", he stressed, "and everything else must be subordinated to this priority."[29] The Communists called on the people to take "the defence of Poland" into their own hands. The Polish army had to be transformed into "a conscious guardian of the independence of the nation, liberated from Fascist dictatorship".[30] And when the issue of German claims to the Czech Sudetenland arose in the spring of 1938, after the Anschluss, exciting Polish ambitions to seize Teschen from the encircled prey, *Le Journal de Moscou* issued an ominous warning to the Poles that there might be more to lose than to gain from raising the issue of ethnic frontiers: "Berlin and Warsaw must understand that, in the eyes of European public opinion, the question of the oppression in Poland of six and a half million Ukrainians and of two million or so Byelorussians has much greater weight than the question of the fate of a small group of Poles in Czechoslovakia, who anyway enjoy all their rights." "In speculating on the national problem", the paper threatened, "the Fascist warmongers are indulging in a game dangerous not only to the cause of peace, but to themselves."[31]

The issue of ethnic frontiers was something the Russians were prepared to bury when co-operation with the Power concerned was in sight, but it was also an instrument of last resort when such a Power had to be called into line. Having held back on the delicate issue of Bessarabia, even to the extent of silencing hitherto a vociferous campaign on the matter after Titulescu broached the subject of a pact,[32] the Russians plucked it out of the bag in January 1938 after the formation of a new Romanian cabinet under "the notorious Germanophile Goga": "For its part", *Le Journal de Moscou* warned, "the Soviet Union cannot be indifferent to events in a neighbouring country. Moreover, Romania is the only[33] neighbouring state with which the Soviet Union has not regulated certain fundamental questions." "There is reason to fear that Romania's fixed orientation towards a rapprochement with the aggressors might destroy the reciprocal tranquillity which has been established in latter years in relations between Romania and the USSR", the paper added menacingly.[34]

This was the bleak background against which the Czechs sought reassurance that Moscow would observe the terms of its pact with Prague. They were to be disappointed. When questioned by Czechoslovakia's ambassador, Fierlinger, Potemkin was somewhat irritated and retorted that the French were the ones to press as to whether they would live up to their obligations, for no one could accuse the USSR of not doing so.[35] In Prague

Foreign Minister Krofta approached polpred Alexandrovsky and elicited an equally acid response. Krofta spoke rather too freely of the Red Army defending Czechoslovakia against the Germans, and Alexandrovsky replied that the Czechs were looking for excuses to avoid doing anything to defend themselves against possible attack, adding that the defence of Czechoslovakia's freedom and democracy was "above all a matter for Czechoslovakia itself". France and the USSR could "*aid* Czechoslovakia" but only on the condition that Czechoslovakia defended itself. Alexandrovsky drew the conclusion that the Czechoslovakian leaders themselves were reluctant to fight, even if the population were willing.[36] This concern eventually drew the Russians out into the open, since without encouragement Prague was unlikely to resist.

In the meantime, however, Litvinov's hands were still tied. The furthest he could go was revealed at a press conference he summoned on the 17 March. Here he condemned the German invasion of Austria and announced that the Soviet Government "is, as before, ready to participate in collective action" to be decided on with France and Czechoslovakia to halt the growth of aggression and remove the danger of world war. He added that the Soviet Government was willing "to enter immediately into discussions with other Powers in the League of Nations or outside, on practical measures dictated by circumstances. Tomorrow may already be too late", he warned, "but today the time for this has not yet passed, if all states, particularly the Great Powers, adopt a firm, unambiguous position with respect to the problem of collectively saving peace".[37] The offer was never formalised in a diplomatic note, much to the relief of the Entente Powers who, upon being handed a copy, immediately stuffed it into a back pocket and promptly dismissed it from their minds.[38]

This tentative reassertion of Litvinov's line had met with an immovable obstacle in the form of Neville Chamberlain; and since French policy depended on British policy – the British guarantee reasserted in 1936 underlined that unhappy fact – and Czech policy depended upon French policy, there were no great prospects for improvement except, perhaps, in the event of a shift within Britain's domestic political situation. Soviet policy had ground to a halt in the face of a British road-block. The leadership under Stalin retreated into domestic affairs. "You complained at the absence of any orientation from us on questions relating to the international situation in one of your telegrams", Stomonyakov wrote to polpred Luganets-Orel'sky, Bogomolov's replacement in distant and troubled Nanking, on the 17 April 1938. "Comrade Litvinov has given you the reply that currently we are conducting no international negotiations and we are not discussing any international problems and that therefore he can tell you nothing", Stomonyakov added.[39] Instead he offered an outline of the international situation as viewed from Kuznetsky Most. Britain was at the root of the problem. Since Eden's departure from the Foreign Office in February 1938 – "at bottom Anthony did not want to talk either with Hitler or Mussolini and, as I did, he was right to go", noted Chamberlain[40] – Britain had reached an agreement with Italy on the 16 April,[41] whose significance, Stomonyakov remarked, went far beyond its relatively limited content. It was a sign that Britain had moved decisively "in favour of an agreement with the aggressors". Worse than that: "The strengthening of Germany and its co-operation with Italy, the about-turn in English policy noted above, the universal fear of war in France and above all the fear of revolution on the part of ruling circles in the French bourgeoisie, and events in Spain, are also increasing the tendency of France to follow in England's footsteps towards a rapprochement with the aggressors." "The reactionary bourgeoisie of France exemplifies even more glaringly than that of England the betrayal of the national interests of its country under the pressure of a deeply rooted fear of revolution", Stomonyakov concluded.[42]

This analysis was not far short of the mark. Neither Britain nor France showed any real interest in measures to protect Czechoslovakia. Britain was ready to allow Germany to take territory provided no force was used. From this position British policy slid inexorably into the invidious role of exerting pressure on Czechoslovakia to accede to German demands as a means of forestalling the use of force. Towards the end of November 1937 Neville Chamberlain wrote: "I don't see why we shouldn't say to Germany give us satisfactory assurances that you won't use force to deal with the Austrians and Czecho-Slovakians and we'll give you similar assurances that we won't use force to prevent the changes you want if you can get them by peaceful means . . . for the Germans want much the same things for the Sudetendeutsche as we did for the Uitlanders in the Transvaal."[43] Chamberlain did not have much understanding of Hitler. And when the Germans did employ force – as in Austria – the British Government found other reasons for doing nothing.

At the very least Chamberlain's policy implied that a fundamental alteration in the European balance of power to Germany's advantage was no threat to British interests, and, given Hitler's unwavering hostility towards the Russians and his apparent determination to continue eastwards, Chamberlain's policy also amounted to tacitly directing the Germans towards the Russians. His viewpoint, translated into a fatalistic belief that the Germans and the Russians were natural enemies, went unchallenged in the Foreign Office and was endorsed by the Chiefs of Staff, themselves fixated by the unreal and defeatist assumption that not only could one not call Hitler's bluff, but that Britain would have to fight Germany, Italy and Japan, simultaneously and entirely alone, if the decision was taken to oppose Hitler.[44] In fact Chamberlain's policy eventually led to the very disaster he sought to avoid. It did not prove sufficient to appease Hitler; it resulted in others being thrown wastefully to the wolves; it undermined what remained of the French will to resist; and it entirely alienated the Russians.

Having ruled out the feasibility of confronting the aggressors for fear of provoking war, Chamberlain – with the pliable Halifax in train – chose a policy of wringing concessions from Hitler's chosen victims as a means of staving off a conflict, a policy which he never entirely abandoned until early September 1939 when it finally proved impossible to continue. Chamberlain naturally regarded all Soviet efforts in the contrary direction – and Litvinov's policy was the exact reverse of Chamberlain's, though both aimed to prevent war – as warmongering. Chamberlain never accepted Litvinov's view that Hitler's bluff could be called. "Again and again Canning lays it down that you should never menace unless you are in a position to carry out your threats", he wrote.[45] As a result of this philosophy and an underlying ideological hostility towards the USSR stemming from the days when as Health Minister he watched and worried as the Russians fished in the troubled waters of British domestic and imperialist unrest, Chamberlain placed a mischievous misconstruction on Soviet aims, a view reinforced by misleading Secret Intelligence Service assessments: to him the Bolsheviks were "stealthily and cunningly pulling at the strings behind the scenes to get us involved in a war with Germany".[46]

Faced with Chamberlain's deluded obduracy and beset with

piercing doubts about the reliability of France and its allies, it was scarcely surprising that Stalin chose to do next to nothing; but the near paralysis which afflicted Soviet foreign policy could not continue indefinitely. There was no prospect of achieving even normal relations with Germany, and, since Hitler appeared intent on moving against Czechoslovakia if nothing barred his way, Litvinov's line began to re-emerge, uncertainly but inevitably. Although Chamberlain was viewed as an unmitigated disaster, there was no reason to assume he could remain in power indefinitely. It was evidently this hope which brought Stalin round to seeing that something could still be done. In his opinion as expressed to the US ambassador – the only foreign diplomat he would agree to see at this stage – "the reactionary elements in England, represented by the Chamberlain government, were determined upon a policy of making Germany strong, and thus place France in a position of continually increasing dependence upon England; also with the purpose of ultimately making Germany strong against Russia. He stated that in his opinion Chamberlain did not represent the English people and that he would probably fail because the Fascist dictators would drive too hard a bargain. He said that the Soviet Union had every confidence that it could defend itself".[47] Thus although Stalin saw British policy as inimical to Russian interests, he also viewed it as open to change. This judgement, at root correct, but not within the limited span of time the Russians had to work within, was undoubtedly a product of the Bolsheviks' exaggerated appreciation of Britain's power and self-esteem – an appreciation which had temporarily been invalidated in 1931–2 only to reappear from 1933. It was also a product of Stalin's longstanding respect for Winston Churchill,[48] the single most articulate opponent of Chamberlain's policies. Maisky's despatches clearly did much to bolster Litvinov's argument that collective security, if not immediately practicable, could soon be effected with men like Churchill in power.

On the 23 March 1938 Churchill had invited Maisky to lunch; the two had been meeting intermittently since Hitler came to power. Churchill was alarmed at the damaging reports in the British press concerning the terror in Russia and at the prospect that, with Hitler on the rampage, the USSR was backing away and seeking to disengage itself from the approaching battle: "Please explain to me what is going on in your country. As I've told you more than once in the past, I hate Nazi Germany and I'm working unceasingly towards the creation of a 'grand alliance' within the framework of the League of Nations to fight Germany and the aggressors in general. The 'grand alliance' must, in my opinion, encompass all the peace-loving states, but the main role in it must naturally be played by England, France and Russia. We desperately need a strong Russia; many tell me that as a result of recent events Russia has ceased to be a serious factor in international politics." Churchill's whole manner convinced Maisky that his concern was genuine. Maisky did his best to set Churchill's mind at rest, but clearly the only thing that would satisfy him would be deeds, not words. The Soviet Union's retreat into isolation was weakening the case he was putting in Parliament and the country. It was vital, Churchill insisted, "that the USSR demonstrate, by some firm act or other before the entire world, that all the cock-and-bull stories about would-be weakness are entirely without foundation". When Maisky asked what he had in mind, Churchill, after momentary reflection, "said that, for example, our solemn and totally firm statement that we would render serious aid to Czechoslovakia in the event of aggression against it could have such an effect". Churchill also sugared the pill with some flattering remarks about Stalin, which Maisky doubtless skilfully embroidered in his despatch.[49] The despatch evidently awakened considerable interest in gloomy Moscow. After further enquiries from the Soviet capital, Maisky sent another telegram on the 8 April, in which he explained: "In evaluating Churchill's political line one must bear in mind that his point of departure is defence of the integrity of the British Empire and that now the main danger to the latter he sees as Germany. Churchill is extremely Germanophobe by nature, and he is prepared to subordinate everything to the goal of fighting Germany."[50]

Churchill's move came at an opportune moment. The Russians were soon preoccupied by news "that Anglo-French 'mediation' between Czechoslovakia and Germany" was in preparation, "mediation which will very likely lead to joint pressure on Czechoslovakia, with the aim of forcing it to make far-reaching concessions to Germany".[51] Soviet diplomats were already sounding the Romanians as to whether co-operation to aid Czechoslovakia was on the cards. But the Romanians faced an awkward dilemma and they saw themselves as impotent. The best statement of their predicament was made in late May 1938 by Minister of Internal Affairs, then de facto head of the government, Calinescu: "we are in a difficult position. 1. We cannot be sure of Poland. Treaty relations with it are anyway in doubt; they are in force only against Russia. 2. Yugoslavia will never move against Germany. 3. An attack by Germany on Czechoslovakia will for us be casus foederis. In the event of the Soviets intervening, we will find ourselves in a difficult position".[52] Nonetheless, the Romanians did not wish to alienate the Russians entirely; by the end of March they had evinced an interest in resuming contact. However, polpred Ostrovsky was now languishing in an NKVD prison; furthermore chargé d'affaires Butenko, fearing his turn would be next, "chose freedom" and defected. Litvinov therefore instructed Alexandrovsky to visit Bucharest to reassure the Romanians that a new polpred would shortly be appointed. Alexandrovsky would then return to Moscow for discussions with the leadership on the overall situation. Litvinov also asked Krofta, the Czech Foreign Minister, "to urge Romania to co-operate and sign a pact with us, which we always were and are ready for".[53]

However, the Romanians were unprepared for any concrete commitment, as Alexandrovsky discovered when he met Comnène, their Foreign Minister, on the 14 April 1938.[54] When he returned to Moscow a meeting was held with Stalin, Molotov, Voroshilov, Litvinov and Kaganovich. Here Litvinov in effect received endorsement for his policy. It was decided that, if asked, the USSR would undertake every measure to guarantee Czechoslovakia's security along with the co-operation of the French and the Czechs themselves. Voroshilov was reportedly optimistic about the ability of the Red Army and Air Force to fulfil Soviet obligations.[55] But Romania was still unwilling to grant passage.[56] The Russians never regarded this as an insoluble problem, however. On the 26 April Kalinin made the first statement indicating that the USSR might be ready to aid Czechoslovakia even if the French abstained, pointing out to a Soviet audience that the Soviet–Czech pact "does not prohibit either party from rendering assistance without waiting for France".[57]

The Russians certainly did not want this suggestion broadcast far and wide. Kalinin's indiscretion was not printed in the Soviet press. It might have given the French the idea that they could wash their hands of their obligations to Prague and leave the

Russians in direct confrontation with the Germans without any aid from the West. On the other hand, the Russians were not prepared to see Czechoslovakia go under and were certainly not prepared to see Poland pick at Prague's bones. The Poles were sharpening their knives now that Berlin had chosen Czechoslovakia as its victim. The Soviet press had already reminded the Poles that there were far greater numbers of ethnic Ukrainians and Byelorussians in Poland than Poles stranded in Czechoslovakia. Litvinov broached the issue of Polish irredentism with Bonnet, the French Foreign Minister, at Geneva in mid-May, but we have no record of the discussion, only references to it made retrospectively. Litvinov raised the matter once more, this time with ambassador Coulondre on the 8 June 1938,[58] and then again on the 10 June. That day Coulondre sent the following despatch to Bonnet in Paris:

> During the course of a chance conversation I had yesterday with Mr Litvinov and my Czech colleague, I asked the People's Commissar what had induced him to question Your Excellency as to how the French Government understood the state of play with respect to our alliance with Poland in the event of the later attacking Czechoslovakia and, as a result of this, the USSR coming into conflict with it. For the purpose of provoking a reaction, I added that, with the Czech-Soviet pact subordinated to the Franco-Soviet pact, France, in the hypothesis envisaged, would also find itself in conflict with Poland.
>
> "There is", he replied, "another possible outcome: wherein for one reason or another, France did not intervene and the USSR all the same rendered assistance to Czechoslovakia". . . . One may also ask oneself whether they [the Russians] do not envisage the possibility, not covered by the agreements, of aggression undertaken by Poland alone. Would the USSR not go beyond its contractual obligations and indicate to Poland that it would not be permitted to expand into Czechoslovakia at the expense of territory inhabited by Ukrainians.[59]

Coulondre was surely right.

While the Western Powers did nothing to shore up the defences of Central and Eastern Europe against aggression from Germany, let alone Poland, the Russians were busy trying to do what they could for themselves. Litvinov pressed the Czechs that "in the current situation it is important that Soviet forces are allowed to pass through Romania, quite apart from providing immediate assistance in the air".[60] Yet it was most unlikely that Romania would alter its position except under heavy pressure from the Entente, and the Romanians were looking to London for a lead; but none was forthcoming.[61] All Soviet efforts had therefore to be directed towards encouraging anti-appeasement elements within the Western camp.

One obvious focus, as Stalin came to realise, was the working-class of the bourgeois world. In its declaration of the 1 May 1938 the Comintern executive committee claimed that never before, since the end of the world war, was the international situation so tense. With events in Austria, Spain and China as illustration, it accused "the reactionary circles" amongst British Conservatives of responsibility for this state of affairs, and of attempting to direct aggression eastwards towards the USSR. With respect to Spain, the Second International had acquitted itself as badly. The declaration went on to press for collective action against aggression, arguing that war was not to be avoided by allowing it to flourish, but by adopting a "firm policy" to combat it. The governments of Britain, France and the USA were not too weak to stop the international Fascist onslaught. What was required was that they accept the USSR's offer of "joint action by all states interested in preserving peace".[62] *Kommunisticheskii Internatsional* appeared with an editorial in May on "The Struggle for Peace and the League of Nations", reminding readers of their "elementary duty" to strengthen the League and transform it into "a real obstacle" to those inciting war. "One thing alone", it argued, "which is absent now would be sufficient to prevent the outbreak of a war prepared by Hitler and to guarantee the security of small nations, and that is the decision of the democratic Powers to defend the cause of peace together with the Soviet Union." As regards Britain, events of the previous months had shown that there existed a mass movement against Chamberlain's policy of appeasement, but "the reactionary leaders of the English Labour movement, the Citrines, the Bevins, the Daltons and their assistants, are trying by every means to hinder the unification of the popular masses and the creation of an English front against Fascism and war. This movement", the editorial continued, "will create real possibilities for turning English foreign policy in the direction of collective security and thus the salvation of the cause of peace". British workers were told to overcome the "sabotage" of the Citrines, Bevins and Daltons, and to "attain a decisive influence over the foreign policy of the country, to attain the implementation of that policy which corresponds to the vital interests of the popular masses and the maintenance of universal peace".[63]

Despite the brave words which heralded this campaign, it would take time to produce results. Meanwhile, Moscow was reluctant to over-extend existing commitments. Chamberlain's rapprochement with Italy necessitated the abolition of League sanctions imposed during the Abyssinian war, and the Russians decided this was not an issue upon which they were prepared to offer direct opposition. When the votes were cast at Geneva, the Soviet delegation abstained. The decision could not have come easily to Litvinov. Whilst abstaining on the vote, he admitted that the Soviets had taken no part in creating the Covenant in the first place, but he attacked those who were destroying its value – Chamberlain was in favour of neutering it – and pointed to its "usefulness and necessity in the role of a weapon for the maintenance of peace".[64] In private he berated the British and the French. He reminded Bonnet that the USSR was not contiguous with Czechoslovakia and Germany, that the Baltic states, Poland and Romania stood in between, and that "our pressure on these countries is insufficient to allow us to offer co-operation to Czechoslovakia". He told Bonnet what was required: "Stronger diplomatic measures to exert pressure, to which other states must also be a party"; this clearly referred to the British. He bearded Halifax in a similar fashion, attacking British policy towards Berlin. In particular, he "explained that England is making a big mistake in accepting Hitler's motives in the Spanish and Czechoslovakian question as valid tender"; it was, in fact, a question of annexing territory and attaining strategic and economic positions in Europe. The Soviets were also disturbed by the fact that Romania was now ignoring an invitation to attend talks along with the Czechs on the establishment of aviation links between Moscow and Prague; this was the result of pressure exerted by Warsaw on Bucharest.[65] But Soviet diplomacy was, as always, caught in a tangle; foreign Communist parties were fighting in their own corner, against governments which the Russians needed as allies. After coming to power on the 10 April 1938 Daladier's Government had attempted to reverse the victories in wages and working conditions won by the trade unions and the Communist Party in the struggles of June 1936. The Popular Front had by now ceased to be a real force in French politics and the French Communists stood out as the main line of defence against Daladier's onslaught. He blamed the failure of arms deliveries to the USSR on the PCF and the forty-hour week, evidently hoping Moscow's restraining hand would descend on the French Communists: "Tell Stalin that in France they are disrupting the cause of military defence", Daladier told Surits.[66] But this was a nettle Stalin was loath to grasp without greater incentive.

Soviet caution was also evident when a new crisis arose. On the basis of faulty conclusions drawn from Intelligence reports, the Czech Government ordered a partial mobilisation of its armed forces on the 20 May 1938.[67] The Czech Communist Party immediately issued a declaration approving and offering full support for "all the measures directed towards maintaining the security, integrity and independence of the republic";[68] but the Russians themselves were stubbornly silent. They clearly wished to see how the Entente would react, before committing themselves. The British did, to the surprise of many, warn Germany against moving on Czechoslovakia;[69] but it was also made clear to the French that Britain would not join in military action against Germany should Hitler proceed with aggression.[70] The Russians were therefore not wrong in their assessment that: "The situation in which Europe finds itself at the end of May 1938, confirms the most pessimistic predictions'.[71] They themselves retreated under cover as the storm broke.[72]

Litvinov had to be careful. A US journalist, obliged, as was the rule, to submit despatches to the Narkomindel's Press Department for censorship, presented Gnedin with a telegram categorically denying rumours of Soviet–German negotiations and ruling out even the possibility of any kind of talks whatsoever. Gnedin was not slow to see what the correspondent was trying to elicit. The telegram was passed to Litvinov, who never allowed himself to be trapped by anybody. "On the following day", Gnedin relates, "or the day after, on Litvinov's instructions, I composed the second half of the telegram submitted to me in such a way that the USSR would look favourably upon offers from Germany contributing to universal peace, and would reject any offer, directed at the expense of universal peace."[73] It was not easy to outwit Litvinov, and this was a time when he very much needed all his wits about him. He was having to fight a battle for collective security in Moscow as well as Geneva. On the 23 June 1938, in addressing an election meeting in Leningrad, he mustered his arguments against the isolationists, who evidently asked why the Russians had to defend the postwar status quo, when they had played no part in its creation, and when its iniquities were largely responsible for the aggression now in train. Litvinov's answer was this:

> Does this mean that the Soviet Union stands completely aside from these events . . . ? Of course not. No one can suggest that we are locked into the struggle for imperialist interests. We remain foreign to the idea of conquering anyone's territory; furthermore, we are indifferent to the fact that one Power rather than another exploits this or that colony, takes hold of this or that foreign market, subjugates this or that weak state. But Germany is not merely looking to re-establish its rights trampled underfoot by the Versailles treaty, to re-establish the frontiers of the Reich's pre-war frontiers. Its foreign policy is based on unlimited aggression and even goes so far as to talk of subordinating to the so-called German race every other race and nationality. It is openly conducting a furiously anti-Soviet policy, suspiciously raising memories of the time when the Teutonic Order dominated the Baltic region; it has wild dreams about conquering the Ukraine and even the Urals. And who knows what other dreams obsess it?

Returning ominously to the USSR's role in the situation, Litvinov added:

> Quite recently the government of the USSR reminded the peaceful Powers of the need for urgent collective measures to save humanity from a new and bloody war which is on its way. This appeal was not listened to, but [sic] the Soviet Government has released itself from all responsibility for future developments.[74]

The message was not lost on those at the French embassy. In a despatch dated the 12 July Coulondre warned that the "current tending towards the consolidation of the pacific Powers and which is represented by Mr Litvinov is now meeting with resistance. Other currents are in opposition, less favourable to the maintenance of the status quo. Several of the USSR's diplomatic representatives . . . appear to be banking on the failure of collective security''.[75]

* * *

Europe was tense but quiet. By mid-June Hitler had decided to act against Czechoslovakia if it was certain that France and Britain would not go to war.[76] The deadline had been fixed for the 1 October 1938, by which time he would move against Czechoslovakia if the West appeared quiescent. The decision must have been monitored by Soviet Intelligence. On the 26 June the Chief Military Council of the Red Army took measures to re-form the Kiev and Byelorussian commands – those nearest Czechoslovakia – into a special military command. These measures were due for completion by the 1 September.[77]

But trouble now came from the East. A report from the Soviet Far Eastern Border Forces headquarters said the following: "In connexion with the arrival in the Digasheli Khomok region of Japanese to platoon level, who have begun to construct telephone lines and also survey our territory in this region, which had not been surveyed prior to the 6 July, a detachment was given the order on the 8 July to hold the hill-top with a permanent detail, which was carried out at 7.00 on the 9 July by troops of the reserve post amounting to 30 men, which have been billeted in open trenches . . . The implementation of these measures in taking the hill-top is bound up with preventing the Japanese from taking this hill-top, advantageous as it is for continual surveillance over our territory. There was no breach of the frontier."[78] These were the heights above Lake Khasan, on the border with Japanese-occupied Manchuria. Tension in the Soviet Union's relations with Japan had been rising since the Russians decided upon a firmer line at the beginning of the year. After heated exchanges between Litvinov and Shigemitsu, the Japanese ambassador, Japanese forces launched an assault on Soviet forces in an attempt to take the heights on the 29 July.[79] But the Japanese in Tokyo, at least, were reluctant to risk open war, and the Russians knew that to be the case. Fighting ended, after a ceasefire, on the 11 August, with Soviet forces still in position. That very day Litvinov telegraphed Soviet representatives abroad that "the Japanese Government was extremely afraid that the conflict would develop into a war", hence they brought the fighting to an end as soon as possible, despite opposition from the military, especially Shigemitsu. "Japan has received a lesson, is assured of our firmness and will to resist, and also of the illusory nature of aid from Germany."[80]

The incident was important for what it illustrated. The Soviets were confident that it would not develop into war, evidently as a result of information from Intelligence sources.[81] The Red Army had held off Japanese forces, though Voroshilov found that the engagement had revealed serious deficiencies on the Soviet side.[82] The victory was essentially a political one: the Russians had publicly succeeded in calling the bluff of the aggressor, and had shown to the world that the supposed alliance between the Japanese and the Germans was not yet a reality. This had important repercussions on Soviet policy in Europe. The Soviet victory in the East was held up as an example of what could be done here *vis-à-vis* Germany. When, on the 10 August, Maisky saw Oliphant, Permanent Under-Secretary Cadogan's deputy at the Foreign Office, he attacked British policy on Czechoslovakia – Chamberlain's emissary, Runciman, was already in Prague "mediating" – arguing that the Runciman mission was "directed not at curbing the aggressor, but at curbing the victim of aggression". He repeated this to Halifax a week later, adding strong criticism of British attempts to surrender article 16 of the League Covenant, and he found both men unwilling to defend British policy.[83] The British were apparently still open to persuasion.

All this undoubtedly made Litvinov's task easier. When the German ambassador, Schulenburg, enquired of Litvinov what the Czechs and the French intended, the Commissar replied that the Czechs would fight and France would inevitably have to come to their aid.[84] *Le Journal de Moscou* emphasised that "German Fascism has put into effect a formidable display of blackmail and bluff". "If German Fascism knew that the pacific states are ready for all surprises, it would find itself forced to give up not only all armed adventures against Czechoslovakia, but even its excessively bold intimidation of other states", the paper continued, adding: "One can only force the aggressor to beat a retreat if one shows oneself resolved to resort to force and resorts to it in deed, if necessary. The recent events in the Far East have shown the best means of cutting short the policy of blackmail and, at the same time, of maintaining peace."[85] This editorial was followed a week later, on the 30 August, with the suggestion that the Powers interested in maintaining order should meet and adopt concerted measures to keep the peace. But the editorial was not consistent in tone throughout; clearly Moscow's tolerance at being totally excluded from Entente–Czech–German discussions was wearing thin. The editorial ended with a repetition of the points advanced by Litvinov in his June speech: the main threat was to the Entente and these Powers would have to bear the responsibility for having failed to take the necessary measures in due time to avert the impending catastrophe.[86]

The Soviet leadership were evidently divided as to how to proceed. As was so often the case in times of crisis, Stalin preferred to diffuse responsibility for the weightiest decisions in order to safeguard his reputation in the event of disaster. He customarily left for the Caucasus in late August until mid to late September; this left the ship of state with an uncertain crew taking turns at the wheel, a fact reflected in total editorial silence on foreign affairs from the 1 to the 20 September 1938 and in the evident circumspection with which Litvinov responded to Western questions about the USSR's likely response to German aggression, already justified by the Byzantine intrigue of French Foreign Minister Bonnet.

Bonnet was always consistently concerned to ease his burden, hoping to offload the responsibility for unpleasant decisions onto the shoulders of others, particularly the Russians. On the 11 August 1938 he had reassured the Polish ambassador to Paris, Lukasiewicz, that it was "a definite goal of his to come to a full understanding with Poland, eliminating Soviet Russia as a partner in current policy, retaining with it only the contact necessary to counteract [a] Soviet–German rapprochement". At no point did he seriously attempt to persuade the Poles that Soviet forces should be allowed through Poland to aid the Czechs.[87] There is also little to show that Bonnet tried very hard to persuade the Romanians either; the French confined themselves to polite enquiries and dropped the issue in embarrassment when it evoked displeasure. Thus when Bonnet asked chargé d'affaires Payart to press Litvinov as to how precisely the USSR proposed to aid the

Czechs, this only roused the Commissar's suspicions, backed as it was by the assertion which Daladier himself noted to be "false", that "in spite of all my efforts I have not been able to obtain thus far an affirmative response either from the Polish Government or the Romanian Government".[88] In these circumstances, and without any prior assurances from France as to how it would fulfil its obligations to Czechoslovakia, the Russians were right to be wary. "French chargé d'affaires Payart, on instructions from Bonnet, today officially, put to me the question: what assistance from the USSR can Czechoslovakia count on, given the difficulties involving Poland and Romania", Litvinov recorded. "I reminded Payart, that France is obliged to assist Czechoslovakia independently of our aid, at the same time our aid is conditional on that of the French, and that therefore we have more right to take an interest in the aid from France. To this I added that on condition France renders aid, we are fully resolved to fulfil all our obligations according to the Soviet–Czech pact, utilising every means at our disposal to this end."[89] In response to the issue of continued Polish and Romanian hostility, Litvinov suggested that the League Council be mobilised immediately so that as soon as aggression occurred, the machinery could be brought into action. Even a majority decision in favour of Czechoslovakia could effect "a favourable psychological influence on Romania". Litvinov reminded Payart that Comnène, Romania's Foreign Minister, had already indicated his country would close its eyes to Soviet aircraft flying overhead. When the question was repeated, this time by Paul-Boncour at Geneva on the 14 September, Comnène replied: "If you are asking that we let them pass, our government cannot but give a negative response in order to avoid massive internal and foreign difficulties which you know about. But given that we do not have the means to prevent their passage . . .". "I did not finish", Comnène recalls, "Paul-Boncour understood."[90] Litvinov raised with Payart the idea of a conference of the Powers most concerned with the Czech problem, a reiteration of the proposal he made after the Anschluss. "A consultation among the interested states (notably France, England and the USSR) followed by a solemn and categorical declaration", Payart recorded, "seemed to him liable to stop Hitler, who bases all his calculations on the double hypothesis that 'France will move, but only if England moves, and England will not move'."[91] Yet Payart's account omits Litvinov's proposal for "a meeting of the representatives of the Soviet, French and Czech armies". "It was", the Commissar said, "difficult to imagine the common defence of Czechoslovakia by the three states without prior discussion of practical measures by their military experts."[92]

Litvinov had, in fact, gone a little further than the position adopted in March 1938 and in so doing – suggesting military conversations – he may well have exceeded his brief. He appears to have covered himself by asking polpreds to relay to contents of the Payart conversation only informally. The Russians were certainly inhibited by the alarming prospect of being left exposed and alone in the path of the storm. As Maisky relates in one of his several memoirs, Litvinov wanted political circles in Britain to know of his statement to Payart, but Maisky "did not have instructions to publish the contents of the talk".[93] Litvinov's position was a delicate one and the response his statement to Payart elicited in Paris only made matters worse. There his words were interpreted as "evasive" and as marking "a tendency to flee behind procedural arguments, which makes a bad impression".[94] He feared something like this might happen. As a precaution he sent Surits a copy of the record of the Payart conversation with the caution: "I am not confident that Payart will relay it accurately", and instructed Surits to acquaint Bonnet personally with the record. "It seemed to me", Litvinov wrote, "that Payart attempted to elicit from us an evasive or negative reply, so that the responsibility would then fall on us."[95] Coulondre, then in Paris, sensed Litvinov's remarks may have been misconstrued; he therefore hurried to Moscow to clear the matter up.[96] But the damage had already been done; the myth was born that the USSR was not willing to aid Czechoslovakia, presenting the Entente with an alibi for a policy of surrendering part of Czechoslovakia to the Germans. This capitulation had essentially been decided upon in advance without, of course, consulting the Russians.

On the 3 September 1938 Surits replied to Litvinov; Bonnet was out of town. "From a very solid source", he wrote, "I know that each time the question is raised in cabinet about establishing real contact with us on the Czechoslovakian question, particularly with respect to military staffs, the fear is expressed that this will meet with an unfriendly reception in London. One of the Ministers (I don't know who, but I think it's Chautemps) said at the council that from discussions with authoritative Englishmen, he gained the distinct impression that above all they fear the intervention of the USSR in European affairs, apprehensive lest the success of Soviet arms may pave the way towards Communism in Central Europe. Nonetheless", he continued, "at the last meeting of the cabinet, a group of Ministers insisted that contact with us should be established; Payart's démarche was a result of their pressure. I fully allow that, having made this démarche under pressure, Bonnet may have secretly counted on our giving a negative reply or, in any case, a reply bolstering his conclusions against contact."[97]

When he arrived back in Moscow – on the 9 September – Coulondre realised that Litvinov's assurances had been misconstrued.[98] The Russians had good reason to be suspicious of Bonnet. On the 5 September Maisky saw his French counterpart Corbin; "from the conversation it transpired that Paris told him nothing of Litvinov's conversation with Payart of the 2 September", and Maisky also found it odd, given French garrulousness, that practically no trace of the conversation had been leaked to the British press. "One has the impression", Maisky wrote, "that the French Government wants to hush up the conversation and thereby reduce its immediate political impact to a minimum."[99] This impression was certainly not dispelled when Litvinov met Bonnet at Geneva on the 11 September. Bonnet pressed Litvinov as to how the USSR would aid Czechoslovakia and Litvinov reiterated the assurances given Payart. But in Bonnet's account of the exchange great stress is laid upon Litvinov's apparent insistence on proceeding via the League;[100] this issue barely emerges from Litvinov's record.[101] Bonnet's conclusion, which one suspects predated the conversation, was that "it would appear that the Soviet Government could easily find an escape clause to justify its abstention at a moment when France itself is already committed"[102]. This was a projection of his own mode of thinking rather than an accurate judgement of Soviet intentions. On the issue of the Soviet offer of a joint meeting of the interested Powers – the true test of Bonnet's concern for co-operation – Bonnet said he had passed the offer on to the British, who had rejected it. This was true; but he went on to say that he had tried to obtain some sort of démarche to Berlin from the British, but he had failed, which was untrue and which Bonnet carefully omitted this from his own account of the conversation.[103] In fact the reverse was true. Bonnet was horrified when it appeared for a moment that London was toughening its stand *vis-à-vis* Berlin. He vehemently opposed such a move. On the 11 September – the very day Bonnet was busy misleading Litvinov – Chamberlain warned Berlin against the illusion that it could embark on a brief and victorious campaign against Czechoslovakia without running the risk of Anglo-French intervention.[104] Bonnet was not merely piqued by the brusque and unilateral reversal of a position secretly agreed between the two Powers, a reversal which accorded more with Soviet than French policy. He was even more concerned at the effect this might have on public opinion which, "falsely convinced of a superiority in armaments", would "blindly push the governments into a war which might be a disaster". In fact, as Britain's ambassador to Paris, Phipps, assured Bonnet, "the real position" was still that agreed in secret conversations with Corbin;[105] Chamberlain was merely playing blind man's bluff, a game from which the Russians were as ever entirely excluded, and not merely excluded. On the 13 September Chamberlain wrote to King George VI advising him of his forthcoming trip to meet Hitler in Germany to establish "an Anglo-German understanding" and the settlement of the Czechoslovakian problem; he intended, he wrote, to outline to Hitler "the prospect of Germany and England as the two pillars of European peace and buttresses against Communism".[106]

The Litvinov-Bonnet conversation at Geneva thus ended without result; Bonnet "made no offers and I was also reserved", Litvinov noted on the 11 September.[107] Bonnet then put it about that the Russians were not fully committed to the defence of Czechoslovakia. Not only did Litvinov discover that Herriot, president of the Chamber of Deputies, know little of the assurances given Payart,[108] but Coulondre informed the Czech ambassador in Moscow, Fierlinger, that there was dissatisfaction – evidently in Paris – at the results of the Bonnet-Litvinov meeting; clearly Bonnet's account had done its work. According to Coulondre, Litvinov is supposed to have declined to say whether the USSR would fully support the Czechs; unaware of Bonnet's antics, the French ambassador concluded that there had been a misunderstanding. To clear up the matter Potemkin showed Fierlinger Litvinov's despatch from Geneva; the Czechs were thus left in no doubt that Bonnet was the obstacle, that Litvinov had endeavoured to get matters moving.[109] Potemkin then telegraphed Litvinov at Geneva to warn him of what had happened.

"Once again the mendacious story is being repeated, that they have waited for confirmation of our readiness to help Czechoslovakia from us, and have received only an offer of diplomatic action." Potemkin emphasised to Fierlinger that in the event of France aiding Czechoslovakia, the USSR would "render support to the last by every means at its disposal". It was clear to Potemkin that the French were "continuing to play the fool, pretending that they did not understand our reply, and reducing it merely to an offer to act through the League of Nations or coming out with a declaration in the name of the USSR, England and France".[110] In this the French were joined by the British. From Berlin chargé d'affaires Astakhov reported that "the English . . . are spreading the story that the position of the USSR in the event of war is unclear and even less decisive than the position of France".[111]

* * *

These setbacks on the diplomatic front were scarcely compensated for by advances on the Comintern front. Although Dimitrov himself was undergoing medical treatment in the Caucasus, the Comintern had also been busy.[112] Early in August Communist deputies in Czechoslovakia's national assembly warned against "any kind of negotiations about the so-called neutralisation of Czechoslovakia" and against efforts towards the conclusion of "a Four-Power Pact, which would mean decisions about our internal affairs taken without our participation, a diktat by the four Great Powers including Italy and Germany, and the alienation of the USSR".[113] On the eve of the Party's dissolution, the Polish Communist leadership called on the Polish people to prevent their government from colluding with the Germans in an assault on Czechoslovakia.[114] The 30 August saw a manifesto issued by the French Communist Party containing the following appeal:

> Frenchmen, concerned with the security of the country, who want France to be free and honourable: Democrats, Radicals, Socialists, Communists, trade unionists, Catholics, men and women of feeling, unite to save civilisation and peace! If Hitler attacks Czechoslovakia, he will find himself opposed by France faithful to her engagements. If he lets loose on Europe the

> scourge of war, he will break himself against the might of the united peaceful forces. Long live the independence of Czechoslovakia! Long live the pacific forces to save peace![115]

On the 4 September the Romanian Communist leadership called on the people to save Czechoslovakia:

> A decisive statement by Romania in defence of collective security on the side of Czechoslovakia, France, England and the Soviet Union, a clear declaration of the Government to the effect that, in the event of aggression against Czechoslovakia, Romania will be an ally of the victim of aggression and will render Czechoslovakia immediate and decisive aid – this is what the situation requires.[116]

The French and German Communist Parties issued a joint declaration three days later, calling on both French and German nations to fight Fascism and the threat of a world war.[117] The Czech Communist Party, worried at the secret negotiations in train, despatched a deputation to the government in Prague emphasising, inter alia, that "(1) Nothing must be allowed which would threaten the sovereignty and indivisible unity and the defensive forces of Czechoslovakia; (2) Nothing can be permitted which might weaken the alliances with France and the Soviet Union."[118] On the 13 September this was followed by the slogan "Everything for the defence of peace, everything for the defence of the homeland".[119] But this campaign was an uphill struggle, particularly in Britain, its most important target. Referring bitterly to Neville Chamberlain's professions of peace, an editorial in the Comintern's *World News and Views* reflected with evident disappointment on the fact that: "The unbounded longing for peace felt by the democratic parties favours this demagogy." But this could not go unchallenged. "It is the duty of the democratic people, both in France and Great Britain, to bring the greatest pressure to bear upon their governments in order to check them at the last moment on the fateful path on which they have entered."[120] It was some measure of the overriding concern to save Czechoslovakia that the proposals of the once dreaded Winston Churchill for a joint or simultaneous démarche to Hitler from Britain, France and Russia, which he had put forward in *The Daily Telegraph* on the 15 September, were publicised in the

Comintern weekly.[121] "The peace of Europe will be betrayed unless the undermining activities of Chamberlain's emissary – Runciman – are stopped once and for all", the British Communist Party leadership declared.[122]

* * *

On the 15 September 1938 Chamberlain flew to Berchtesgaden to reason with Hitler. There he "got the impression that here was a man who could be relied upon when he had given his word".[123] All hope was slipping inexorably through Litvinov's fingers. "Faced with these events", Litvinov warned the French through an intermediary, "Russia must of course proceed to reverse its policy and ask itself whether it would not be preferable to abandon the principles of collective security and perhaps the League of Nations to retire within itself."[124] This was evidently a belief fast gaining ground in Moscow since the spring. With Stalin returned from the Caucasus Litvinov found the backing he needed, but it was still only conditional. Beneš asked for and received from the Russians an assurance that the USSR would take action under articles 16 and 17 of the Covenant, should Prague appeal to the League.[125] The decision came from the top.[126] Litvinov now had a measure of solid support behind him. On the day after this decision – the 21 September – he spoke at the League, rejecting any weakening of the Covenant. Referring to the aggressor Powers he stated:

> They are now still weaker than a possible bloc of peace-loving states, but the policy of non-resistance to evil and bartering with the aggressors, which the opponents of sanctions propose to us, can have no result other than further strengthen and increase the forces of aggression, a further expansion of their field of action. And the moment might actually come when their power has grown to such an extent that the League of Nations, or what remains of it, will be in no condition to cope with them, even if it wants to . . . with the slightest attempt at actual perpetration of aggression, collective action as envisaged in article 16 must be brought into effect progressively in accordance with the possibilities of every League member. In other words, the programme envisaged in the Covenant of the

> League of Nations must be carried out against the aggressor, but decisively, resolutely and without any wavering.[127]

Litvinov went on to reject any attempt to dispose of articles 10 and 16, vital to the League's role as a collective instrument against aggression, and he reiterated the USSR's commitment to Czechoslovakia and France. But the speech never mentioned any threat to the USSR. A *Pravda* editorial on the 21 September took pains to emphasise that the USSR was indifferent to the division of spoils amongst the imperialists; it stressed that the "democratic" states (the word democratic appearing in between inverted commas) could not afford to adopt such a stance. England and France were "playing with fire".[128]

The Russians might de-emphasise the threat to themselves from Germany, but they were in no mood to countenance an expansion of Polish power in the region. On the day Litvinov addressed the League, Voroshilov ordered manoeuvres in the frontier region of Volochisk, Proskurov, Kamenets-Podol'sk.[129] The Poles were demanding the annexation of Teschen. When Romanian Foreign Minister Comnène met Lubiensky, head of Colonel Beck's private office, on the 16 September, the Pole astonished him with "a spirited indictment of what he called 'Prague's inhumane policy towards the minorities' ". "I thought I was hearing Goebbels' megaphone", Comnène recalls: "the same accusations, the same tone, almost the same phrases; what struck me about Lubiensky was that now he did not restrict himself to talking of the Teschen district . . . but made transparent allusions to the possibility of Hungary annexing the *whole* of Slovakia."[130]

As in the spring, signs of Polish irredentism spurred the Soviet leadership into a more positive attitude towards Litvinov's line. On the 22 September *Pravda* appeared with an editorial which largely overshadowed that of the previous day. Entitled "The Forces of War and the Forces of Peace", it reiterated Litvinov's words to the League, adding, revealingly, that this viewpoint represented the "unanimous opinion of the whole Soviet people", which suggests that Moscow was hitherto not so "unanimous". On the other hand news that Chamberlain had, on the 22 September, flown once more to see Hitler came as a further blow to Litvinov. Litvinov attempted to keep his policy afloat by holding to the argument he had long deployed with great effectiveness in Moscow: Hitler was a pastmaster at bluff and blackmail. A united opposition would force him to back down; his military were nervous at the prospect of a general war. But Stalin clearly had his doubts. Evidently in response to the expression of such doubts, Litvinov sent the following to Moscow on the 23 September:

> Although Hitler has committed himself to such an extent that it is difficult for him to retreat, I still think he would retreat if he was certain beforehand of the possibility of joint Soviet–French–English action against him. We are at a stage when no declarations, even joint ones, or meetings, will produce any impression on him. More persuasive evidence is needed. Believing that a European war in which we would be drawn is not in our interests, and that we need to do everything necessary to prevent one, I pose the question: should we not declare even partial mobilisation and conduct a campaign in the press that would be such as to force Hitler and Beck to believe in the possibility of a major war involving ourselves. De la Warr [Britain's Lord Privy Seal] told me that the mood in Paris is strengthening. It is possible that France would also agree to declare partial mobilisation simultaneously with us. We need to act quickly.[131]

It was on the 23 September that De la Warr and Butler, Halifax's deputy, came to see Litvinov. They felt the talks with Germany would break down, which would leave Britain and France faced with the need to take substantial measures; the British wanted to know the Soviet position. The result was a replay of the Bonnet-Litvinov conversation of more than a week before; as soon as they lobbed a ball into Litvinov's court, he knocked it back into theirs. "I replied", Litvinov telegraphed Moscow, "that our position is outlined in the declaration made by me in Geneva on the 21 and today, where I made public the official replies we had given to the relevant enquiries from the French and Czechoslovakian Governments. In turn I asked them to give me details of the Chamberlain negotiations, but my interlocutors replied that at present they knew nothing. I pointed out to them that up to now, despite the fact that the fate of Europe is at stake, and perhaps even more, they have ignored us and now want to receive a reply from us without giving us any information.

We would also like to know what England and France intend to do. I referred to our offer concerning a conference of the Great Powers. In reply to De la Warr's question as to the venue for the conference, I said that this is of no concern to us – let it be London or Paris, but not Geneva, because negotiations here will be looked upon as the usual League of Nations exchange of opinions and will produce no impression on Germany. Independently of a conference elsewhere, the question must be put in the League of Nations. De la Warr asked under what conditions we would set our forces in motion, would we wait for prior movement from France and a decision by the League, which would require a significant period, whereas Hitler would not wait. I replied that one scarcely moves and mobilises forces faster than one can take a decision at Geneva, but that we would anyway not act before France, particularly after what has happened in the last few days. De la Warr further tried to ascertain whether our forces are ready, whether there are appropriate rail links through Romania, whether we already have aeroplanes in Czechoslovakia, whether reserves have been called up. My reply to this was that these questions concern the relevant military departments and I can say nothing, especially since I left Moscow over two weeks ago." For the Kremlin's further information, Litvinov added that De la Warr belonged to "that group of young members of the Cabinet which up to now has objected to Chamberlain's policy".[132] That same day a reply came from Moscow pointing out that it was doubtful whether France and Britain would agree to a joint conference with the USSR given the fact that they had hitherto ignored the USSR.[133]

Moscow was correct. In London Chamberlain was determined to pursue appeasement and the elusive goal of Anglo-German friendship to its logical conclusion, though he was to meet with several obstacles along the way. According to information that reached the Czechs, presumably through Masaryk in London, Chamberlain was appalled at De la Warr's approach to Litvinov, and warned of the great danger that would arise from the presence of Russian forces in Central Europe, since it would strengthen Bolshevism throughout the world.[134] "Meeting of 'Inner Cabinet' at 3.30 and P.M. made his report to us", Cadogan recorded in his diary on the 24 September. "I was completely horrified – he was quite calmly for total surrender. More horrified still to find that Hitler has evidently hypnotised him to a point. Still more horrified to find P.M. has hypnotised H.[alifax] who capitulates totally. P.M. took nearly an hour to make his report, and there was practically no discussion."[135] After pressure from Cadogan, Halifax then opposed acceptance of Hitler's terms on the 25 September – "a horrible blow" to Chamberlain, who now said of the French: "If they say they will go in, thereby dragging us in, I do not think I could accept responsibility for the decision".[136]

In the meantime it was Polish behaviour that prompted Moscow's immediate moves. On the 23 September Voroshilov and the General Staff brought forces in the Byelorussian and Kiev military districts to a state of readiness, and moved a number of operational units to the Western frontier. Measures were also taken to bring into readiness the Kharkov and Moscow military districts. The total made ready for action amounted to an armoured corps, 30 rifle and 10 cavalry divisions, 7 tank, motorised rifle and 12 aviation brigades, plus anti-aircraft batteries and logistical support.[137] The partial mobilisation did not result from Litvinov's telegram. On the 22 September Czech Foreign Minister Krofta pointed out to Alexandrovsky in Prague that Poland had concentrated its forces along the entire length of the frontier in preparation for an attack, and he asked whether Moscow could "draw Warsaw's attention to the fact that the Soviet–Polish pact of non-aggression would cease to operate the moment that Poland attacks Czechoslovakia".[138] This certainly appears to have been an issue the Russians were less divided upon. It was in this context that Potemkin apparently expressed surprise and regret that the Czechs had not asked for military assistance from the USSR independently of the Franco-Czech pact coming into effect – an odd remark since Soviet officers refused to open discussions with the head of the Czech air force when he arrived in Moscow earlier that month, until the French also participated.[139] Potemkin followed this by raising the question touched on in June concerning the operation of the Franco-Polish alliance in the event of a Polish attack on Czechoslovakia.[140] Then at about four in the morning of the 23 September – Stalin often conducted meetings into the early hours – Potemkin summoned the Polish chargé d'affaires to hand him a note informing Warsaw that the Russians would denounce the non-aggression pact if the Poles attacked Czechoslovakia.[141] Expressions of Polish indignation were later met with the blunt retort that: "Had such measures been taken by the Polish Government on the border between Poland and the USSR, the most likely consequence would have been not a diplomatic démarche, but appropriate counter-measures on the part of the government of the USSR."[142]

In London Chamberlain momentarily appeared to give way to pressure from his colleagues; at eight in the evening on the 26 September a communiqué was issued by the Foreign Office, but it had not been approved by Chamberlain, only by Halifax. It pointed out that: "If, in spite of the efforts made by the British Prime Minister, a German attack is made upon Czechoslovakia, the immediate result must be that France will be bound to come to her assistance, and Great Britain and Russia will certainly stand by France."[143] On the 27 September Chamberlain made his notorious broadcast: "How horrible, fantastic, incredible it is that we should be digging trenches and trying on gas-masks here because of a quarrel in a far-away country between people of whom we know nothing." It was this that epitomised Chamberlain's continuing search for a solution, despite the pressures exerted by those around him. In Germany his unofficial foreign policy adviser and official industrial adviser, Sir Horace Wilson, reported Hitler's menaces and then Hitler's apparent reasonableness when he agreed to a conference to settle the problem, on basically the same terms Chamberlain had brought back from Bad Godesberg on the 24 September, and which the Cabinet had rejected. Hitler had demanded immediate occupation of the Sudetenland. These were terms the Czechs were now forced to swallow. Halifax was unable to resist Chamberlain for more than a matter of days.[144]

In Moscow Litvinov's exhortations and Polish belligerence had resulted in a firmer front. *Pravda* published a "letter from Berlin" entitled "A Policy of Blackmail and Bluff" on the 27 September under the name of A. Belkin (probably a pseudonym for Litvinov).[145] It boldly asserted:

> The annexationist plans of German Fascism, according to the impression of observers who are at all objective, in no way correspond to the military–political power of Germany or to the mood of the mass of the German people. Never before was it so clear as now that Germany cannot contemplate a serious military struggle against a coalition of peaceful Powers. Even a

> struggle against Czechoslovakia alone would not be easy for her and would drag on for months.

The writer went on to criticise the state of the German armed forces and to emphasise the unpopularity of a long war amongst the German public. He cited opposition even among the new leaders of the Reichswehr and also in economic circles. This was evident in Hitler's speech at Nuremberg earlier in the month. The worsening of the economic situation in Germany was said to be working in the same direction.

Up to the very last the Russians were working to draw together a common front against Hitler, based on Litvinov's judgement that this would force Germany into retreat, and might even bring Hitler down as a result of a loss of face. On the same day the 28 September, that Chamberlain told the House of Commons that the Four Powers – Britain, France, Germany and Italy – would meet in Munich without the Russians, the PCF launched yet another desperate appeal to all political parties in France:

> How can peace be saved?
> To save peace international Fascism must be reminded that there is a limit to everything.
> To leave Czechoslovakia without aid would mean not avoidance of war, but bringing it closer.
> If the democratic countries show cowardice and apathy, war is inevitable. But if France and England unflinchingly unite in the struggle against the aggressors, if they carry on talks to save peace, but not in a spirit of capitulation when faced with the warmongers, they can, with the firm support of the Soviet Union and the USA, deliver the world from a new war and bring to life the stirring message of President Roosevelt.[146]

Roosevelt's message, announced on the 26 September 1938, also elicited a statement of support from the Soviet Government, agreeing on the need for an international conference on Czechoslovakia.[147] But Chamberlain sought to reach an agreement with Germany to avoid a confrontation. Knowing the Soviet attitude, he endeavoured to exclude Moscow from all involvement. Even American participation appeared undesirable.

The Russians accordingly went ahead with military preparations. On the 28 September Voroshilov reported to the Politburo and Council of People's Commissars on the air squadrons which could be sent to Czechoslovakia on the 30 September – the eve of Hitler's planned invasion should he fail to achieve concessions by other means. The total made ready included 123 high-speed bombers from the Byelorussian military district, 62 high-speed bombers from the Kiev military district and 61 from the Kharkov military district, plus 302 fighters (I–16's).[148] Those serving in the armed forces were not to be discharged until further notice.[149] To reinforce the measures already taken on the 22–23 September a further 17 infantry divisions, the commands of three tank corps, 22 tank and 3 motorised infantry brigades and 34 air bases were also brought to a state of readiness, from Leningrad down to the south-west frontier region. In addition, mobilisation was effected as far into the interior as the Volga and the Urals; some 330 000 reservists were also called to the colours.[150]

When Halifax saw Maisky on the 29 September he still cautiously held open the possibility of an Anglo-French-Soviet conference. But in the circumstances this was highly misleading,[151] and merely gave the term 'perfidious Albion' new relevance. Maisky nevertheless rejoiced at the extent of apparent opposition to Chamberlain even within the Cabinet – Maisky was the eternal optimist – and it was these continual reminders that the British Government and Conservative Party were by no means united behind the current line of appeasement that gave Litvinov and others hope that a firm Soviet position would put some spine into British policy.[152]

As events continued to drift inexorably in the wrong direction the awkward question had to be faced in Moscow: what would happen if both Britain and France abandoned Czechoslovakia to its fate? An article in *Pravda* on "The Defence Capability of Czechoslovakia", evidently drawn from the evaluations of the Defence Commissariat, was forced to acknowledge:

> It is impossible to deny the imbalance of forces between Czechoslovakia and Germany and to underestimate the military power of the latter. However, the world war has shown that a simple superiority of forces is insufficient to defeat an army occupying a defensive position and well armed. In order to achieve victory what is required is overwhelming superiority of forces. Does the German army have this overwhelming superiority? Czech military circles do not think so. In all

> caution and despite widely held opinion, one can draw the following conclusion: if Germany starts a war against Czechoslovakia, then this war could continue for an unforeseen period as has the war in Spain.[153]

This article appeared on the 29 September. The Czechs had not yet asked the Russians what they would do in such circumstances. But on the following day the question arose; Alexandrovsky informed Moscow of Beneš' enquiry as to whether the USSR would support him if he chose war without French and British backing, as an alternative to the option of accepting the Anglo-French ultimatum to cede the Sudetenland to Germany.[154] Before the Russians had time to reply, another message from Alexandrovsky reached Moscow that same day announcing that Beneš had decided after all to capitulate and that no reply to the first telegram was therefore required.[155] Inevitably Stalin and the others were suspicious. Potemkin telegraphed to Prague asking Alexandrovsky whether Beneš had used the interval between his request and the expected Soviet reply to claim to the rest of the Czech cabinet that no Soviet response had been forthcoming, as a justification for capitulation to the Four Powers.[156] Alexandrovsky was able to assure Potemkin that Beneš had made no such claim.[157]

The Munich settlement concluded on the 30 September 1938 thus forestalled the issue of Czech resistance and Russian aid. The Russians were deeply disturbed by the whole affair. When Litvinov arrived in Paris on the 2 October, he avoided an invitation from Bonnet to visit him, because he did not want to betray just how worried he was. But Bonnet turned up at the Soviet embassy and Litvinov, unable to restrain himself after weeks of frustration and humiliation, launched into a tirade attacking him for unnecessary capitulation to the Germans: "Hitler, who himself evidently feared war even more than Chamberlain and would probably have conceded, has been saved from such a retreat by the Munich conference", he remonstrated.[158] We shall probably never know whether this was so. Chamberlain acted on the assumption that whatever resistance the Germans encountered, Hitler's entourage would stand by him even in the event of war. Litvinov believed that what the other Powers did would affect the course of internal German politics as well as its foreign policy. Whereas the Entente saw Germany as essentially strong, the Russians saw it as fundamentally weak. Litvinov and Stalin both shared a belief in the fragility of Fascism in Germany; Litvinov argued, and Stalin appears to have been on the whole convinced, that by resisting Hitler's demands, war could be averted. Whether the Russians would have come to the aid of the Czechs had they refused to accept the ultimatum is difficult to say. Their military preparations indicate that they were prepared to move against Poland in force if the Polish Government attacked Czechoslovakia. They indicate that the Soviet air force, facilitated by Romanian myopia, would have come to the aid of the Czechs. The parallel drawn in the *Pravda* article of the 29 September between Spain and Czechoslovakia is illustrative of the direction of Soviet thinking on this issue. But Czech acceptance of the Munich diktat closed the matter once and for all. By orchestrating the affair in this manner, by relegating Russia once more beyond the pale of international settlements as it had been during the twenties, Chamberlain not only opened the fortified gates of Eastern Europe to German tanks, he also left Litvinov stuggling to preserve the few bare threads of the policy he had so painstakingly pursued. Munich did not lead directly and immediately to a drastic reversal of Soviet policy, but it certainly created an atmosphere in which such a reversal could appear both reasonable and inevitable.

10 The Collapse of Collective Security, 1938–39

The Munich settlement completely disoriented the Soviet regime. The rickety platform of collective security so assiduously assembled by Litvinov with whatever lay to hand – and building materials were in hopelessly short supply while Britain steadfastly refused to help – crumpled into an undignified heap as the British, aided and abetted by the French, wrenched out the main pillars of support from underneath.

By the 4 October 1938 the resulting sense of betrayal had broken through the façade of silence with an editorial in *Izvestiya* sarcastically entitled "The Policy of Awarding Prizes to the Aggressor". It was not the first time that people had had to face Fascist aggression, the paper argued:

> But it is the first time we know of that the seizure of someone else's territory, the transfer of borders guaranteed by international treaties to foreign armies, is nothing less than a "triumph" or "victory" for peace.
>
> But you know this is what the Munich "peacemakers" are trying to assure nations. They are in raptures about their successes, they are prepared to lavish flattering compliments on one another. Chamberlain has addressed a special message to Daladier in which he is "delighted by the boldness and dignity" with which Daladier represented France at Munich. If this formula had not emanated from an official figure it would be easy to take it as a malicious gibe. One imagines that many Englishmen and Frenchmen will be asking themselves in bewilderment: in what sense can one call the rape of the weak by the strong "dignity"? In truth, it takes great courage to hand over a whole state to be torn to pieces!

Hearing news that Chamberlain had promised further moves to

consolidate peace, *Izvestiya* went on to ask acidly whether London and Paris were now about to discover German national minorities in Romania – in truth such a minority existed – or Italian minorities in Spain: "small states will be destroyed one by one, but war will not be needed for this, and as a consequence 'European peace will be consolidated' ". The editorial then repeated the familiar warning that by capitulating to the aggressor, Britain and France were merely bringing war closer and in conditions which would be far more disadvantageous than before.[1]

This was true, but it was the USSR that was now dangerously isolated and vulnerable to the threat from Germany. Czechoslovakia had been obliged to cede to the Germans the better part of its defences and in so doing had opened the road to the East. The British and French Governments had shown themselves prepared to facilitate Hitler's progress in this direction. The Japanese may well have been dealt a serious blow at Lake Khasan in August, but this was more of a political than a military victory. The Russians were therefore still nervous lest Tokyo and Berlin coordinate an offensive against them. The Red Army, though stronger than the West would acknowledge, was certainly in no condition to fight a war on two fronts. Moreover, an alternative to collective security had always found advocates within the Soviet regime. Hopes for a revival of Rapallo had faded but not died. The attempt to win over the Germans via trade had last been tried in February 1937 and, although Hitler evinced no interest, this alternative always lay nestled in the womb of Soviet foreign policy awaiting German fertilisation. The failure of Litvinov's policy evidenced by the Munich settlement naturally played into the hands of those arguing that co-operation with the West against Hitler was unattainable. The spirit of isolationism had re-emerged with a vengeance. The Austrian Communist Ernst Fischer recalls an outburst by Manuilsky, head of the Soviet delegation to the Comintern. After enumerating the succession of failures on the part of foreign Communists and the working class of the West, Manuilsky is reported to have said:

> The Soviet Union will stand alone. Alone and unaided she will have to wage war against Hitler – against Hitler who has the support of every government in Europe – a desperate war whose outcome cannot be predicted. The Soviet people, alone

in the hour of decision, always sacrificing themselves for everyone else, always paying for everyone else in blood and suffering, always alone, without effective international solidarity; the Red Army, and the Red Army alone, will pit its strength against Hitler. To save our country from this war, I would be prepared to treat with the devil – but even the devil is hobnobbing with the others.[2]

A deal with the devil would, of course, be at the expense of others, and the most likely victim was Poland. The Soviet Union had become increasingly exasperated at Colonel Beck's German orientation. During the crisis over Czechoslovakia the Red Army had mobilised when Warsaw threatened to annexe Teschen. The Munich agreement outflanked Russian efforts here, as elsewhere, and the Polish Government was able to help itself to a slice of the carcass. That the Russians contemplated a similar fate for Poland is indisputable. Deputy Commissar Potemkin, increasingly the spokesman for isolationist sentiment within the Narkomindel, several times warned French diplomats that "Poland is preparing its fourth partition."[3] An article in *Le Journal de Moscou* on the 11 October, under the ominous title "What the Polish Aggressors Can Expect", concluded that: "In embarking upon the path of aggression and imperialist annexations, Poland is taking the risk of herself becoming a victim of this policy in the near future.'[4] As a reminder, in early November the same paper pointed out to the Poles that they possessed minority nationalities on their soil as well – particularly the Ukrainians.[5] But while the Russians talked threateningly of a fourth partition, they were in no position to act on it. A partition implied collusion with Germany and there were as yet no signs of an impending detente, let alone a rapprochement, between Berlin and Moscow. Soviet hostility was thus curbed by impotence. The Polish ambassador showed no evident signs of anxiety; he merely reported Potemkin disoriented and depressed.[6] At this stage the grave deterioration in the USSR's international position consequent upon exclusion from the Great Power Concert ruled out any new and dramatic departures in Soviet foreign policy. The Poles, well aware of this fact, though oblivious to its more far-reaching consequences, saw some advantage in easing tension in relations with the Russians, but no more than that. A joint communiqué was issued on the 28 November 1938 reaffirming the continuing validity of the Polish-

Soviet non-aggression pact (1932),[7] and although the Russians made considerable efforts to expand trade and worked hard to win over the Poles as future allies against Hitler, Warsaw was simply uninterested. Insecure at home in the face of domestic unrest, the Polish Government could never bring itself to contemplate an alliance with the major catalyst to revolution in Europe.

* * *

Isolated and alone, Moscow naturally looked to the potential of Communist Parties elsewhere for support. The Popular Front strategy was maintained, but tactics became more abrasive. After Munich Dimitrov suggested that the Comintern executive committee should re-evaluate the position, taking into account "the present essential changes in the international situation following the piratical conspiracy in Munich and as a result of the formation of the anti-democratic counter-revolutionary bloc between German and Italian fascism and the imperialist reactionaries in Britain and France".[8] When asked by a French diplomat what the Soviet Union now intended to do – this was the beginning of October 1938 – Potemkin replied: "We are still counting on the working masses to carry on the good fight", adding, after a moment's reflexion, "and on the inexorable consequences of the economic crisis."[9] Whenever they were excluded from the European Concert the Bolsheviks always turned back to fundamentals, though with how much conviction it is impossible to say. The day after the Munich settlement the French, British, German and Czech Communist Parties all issued a joint declaration "For Peace Throughout the World", condemning the agreement that had been reached by the capitalist Great Powers and calling on the forces of peace to end "the policy of capitulating to Fascism".[10] This was then followed in October by a KPD announcement calling for Hitler's overthrow and linking Chamberlain's capitulationism to his supposed fears that only by saving Hitler could he forestall "the victory of the German people's revolution" – a somewhat sanguine prospect for an enfeebled Communist Party.[11] This theme, which reflected a tendency in Moscow to retreat behind the revolutionary barricades and spit at the world on the other side, was further elaborated in another joint declaration, signed by the leaders of most Western Communist Parties. It appeared in *l'Humanité* on the 9 October 1938:

> What was done at Munich expresses the wishes of the big capitalists of England and France, whom Chamberlain and Daladier serve, to save Fascism, in which they see the guarantee of their class interests, more important to them than the nation's interests.[12]

Later that month the Comintern went one step further. It threatened to withdraw support from the French national defence efforts. Tucked away in an article published by *Kommunisticheskii Internatsional* were the following lines:

> None of the democratic states' armaments are a means of defence against the Fascist aggressor, while these armaments are in the hands of the reactionary bourgeoisie. Armaments can only serve the defence of the country from Fascist aggression, serve the cause of peace, when the people have them in their power.

The article went on to urge the workers to remove "pro-Fascist cliques" from their governments and to join in a united front against the Fascist aggressor, side by side with "the great Soviet people".[13]

* * *

However, Comintern fireworks burst onto the gloom without leaving any lasting impression; Soviet influence on the European labour movement was still minimal. The sense of isolation inflicted on the Soviet regime was relieved only – and temporarily as it turned out – by reassuring signs that Hitler had shifted his ambitions westwards. In a speech at Saarbruchen on the 9 October Hitler raised the issue of German demands for colonies from Britain and France; this demand was reiterated by the official *Deutsche diplomatisch-politischen Korrespondenz* on the 24 October,[14] and in further speeches at Weimar on the 6 November, and in Munich on the 8 November, culminating in his address to the Reichstag on the 30 January 1939. This was good news to the Russians. The Soviet press broke its self-imposed silence on the 23 October with an article in *Izvestiya* entitled "The Munich Balance" and written under his usual pseudonym, E. Alexandrov, by Gnedin, head of the Press Department at the Narkomindel.[15] Gnedin warned that "*the Munich agreement is not the end, but the beginning of a new period of activity by the aggressors and*, furthermore, directed right at England and France".[16] The same hand, this time writing in *Kommunisticheskii Internatsional*, repeated the message for the benefit of the foreign Communist readership:

> despite the savage hatred of Fascist Governments for the USSR, despite the fact that hatred and fear of the USSR unite both the Fascist aggressors and the bourgeois-democratic capitulationists retreating before them, at the present stage the second imperialist war is primarily threatening the interests of a range of capitalist countries.[17]

Hitler's about-turn against the West certainly took much of the sting out of the Munich settlement, largely redeeming Litvinov's position. Logically the Entente would soon be driven into the Russian embrace by Nazi demands. As *Le Journal de Moscou* noted: "Sooner or later England and France will see clearly the abyss towards which they are sliding fatally down the slippery slope of capitulationism, and they will begin to look for other positions from which to talk with the aggressors."[18]

In these more propitious conditions Moscow pressed what it conceived to be its advantage. "Will the world await the ultimate development of the Munich tragedy fatalistically or will the Powers which have still maintained their independence instead make a supreme effort and gather together at least to discuss collective action? Will they gather together before Hitler has forbidden international meetings?", the Russians asked petulantly.[19] The pendulum at last appeared to be swinging in their direction. "It is impossible to isolate the Soviet Union from Europe", Gnedin asserted in a further *Izvestiya* article. "Bourgeois-democratic Governments can isolate themselves from the support of the Soviet Union and go cap in hand to the Fascist aggressors. But European democracy cannot be isolated from a country which is the beacon for all nations thirsting for peace and independence."[20]

This volte-face in Hitler's position proved to be a mere interval, a temporary aberration in Hitler's programme for expansion to the East. This breathing-space may have eased Litvinov's position but it appears not to have silenced his critics. Such dissent could find no explicit public outlet. Until the late spring of 1939, therefore, few were aware of the depth of dissatisfaction with him at the top. Stalin was evidently still loath to dispense with his Commissar, but other Party leaders, most notably Zhdanov and Molotov, were more openly hostile. At this stage criticism could be found only in the subtle shift of emphasis or the words left unsaid in a speech printed in the press. At a time when, towards the end of October, *Le Journal de Moscou* was calling once more for collective security, Zhdanov chose to speak disparagingly of the Western Powers as "the so-called 'great' democratic countries", and, omitting any reference to anti-Fascism or collective security, he went on to speak of the Red Army's victory at Lake Khasan, emphasising the USSR's reliance on its own armed forces.[21] Munich had hurt Russian pride and kindled the tinder of Russian nationalism.

The most damaging charge against Litvinov from such quarters was that, in pursuit of anti-Fascism, the Commissar was naively playing into the hands of the Entente, who were inciting Hitler to move eastwards. Less than one year later, in a transparent reference to Litvinov, Molotov pointed out that "there were some short-sighted people even in our country who, carried away by vulgar anti-Fascist agitation, forgot about this provocative work of our enemies".[22] Matters were made worse by the rumours spreading across Europe in December 1938 to the effect that the Ukraine, not the West, was Germany's more likely goal. Quite naturally this abrupt reversal in the apparent direction of German expansion aroused Soviet suspicions "Possibly ... it is the followers of Bonnet and Chamberlain who are fanning the campaign and prompting Hitler to make a subversive move against the East", Litvinov noted with exceptional mistrust on the 31 December.[23] Although more Anglophile, Maisky also took this line, probably only too aware that in existing circumstances he should not appear to be too generous in estimates of Entente intentions. He wrote of Chamberlain "deliberately encouraging the 'Ukrainian direction' of German aggression":[24] a mirror image of Chamberlain's own conviction that the Russians were "stealthily and cunningly pulling at the strings behind the scenes to get us involved in [a] war with Germany".[25] Regardless of the truth behind these assertions – and doubtless there was a good deal of loose talk in private on both sides – it was sufficient that both the Russians and the British should believe them to prevent any real trust and thus true co-operation from being established between them.

There can be little doubt that the sudden and mysterious sprouting of what *Le Journal de Moscou* referred to as "the artificial and fragile plant of the 'Ukrainian problem' ",[26] prompted a positive Soviet response to enquiries from the Germans concerning the reactivation of trade relations. This move was made on the 22 December. The decision to take up the offer followed a fortnight's delay and, as is evident below, a struggle by Litvinov to have it rejected. It represented the first hesitant step down the ladder into the arms of the Germans. On the 10 January 1939 polpred Merekalov informed the Germans that negotiations on trade credits broken off in March 1938 at the time of the Anschluss should be resumed immediately. Significantly he was also most insistent that the talks take place in Moscow rather than Berlin.[27] The Germans interpreted this to mean that "the Soviet Government would like to demonstrate to the outside world the value placed also by the Third Reich on the continuation of economic relations".[28] However, this was only partly true. The Soviet move also appears to have represented a reassertion of attempts to revive the "tactical line", foiled by Hitler in February 1937, which aimed at throwing an economic bait to the needy Germans in order to land a political catch. Mikoyan, as Commissar of Foreign Trade, was to conduct the negotiations on the Russian side. According to Schulenburg "Litvinov does not regard Mikoyan's negotiations with a friendly eye at all."[29] Although reluctant, the Germans finally conceded that Schnurre, a senior official at the Ausamt's economic policy department, should visit Moscow on the 30 January 1939 for preliminary negotiations.[30] Up to that moment the Soviet press had observed the strictest silence on the subject, though Litvinov did warn the British embassy in Moscow of the impending event.[31] But when Schnurre failed to materialise, evidently due to a last minute veto by Hitler, the Russians decided to make use of the visit which never took place as a means of exerting pressure on the Entente.

On the 1 February 1939 *Izvestiya* appeared with an article provocatively entitled "*The News Chronicle* on a Soviet–German Rapprochement". Summarising the views of Vernon Bartlett, the paper's diplomatic correspondent, TASS ended its report with the following: "It would be extremely imprudent to suggest, Bartlett concludes, that disagreements now current in Moscow and Berlin will of necessity remain an unchanging factor in international politics." Similarly, in an article published under a pseudonym in *Bol'shevik* on the 14 February and disingenuously phrased as though Schnurre was still expected, Potemkin raised the spectre of Soviet–German collaboration in an attempt to startle the Entente into action. After an eclectic and dazzling survey of the international situation Potemkin turned to the position of France at some time in the future when, having lost its allies, it was assured by Chamberlain that surrender was the only option:

> The Soviet Union? But France herself has done everything to belittle the significance of the Franco-Soviet pact of the 2 May 1935 . . . [punctuation as in the original] On the other hand the Rapallo agreement between the USSR and Germany still exists. Does this not mean that it is being kept in reserve for any eventuality? Allegedly Hitler does not object to a Polish-Soviet rapprochement. He is paying polite attention to the Soviet ambassador. Finally Schnurre is preparing for Moscow. And this is a man trusted by Hitler. He has been entrusted with important negotiations with the Bolsheviks.

The article also reflected continuing mistrust of Berlin: talk of reviving trade with Moscow was, Potemkin suggested, Germany's means of "distracting the attention of the USSR from Western affairs".[32]

Although Schnurre's visit had been abruptly cancelled, the Russians felt they could little afford to reject German offers to conduct trade negotiations via Schulenburg, for they were still extremely anxious lest there be a deal between Germany and the Western Powers. "So far", Litvinov wrote to Maisky on the 19 February 1939, "Hitler has been pretending not to understand Anglo-French hints about freedom of action in the East, but he may understand them if, in addition to the hints, something else should be offered to him by England and France at their own expense or else if he is promised, in the event of a conflict in the East, not only neutrality, but also some active assistance, which I on no account consider to be ruled out."[33] And if the Anglophile Litvinov could not rule this out, others in the Kremlin with an even less generous view of Entente intentions were probably taking this as a working assumption. Potemkin's article was only one sign of Moscow's restlessness. On the 24 February the new

French ambassador, Naggiar, evidently on the advice of his perspicacious assistant, Payart, informed Paris of a "marked tendency in the Soviet press, radio and other means of propaganda giving to understand that today there is no great difference between Chamberlain, Hitler or Mussolini".[34] In addition, the Russians were now calling into question Britain's utility as a potential ally. "It is beyond doubt", *Le Journal de Moscou* concluded at the end of February, "that the orientation of Neville Chamberlain's foreign policy, contrary to the vital interests of the British empire, is also explicable in terms of the military weakness of Great Britain."[35] Then came Stalin's speech to the XVIII party congress on the 10 March 1939.

Stalin had yet to reach a final decision as to whether Soviet interests demanded an alignment with Germany or an alliance with the Entente; indeed, it would be a mistake to see him as anything other than indecisive on this vital issue for the greater part of the spring and summer of 1939. In his speech to the congress he attacked Britain and France for rejecting the policy of collective security. The two Powers were guilty of giving way over Austria, "despite the existence of obligations to defend its independence", and for sacrificing the Sudetenland, leaving Czechoslovakia to its fate. After having reneged on any and every obligation, Britain and France "then began to lie loudly in the press about 'the weakness of the Russian army', about 'the decomposition of Russian aviation', about 'disorder' in the Soviet Union, pushing the Germans further to the East, promising them easy spoils and saying again and again: just start a war with the Bolsheviks and henceforth everything will work out well". As an example he referred to what had by now become an idée fixe: "the commotion which the Anglo-French and North American press raised on the subject of the Soviet Ukraine. . . . It is as though this suspicious commotion had as its aim to make the Soviet Union enraged at Germany, to poison the atmosphere and provoke a conflict with Germany without any evident grounds". "Far be it from me to moralise on the subject of the policy of non-intervention, to talk about betrayal, treachery, etc.", he said; "Politics is politics, as inveterate bourgeois diplomats say. However, one must point out that the great and dangerous political game begun by the supporters of the policy of non-intervention may end for them in serious failure." Furthermore, in enumerating the Party's tasks, Stalin indicated the need to strengthen "business-like contacts with all countries" – leaving unsaid whether this included political links – and to "observe caution and not let our country be drawn into conflicts by warmongers urging others to take the chestnuts out of the fire".[36]

Stalin's instinct for the ambiguous turn of phrase to cover his own indecision left even the foreign department of *Izvestiya* in the dark. "Such important documents as the stenographic report of the CC VKP(b), were handed over for type-setting by the editorial secretariat, but those working at the foreign department looked for anything that touched on the international situation, and then, having gathered together in Shpiegel's [head of the department] little room, discussed what appeared to be the most important or what was new", relates a former employee. But, he recalls, "we did not find substantial changes in the foreign policy course of the country" in Stalin's speech. "Only Yanovsky, who was by nature a sceptic and doubted practically everything, called our attention to the warning that the 'great and dangerous political game . . . may end in serious failure'. He saw in these words a hint at important changes in our relations with respect to Germany as well as England and France. Shpiegel considered this suggestion 'too bold', and we – Magram, the observer on economic questions Glushkov, Keith and myself – supported him. Although the Western Powers deliberately excluded the Soviet Union from European affairs, deciding them with Hitler and Mussolini, we never thought for a moment that any sort of reconciliation with Nazi Germany was possible."[37] This assumption was duly reflected in *Izvestiya* and *Pravda* editorials on the 13 March 1939;[38] and the delay in their appearance may perhaps be accounted for by the difficulties encountered in unravelling the finer threads of Stalin's pronouncement and in obtaining requisite clarification from Stalin's secretariat. The Germans, however, were more perceptive[39]; this was a moment that Schulenburg had long been waiting for. But there was no sign that those governing France or Britain showed any concern. It took the German invasion of truncated Czechoslovakia on the 15 March to shake them from their insular indifference.

The Soviet response to the invasion reflected Stalin's line of greater caution. Instead of a vigorous outburst from Moscow or even a delayed call for a conference of interested Powers, as after the Anschluss in March 1938, the invasion prompted only a sharply worded note from the Soviet Government despatched to the Germans on the 18 March, its significance belittled even by Litvinov.[40] A subsequent scare over German intentions with regard to Romania – Berlin was indeed attempting to turn the country into an economic satellite – led to British enquiries about possible Soviet aid and finally caused Moscow to call for a meeting of the Powers;[41] typically the British then ignored the suggestion,[42] blithely unaware that this kind of treatment was slowly but surely destroying whatever credibility they still possessed in Moscow.

Litvinov was already on borrowed time at Kuznetsky Most, his position crumbling by the hour. Writing to Maisky of "the suspicions and mistrust that exists here", Litvinov summarised the Kremlin's current outlook as his own:

> For five years in the foreign policy field we have been making suggestions and proposals for the organization of peace and collective security, but the Powers have been ignoring them and acting in defiance of them. If England and France are really changing their line, let them either make known their views on our previously advanced proposals or else make their own proposals. The initiative must be left to them.[43]

Litvinov had not, however, entirely given up. The Russians were as yet unable to sustain such a tough stance; they were still only too conscious of the fact that while the Germans were unalterably hostile, they had little choice but to draw the Entente into a satisfactory alliance to deter, and if necessary defend Soviet soil from, Nazi aggression. Thus, not long after making this seemingly determined decision, Soviet leaders were prepared to countenance a further initiative – a joint declaration by Britain, France, Poland and the USSR on the indivisibility of peace in Europe and a commitment to consult about resistance to any aggression.[44] But Poland, still precariously poised between Moscow and Berlin, terrified of provoking Hitler and at the same time desperately anxious to avoid falling into Bolshevik hands, refused to have any part in such a plan;[45] and this provided Neville Chamberlain with just the excuse he needed. "Was it worth while to go on with Russia in that case?", he asked rhetorically on the 26 March; "I must confess to the most profound distrust of Russia. I have no belief whatever in her ability to maintain an effective offensive even if she wanted to. And I distrust her motives which seem to me to have little connection with our ideas of liberty and to be concerned only with getting every one else by the ears. Moreover she is both hated and suspected by many of the smaller states notably by Poland, Rumania and Finland so that our close association with her might easily cost us the sympathy of those who would much more effectively help us if we can get them on our side."[46]

* * *

The Russians were by now alarmed at the German seizure of Memel from Lithuania on the 23 March 1939 – yet another slice of territory nominally guaranteed by the Entente.[47] The Lithuanians had, in fact, surrendered the region under threat. The Russians were naturally alarmed lest this practice be repeated on a larger scale elsewhere in the Baltic and at the very least that the Germans might seek to dominate the area economically through the exertion of pressure along the lines they had pursued in Romania. The Baltic was an area of vital strategic importance to the Russians. During the Allied war of intervention the near collapse of Petrograd in the spring of 1919 forced the Soviet Government into recognising the Baltic republics as separate states in order to win them over to neutrality from the Entente. Thereafter the Russians had been exceptionally sensitive to foreign influence in the region, whether Polish, British or, latterly, German. In November 1936 Leningrad Party secretary and candidate Politburo member Zhdanov, using his newly acquired role in foreign affairs, warned the Baltic states not to surrender their independence to others:

> The geographical position of Leningrad is well known to all workers in the Soviet Union. Leningrad is an outpost of our socialist country on its north-western borders. Sitting by the "window" onto Europe and observing what is happening on the other side . . . we hear the savage howling and grinding of teeth of Fascism, which is preparing for war against the Soviet Union, growing louder and louder.
>
> As everyone knows, the USSR's borders with Finland, Estonia and Latvia, countries with whose people the USSR has

> normal peaceful relations, run alongside the Leningrad region. And if in certain of these small countries as, for example, in Finland, feelings of hostility towards the USSR are stirred up by great adventurers [sic] and preparations are made to hand over the territory of their countries for aggressive activities by the Fascist Powers, then in the final analysis these countries can only lose as a result. It is not worth while for small countries to become embroiled in great adventures.[48]

Thereafter, and evidently at Zhdanov's insistence, Soviet pressure was intermittently applied to Finland to join in the co-ordination of defence measures against a probable German offensive. Initially circumventing Litvinov, the Soviet leadership used the second secretary at the Soviet legation in Helsinki to cajole the Finns into accepting a pax sovietica. On the 14 April 1938 Foreign Minister Holsti was surprised to receive a visit from second secretary Boris Yartsev, who warned him that if German forces were permitted to operate freely on Finnish territory, "the Red Army would not remain on the border to wait for the enemy, but would advance as far as possible to meet him". The Russians wanted "guarantees" that Finland would not side with Germany.[49] The Finns, however, sought to maintain their independence from Soviet influence as much as German expansionism, and to this end attempted to forge closer links with neighbouring Sweden. It was with this in mind that the Finns began sounding the Swedes on the projected fortification of the Åland islands – demilitarised in 1921 by an international convention from which the Russians were excluded.[50] The Russians persistently pressed for participation in any such arrangements and also demanded air and naval bases on other islands closer to the Leningrad coastline. Although Field-Marshal Mannerheim, a longstanding anti-Communist, considered these demands justified and of little loss to Finland (materially rather than in terms of dignity), the government viewed them as too offensive to national pride to be acceptable. As a result, by early 1939, relations between Moscow and Helsinki had reached impasse.[51]

Appointed commander of the Leningrad military district in February 1939,[52] Meretskov was advised that "the Politburo of the Party's Central Committee and Stalin personally are very interested in the situation on our north-western frontier". As a result of the reports he submitted after assuming command, the border region was reinforced with men and equipment.[53] The German annexation of Memel then injected a note of urgency into the situation. Five days after its surrender, on the 28 March, Litvinov issued a statement to the Ministers of the Latvian and Estonian embassies in Moscow. It stressed that "the Soviet Government . . . continues to attach immense importance to the preservation of the complete independence of . . . the Baltic republics, which meets not only the interests of the peoples of those republics but also the vital interests of the Soviet State". Any agreement, "whether concluded voluntarily or under external pressure, that would result in even the derogation or restriction of the independence and autonomy" of the republics "would be regarded by the Soviet Government as intolerable" and would be viewed as a violation of the peace treaties and non-aggression pacts concluded with the USSR, "with all the consequences this would entail".[54] This warning showed the true measure of Soviet concern for the delicate security situation along these frontiers and must be borne in mind later when the issue of a Baltic guarantee arises in negotiations with Britain.

* * *

On the 31 March the Spanish Republic finally fell to Franco's forces. By then such negotiations as there were with London had fallen victim to Chamberlain's unremitting hostility. Forced by the weight of public opinion to do something to deter Hitler from further adventures, but reluctant to draw in the Russians, and faced with rumours of an impending German assault on Poland, Chamberlain announced a unilateral guarantee for Polish (and Romanian) independence on the 31 March. This was done against the advice of the Chiefs of Staff, who insisted that the USSR would have to be brought in to make assistance to Poland effective in the event of hostilities.[55] The Soviet Government was irate. Halifax's clumsy attempt to obtain Soviet approval at the last minute merely in order to deflect opposition in the House of Commons at failure to consult the USSR beforehand only further fuelled existing Soviet suspicions. Indeed Chamberlain's guarantee only complicated Moscow's position. Firstly, it provided a mere paper guarantee, and the

Russians, after seeing what had happened to Czechoslovakia and Memel – also nominally guaranteed by the Entente – looked for "a precise definition of military commitments".[56] Secondly, by providing a unilateral guarantee to the Poles, the British made it easier for Poland to resist Soviet pressure for a multilateral alliance and, in Soviet eyes, provided Beck with an opportunity to "strike a bargain" with Hitler "at the expense of Lithuania and the Baltic area".[57] And, thirdly, as Litvinov wrote in a letter to Maisky on the 4 April: "it is possible that by his unexpected readiness to come to the aid of Poland and Romania Chamberlain is prompting Hitler to direct his aggression to the north-east. Chamberlain is counting on us to resist the occupation of the Baltic area and expecting that this will lead to the Soviet-German clash he has been hoping for".[58] Unjustified though these suspicions appear to have been – no evidence can be found to sustain them in British archives – they were nonetheless by now deeply rooted in Soviet thinking. "Perhaps a policy of isolation would after all be better for the USSR", a disconsolate Litvinov told Payart, voicing a sense of grievance held even more strongly at the very top.[59]

Although the Russians doubted whether Britain would live up to its guarantee to Poland, to all intents and purposes they henceforth – at least until early August 1939 – tended to assume that Hitler would probably redirect his expansion north-eastwards to avert a head-on collision with Poland. This left the Baltic states in the front line. All Soviet policy was now focused on ensuring that this open pathway should be blocked. The extent of British willingness to facilitate these efforts thus became the litmus by which the sincerity of London's good intentions was to be tested. Only when it became crystal-clear in early August that Hitler was unalterably determined to strike at Poland, did the Soviet Government then switch all its attention to reaching a modus vivendi with Berlin.

Until August the British and the French remained unsympathetic to Soviet entreaties concerning an adequate Baltic guarantee. This is not to say that Entente policy was static. On the contrary, the period from April to August saw enormous changes in policy on both sides of the Channel, particularly in France. As a consequence of the events in March Bonnet, hitherto desperately throwing overboard every commitment in Eastern Europe France had acquired since 1920, had been forced by growing discontent within the *conseil d'état* and outside to reconsider.[60] However, the proposals he handed Surits on the 14 April 1939 – the last that the French were able to put forward on their own initiative – scarcely answered Moscow's needs. They amounted merely to a commitment from both sides to aid one another in the event of war with Germany as a result of coming to the assistance of Poland or Romania; there was no mention of the Baltic states.[61] Nevertheless, appearing at a time when a further crisis with Japan was brewing, and with disturbing news reaching Moscow that "in the event of Germany and Italy starting a war with the USSR Japan will join them at any moment without raising any conditions",[62] the Russians were in no position to brush the French offer aside. The occasion also gave Litvinov an opening he could exploit.

Taking the French proposals as a basis Litvinov then suggested the following plan, which in fact proved to be the furthest the Politburo was now prepared to go in an attempt to reach agreement with the Entente:

1. That England, France and the USSR conclude with one another an agreement for a period of five or ten years, by which they would take on the obligation to render mutually forthwith all manner of assistance, including that of a military nature, in case of aggression in Europe against any one of the contracting Powers.
2. That England, France and the USSR undertake to render all manner of assistance, including that of a military nature, to the Eastern European States situated between the Baltic Sea and the Black Sea and bordering on the USSR, in case of aggression against these States.
3. That England, France and the USSR undertake to discuss and to settle within the shortest possible period of time the extent and forms of military assistance to be rendered by each of these States in fulfilment of paragraphs 1 and 2.
4. That the English Government announce that the assistance promised by it to Poland concerns exclusively aggression on the part of Germany.
5. That the treaty of alliance which exists between Poland and Romania be declared operative in case of aggression of any nature against Poland and Romania, or else be revoked altogether as one directed against the USSR.
6. That England, France and the USSR undertake, following

the outbreak of hostilities, not to enter into negotiations of any kind whatsoever and not to conclude peace with the aggressors separately from one another and without the common consent of all three Powers.

7. That an agreement on the above lines be signed simultaneously with the convention to be elaborated in accordance with paragraph 3.
8. That the necessity be recognized for England, France and the USSR to enter into joint negotiations with Turkey for a special agreement on mutual assistance.[63]

This was Litvinov's last throw. The Soviet Government simultaneously took the precaution of reopening lines to Berlin. On the very day that ambassador Seeds was presented with the alliance proposals, Merekalov called on Weizsäcker at the Ausamt and suggested normalising Soviet-German relations with prospects for their further improvement.[64] The Russians were certainly wise to take such measures. The French at first appeared interested in the Soviet offer,[65] but it had met with an awkward and embarrassed silence in London. As April drew to a close, prospects for acceptance worsened rather than improved. Bonnet, – sandwiched between Soviet demands and British reticence, mustered his customary skills to produce a three-Power agreement. In this, as Surits noted, " 'reciprocity' amounts to our being committed to render assistance to France and England in the event of their getting involved in a war as a result of their actions to protect the status quo in Central and Eastern Europe, whereas they would come to our assistance not under comparable circumstances, but only after we were at war with Germany as a result of our coming to the assistance of France and England, i.e. when France and England are already at war with Germany. It appears that whenever France and England consider it necessary to fight Germany to protect the status quo in Europe, we will automatically be drawn into the war on their side. But if we were to defend the same status quo on our own initiative, England and France would not be committed to anything. A strange equality".[66]

Litvinov described the wording as "humiliating".[67] Soviet protests then elicited a revised and more egalitarian set of proposals,[68] but here again a significant lacuna emerged – "Bonnet telephoned me just now . . . and said that the 'countries of Eastern or Central Europe' should be taken to mean Poland, Romania and Turkey", Surits telegraphed on the 29 April 1939.[69] The Baltic states would remain vulnerable to German penetration. Yet at least the French were responsive; the British were simply uninterested. Although the Chiefs of Staff warned of "the very grave military dangers inherent in the possibility of any agreement between Germany and Russia",[70] Chamberlain, even as late as the end of July, "could not bring himself to believe that a real alliance between Russia and Germany was possible".[71] He was "deeply suspicious" of the Russians and considered it sufficiently prudent "to keep Russia in the background without antagonising her".[72] Indeed this was to be the basis of British policy during the spring and summer of 1939, because while his colleagues were less than fully convinced of the need for an alliance, Chamberlain was himself certain that it could be dispensed with entirely. Litvinov's policy was therefore doomed. The symptoms were already there to see for those attentive to subtle changes in the Soviet press.

Stalin's speech to the party congress was followed by the disappearance of Ehrenburg's anti-Fascist despatches published in *Izvestiya* under the pseudonym of Paul Jocelyn[73] up to mid-April 1939. The Soviet embassy in Paris told him that for the time being his correspondence could no longer be printed. When Ehrenburg sought an explanation from Surits, the latter – already under considerable strain – is said to have shouted: "Nothing is demanded of you, and you're worried!".[74] By this time, Litvinov was finished. British equivocation coincided with the absence of any anti-Soviet outbursts in Hitler's speech to the Reichstag on the 28 April. On the 3 May ambassador Seeds finally conveyed to Litvinov a message from London explaining that the British had still not yet reached a decision on the Soviet proposals – after a fortnight. In a clumsy attempt to cover the futility of his own efforts to obtain a more positive response from London, Seeds only made matters worse. By saying that he had delayed passing on this information in order not to "bother" the Commissar during the May Day festivities,[75] Seeds inadvertently revealed the true spirit of British policy. It had by now become blatantly obvious that, with Litvinov as Commissar, the British felt they could treat Moscow as a pliant suitor rather than as an equal partner who had alternative options available. With war approaching, Stalin also wanted more direct control over foreign affairs. Furthermore, Litvinov was a Jew, and it was not to be expected that his intimate identification with the policy of collective security would make him anything other than an obstacle in the way of an understanding with Berlin, should that prove necessary. Thus on the 4 May *Pravda* and *Izvestiya* announced Molotov's appointment as Commissar of Foreign Affairs – on the front page – and Litvinov's resignation – relegated to the back page. This move was then followed by the sudden disappearance of *Le Journal de Moscou* "for technical reasons" and the remaining Litvinovtsy at Kuznetsky Most were removed from their posts.[76] In came new men untried and unfamiliar with the skills of diplomacy, alien to the world outside – "slow 'protocol' diplomacy was being replaced by 'dynamic' diplomacy, as they said at the time",[77] marking a revolution in Soviet diplomacy which the Western Powers would for years have good cause to regret. The reaction of the Poles, who could now ill afford any illusions, was typically blind. Kobylanski, head of the Eastern Department at the Foreign Ministry in Warsaw, suggested that Litvinov's removal was a positive sign, since Molotov was an opponent of Rapallo![78]

In what may have been an over-impetuous response to news of Litvinov's removal, Astakhov, chargé d'affaires in Berlin, "touched upon the dismissal of Litvinov and tried without asking direct questions to learn whether this event would cause a change in our position towards the Soviet Union", the Germans noted.[79] That Astakhov should take the initiative is not so strange; at the Ausamt he was "regarded . . . as a first-class diplomat with an independent mind unlike the average Soviet official".[80] That this move was regarded by his superiors as premature is indicated by the fact that only four days later, when asked about the significance of Litvinov's dismissal, "Astakhov declared that previously too it had, after all, not been a question of a personal policy by Litvinov, but of complying with directives generally laid down. Therefore one could hardly speak of a reorientation of policy at present, particularly since Soviet Russian policy depended on that of others, and not least on that of Germany."[81] Indeed, in what appears to have been a Soviet-inspired article published in the Basel *Nazional-Zeitung* on the 7 May, the Russians revealed the fundamental motive behind Litvinov's removal:

Changes of personnel in the Soviet Commissariat of Foreign

> Affairs currently signify merely a change in method and not in policy itself. The danger of a change in policy will arise if Russian gestures are not understood in Paris and London. Russia has stated that it is ready for talks with the Western Powers. But Russia demands that it is not treated, so to say, like suspicious characters with whom one has business and does not greet in the street. Russia demands a clear and unambiguous position from Paris and London and rejects pacts with dozens of "ifs" and "buts", with the lengthy application of various reservations. The Western Powers must unambiguously state whether they agree to the clear and simple Russian proposals or not.[82]

Litvinov disappeared off stage. He and his wife were still occasionally to be seen at concerts, but apart from this they were obscured from public view.[83] In his place sat Molotov, generally viewed by the diplomatic community as little more than "a good stodgy . . . civil servant" who was respected, by the Germans at least, because "he did not hesitate to speak his mind where another might be silent".[84] But his native reserve, combined with an ignorance of foreign languages, certainly made all diplomatic contact with him more of an ordeal than a pleasure;[85] this became the hall-mark of Soviet diplomacy from now on, and Stalin evidently believed that this was what was required.

Only on the 8 May 1939 did Seeds finally communicate Britain's response to the Soviet proposals, and in the form of a woefully inadequate counter-proposal. It was merely a revision of the previous British offer, suggesting that "the Soviet Government should make a public declaration on their own initiative", with the undertaking that "in the event of Great Britain and France being involved in hostilities in fulfilment of these obligations [to "certain East European countries"] the assistance of the Soviet Government would be immediately available if desired and would be afforded in such a manner and on such terms as might be agreed".[86] This represented a reversion to the original Bonnet formula, already rejected by the Russians and revised by the French under Soviet pressure. "As you see", Molotov wrote to Surits, "the English and the French are demanding of us unilateral and gratuitous assistance with no intention of rendering us equivalent assistance."[87] Not surprisingly Molotov gave Seeds a "most unpleasant ten minutes", prompting the ambassador's belated regret at Litvinov's removal from office.[88] And when Reuters reported an inaccurate summary of the British offer, TASS promptly issued its own account on the 10 May, correcting errors in the Reuters version.[89] The Russians rightly sensed British "unwillingness to get involved" with them "through any formal agreement, an unwillingness to place their signature side by side" with that of the Russians "on any documents, and an unwillingness to go beyond 'parallel' actions". The British proposals would "automatically involve us in a war with Germany whenever England and France choose, to fight Germany under the obligations which they have assumed without our consent and which have not been concerted with us . . . While assigning to us the role of a blind companion in this combination, they do not wish to guarantee us even against the consequences which our obligations would entail for us".[90] These sentiments were forcefully expressed in an editorial, unsigned but in fact by Molotov, which appeared in *Izvestiya* on the 11 May. Its general message was that after Hitler's denunciation of the Anglo-German naval agreement and the Polish–German non-aggression pact, plus news of an impending alliance between Rome and Berlin, the brunt of the German threat had to be faced by Britain and France. The USSR was, however, still willing to join "a united front of mutual assistance", but only on the basis of true reciprocity. "Where there is no reciprocity", Molotov argued, "there can be no true co-operation."[91]

Chamberlain as usual reacted with emotion rather than reason, annoyed that the Russians should "reply to our . . . courteous despatch by publishing a tendentious and one sided retort in the press",[92] oblivious of how insulted the Russians were to receive such one-sided proposals after so many weeks' delay. The formal rejection of the British offer was communicated to the British embassy on the 14 May and followed the lines of criticism already voiced by Molotov.[93]

* * *

Given the lack of serious intent in London it was inevitable that the Russians should turn to the Germans. In Berlin on the 17 May Astakhov emphasised that "there were no conflicts in foreign policy between Germany and the Soviet Union and that therefore there was no reason for any enmity between the two countries".[94] At the same time the Russians still harboured grave suspicions. German efforts to revive economic relations met with the brusque response that the previous negotiations – particularly the abortive Schnurre visit – showed the Germans to be playing at negotiations "for political reasons".[95] "The result of the conversation with Molotov", Schulenburg noted in a telegram to Berlin, "was that the Soviet Government considered economic negotiations as inopportune for as long as no 'political basis' for them had been found. My repeated and determined questions as to what the Soviet Government understood by 'political basis' Molotov repeatedly evaded by saying that both Governments would have to think about it. In the course of the conversation the old Soviet mistrust reappeared, as Molotov expressed the suspicion that our taking up the negotiations again was only a political game and not seriously intended."[96] Nevertheless the Russians still saw signs that they might yet be able to use trade as a lever over German policy. One indication of this was the appearance of an article in *Krasnaya Zvezda* on the 22 May entitled "The Economic Position of Fascist Germany", which concluded "The worsening economic and financial difficulties and the growth of resistance to Fascism on the part of the working masses and the petty bourgeoisie will make the internal situation of Germany still more unstable."[97]

Rumours of an impending Soviet-German rapprochement had inevitably filtered through to London and had an impact on certain quarters, though they were never sufficiently concrete to convince the British that they had little time to play with. The Chiefs of Staff now voiced the need for "a full-blown guarantee of mutual assistance between Great Britain and France and the Soviet"[98] – exactly what Churchill had been arguing for years. The Cabinet were impressed and followed suit, though the hesitancy with which they did so in the face of Chamberlain's bitter and increasingly elaborate and unconvincing objections, left the Prime Minister with an opportunity to dilute and sabotage the proposals that resulted from the discussion. Chamberlain insisted that the offer of an alliance should amount to no more than "a declaration of our *intentions* in certain circumstances in fulfilment of our obligations under Art. XVI of the Covenant. It is really a most ingenious idea", he confided to his sister Hilda, "for it is calculated to catch all the mugwumps and at the same time by tying the thing up with Art XVI we give it a temporary character. I have no doubt that one of these days Art XVI will be amended or repealed and that should give us the opportunity of revising our relations with the Soviet if we want to". Given Chamberlain's proven disdain for the League, which he completely cast aside throughout the Czechoslovakian crisis, he was naive, to say the least, in expressing the belief that the Russians would find the offer "difficult to refuse".[99] Chamberlain persistently over-estimated his own abilities and under-estimated those of others.

Chamberlain's devious caveat thus appeared in the Anglo-French proposals for an alliance which Molotov learned of on the 26 May, the day before Seeds actually presented them to him. Molotov complained to Surits that "the English and the French, after having at a meeting of the League of Nations in the presence of Litvinov recognized as unbinding the most important points of the League Covenant, including Article 16, now want to turn the first point of our proposal into a mere scrap of paper. This means that in the event of aggression mutual assistance will not be rendered immediately as we are proposing, but only after deliberations in the League of Nations, with no one knowing what the results of such deliberations would be".[100] The Russians naturally voiced the suspicion that both London and Paris "were interested less in a pact itself than in discussions about it".[101]

Negotiations with the Entente had scarcely progressed much since Litvinov's dismissal; by the time Molotov addressed the Supreme Soviet on the 31 May he had little to report. After outlining the state of play in negotiations with the Entente, he now indicated publicly that the Soviet Government would not "abstain from business relations with countries such as Germany and Italy". He also issued a warning to Finland. The Finnish authorities had refused to supply full information concerning the fortification of the Åland islands. Molotov pointed out that "we do not consider that we can reconcile ourselves to the assumption that the interests of the USSR might in any way be neglected in this matter, which is of great significance for the defence of our country". But the most important part of the speech was that dedicated to Japan, whose armed forces had begun systematic violations of the Manchurian frontier with Outer Mongolia from the 11 May. Molotov warned that the USSR would defend these borders as its own, and this section of the speech was uttered in "a more forceful tone, giving the impression that at this moment the USSR is particularly preoccupied with the East''.[102] Not since the summer of 1938 had anxiety at the prospect of a two-front war weighed so heavily in Soviet considerations. Here was one further reason to seek an understanding with Germany.

For the moment, though, collective security was still Soviet policy. The Supreme Soviet formally accepted the government's line of seeking an alliance with the Entente – a sure sign that Stalin was still interested.[103] Accordingly, on the 2 June Molotov handed Seeds and Naggiar (the French ambassador) a revised version of the Anglo-Soviet proposals tailored to the specifications outlined to the Supreme Soviet. Latvia, Estonia and Finland were named as countries to be guaranteed, alongside Belgium, Greece, Turkey, Romania and Poland. It was also stipulated that a military convention should be concluded "within the shortest possible time" so that it could "enter into force simultaneously with the agreement", and that neither side should conclude a separate peace, two provisions provided for in different form within the April proposals.[104]

The Russians were still way ahead of the British. Despite the Cabinet's expressed wish to come to terms with the Russians, they readily accepted Chamberlain's suggestion that a guarantee be denied the Baltic states.[105] The despatch of Strang – formerly at the Moscow embassy and currently head of the Foreign Office Central Department – to facilitate negotiations scarcely sugared the pill. The Russians would have preferred to see someone more senior, like Halifax. But the Foreign Secretary's interest in an alliance with the Russians did not extend to actually associating with them personally. Strang's brief did not meet Soviet needs. The Baltic states were the sticking point. "To avoid misunderstandings", Molotov wrote to Maisky on the 10 June, "we consider it necessary to make it clear that the question of the three Baltic states is a question without whose satisfactory solution it would be impossible to bring the negotiations to a conclusion." The telegram which contained these words also noted the danger of an "indirect attack" on these countries – a Fascist coup fomented from outside which would re-align these states onto Germany's side. This was an issue which re-emerged later in negotiations with the Entente and which was never satisfactorily settled.[106] Three days later an editorial in *Pravda* spoke in similar terms.[107]

The Russians and the British were drifting further apart. As

Soviet insistence on their position grew, the silence from London sounded more disturbing. Once more Soviet diplomats in Berlin were encouraged to make discreet soundings that could safely be disavowed were they to become public. On the 14 June Astakhov, knowing that his words would be passed onto the Germans, indicated to the Bulgarian Minister that the Soviets "were vacillating between three possibilities, namely, the conclusion of the pact with England and France, a further dilatory treatment of the pact negotiations, and a *rapprochement* with Germany. The Soviet Union was most in sympathy with this last possibility, which need not involve ideological considerations". Inter alia, Astakhov suggested the conclusion of a non-aggression pact.[108]

When Strang arrived in Moscow that day, he came with instructions ineptly ill-conceived to meet the extent of Soviet suspicions. The instructions amounted to this: "It is better that agreement should be quickly reached than that time should be spent in trying to cover every contingency."[109] One could scarcely have suggested anything less appropriate. As a result of British equivocation and procrastination, the Russians had become so distrustful of the Entente that only explicit and unambiguous concrete commitments were acceptable. The draft that Strang presented to Molotov on the 15 June once more undermined the case for an alliance with the Entente. The wording carefully left to one side the issue of a guarantee for the Baltic, while at the same time including the states Britain wanted under guarantee[110] – a sleight of hand that simply worsened relations with Moscow, without achieving anything at all. Molotov was furious. "We feel that the English and French want to conclude a treaty with us which would be advantageous to them and disadvantageous to us", he wrote to Maisky and Surits.[111] Accusing the British and French of treating the Russians as "fools",[112] Molotov suggested reverting to the idea of a triple alliance tout court, with merely a provision against a separate peace.[113]

The British were not interested. Furthermore they also refused to concede an unequivocal guarantee for the Baltic states. The proposals they gave the Russians on the 21 June referred only to joint action in the event of aggression "which, being directed against another European state thereby constituted a menace to the security of one of these three countries".[114] Seeing through this, Potemkin immediately pressed British and French representatives to explain who exactly would decide whether or not aggression against a European state constituted a menace to the security of one of the three Powers.[115] The deliberate ambiguity in the wording of the Entente proposals continued to fuel Soviet suspicions. The British and French ambassadors were unable to reply. London was still reluctant to accept the need to deter German expansion into Eastern Europe at the price of risking Soviet hegemony in the region. The Poles, who had more at stake, still lived in a world of grandiose illusions. On the 26 June Grzybowski, their ambassador in Moscow, expressed the view that rumours of German–Soviet talks could safely be discounted; the Russians could not afford to see Germany succeed, he asserted, and they would never agree to a frontier with the Germans. As far as Grzybowski was concerned, and there are no signs that anyone disagreed with him, the Russians were merely bluffing.[116]

In the meantime Finland, in particular, showed itself the willing recipient of German favours, thus alarming the Russians even further and placing an even greater strain on the Anglo-Soviet negotiations. On the 26 June 1939, as the polpred in Estonia reported, "Chief of Staff Halder [of the Wehrmacht] will arrive in Tallinn from Berlin to inspect Estonian military units. From Estonia Halder will go on to Finland. A lavish reception is being prepared for him there".[117] Halder was due at Helsinki on the 29 June. On the 28 June the Soviet embassy in Finland reported: "The visit of Halder and five German military officers to Vyborg and Parkejarvi (the central point of the fortifications being erected on the Karelian Isthmus) and then to Kemi and Rovaniemi (the point from which the extension of the railway between Rovaniemi is to be built in the future so as to connect Kemi and Petsamo) shows fairly clearly the purpose of this visit."[118] At the end of the month Stalin called in Meretskov to discuss the situation.

Meretskov's record of what occurred is unfortunately all we have. Comintern secretary Kuusinen, a Finn, was also present, and participated in the briefing on the overall political situation, including the Soviet leadership's fears concerning the "anti-Soviet line of the Finnish Government". When Kuusinen had left, Stalin returned to the question of Leningrad. The situation on the Finnish frontier was "disturbing". Talks with Britain and France had yet to reach a successful conclusion. Germany was poised to pounce in any direction; both Poland and the USSR were vulnerable. Finland "may easily become the springboard for anti-Soviet moves for either of the two main bourgeois-imperialist groupings – the German and the Anglo-French-American". It could "not be excluded" that they were plotting together for "joint action against the USSR". Finland might well become small change in someone else's game, "urged on against us as a skirmisher for a major war". Intelligence reported that the accelerated construction of fortifications and roads on the Finnish side of the frontier were still under way. Meretskov was instructed to prepare a memorandum on counter-measures to be taken in the event of a future attack from Finland. This had to be ready within two to three weeks since Germany was expected to move in the summer and both the USSR and Finland would be involved either directly or indirectly in the conflict. At the same time troops were to be prepared for action and fortification construction speeded up in the Leningrad military district. All this had to be done in secret to avoid sowing panic among the population. Zhdanov was to be kept informed of the situation.[119]

Not surprisingly Zhdanov's longstanding concern with the security of Leningrad drove him to the forefront of those dissatisfied with the tortuous lack of progress in the negotiations with Britain. On the 29 June an article appeared under his name in *Pravda* entitled "The English and French Governments Do Not Want an Equal Agreement with the USSR". Although he emphasised that the article expressed only his "personal opinion" and that his "friends" did "not agree with it", and it was published in *Pravda* but not *Izvestiya*, the views expressed were common currency in the Kremlin, as Stalin's comments to Meretskov indicate. Zhdanov was particularly suspicious of Britain's refusal to guarantee the Baltic states. The refusal to provide such a guarantee was, he asserted, "dictated by only one aim: that of complicating the negotiations with the goal of disrupting them". Britain appeared to be willing to have Moscow guarantee Switzerland and the Netherlands when these Powers did not even have diplomatic relations with the USSR, yet hesitated where an area vital to Soviet security was concerned. Zhdanov expressed the belief that "the English and French do not want a real agreement acceptable to the USSR, but merely *talks* about an agreement so that, by leading the public opinion of their countries to believe in the apparent inflexibility of the USSR, they might ease the way towards a deal with the aggressors".[120]

At last the British Cabinet had begun to realise that little was to be gained by stalling on this point. In deference to Soviet objections, they finally dropped their refusal to accept a Baltic guarantee against (direct) aggression and this necessary concession duly appeared in the new draft presented to the Russians on the 1 July.[121] However, the interminable wrangling on points which bore little relationship to British and French vital interests, but which directly affected crucial Soviet interests, had only served to harden existing Soviet suspicions, as Zhdanov's article unequivocally indicated. This now had the unfortunate effect of making Molotov's negotiating position more unyielding and more demanding than before. To appease Stalin and the Politburo he was clearly determined to squeeze every last drop of commitment from the Entente. If this was intended to test the depth of resolve with which the British Government sought an alliance on equal terms, then it served its purpose, but it had the unforeseen and disastrous result of weakening the position of the USSR's uneasy supporters within the British Cabinet and thereby of strengthening Chamberlain's restraining hand. At his meeting with the British and French ambassadors Molotov indicated that he found the inclusion of the Netherlands, Switzerland and Luxembourg unacceptable. Furthermore, he wanted the Baltic guarantee to cover "indirect aggression" as well, which would be tantamount to creating a pax sovietica in the region.[122]

* * *

Without any assurance that Germany was interested in a rapprochement, let alone anything more ambitious, the Russians had clumsily upset the delicate balance of opinion in London to the disadvantage of an Anglo-Soviet alliance. Diplomacy under Molotov was largely insensitive to Western opinion, and in Stalin's deeply rooted suspicions Chamberlain had found an unwitting ally in his opposition to an alliance. Henceforth British decisions were once again based on the idea of negotiating merely in order to hinder a Soviet–German agreement rather than to secure an alliance. On receipt of the news that the Russians had increased their demands, Chamberlain remarked on the fact that "even Halifax is beginning to get impatient with them while I grow more and more suspicious of their good faith". He personally did not consider the British position "greatly worsened if we had to do without them".[123] Halifax was indeed downcast, but still oblivious of the extent to which his own actions had undermined the very goal he had originally sought. The legacy of suspicion and mistrust endowed by years of friction in relations between London and Moscow played a crucial role in shaping the course of developments in the summer of 1939. Halifax now retreated to the base line from which Britain had originally embarked on the negotiations: "our *main object* in the negotiations was to prevent Russia from engaging herself with Germany".[124] He therefore wanted talks to continue. But the Cabinet accepted Chamberlain's arguments for resisting Molotov's demand on indirect aggression, confident in the false assumption that the Russians would never risk breaking off negotiations.[125]

In Moscow, reports of German activities in countries such as Estonia acted as a constant reminder that carte blanche must be obtained for action against potentially hostile Baltic neighbours capable of inviting in the Wehrmacht.[126] Obsessively concerned with this threat, Molotov and Stalin were blind to opinion in London. Molotov contented himself with bemoaning the "trickery and disgraceful subterfuge" of the Entente. "It seems that nothing will come of the endless negotiations", he concluded gloomily on the 17 July.[127] The scene was thus set for another approach to Berlin. On the 18 July deputy torgpred Barbarin called on Schnurre at the Ausamt and spoke of the need to extend and intensify trade relations.[128] This had some effect, and not only in Berlin. News of the subsequent talks appeared in the Soviet press a few days later, a rather obvious reminder to the Entente that Moscow had alternative options to hand.[129] True to Halifax's line, the British Cabinet agreed to open staff conversations with the Russians as a means of preventing the complete breakdown in negotiations: "so long as the military conversations were taking place we should be preventing Soviet Russia from entering the German camp", Halifax is reported to have said.[130]

The British had so far still conceded nothing on indirect aggression in the Baltic. Meretskov had reported to Stalin on contingency plans for action against Finland[131], and the Russians therefore now turned to Berlin to see whether they could pre-empt any further German moves in that direction. Clearly Stalin had yet to make up his mind on the line to take. He always had a tendency to drift towards decisions, to allow alternative options to be followed simultaneously, cautiously waiting to see which would bear fruit first before finally making his choice. In Berlin Astakhov pressed Schnurre repeatedly on the issue of the Baltic and "whether, besides economic penetration", the Germans had other far-reaching political aims in the region.[132] Soviet probing on this and other delicate issues now secured a German response. On the 29 July – only three days after Astakhov's conversation with Schnurre – Weiszäcker briefed Schulenburg as follows: "We would be prepared, however the Polish question may develop, whether peacefully as we desire, or in some other way that is forced upon us, to safeguard all Soviet interests and to come to an understanding with the Government in Moscow. In the Baltic question too, if the talks took a positive course, the idea could be advanced of so adjusting our attitude . . . as to respect vital Soviet interests in the Baltic Sea".[133] The Germans were now prepared to concede what the British were still reluctant to contemplate; the substance of this was duly communicated to Molotov on the 4 August.[134]

The British military mission, headed by the hitherto unknown Admiral, the Honourable Sir Reginald Plunkett Ernle-Erle-Drax, left London on the 5 August without plenipotential authority, travelling by slow-boat – an aeroplane could not be found! – along with their French counterparts, and not arriving in Leningrad until the 10 August and not reaching Moscow until the following day. As a member of the US embassy recalls: "Members of the British embassy were appalled by this low-level delegation. It should have been headed by the French and British Foreign Ministers to demonstrate Paris's and London's seriousness about making a deal. The half-hearted British–French approach had the mark of failure on it right from the beginning."[135] Strang left by air for London, having failed to accomplish anything on the political front with his restricted brief. The contrast between his and the mission's mode of transport – the former leaving by the fastest and the latter arriving by the slowest route – could hardly have impressed the Russians with British goodwill.

Serious Soviet doubts about the earnestness of the British were only partly offset by lingering mistrust of the Germans[136] and the likelihood that if Berlin was really interested in an agreement, the arrival of the Anglo-French delegation would propel the Germans into action, as it certainly did. The German Government was soon straining after the Soviet bait with an eagerness bordering on desperation. Nonetheless as late as the 8 August a sceptical Astakhov sent warning that the Germans had no intention of observing any obligations they undertook, "seriously or for long". In his opinion they merely wished to reach "a limited understanding" and "to neutralise us at this price" for the immediate future.[137] But as soon as the military talks opened in Moscow on the 12 August, when Voroshilov asked to see Drax's credentials and it transpired that he had none,[138] the Russians had their worst fears confirmed. "According to N.G. Kuznetsov", head of the Soviet navy and member of the Soviet delegation, "in the ranks of the Soviet delegation the conduct of English and French plenipotentiaries . . . soon after the opening of the negotiations prompted serious mistrust and this mistrust grew as the negotiations progressed. This was I.V. Stalin's opinion, to whom the Soviet delegation reported on the course of the negotiations each day."[139]

It was on the 14 August – the third day of the negotiations – that Voroshilov bluntly called the bluff of the British and French missions. "I am interested", he said, "in the following question . . .":

> Do the French and British General Staffs think that the Soviet land forces will be admitted to Polish territory in order to make direct contact with the enemy in case Poland is attacked? And further:
>
> Do you think that our armed forces will be allowed passage across Polish territory, across Galicia, to make contact with the enemy and to fight him in the south of Poland? And one more thing:
>
> Is it proposed to allow Soviet troops across Romanian territory if the aggressor attacks Romania?
>
> These are the three questions which interest us most.[140]

These awkward questions were never answered. While the British and the French made unhurried and courteous enquiries of the Poles without much conviction, the Germans arrived with the sort of arrangement which the Russians could scarcely reject. On the very day Voroshilov issued his ultimatum, Schulenburg received instructions to inform Molotov as follows: "The Reich Government are of the opinion that there is no question between the Baltic Sea and the Black Sea which cannot be settled to the complete satisfaction of both countries" and to argue for "a speedy clarification of German–Russian relations". Foreign Minister Ribbentrop would have to come to Moscow for talks.[141] Molotov was pleased to hear this, but native caution led him to stress that "adequate preparation" would be required before Ribbentrop could come.[142] Suspicions that the Germans might still be aiming merely to sabotage the talks with the Entente were not yet buried. In response, Berlin continued to call for quick results, agreed to Molotov's demands, including the all-important guarantee for the Baltic states, and gave every indication that war with Poland was imminent.[143] Hitler was impatient. On the 20 August he wrote to Stalin, appealing that Ribbentrop be permitted to arrive on the 23 August at the latest, to sign a non-aggression pact and a secret protocol defining spheres interest between the two Powers.[144]

The Entente had still produced no satisfactory answer to Voroshilov's questions. In London Chamberlain was, as he later described, conducting "secret communications . . . with Goering and Hitler through a neutral intermediary" (Dahlerus). Chamberlain hoped "to persuade Hitler to accept a peaceful and reasonable solution of the Polish question in order to get an Anglo-German agreement which he continually declared to be his greatest ambition".[145] On the 21 August Halifax approved a letter to Hitler following these lines and the head of the Secret Intelligence Service told Halifax and Chamberlain "that he has received an approach suggesting that Göring should come over to London if he can be assured that he will be able to see the Prime Minister. It was decided to send an affirmative answer to this curious suggestion, and arrangements were accordingly set in hand for Göring to come over secretly on Wednesday, the 23rd. The idea is that he should land at some deserted aerodrome, be picked up in a car and taken direct to Chequers".[146] Whether Poland's fate would have been something similar to that of Czechoslovakia in September 1938 is impossible to say. Stalin was one step ahead of the British. He accepted Hitler's offer, and on the 23 August the Nazi–Soviet pact and secret protocol were duly signed. The non-aggression pact differed little from its less notorious predecessors. The most important part of the agreement was, of course, the secret protocol, which ran as follows:

1. In the event of a territorial and political transformation in

the territories belonging to the Baltic States (Finland, Estonia, Latvia, Lithuania), the northern frontier of Lithuania shall represent the frontier of the spheres of influence both of Germany and the USSR. In this connection the interest of Lithuania in the Vilna territory is recognized by both Parties.

2. In the event of a territorial and political transformation of the territories belonging to the Polish State, the spheres of influence of both Germany and the USSR shall be bounded approximately by the line of the rivers Narev, Vistula, and San.

The question whether the interests of both Parties make the maintenance of an independent Polish state appear desirable and how the frontiers of this State should be drawn can be definitely determined only in the course of further political developments.

In any case both Governments will resolve this question by means of a friendly understanding.

3. With regard to South-Eastern Europe, the Soviet side emphasizes its interest in Bessarabia. The German side declares complete political *désintéressement* in these territories.[147]

Negotiations with the Entente were thus ruptured. Clearly the British and the French had themselves to blame for missing an opportunity which, judging by their reaction, they would not have let slip had they been more aware that Berlin intended an agreement with Moscow. "The fact remains that we were never told that the Germans and the Russians had started negotiations with one another – which was the only thing that mattered", was the bitter comment from Sir Orme Sargent on the 3 September.[148] Yet it was he, amongst others, who had, over the course of the previous three years, done so much to ease Germany's path eastwards and undermine Litvinov's genuine attempts to construct a collective security system that would embrace both halves of Europe. Just as the Soviet decision to reach agreement with the Germans in August 1939 cannot be attributed merely to last-minute breakdown in negotiations with the Entente, so too London's failure to grasp the nettle of an Anglo-Soviet alliance earlier that year cannot be attributed merely to lack of information on German or Soviet intentions. The deeply rooted mistrust between Britain and the USSR which antedated Hitler's assumption of power had at least as much to do with the failure of both to reach agreement in 1939 as the missed opportunities and Intelligence failures of that year.

11 Conclusion

The book began with the initiation of the struggle for collective security; it ends with its failure. The story opened with the collapse of Rapallo; it closes with its reaffirmation.

Certainly the ever-suspicious Stalin found an isolationist policy more congenial than either the revolutionary internationalism of Lenin and Trotsky, or the more conservative and statist cosmopolitanism of Litvinov. Stalin's whole philosophy was one of fortress Russia, an outlook nurtured by the very isolation of the October revolution in an alien world. Furthermore, the Nazi–Soviet pact undoubtedly had roots in the Rapallo tradition which predated Litvinov's ascendancy and which he had attempted to supplant.

Yet at a crucial moment, in 1933, the USSR had stepped out into the world under Litvinov's forceful direction. And what is so striking from 1933 to 1939 is less the tentative soundings in Berlin – the echoes of Rapallo – than the merciless persistence with which the Russians so doggedly clung to the policy of collective security, a policy which so rarely showed any promise of success. Unrelenting German enmity was indeed Litvinov's best ally, an ally he lost in 1939. It was this that made the policy so necessary; though ironically it was also this which made the USSR's potential allies so complacent in their indifference.

The intractable obstacles which the policy of collective security encountered abroad finally destroyed its credibility at home. The Entente were unwilling, at least when Litvinov remained in power, to engage directly with the Russians in containing the expansion of Germany. The French had signed and later ratified a pact of mutual assistance with Moscow; but Laval blasted enough holes in it to throw its utility into grave doubt. France consistently saw the pact as a means of blocking the Russian path back to Rapallo rather than as a truly positive measure. Yet at least the French recognised the possibility of a return to Rapallo; to the very last the British blindly referred to this danger as a mere "bogey", refusing to see that if the Russians were not with them, they would necessarily be against them.

In large part French reluctance to extend the boundaries of their pact with Moscow stemmed from their tragic reliance upon the British for their security; but French fears of Communism also played a significant supporting role. Similarly, Britain's reluctance to confront Germany by aligning or allying with the USSR can plausibly be attributed to pacifism or military impotence; but there was certainly more to it than this. The British were always too conscious of their previous collisions with the Russians in the days of imperial and industrial unrest during the twenties to view Moscow with anything other than acute suspicion. Even though the inauguration of the Popular Front strategy at the seventh and last Comintern congress in 1935 spelt an end to any immediate attempts at revolution in metropolis or colony, unrest continued as before and Communists naturally exploited every opportunity when the great restraining hand was engaged elsewhere. Granted, they were never permitted, let alone encouraged, to agitate and organise to the point of insurrection – the behaviour of the PCF in the heady days of June 1936 made this notoriously clear – nonetheless they were still sufficiently identified with the forces of radical change to evoke the suspicions of socialist collaborators and, of course, the anxieties of the Right. The Spanish civil war brought these fears to a head and revealed the common thread which bound the Fascist Powers to the bourgeois democracies of the West, and separated both from the Soviet Union. However much Mother Russia attempted to conceal the fact, her revolutionary petticoat kept dropping below the hemline of her ill-fashioned dress. Anti-Communism, with few exceptions, was rarely a conscious matter in Western counsels of state; yet it drifted through the clubs and dinner parties as did the air they breathed. It was all the more powerful as an unstated, instinctive and rooted aversion, tending to reinforce decisions made at Soviet expense for other and seemingly more exalted reasons.

Confronted with the evident unwillingness of the Entente to provide immediate, concrete and water-tight guarantees for Soviet security in Europe, let alone Asia, at a time when storms heralding untold destruction were rapidly approaching from both East and West, the Russians were left with little alternative but an agreement with Germany creating a condominium in Eastern Europe. Nonetheless, the Nazi–Soviet pact was unquestionably a second-best solution. Even into the autumn of 1939 the rapprochement with Berlin remained an uncertain victory. Molotov had apparently wrung from the Germans in a matter of months what Litvinov had over six hard years failed to win from the Entente. Yet Molotov's achievement could only be an interim solution. Stalin undoubtedly recognised the transitory nature of the victory – he was by nature too suspicious to do otherwise – but he gravely overestimated the length of the breathing-space it afforded (as did many others). The Soviet Union thus gained valuable time, but then squandered it unprofitably in a desperate, unseemly and short-sighted attempt to win space. By pushing Soviet frontiers north and westwards in Europe, Stalin and his entourage – with Zhdanov to the fore – took in hostile populations, sapped the army's vitality, and uprooted defences long consolidated for new fortifications that would take time to implant and reinforce. In the short-term the policy of isolation and expansion rendered the USSR more rather than less vulnerable to attack; the tragedy was that the short-term turned out to be the only time available.

The collapse of collective security had led the USSR into policies which the Entente had good reason to regret. But the root causes were never entirely understood; and although the Western Powers and the USSR were ultimately forced into collaboration against the common and immediate threat from Nazi Germany, the fundamental differences which still divided them and the deep mistrust which grew out of these differences were only suppressed, not eliminated, in the name of a higher cause.

Appendix 1: The Soviet Press and Soviet Foreign Policy, 1933–39

The revolution of November 1917 resulted almost immediately in the seizure of the press as a vital instrument in the transformation of Russian society. "Hitherto", Lenin wrote in March 1918:

> our press has to a significant extent still been under the influence of old habits and old traditions of bourgeois society . . . our press, like the old bourgeois press, continues to devote an inordinate amount of space and attention to petty politics and the question of personalities in the political leadership, with which the capitalists of every country attempt to distract the attention of the masses of the people from the really serious, the deep and fundamental issues affecting their lives.[1]

The press therefore became "a weapon of socialist construction"[2] in the hands of the Bolsheviks. As such it was transformed into a precisely fashioned prism through which the Russian people glimpsed the world outside; as such it mirrored the regime's attitude on the international situation.

The raw material of Soviet news on foreign affairs came from several sources. A fairly limited source was the foreign department, INOTASS, of the official Soviet news agency TASS. Its correspondents were stationed in most parts of the world of real interest to the Soviet regime. Its telegrams were classified on receipt in Moscow into two categories: "white TASS" (for publication) and "red TASS" (not for publication).[3] Red TASS went to Central Committee members and at Litvinov's level. "But", as former head of the Narkomindel Press Department Gnedin writes, "at the beginning of 1939 much information was not included even in the 'red' summaries. The NKID and the

Central Committee were sent a list of Politburo members who could be sent a daily summary of the more interesting telegrams from foreign correspondents. Thus it was by no means every member of the Politburo and government who received full information".[4] "Aside from official news from TASS, very modest in total, and the reports of information which were transmitted by radio from foreign telegraphic agencies", records a former member of *Izvestiya*'s foreign department, "foreign newspapers were the source of our information." These broadcasts were picked up by special equipment – there were several systems – and, after being taped, they were then transcribed onto paper; this was facilitated by the fact that the most important transmissions were so slow that they could be recorded directly by hand.[5]

Another obvious and vital source of news was the Commissariat of Foreign Affairs, particularly its press department. "The international specialists of *Izvestiya* were in constant touch with the Narkomindel. Not only its employees, but also those in charge, published their articles in the pages of the newspaper to explain the position of the Soviet Government on this or that question. We sought advice from them almost daily about material ready for publication", *Izvestinets* Kraminov recalls. "Personal contacts which had grown up between us made possible a more precise and up-to-date representation of events, which at that time unfolded with staggering speed and unexpected turns. From time to time they informed those running the newspaper, and those running the foreign department in particular, of the important moves made by Soviet diplomacy, so that we could judge what was right and what was wrong in the responses of the foreign press".[6] Guidance also came, of course, from Stalin's personal secretariat, though what is striking is the lack of authoritative directives from that quarter after Stalin's speech to the XVIII party congress and also after the signature of the Nazi–Soviet non-aggression pact.[7]

The somewhat disorderly process by which the Party-state apparatus functioned had not been improved by the impact of the terror. Former head of the Narkomindel Press Department, Gnedin, relates an anecdote about *Le Journal de Moscou*, for which he held ultimate responsibility. Its editors disappeared one by one: Luk'yanov, Raevsky, Kin, etc. "When it was the turn of the next editor to be arrested", Gnedin relates, "I instructed that in the space on the first page where the name of the editor had hitherto appeared, the day of issue should now be specified. At that time Litvinov was abroad. When he returned, I met him at the station. On greeting me, Maxim Maximovich said: 'Does this mean that the editor of *Le Journal de Moscou* is now . . . Tuesday?' "[8] *Izvestinets* Kraminov was posted to Stockholm in the autumn of 1939. Prior to departure Khavinson, then head of TASS, arranged for him to be briefed at the Narkomindel: at the department dealing with Scandinavian affairs, the Press Department and by the Deputy Commissar responsible for the area. "There turned out to be no one amongst the 'Scandinavians' who had worked in Stockholm. . . . Comparatively recently a professor of philosophy had been appointed head of the Press Department [Gnedin's replacement], who had a very vague impression about the press in general and who knew nothing at all about the Swedish press, which he admitted to me with disarming frankness. His two young and cheerful assistants had still not once crossed the frontier." The Deputy Commissar was not much more helpful either.[9] With several ruthless strokes of the sword, the terror had physically liquidated the most valuable expertise accumulated over two decades' hard experience; this was a price that need not have been paid, and which cost the USSR dearly in international affairs.

Appendix 2: The Soviet Union and the Defence of Leningrad, 1936–39

It is easy in retrospect to discount Soviet alarm at the prospect of a German advance through the Baltic. Indeed, at the time not only the British but also the Finns foolishly refused to acknowledge what to them appeared archaic geostrategic concerns expressed by the Soviet Government.

The Russians expected the Germans to attack through the Baltic. The best account of their thinking on this can be found in publicist Ernst Henri's book, *Hitler Over Europe?*, published in 1936. Concurrently employed as an agent of Soviet military Intelligence, Henri (Rostovskii) almost certainly drew upon the Red Army's assessments about Germany's likely lines of advance.

The map in the frontispiece to the volume illustrates two main lines of advance: "The March of the Southern Fascist Army", which does not concern us here, and "The March of the Northern Fascist Army" – from Berlin, via Kovno (Lithuania) and Pskov, to Leningrad, supported by the Baltic fleet and pincer movements on land via Finland and Estonia. It was assumed that Poland would stand at Germany's side. With respect to an attack on land, Henri focused on the danger of a "*Memel war*": "*Memel is the lever to the isolated war with Lithuania*, and the isolated war with Lithuania – leading within twenty-four hours the disappearance of the Lithuanian army – is the lever to the military absorption of the whole of the Baltic by Germany".[1]

With respect to sea defences, Henri broached the issue of the Åland islands and their proposed fortification by Finland and Sweden: "the German Admiralty, which since 1934–5 has been stirring up the waters of the Baltic, has turned its hand to the position here too".[2] The Russians did not take up the issue until April 1938 and by then Zhdanov's malign influence on Soviet foreign policy was increasingly overshadowing Litvinov's own position. On the 27 March Sweden's *Dagens Nyheter* dismissed denials that Finland was determined to fortify the islands and two days later the same newspaper said it was time the question was raised in the Riksdag.[3] The first step was taken by the Russians on the 8 April, when Heidenstam, the Swedish envoy in Helsinki, learned from Derevyanskii, his Soviet counterpart, that the Russians had no objection to fortification provided the USSR could "control" construction so that it would not fall into German hands.[4] In fact, as polpred Kollontai revealed in a telegram to Moscow on the 10 April, Sweden had informed Finland that it would only consent to fortification if control lay in Swedish hands.[5] It was against this background that Yartsev raised the issue in Helsinki on the 14 April, warning the Finns of the consequences of allowing German forces into their country and encouraging them to accept Soviet military and economic assistance against Germany.[6] The employment of a second secretary to relay such a warning suggests that this was an initiative circumventing normal channels, preliminary soundings which could be disavowed if they became public. But Litvinov could not long be excluded. On the 19 April he told Winther, Sweden's Minister in Moscow, that the Russians were totally opposed to any fortification of the Åland islands. The issue was further discussed at Geneva in May between Litvinov and Sandler, Sweden's Foreign Minister;[7] and, in the knowledge that "in some form or other negotiations about Åland are evidently taking place",[8] Kollontai reminded Sandler of Soviet opposition on the 27 July.[9] No progress was made when Yartsev discussed the matter with Cajander, the Finnish Premier, at the end of June and on the 11 July.[10] The Swedes continued to reassure the Russians,[11] but continued Soviet concern obliged Yartsev to offer concrete proposals to the Finns to forestall measures taken to Soviet disadvantage. The USSR wanted a written undertaking that Finland would "ward off all possible attacks and, to that end . . . accept Russian military aid". Soviet policy now reverted to the position originally outlined by Derevyanskii on the 8 April: "Moscow can assent to fortification of the Åland Islands if Russia is enabled to take part in their arming and if it is permitted to send its own observer to follow the work and subsequently to maintain surveillance over the use of the fortifications." The Russians also sought Finland's consent to the erection of a fortified air and naval base on Suursaari Island. In return Moscow offered a guarantee of Finland's frontiers, military assistance in the event of war, and exceptionally favourable terms of trade.[12] On the 29 August the Russians were informed that this was unacceptable.[13] Litvinov met both the Finnish and Swedish Foreign Ministers in Geneva in mid-September and found them unalterable in their determination to fortify the islands.[14]

Further discussions proved fruitless. Increasingly the Russians came to regard the Åland islands issue as a lost cause. In public the matter was raised as a symptom of Finland's untrustworthiness. In private the Russians sought compensation elsewhere. After Meretskov received Stalin's instructions to reinforce the north-western frontier region (see pp. 208–9, above), on the 5 March 1939 Litvinov suggested to the Finns that the USSR lease the islands of Suursaari, Lavansaari, Tyrtärsaari and Seiskari for thirty years, as a means of guarding the sea approaches to Leningrad. Faced with a refusal, Litvinov then suggested their exchange in return for some 183 square kilometers of Soviet eastern Karelia. But the Finns were not prepared to accept this either.[15] Not until the Nazi–Soviet pact of August 1939 gave the USSR carte blanche in the Baltic did the Russians reassert their claims; but that is the subject of a future volume.

Notes and References

CHAPTER 1 THE STRUGGLE FOR COLLECTIVE SECURITY, 1933–39

1. See J. Haslam, *Soviet Foreign Policy, 1930–33: the Impact of the Depression* (London, 1983) ch. 2.
2. Statement to French press correspondents, 7.7.33: *Izvestiya*, 9.7.33, reprinted in M. Litvinov, *Vneshnyaya Politika SSSR: Rechi i Zayavleniya 1927–1935* (Moscow, 1935) p. 256.
3. See Litvinov's speech to the world disarmament conference, 29.5.34: ibid., pp. 306–14.
4. Ibid., p. 314; also Litvinov's conversation with the French journalist, Zauervein: *Izvestiya*, 29.6.34, reprinted in Litvinov, *Vneshnyaya Politika*, pp. 318–20.
5. "Po Rossii", *Sotsialisticheskii Vestnik*, 25.4.34; further such sentiments were reported later: ibid., 25.5.35. Their reports from Moscow on foreign affairs appear to have been fairly reliable; much has now been confirmed by material since published from the Soviet archives.
6. G. Hilger, (with A. Mayer), *The Incompatible Allies: a Memoir-History of German–Soviet Relations 1918–1941* (New York, 1953) p. 269.
7. See chapter 4.
8. *Pravda*, 5.3.36.
9. Editorial, "Soviet Diplomacy and Its Social-Fascist Critics", *International Press Correspondence* (hereafter *Inprecorr*), 15.12.33.
10. Bullitt (Moscow) to Hull (Washington), 19.7.35: *Foreign Relations of the United States* (hereafter *FRUS*), *The Soviet Union 1933–1939* (Washington, 1952) p. 225.

CHAPTER 2 THE END OF RAPALLO, 1933

1. Dirksen (Moscow) to Bülow (Berlin), 31.1.33: *Documents on German Foreign Policy 1918–1945* (hereafter *DGFP*), Series C (1933–1937), vol. 1 (London, 1957), doc. 6.
2. See J. Haslam, *Soviet Foreign Policy, 1930–33: the Impact of the Depression* (London, 1983) pp. 101–4 and 113–14.
3. Hitler, *Mein Kampf*, ed. D. Watt (London, 1969) ch. 14.
4. G. Hilger (with A. Mayer), *The Incompatible Allies*, pp. 254–5.

5. Haslam, *Soviet Foreign Policy*, pp. 102–4.
6. Dirksen (Moscow) to Berlin, 28.2.33: *DGFP*, doc. 41. In a further despatch Dirksen describes Krestinsky as "a moderate, conciliatory, and reliable advocate of good German-Soviet relations" – Dirksen (Moscow) to Berlin, 14.8.33: ibid., doc. 404. There are other reports to the same effect: for example, Dirksen (Moscow) to Berlin, 3.11.33: *DGFP*, vol. 2 (London, 1959), doc. 44. For Krestinsky's background: Haslam, *Soviet Foreign Policy*, pp. 15–16.
7. For the text of his speech: *Izvestiya*, 8.2.33; *Dokumenty Vneshnei Politiki SSSR* (hereafter *DVP SSSR*), vol. XVI, ed. F. Dolya *et al.* (Moscow, 1970), doc. 32; supportive comment appeared in an article by E. Gnedin, then working in *Izvestiya*'s foreign department, "Auf den Spuren des Krieges", *Moskauer Rundschau*, 12.2.33.
8. Litvinov's record of a conversation with Neurath, 1.3.33: *DVP SSSR*, doc. 54.
9. "Presseschau", *Moskauer Rundschau*, 5.3.33.
10. Editorial, "Pravitel'stvo fashistskoi kontsentratsii v Germanii", *Kommunisticheskii Internatsional*, no. 4–5, 10.2.33, pp. 3–7.
11. Broadcast dated 1.2.33: *Keesing's Contemporary Archives*, vol. 1, p. 657.
12. Political police instructions, 28.3.33: *Protsess o Podzhoge Reikhstaga i Georgii Dimitrov: Dokumenty*, ed. G. Berngard *et al.*, vol. 1 (Moscow, 1981), doc. 17.
13. "Shuty na trone", *Pravda*, 4.3.33.
14. The first quotation is from an unnamed Soviet diplomat. The reference to Stalin comes from yet another, who had just returned from Moscow where he spoke to Stalin – François-Poncet (Berlin) to Paul-Boncour (Paris), 11.2.33: *Documents Diplomatiques Français 1932–1939* (hereafter *DDF*), 1er Série (1932–35), vol. 2 (Paris, 1966), doc. 289. Soviet sensitivity about Moscow's neglect of the KPD is apparent in a counterblast to criticism from Fenner Brockway of the British ILP. The Soviet justification for the policy of non-intervention was lame but revealing:

   > Any worker would understand *that Hitler will prepare for war shouting that the Soviet Union wants to attack innocent Fascist Germany. It is precisely because Hitler is trying to strengthen his influence over the nationalist petty bourgeois masses with tales of the Soviet Union's military preparations, that the signature* [sic] *of the Berlin agreement by the Soviet Government is a blow to these military manoeuvres of Hitler's.*

   – editorial, "Antisovetskaya politika germanskogo fashizma i mezhdunarodnyi proletariat", *Bol'shevik*, no. 11, 15.6.33, pp. 1–15.
15. Hitler's words, spoken at a conference of Ministers, 28.2.33: *DGFP*, doc. 42.
16. Attolico (Moscow) to Rome, 7.3.33: Ministèro degli Affari Esteri, *Archivio Storico Diplomatico* (hereafter *ASD*), Affari Politici (1931–35), Russia (1933), busta 8, fascicolo 1.1.
17. Ex-Insider, "Moscow-Berlin 1933", *Survey*, no. 44–5, October 1962, p. 164.
18. Attolico (Moscow) to Rome, 7.3.33: *ASD*, URSS (1933), b.9, f. 1.9.
19. For the best account of the Comintern in this period, turn to E. H. Carr, *The Twilight of Comintern, 1930–1935* (London, 1982); but he has mis-dated the Paris meeting (p. 84).

20. The parties involved were the Norwegian Labour Party, the British Independent Labour Party, the Dutch Independent Socialist Party, the Polish Independent Socialist Labour Party, the German Socialist Workers' Party, the French Party of Proletarian Unity and the Italian Socialist Party: *The New Leader*, 10.2.33.
21. *l'Humanité*, 13.2.33; *Kommunisticheskii Internatsional: Kratkii Istoricheskii Ocherk* (Moscow, 1969), p. 350. This may well have originated with the Bulgarian Georgii Dimitrov, who headed the Comintern's West European Bureau in Berlin.
22. *Pravda*, 6.3.33.
23. *Kommunisticheskii Internatsional: Kratkii*, p. 354.
24. Quoted in *Istoriya Vneshnei Politiki SSSR 1917–1945*, ed. A. Berezkin et al. (Moscow, 1980), pp. 290–1.
25. Listed in the Soviet embassy's annual report for 1933, and cited in *DVP SSSR*, p. 814. A despatch from polpred Khinchuk on the 12 March is illustrative of the conditions in which Russians were living in Germany at the time: "I have tried to create a calm atmosphere, I am struggling with the slightest sign of nerves among any Soviet employees" – Khinchuk (Berlin) to Krestinsky (Moscow), 12.3.33: ibid., doc. 74.
26. K. Radek, "Kuda idet Germaniya?", *Izvestiya*, 22.3.33.
27. Krestinsky's record of the conversation, 3.4.33: *DVP SSSR*, p. 824.
28. For the protocol: Haslam, *Soviet Foreign Policy*, pp. 62–4.
29. *DVP SSSR*, doc. 139.
30. Khinchuk (Berlin) to Moscow, 28.4.33: *DVP SSSR*, doc. 138.
31. *DGFP*, doc. 212; comment in the Narkomindel's German language weekly reflected continuing mistrust of the German Government: "Berliner Vertrag", *Moskauer Rundschau*, 14.5.33.
32. Haslam, *Soviet Foreign Policy*, p. 105.
33. Laroche (Warsaw) to Paul-Boncour (Paris), 8.2.33: *DDF*, doc. 276.
34. See J. Lipski, *Diplomat in Berlin 1933–1939*, ed. W. Jedrzejewicz (London, 1968), pp. 46–59.
35. Source cited in note 33.
36. An extract appears in Col. J. Beck, *Dernier Rapport: Politique Polonaise, 1926–1939* (Paris, 1951) p. 279.
37. Lipski, *Diplomat*, p. 71.
38. See Litvinov's conversation with ambassador Dejean and counsellor Payart, 10.4.33: *DVP SSSR*, doc. 114.
39. B. Miedziński, "Droga do Moskwy", *Kultura* (Paris), 1963, no. 188, p. 77.
40. Ibid., pp. 81–6. Radek is described as having "always" had "close relations" with the Polish embassy in Berlin by one of its former secretaries, Zabiello: S. Zabiello, "Rokodwilzy", *W Kregu Historii* (Warsaw, 1970) pp. 140–1.
41. V. Krivitskii, "Iz vospominanii sovetskogo kommunista", *Sotsialisticheskii Vestnik*, no. 7, 15.4.38; L. Fischer, *The Life and Death of Stalin* (London, 1953) p. 142; A. Orlov, *The Secret History of Stalin's Crimes* (London, 1954) p. 204; and E. Gnedin, *Iz Istorii Otnoshenii Mezhdu SSSR i Fashistskoi Germaniei: Dokumenty i Sovremennye Kommentarii* (New York, 1977) p. 23.
42. It is said that Radek edited the "Secret Bulletin of the CC", which put together a review of foreign press coverage of the USSR for Central

Committee members: A. Avtorkhanov, "Pokorenie Partii . . .", *Posev* (Munich), 29.10.50.

43. Early in 1922 Radek gave an interview to *Le Matin* in which he made an indiscreet attack on the British. On the 18 February Chicherin, then Commissar of Foreign Affairs, wrote to Lenin complaining that Radek's interview damaged Soviet Russia diplomatically. Two days later, Lenin wrote to Molotov (for all Politburo members): "I think Chicherin is absolutely right, that Radek has in this instance shown yet again that for all his innumerable achievements he is completely unsuited to diplomacy" – V. Lenin, *Polnoe Sobranie Sochinenii*, Vol. 54 (5th edition, Moscow, 1965), doc. 285 and note 291.
44. This was pointed out by Litvinov in conversation with Dirksen – memorandum by the German ambassador to Moscow, 16.5.33: *DGFP*, doc. 245.
45. K. Radek, "Reviziya versal'skogo dogovora", *Pravda*, 10.5.33.
46. Litvinov's record of his conversation with Neurath, 29.5.33: *DVP SSSR*, doc. 167; significantly, comment in the Narkomindel's German language weekly lauded what it called "The Franco-Soviet Rapprochement": Nomad, "Die Franzoesisch-sowjetische. Annaeherung", *Moskauer Rundschau*, 28.5.33.
47. Haslam, *Soviet Foreign Policy*, p. 111.
48. Ibid., p. 107.
49. Ibid., pp. 108–9.
50. Maisky (London) to Litvinov (Moscow), 2.3.33: *DVP SSSR*, doc. 56.
51. Haslam, *Soviet Foreign Policy*, pp. 43–5.
52. T. Gladkov and M. Smirnov, *Menzhinskii* (Moscow, 1969), pp. 322–3; the information comes from OGPU archives, which may not be entirely trustworthy in this matter. However the circumstantial evidence given below indicates the information to be more or less correct.
53. The committee is referred to in Ovey (Moscow) to Vansittart (London), 14.3.33: *Documents on British Foreign Policy* (hereafter *DBFP*) *1919–1939*, 2nd Series, vol. 7, 1929–34 (London, 1958), doc. 219.
54. Information on the activities of this body is not easy to obtain, even after fifty years have elapsed; the only file on the sub-committee which the British Public Record Office was prepared to release for 1932 was concerned with trivia – no other files have been made available to the public. We do, however, have a list of the sub-committee's members for the mid-thirties, which can be found in the Foreign Office files:

Chairman:	Sir Edward Crowe, Comptroller-General, Department of Overseas Trade
Members:	E. Bridges, Treasury
	Ashton-Gwatkin, Foreign Office
	Leak, Board of Trade
	Lt. Col. A. Forster, Assistant Director, Naval Intelligence
	Paymaster Commander V. Eason, Plans Division, Admiralty
	Brigadier D. Anderson, Deputy Director, Military Operations and Intelligence, War Office

Col. L. Hill, Directorate, Military Operations and Intelligence, War Office
Lt. Col. Sir E. Holt Wilson, Directorate, Military Operations and Intelligence, War Office
Wing Commander C. Medhurst, Directorate, Operations and Intelligence, Air Ministry

– *Foreign Office* (hereafter *FO*) 371/19643.

55. F. Hinsley, *British Intelligence in the Second World War*, vol. 1 (London, 1979) pp. 30–1.
56. M. Gilbert, *Winston S. Churchill*, vol. v (London, 1976) p. 298.
57. *FO* 371/19643.
58. Gladkov and Smirnov, *Menzhinskii*, pp. 322–3; Thornton confessed under OGPU questioning (no force was applied) and refused, in court, "to bring himself to a clear-cut denial", which left all those not privy to the truth somewhat baffled – see, for example, "Report on the TRIAL of the METROPOLITAN-VICKERS ENGINEERS at Moscow, 12th to 19th April 1933", by the company's solicitor Robert R.J. Turner, 24.5.33: *DBFP*, appendix III, iv; the British Government itself insisted that none of the accused was a member of or had worked for the Intelligence Service – which was, of course, technically true, though untrue in every other sense: *Parliamentary Debates: the House of Commons*, 5th Series, Vol. 276, col. 2808.
59. Ovey (Moscow) to Vansittart (London), 14.3.33: *DBFP*, doc. 219.
60. Monkhouse (Moscow) to Richards (London), 14.3.33: *DBFP*, appendix III. At the time Richards was disingenuously denying that the company ever "made a practice of asking their men for reports on conditions in Russia"! – an extraordinary statement to make, given the importance of the company's operations there: memorandum by Sir L. Oliphant, 15.4.33: ibid., doc. 409.
61. For Ovey's initial reaction – Ovey (Moscow) to Vansittart (London), 12.3.33: *DBFP*, doc. 207; also *Cmd.* 4286. Some at the Foreign Office felt he may have gone too far – comment by Fitzmaurice, 24.3.33: *FO* 371/17266.
62. Fitzmaurice to Collier, 25.3.33: ibid.
63. The United Press correspondent in Moscow believed Thornton's confession pointed to some sort of guilt. He noted: "The GPU and the prosecution, I came to feel, had a club over the heads of some of the Britishers. British guilt was involved (whether of the British Intelligence Service or of individual Britishers, I dare not surmise), but that guilt referred to matters which were not even mentioned at the trial" – E. Lyons, *Assignment in Utopia* (London, 1938) pp. 565–6.
64. Editorial, 26.4.33: quoted in W. and Z. Coates, *A History of Anglo-Soviet Relations* (London, 1943) p. 499.
65. E. Carr, R. Davies, *Foundations of a Planned Economy 1926–1929*, vol. 1, 2 (London, 1969) pp. 584–90.
66. Haslam, *Soviet Foreign Policy*, p. 46.
67. Editorial, "Reviziya dogovorov i bor'ba za peredel mira", *Krasnaya Zvezda*, 2.4.33.
68. *DGFP*, doc. 312. For the background to the affair, and the subsequent fate

of Hugenberg: G. Weinberg, *The Foreign Policy of Hitler's Germany: Diplomatic Revolution in Europe 1933–36* (Chicago, 1970) pp. 79–80.
69. Presented to the world economic conference, 20.6.33: *DVP SSSR*, doc. 187.
70. Dirksen (Moscow) to Berlin, 19.6.33: *DGFP*, doc. 325.
71. Editorial, "Nuzhna polnaya yasnost'", *Izvestiya*, 20.6.33.
72. Delivered to Bülow, state secretary at the Ausamt, by Khinchuk, polpred in Berlin, 22.6.33: *DVP SSSR*, doc. 189; subsequently published in *Izvestiya*, 24.6.33.
73. Hartmann (Moscow) to Berlin, 28.6.33: *DGFP*, doc. 339; but not until the 15 September were Russo-German military stations actually closed down – Hartmann (Moscow) to Berlin, 19.9.33: ibid., doc. 439 (annexe i).
74. Khinchuk (Berlin) to Moscow, 19.7.33: *DVP SSSR*, doc. 249.
75. Dirksen (Moscow) to Berlin, 4.4.33: *DGFP*, doc. 136; for published Soviet suspicions: E. Gnedin, "Pakt – gegen Wen?", *Moskauer Rundschau*, 9.4.33.
76. Dejean (Moscow) to Paul-Boncour (Paris), 11.4.33: *DDF*, vol. 3, (Paris, 1967) doc. 115; for Litvinov's record of the conversation, 10.4.33: *DVP SSSR*, doc. 114.
77. B. Miedziński, "Pakty wilanowskie", *Kultura*, 1963, no. 189–90, pp. 115–19.
78. Radek told Zabiello that Tukhachevsky was the author: S. Zabiello, "Rokodwilzy", p. 141.
79. Duo, "Ekonomicheskoe i strategicheskoe znachenie pol'skogo koridora", *Bol'shevik*, no. 15–16, 31.8.33, p. 30.
80. "Note de la direction politique", Paris, 19.7.33: *DDF*, vol. 4, (Paris, 1968) doc. 20.
81. For earlier attempts by the Russians to obtain a pact, at the end of 1930: Haslam, *Soviet Foreign Policy*, pp. 49–50.
82. *DVP SSSR*, doc. 277. It was ratified by the USSR on the 7 October, and by the Italians on the 19 October; instruments of ratification were exchanged on the 15 December 1933. Moscow was at this stage keen to stress that: "The foreign policy interests of both states do not conflict at any point" – Jur, "Nichtangriffspakt mit Italien", *Moskauer Rundschau*, 10.9.33.
83. K. Niclauss, *Die Sowjetunion und Hitlers Machtergriefung. Eine Studie über die deutsch-russischen Beziehungen der Jahre 1929–1935* (Bonn, 1966), p. 120. Louis Fischer refers to Yenukidze as "among those who used to eat and drink in Stalin's Kremlin apartment late at night when he returned from a long day's work"; he portrays him as "a tall, plump, blond, jovial Georgian who had been Stalin's friend since 1900": L. Fischer, *The Life and Death of Stalin*, p. 60.
84. Molotov's record of the conversation, 4.8.33: *DVP SSSR*, doc. 266.
85. K.R. "Eshche raz o germano-sovetskikh otnosheniyakh", *Izvestiya*, 9.8.33.
86. Dirksen (Moscow) to Bülow (Berlin), 17.8.33: *Auswärtiges Amt* (hereafter *AA*), PA, IV Ru, Bd.II, 6609/E497125–32. It is possible that soundings such as this led former counsellor at the Rome embassy, Guelfand, to refer retrospectively to Stalin "nibbling for an agreement with Hitler since 1933" – Butler (Washington) to Sargent (London), 13.9.40: *FO* 371/2485. It is also possible that Guelfand only learned of such moves in the USA after his defection.
87. The record of the conversation on the 14 September can be found in Twardowski (Moscow) to Berlin, 19.9.33: *DGFP*, doc. 438 (enclosure).

88. Alphand (Moscow) to Paul-Boncour (Paris), 12.9.33: *DDF*, doc. 204.
89. Litvinov (Moscow) to Rozenberg (Paris), 19.9.33: *DVP SSSR*, doc. 291.
90. Litvinov's record of the conversation, 22.9.33: ibid., doc. 297.
91. Head of the department, Stern, told Twardowski that "the feeling in Soviet circles was growing worse every day, and it has already come to the point where the Foreign Commissariat is laughed at when it tries to counsel calm and keeps repeating that it is necessary to wait and see", adding that his department was no longer able to make its point of view prevail – Twardowski (Moscow) to Berlin, 19.9.33: *DGFP*, doc. 438 (enclosure 2).
92. For an account of the trial: Carr, *The Twilight*, pp. 101–2.
93. Note from Litvinov to Twardowski, 26.9.33, published in *Izvestiya*, 27.9.33, and reprinted in *DVP SSSR*, doc. 300.
94. "While German-Russian relations could not in practice be maintained in the long run", Hitler stated, "it would perhaps be advisable tactically, by means of the requested statement, to deprive them of an opportunity to get away from us" – minutes of a conference in the Reich Chancellery, 26.9.33: *DGFP*, doc. 456.
95. The dates given in the German documents, for which no Soviet counterparts are available, are confusing. But, judging from the record of a conversation between Italian ambassador Cicconardi and Deputy Director of the East European and Scandinavian Department, Hey, which took place on the 25 September, Krestinsky had already passed through Berlin en route to Kissingen: *AA* 9526/E671744. On the other hand, the record of the discussion at the Reich Chancellery on the following day suggests that Khinchuk's request concerning Krestinsky's "impending visit" was made on the 26 September: *DGFP*, doc. 456. The assumption that Khinchuk's request was made earlier is borne out by the absence of any reference to it in Bülow's record of a conversation with the polpred on the 26: ibid., doc. 455.
96. Bülow's record of a conversation with Khinchuk, 27.9.33: ibid., doc. 461.
97. Another note by Bülow, concerning a conversation with Khinchuk, 27.9.33: *AA* 9526/E671745.
98. As Bülow noted on the 27 September:

    > In the course of the conversation the Ambassador mentioned that he had intended to go to Moscow in order to discuss German–Russian relations thoroughly. Since Stalin was on vacation this trip had no purpose, for to deal with the Foreign Ministry alone would lead to nothing. However, he was sending his Counselor of Embassy to Moscow by plane in order to try to bridge the present acute tension in some way or other.

    – *DGFP*, doc. 455.
99. Twardowski (Moscow) to Berlin, 2.10.33: ibid., doc. 477.
100. Source as cited in note 97.
101. When Bülow saw Khinchuk on the 6 October, the polpred said that he did not know whether Krestinsky would come to Berlin since he had to visit a doctor in Vienna – Bülow's record of the conversation is referred to in *DGFP*, p. 902. But this was plainly an excuse. In conversation with Twardowski, Stern explained Krestinsky's movements by the fact that his long absence from Moscow meant he was insufficiently informed on the current state of relations – Twardowski's memorandum, 7.10.33: ibid., doc. 487 (enclosure).

102. Editorial, "Vykhod Germanii iz Ligi Natsii", *Izvestiya*, 16.10.33.
103. Twardowski (Moscow) to Berlin, 17.10.33: *DGFP*, vol. 2, doc. 12.
104. Göring rescinded the prohibition on Soviet journalists attending the Leipzig trial – memorandum by Neurath, 22.10.33: ibid., doc. 21. The agreement on cutting press polemics was recorded in another memorandum by Neurath, 24.10.33: ibid., doc. 25; and Khinchuk's commitment to follow suit with regard to radio broadcasts was noted in a memorandum by Meyer, director of the East European and Scandinavian Department, 27.10.33: ibid., doc. 30. All this is omitted from the published Soviet documents.
105. K. Radek, "Dinamit na Dal'nem Vostoke", *Izvestiya*, 26.9.33.
106. The recognition of the USSR by the United States will be dealt with in a subsequent volume; the Narkomindel's German language weekly referred to the recognition as "A Great Triumph for the Soviet Peace Policy" – "Ein grosser Sieg der sowjetischen Friedenspolitik", *Moskauer Rundschau*, 26.11.33.
107. Twardowski (Moscow) to Berlin, 6.11.33: *DGFP*, doc. 47.

CHAPTER 3 THE ORIGINS OF THE FRANCO-SOVIET PACT, 1933–35

1. Dovgalevsky (Paris) to Moscow, 20.10.33: *DVP SSSR*, doc. 322.
2. Rozenberg (Paris) to Moscow, 25.10.33: ibid., doc. 325.
3. Potemkin told the French ambassador to Rome that: "One does not have to be particularly [well] informed to see that the most intelligent amongst the capitalists will have to look to China today for the clientele and new avenues for trade which they are unable to find in Europe and America. Have you considered that an entente on the subject of the Far East such as you seem to envisage would require an alliance between the Bolsheviks and the capitalists?" – M. de Jouvenal (Rome) to Paul-Boncour (Paris), 17.7.33: *DDF*, vol. 4, doc. 7. Soviet insistence on the importance of an agreement encompassing Asia was reiterated on every possible occasion. When Paul-Boncour broached the idea of mutual assistance in conversation with Litvinov at the end of October 1933, the Commissar emphasised: "we have to think not only of the West, but also of the East . . . France must have an interest in our avoidance of complications in the East" – Litvinov (Paris) to Moscow, 31.10.33: ibid., doc. 332.
4. In conversation with the Russians, Paul-Boncour "stressed that there is no time to lose and that the elaboration of the shape mutual assistance or some other form of co-operation might take, must be a matter of weeks" – Dovgalevsky (Paris) to Moscow, 1.11.33: ibid., doc. 337.
5. "We have an ambassador in Berlin; Germany has an ambassador in Paris", he emphasised, adding that any "concrete proposal" from Germany would be considered: *Journal Officiel: Chambre des Députés*, No. 13, 14.11.33, p. 4104. For the German reaction – François-Poncet (Berlin) to Paul-Boncour (Paris), 15.11.33: *DDF*, vol. 5 (Paris, 1970), doc. 12.
6. François-Poncet (Berlin) to Paul-Boncour (Paris), 24.11.33: ibid., doc. 52.
7. Rozenberg (Paris) to Krestinsky (Moscow), 25.11.33: *DVP SSSR*, doc. 390.

8. Krestinsky (Moscow) to Dovgalevsky (Paris), 29.11.33: ibid., doc. 396. On the 3 December, Litvinov insisted to Mussolini that "the USSR has reason to fear a Franco-German entente which would necessarily be turned to her disadvantage" – Mussolini's record of the conversation, 3.12.33: *ASD*, URSS (1933), b. 8, f. 1.4. "We aim to prevent France from allying with Germany against us, by means of a rapprochement with France" – Litvinov's record of the conversation, contained in Litvinov (Rome) to Moscow, 4.12.33: *DVP SSSR*, doc. 405.
9. TASS reported rumours of such talks on the 30 November, basing its news on German newspaper speculation. The conclusion as to the existence of talks other than those between Hitler and the French ambassador, appears in the accompanying editorial comment: *Izvestiya*, 2.12.33.
10. Alphand (Moscow) to Paul-Boncour (Paris), 4.12.33: *DDF*, doc. 77; and the comment: "They are as worried here about Franco-German conversations as they were previously about the Four Power Pact" – Alphand (Moscow) to Paul-Boncour (Paris), 5.12.33: ibid., doc. 86.
11. Paul-Boncour (Paris) to Alphand (Moscow), 6.12.33: *DDF*, doc. 88.
12. Dovgalevsky (Paris) to Moscow, 6.12.33: *DVP SSSR*, doc. 413.
13. Reported in *Izvestiya*, 8.12.33; also Alphand (Moscow) to Paul-Boncour (Paris), 20.12.33; *DDF*, doc. 158.
14. Referred to in Litvinov (Moscow) to Dovgalevsky (Paris), 9.12.33, which is quoted in *DVP SSSR*, p. 872.
15. *Pravda*, 10.12.33.
16. Krestinsky (Moscow) to Litvinov (Rome), 2.12.33: *DVP SSSR*, doc. 400; also Krestinsky (Moscow) to Dovgalevsky (Paris), 2.12.33: ibid., doc. 401.
17. Litvinov's record of the conversation is dated 13.12.33, although it took place two days earlier: ibid., doc. 424.
18. *Istoriya Vtoroi Mirovoi Voiny*, vol. 1 (Moscow, 1973), p. 283.
19. *Istoriya Vneshnei Politiki SSSR 1917–1976*, vol. 1 (1917–45) (4th edition, Moscow, 1980), p. 302–3; also *DVP SSSR*, pp. 876–7.
20. Litvinov saw Bullitt on the 21 December – Marriner (Paris) to Washington, 24.12.33: *Foreign Relations of the United States* (*FRUS*), *The Soviet Union 1933–1939* (Washington, 1952) pp. 53–4.
21. Speech to the central executive committee, 29.12.33: *DVP SSSR*, p. 782. Molotov's speech is reprinted in the same volume, pp. 781–97.
22. Editorial, "Yasnost' i opredelennost'", *Izvestiya*, 30.12.33.
23. Litvinov's record of the conversation, 3.1.34: *DVP SSSR*, vol. XVII (Moscow, 1971), doc. 2.
24. Editorial, "Na styke dvukh epokh", *Pravda*, 7.1.34. This was noted by keen observers at the Italian embassy – Attolico (Moscow) to Rome, 9.1.34: *ASD*, URSS (1934), b. 12, f. 1.1.
25. This took place sometime just prior to 10.1.34, the date of Nadolny's despatch to Berlin: *DGFP*, doc. 173.
26. Dovgalevsky (Paris) to Moscow, 4.1.34: *DVP SSSR*, p. 773; and "Note du Département", 4.1.34: *DDF*, doc. 193.
27. Editorial, "Vazhny etap vo franko-sovetskom sblizhenii", *Izvestiya*, 12.1.34. The text has for some reason been omitted from the published Soviet documents.
28. Kaganovich's speech to the fourth regional and third city party conference

in Moscow, 17.1.34: *Pravda*, 22.1.34.

29. S. Kirov, *Izbrannye Stat'i i Rechi* (Moscow, 1937) pp. 472–3.
30. This was first pointed out by F. Benvenuti in his "Kirov nella politica sovietica", *Annali dell'Istituto Italiano per gli Studi Storici*, IV, 1973/1975 (Naples, 1979) p. 344.
31. Dovgalevsky (Paris) to Litvinov (Moscow), 25.1.34: *DVP SSSR*, doc. 26.
32. Reprinted in the Soviet diplomatic documents, doc. 28; also J. Stalin, *Works*, vol. 13 (Moscow, 1955) pp. 297–312.
33. Alphand told Stomonyakov that "there is resistance against rapprochement within our civil service" – Stomonyakov's record of the conversation, 13.2.34: *DVP SSSR*, doc. 54; for illustration, see Haslam, *Soviet Foreign Policy*, chs 4 and 6.
34. "Note de la Direction politique", 26.1.34: *DDF*, doc. 277.
35. Dovgalevsky (Paris) to Moscow, 29.1.34: *DVP SSSR*, doc. 36.
36. S. Berstein, *Le 6 février 1934* (Paris, 1975) and D. Brower, *The New Jacobins: The French Communist Party and the Popular Front* (New York, 1968); also Haslam, "The Comintern and the Origins of the Popular Front 1934–1935", *The Historical Journal*, 22, 3 (1979) pp. 673–91, and Carr, *The Twilight*, p. 189.
37. M. Hajek, *Storia dell'internazionale comunista (1921–1935): la politica del fronte unico* (Rome, 1969) pp. 240–1.
38. Haslam, "The Comintern", p. 678.
39. Ibid., pp. 679–80.
40. Stomonyakov's record of the conversation, 13.2.34: source cited in note 33.
41. On the 6 March Dovgalevsky briefed Barthou on the current state of negotiations: ibid., pp. 781–2.
42. This conversation, recorded by Stomonyakov on the 17 March, took place at Nadolny's: ibid., doc. 82.
43. Ibid., doc. 85, and *DGFP*, doc. 342.
44. Note to the German Government, 24.3.34: *DVP SSSR*, doc. 88 and pp. 786–7.
45. This was raised by Colonel Beck, Poland's Foreign Minister, in conversation with Antonov-Ovseenko, polpred in Warsaw, on or before the 1 December 1933: *Dokumenty i Materialy po Istorii Sovetsko-Pol'skikh Otnoshenii*, vol. 6 (Moscow, 1969), doc. 81.
46. Litvinov raised this in conversation with ambassador Lukasiewicz, 14.12.33: ibid., doc. 87; also *DVP SSSR*, doc. 426.
47. Lukasiewicz hinted as much to Litvinov, 1.2.34: *Dokumenty i Materialy*, doc. 102. Sure enough, two days later, he conveyed Colonel Beck's instructions to the effect that the "Baltic declaration has turned out to be tactically inopportune and has precipitated many complications": ibid., doc. 103.
48. Litvinov's record of a conversation with Nadolny, 28.3.34: *DVP SSSR*, doc. 94.
49. This only appears in Nadolny's account of the conversation – Nadolny (Moscow) to Berlin, 29.3.34: *DGFP*, doc. 364. Its omission from Krestinsky's account suggests Litvinov would not have approved of the sentiments expressed: *DVP SSSR*, doc. 95.
50. Neurath (Berlin) to Nadolny (Moscow), 9.4.34: *DGFP*, doc. 390. He told Khinchuk that Germany attributed no significance to "paper pacts",

which contrasts oddly with the conclusion of the Polish–German agreement in January 1934 – Khinchuk's record of the conversation, 11.4.34: *DVP SSSR*, doc. 122. Litvinov was informed of this by Nadolny three days later: ibid., doc. 126.

51. Ibid., doc. 139 (enclosure).
52. Krestinsky (Moscow) to Khinchuk (Berlin), 17.4.34: ibid., doc. 128.
53. Alphand (Moscow) to Paris, 20.4.34: *DDF*, vol. 6 (Paris 1972) doc. 119; also Litvinov's record of his conversation with Alphand, 20.4.34: *DVP SSSR*, doc. 136.
54. *Izvestiya* and *Pravda*, 27.4.34, and *Le Journal de Moscou*, 9.5.34; reprinted in *DVP SSSR*, source cited in note 51.
55. Editorial, "Germaniya i Pribaltika", *Izvestiya*, 28.4.34.
56. Rozenberg (Paris) to Moscow, 20.4.34: *DVP SSSR*, doc. 138.
57. Litvinov (Moscow) to Rozenberg (Paris), 28.4.34: ibid., doc. 149.
58. This was true as late as the 28 April, when Léger spoke to Rozenberg about the projected Eastern Locarno – Rozenberg (Paris) to Moscow, 28.4.34: ibid., doc. 151.
59. Under pressure from Litvinov on the 18 May Barthou agreed to reconsider, but nothing came of this – Litvinov (Menthon) to Moscow, 18.5.34: ibid., doc. 168; for the French account of the conversation: *DDF*, doc. 221.
60. *DVP SSSR*, doc. 193.
61. Ibid., doc. 194. An editorial on the dual recognition was suitably entitled "A New Success for Our Peace Policy", *Izvestiya*, 10.6.34. The decision to recognise the USSR followed an agreement on the subject between members of the Little Entente (Czechoslovakia, Romania and Yugoslavia) at Zagreb in January; the delay in granting recognition was to allow for Romanian negotiations with the USSR which would not directly compromise possession of Bessarabia, seized from the Russians in 1919: telegraphic circular from Beneš to missions, abroad, 28.1.34: *Dokumenty i Materialy po Istorii Sovetsko-Chekhoslovatskikh Otnoshenii*, vol. 2, ed. Ch. Amort, *et al.* (Moscow, 1977), doc. 458.
62. Interview with Duranty of the *New York Times*, 25.12.33: *Pravda*, 4.1.34.
63. From an informal discussion at a dinner arranged by Litvinov for Avenol, 11.6.34. Only Avenol's record of the discussion is available: *DDF*, doc. 324.
64. Foreshadowed in an unsigned article: xxx, "Graves Difficultés Intérieurs et Extérieurs du Reich (Lettre de Berlin)", *Le Journal de Moscou*, 27.6.34.
65. This is a legend first put into circulation by Krivitsky, formerly *rezident* for Soviet Intelligence in the Netherlands. He claims that Stalin considered the 30 June events would strengthen Hitler's power rather than weaken it: V. Krivitskii, "Iz vospominaniya sovetskogo kommunista", *Sotsialisticheskii Vestnik*, no. 7, 15.4.38. It would appear that this was merely a deduction he made in order to make sense of information he later acquired concerning Soviet soundings for an improvement in relations with Germany; for an evaluation of some of Krivitsky's wilder claims by someone who knew him: E. Poretsky, *Our Own People: A Memoir of 'Ignace Reiss' and His Friends* (London, 1969). In the spring of 1939 more elaborate memoirs, ghosted by Isaac Don Levine, an American journalist, appeared in the *Saturday Evening Post*. In the face of a paucity of information, too many Western writers have relied upon him for evidence.
66. K. Radek, "Deux sons de cloche", *Le Journal de Moscou*, 7.7.34. A similar

interpretation appears in an unsigned article, "Obrechenny rezhim", *Pravda*, 2.7.34; and by Radek, "Nachalo krizisa germanskogo fashizma", *Bol'shevik*, no. 12, 30.6.34, pp. 37–54.

67. the victory of Fascism in Germany must be regarded not only as a symptom of the weakness of the working class and a result of the betrayals of the working class by Social Democracy, which paved the way for Fascism; it must also be regarded as a sign of the weakness of the bourgeoisie, a sign that the bourgeoisie is no longer able to rule by the old methods of parliamentarism and bourgeois democracy, and, as a consequence, is compelled in its home policy to resort to terrorist methods of rule

– source cited in note 32.

68. Attolico (Moscow) to Rome, 12.7.34: *ASD*, URSS (1934), b. 1.4, f. 1.3.
69. Editorial, "The Bloody 30th of June in Germany", *International Press Correspondence* (*Inprecorr*), 6.7.34.
70. Litvinov (Moscow) to Maisky (London), 19.7.34: ibid., doc. 258.
71. Barthou (Paris) to Alphand (Moscow), 19.7.34: *DDF*, doc. 482; and the subsequent discussion between Payart and Litvinov, 23.7.34: *DVP SSSR*, doc. 266.
72. For Nazi involvement: Weinberg, *The Foreign Policy of Hitler's Germany*, pp. 102–3.
73. Litvinov (Moscow) to Rozenberg (Paris), 26.7.34: *DVP SSSR*, doc. 270; also Payart (Moscow) to Barthou (Paris), 27.7.34: *DDF*, vol. 7 (Paris, 1979), doc. 3.
74. Twardowski's record of the conversation, 17.8.34, enclosed in Twardowski (Moscow) to Berlin, 20.8.34: *AA* 6609/E497526–30.
75. Paterno di Manchi di Bilici (Stockholm) to Rome, 15.9.34: *ASD*, URSS (1934), b. 12, f.1.3.
76. This will be dealt with at length in a subsequent volume.
77. K. Radek, "Pouquoi l'URSS entre-t-elle dans la S.d.N.?", *Le Journal de Moscou*, 15.9.34. The French were also very much aware of and worried by this, and made strenuous efforts to reassure the Japanese – "Note de la sous-direction d'Asie", 5.9.34: *DDF*, doc. 241.
78. Editorial, "SSSR i Liga Natsii", *Kommunisticheskii Internatsional*, no. 26–7, 20.9.34, pp. 3–11.
79. Editorial, *Le Journal de Moscou*, 8.9.34. A symptom of this new trend was the sudden absence of the regular "Letter from Berlin", which usually highlighted the less agreeable aspects of the German situation. The letters did not reappear until the 3 November – the day the Politburo finally came to a decision on relations with Germany.
80. Memorandum, 8.9.34: *DGFP*, Series C, vol. 3, (London, 1959) doc. 200.
81. *DVP SSSR*, doc. 331. In his first speech to the assembly, on the 18 September, Litvinov reiterated his belief in the indivisibility of peace: ibid., doc. 334; originally published in *Izvestiya*, 20.9.34.
82. Editorial, "Liga Natsii i SSSR", ibid., 17.9.34; oddly, the Party daily was more enthusiastic: editorial, "SSSR prodolzhaet bor'bu za mir", *Pravda*, 17.9.34.
83. The complete telegram has not been published. For this quotation: *DVP SSSR*, p. 821.

84. Bullitt (Moscow) to Judge Moore (Washington), 6.10.34: *For the President, Personal and Secret: Correspondence Between Franklin D. Roosevelt and William C. Bullitt*, ed. O. Bullitt (London, 1973) pp. 98–9.
85. When Schulenburg, the new German ambassador, presented his credentials to Kalinin, the latter expressed the hope that relations would improve, and told him not to pay any attention to press polemic. But, as the ambassador noted, Kalinin had only just returned from his vacation and may have been unaware of opinion current in the Kremlin. For when Schulenburg met Krestinsky and Yenukidze, both usually Germanophile, he found them reluctant to say anything. Litvinov was by now back in Moscow, but apparently had not yet returned to work – Schulenburg (Moscow) to Berlin, 7.10.34: *DGFP*, doc. 233. For Litvinov's record of the conversation: *DVP SSSR*, doc. 354.
86. Record of a conversation with Schulenburg by Khinchuk, now Commissar of Internal Trade, 15.10.34: *DVP SSSR*, doc. 361.
87. Bülow (Berlin) to Schulenburg (Moscow), 26.10.34; *DGFP*, doc. 271.
88. Litvinov (Geneva) to Moscow, 25.9.34: *DVP SSSR*, doc. 339.
89. *Le Journal de Moscou*, 13.10.34.
90. See Haslam, *Soviet Foreign Policy*, p. 99; for the Russian reaction to Barthou's death – Alphand (Moscow) to Doumergue (Paris), 12.10.34: *DDF*, doc. 457.
91. Rozenberg (Paris) to Moscow, 19.10.34: *DVP SSSR*, doc. 365. The French Right was particularly disturbed at the prospect of a resurgent Left. "Right-wing circles", Rozenberg reported, "who previously . . . admitted the need for agreement with the Soviet Union in view of the German danger, now think that the Communist danger is nearer than the German" – quoted in "The Struggle of the USSR for Collective Security in Europe During 1933–1935", *International Affairs* (Moscow), no. 7, July 1963, pp. 116–23. For the changes in Communist strategy which gave rise to these fears, see ch. 4.
92. Litvinov (Moscow) to Rozenberg (Paris), 19.10.34: *DVP SSSR*, p. 824.
93. On the 4 November, Litvinov wrote to Surits warning him of the current German practice (which the Russians themselves were shortly to emulate) of using semi-official emissaries to conduct unofficial talks:

> Germany is making desperate efforts to hinder France's rapprochement with us and to draw it into some sort of negotiations. To this end it is intimidating France by spreading rumours – on the one hand about the alleged existence of a German–Japanese agreement and the possibility of joint action against the USSR in the near future, and on the other hand about serious political and economic negotiations with the USSR, which would be bound to result in the re-establishment of Soviet-German relations as they were formerly.

– Litvinov (Moscow) to Surits (Berlin), 4.11.34: ibid., doc. 379.
94. *Istoriya KPSS*, vol. 4, p. 296.
95. Litvinov (Moscow) to Rozenberg (Paris), 6.11.34: *DVP SSSR*, doc. 382; also Alphand (Moscow) to Laval (Paris), 9.11.34: *DDF*, vol. 8 (Paris, 1979) doc. 47.
96. Alphand (Moscow) to Laval (Paris), 13.11.34: ibid., doc. 63; also, Wiley

(Moscow) to Hull (Washington), 18.11.34: *FRUS*, p. 163; and Charles (Moscow) to Collier (London), 20.11.34: *FO* 371/18318.

97. Litvinov (Geneva) to Moscow, 21.11.34: *DVP SSSR*, doc. 397. According to one Soviet account, based on the archives, Laval later suggested an exchange of letters instead, but Moscow – evidently by telegraph to Litvinov – insisted on the proposed protocol, and, when Laval persisted, Litvinov announced that he would return to Moscow immediately: "The Struggle . . .", cited in note 91.
98. This information came from a reliable source – Attolico (Moscow) to Rome, 14.12.34: *ASD*, loc. cit.
99. Editorial, *Le Journal de Moscou*, 1.12.34.
100. *DDF*, doc. 215 (enclosure) and *DVP SSSR*, doc. 417; Litvinov's declaration appeared in *Izvestiya*, 9.12.34, reprinted in *DVP SSSR*, doc. 418.
101. Editorial, *Le Journal de Moscou*, 15.12.34.
102. For the visit: J.-B. Duroselle, *La Décadence 1932–1939* (Paris, 1979), pp. 130–9.
103. Litvinov (Moscow) to Potemkin (Paris), and Shtein (Rome), 7.1.35: *DVP SSSR*, vol. XVIII (Moscow, 1973), p. 614. Soviet press comment was more guarded, welcoming Laval's visit in so far as it gave hope for the reinforcement of a policy of consolidating peace in Europe, though it also expressed concern at the idea that the Rome agreements might substitute from the Eastern pact: editorial, *Le Journal de Moscou*, 12.1.35. This was also the tenor of Litvinov's remarks in conversation with Laval at Geneva – Litvinov (Geneva) to Moscow, 12.1.35: *DVP SSSR*, doc. 16.
104. Weinberg, *The Foreign Policy*, pp. 172–4, and Duroselle, *La Décadence*, pp. 125–9.
105. Litvinov (Geneva) to Moscow, 17.1.35: *DVP SSSR*, doc. 19.
106. Speech, 28.1.35: ibid., doc. 27.
107. Schulenburg (Moscow) to Berlin, 2.2.35: *AA* 6609/E429017-030.
108. Memorandum by Orme Sargent, 28.1.35: *DBFP*, vol. 12 (London, 1972), doc. 380.
109. Memorandum by Sargent, 7.2.35: ibid., doc. 428.
110. In his memoirs Eden refers to what he wrote in his diary:

> In a comment on Hitler's obsession with Russia, I wrote that I was strongly against letting Germany expand eastwards: "Apart from its dishonesty, it would be our turn next".

– Sir A. Eden, *The Memoirs of Anthony Eden. Facing the Dictators* (London, 1962) p. 141. All the evidence shows that Vansittart was violently anti-German and, within the limits imposed on him from above, relatively pro-Soviet.

111. "The object of our present policy is of course to bring the Germans back to Geneva", wrote the Foreign Secretary – Simon (London) to Clerk (Paris), 21.1.35: *DBFP*, doc. 359. "It is essential to improve our contacts with Russia, but in nearly every respect Russia and Germany are fundamentally different propositions to us, and the fitting of Russia into a scheme of European co-operation cannot be done in the same way as Germany" – note by MacDonald, undated: ibid., doc. 515.
112. Quoted in "The Struggle . . .", *International Affairs*, no. 8, August 1963, pp. 132–9.

113. As Léger told Potemkin: "the British were at first persistent in persuading the French to entirely omit an Eastern Pact from the general scheme set out in the London agreements": ibid.
114. For the text: *DBFP*, doc. 400 (annexe); also *Cmd* 4798 (1935).
115. The Narkomindel reaction can be seen in correspondence between Moscow and the embassies abroad – Potemkin (Paris) to Krestinsky (Moscow), 10.2.35: *DVP SSSR*, doc. 46; Litvinov (Moscow) to Potemkin (Paris), 11.2.35: ibid., doc. 48; Potemkin (Paris) to Moscow, 13.2.35: ibid., doc. 54; and for the effect on trade negotiations with Germany – Bessonov (Berlin) to Litvinov (Moscow), 6.2.35: ibid., doc. 38; also "The Struggle . . .", as cited in note 112.
116. Memorandum by Collier, 12.2.35: *FO* 371/19460.
117. A Soviet declaration was issued to the British and French Governments, 20.2.35: *Izvestiya*, 21.2.35, reprinted in *DVP SSSR*, doc. 68.
118. Editorial, *Le Journal de Moscou*, 2.3.35.
119. According to the US embassy, some 1074 suspects were deported from Leningrad to the East – Wiley (Moscow) to Hull (Washington), 20.3.35: *FRUS*, 1935, vol. 2 (Washington, 1952), p. 306.
120. Krestinsky (Moscow) to Surits (Berlin), 17.3.35: *DVP SSSR*, doc. 119.
121. The first detailed and authoritative Soviet survey of Germany's economic difficulties – raw materials shortages and a foreign exchange crisis – appears in an article by Varga, "Rastushchie trudnosti germanskogo fashizma", *Kommunisticheskii Internatsional*, no. 36, 20.12.34, pp. 15–24. Radek and Mikhailsky (of the Narkomindel) pointed to these problems in conversation with US diplomats – Wiley (Moscow) to Hull (Washington), 22.3.35: *FRUS*, pp. 312–14.
122. Litvinov (Moscow) to Potemkin (Paris), 23.3.35: *DVP SSSR*, doc. 132.
123. Editorial, *Le Journal de Moscou*, 30.3.35.
124. Entry, 16.3.35: *Diary of Beatrice Webb*, vol. 49, p. 5944.
125. Radek's sarcastic appraisal of the Berlin visit is worth quoting: "Christopher Columbus departed in search of the route to the Indies and discovered America; but such good luck does not always come to travellers who lose their bearings" – K. Radek, "L'Angleterre et l'Organisation de la Paix", *Le Journal de Moscou*, 30.3.35.
126. Those present included Molotov, Litvinov, Chilston, Strang, Maisky and Stalin. The conversation lasted an hour and a quarter: *DVP SSSR*, doc. 148; also Eden *The Memoirs*, pp. 152–3, and I. Maisky, *Vospominaniya Sovetskogo Diplomata 1925–1945gg* (Moscow, 1971) pp. 294–9.
127. Duroselle, *La Décadence*, p. 136.
128. Potemkin saw Laval on the 6 April – Potemkin (Paris) to Moscow, 7.4.35: *DVP SSSR*, doc. 166.
129. Bessonov, Soviet Counsellor in Berlin, told the British of this – Phipps (Berlin) to London, 13.4.35: *FO* 371/19460. It was evidently as a consequence of this that the Stresa conference received a fairly positive response in the Soviet press: editorial, *Le Journal de Moscou*, 19.4.35.
130. *DVP SSSR*, docs. 171 and 172.
131. Radek, "Khozyaistvennye otnosheniya Germanii i SSSR", *Izvestiya*, 11.4.35.
132. Litvinov (Geneva) to Potemkin (Paris), 10.4.35: *DVP SSSR*, doc. 176.
133. Krestinsky (Moscow) to Litvinov (Geneva), 14.4.35: ibid., doc. 180.

134. Litvinov (Geneva) to Moscow, 14.4.35: ibid., doc. 181.
135. Krestinsky (Moscow) to Litvinov (Geneva), 15.4.35: ibid., doc. 182.
136. Litvinov (Geneva) to Moscow, 18.4.35: ibid., doc. 187.
137. Potemkin (Paris) to Moscow, 20.4.35: ibid., doc. 190. Typically Laval told the British that it was the Russians who were responsible for this eleventh hour hitch – Clerk (Paris) to Simon (London), 19.4.35: *DBFP*, vol. 13, doc. 122. That this was not true is evident even from the somewhat patchy French documentation, which unfortunately does not include an account of what precisely occurred at Geneva; see "Note du Jurisconsulte du Département", 16.4.35: *DDF*, vol. 10 (Paris, 1981), doc. 202, also Laval (Paris) to Alphand (Moscow), 20.4.35: ibid., doc. 231.
138. The news visibly shook Laval – Potemkin (Paris) to Moscow, 20.4.35: ibid., doc. 191.
139. Potemkin was told this by another member of the *conseil d'état*, Mandel, on the 22 April: "The Struggle . . .", *International Affairs*, no. 10, October 1963, pp. 112–20.
140. *DVP SSSR*, doc. 205.
141. *DVP SSSR*, doc. 223.
142. See a telegram from Beneš, evidently to missions abroad, 9.5.35: *Dokumenty i Materialy po Istorii Sovetsko-Chekhoslovatskikh Otnoshenii*, vol. 3, doc. 62; and Litvinov (Moscow) to Alexandrovsky (Prague), 11.5.35: ibid., doc. 63.
143. It is perhaps significant that instead of referring to the pact as a "Soviet–French treaty" – as was the case with the non-aggression pact of 1932 – the Russians wrote instead of a "Franco-Soviet treaty": "Franko-sovetskii dogovor", *Izvestiya*, 4.5.35.
144. Noted by German diplomats – Schulenburg (Moscow) to Berlin, 6.5.35: *DGFP*, doc. 70.
145. Schulenburg (Moscow) to Berlin, 8.5.35: ibid., doc. 78; also Litvinov (Moscow) to Surits (Berlin), 9.5.35: *DVP SSSR*, doc. 215.
146. *Izvestiya*, 16.5.35, and *Le Temps*, 17.5.35; for Laval's account of what happened: Laval (Moscow) to Paris, 16.5.35: *DDF*, doc. 388.

CHAPTER 4 THE SEVENTH CONGRESS OF THE COMINTERN, 1935

1. "V Narkomindele. 1922–1933: Interv'yu s E. A. Gnedinym", *Pamyat'*, no. 5 (Paris, 1982) p. 365.
2. A. Avtorkhanov, "Pokorenie Partii", *Posev*, 29.10.50; the author served in the upper reaches of the Party apparatus in the early thirties. For confirmation concerning Stalin's secretariat: V. Krivitsky, "Iz vospominaniya sovetskogo kommunista", *Sotsialisticheskii Vestnik*, no. 7, 15.4.38; L. Fischer, *The Life and Death of Stalin* (London, 1953) p. 142; A. Orlov, *The Secret History of Stalin's Crimes* (London, 1954) p. 204; and E. Gnedin, *Iz Istorii Otnoshenii Mezhdu SSSR i Fashistskoi Germanii: Dokumenty i Sovremennye Kommentarii* (New York, 1977) p. 23.
3. Haslam, *Soviet Foreign Policy*, pp. 90–1.

4. Quoted in Haslam, "The Comintern . . .", p. 677.
5. Ibid., p. 680.
6. Ibid.
7. Ibid.
8. Ibid.
9. Ibid.
10. Ibid.
11. Ibid., pp. 681–2.
12. Ibid., p. 682.
13. Ibid.
14. Ibid.
15. Ibid., pp. 682–4.
16. B. Leibzon, K. Shirinya, *Povorot v Politike Kominterna* (2nd edn., Moscow, 1975) pp. 101–2, 109; the KPD was particularly resistant to such changes, even after the seventh congress made them mandatory: ibid., p. 363. Also see Togliatti's speech to the fourth conference of the KPD on the 10 October 1935: P. Togliatti, *Opere*, IV, I, ed. F. Andreucci, P. Spriano (Rome, 1979), pp. 3–22; Haslam, "The Comintern . . .", pp. 687–8; and Carr, *The Twilight*, pp. 134–42.
17. Carr, *The Twilight*, pp. 140–1.
18. Haslam, "The Comintern . . .", p. 689.
19. Dzh. Gol'dkhil, "Vostochnyi Pakt", *Kommunisticheskaya Revolyutsiya*, no. 8, August 1934, pp. 43–4.
20. "Po Rossii", 17.6.34: *Sotsialisticheskii Vestnik*, 25.6.34.
21. "Iz zala verkhovnogo suda SSSR", *Pravda*, 16.1.35.
22. Haslam, "The Comintern . . .", p. 689.
23. K. Shirinya, *Strategiya i Taktika Kominterna v Bor'be Protiv Fashizma i Voiny (1934–1939)* (Moscow, 1979) p. 58; for the congress itself: Carr, *The Twilight*, ch. 18.
24. "La preparazione di una nuova guerra mondiale da parte degli imperialisti e i compiti dell'Internazionale comunista", delivered between the 10 and 11 August 1935: P. Togliatti, *Opere*, III, II, ed. E. Ragionieri (Rome, 1973) p. 777.

CHAPTER 5 THE ABYSSINIAN CRISIS, 1935–36

1. Quoted in R. de Felice, *Mussolini il duce 1. Gli anni del consenso 1929–1936* (Turin, 1974) p. 607.
2. Ibid., p. 608.
3. Ibid., p. 645.
4. J-B. Duroselle, *La Décadence*, p. 133; and de Felice, *Mussolini*, p. 615. The fact that Laval left no documentary record of what precisely was said should cause no surprise; and even his "closest collaborators" were left in the dark about his true intentions: G. Tabouis, *Vingt ans de "suspense" diplomatique* (Paris, 1958) p. 222.
5. Ibid., p. 648.
6. Secretary-General Suvich's record of a conversation with Shtein, polpred

in Rome, 3.5.35: *ASD*, URSS (1935), b. 16, f. 1.1; Litvinov's record of a conversation with ambassador Attolico, Moscow, 3.5.35: *DVP SSSR*, vol. XVIII, p. 637; Litvinov (Moscow) to Shtein (Rome), 5.5.35: ibid., doc. 207; and Shtein (Rome) to Moscow, 6.5.35: ibid., p. 636.

7. Karakhan (Ankara) to Litvinov (Moscow), 8.5.35: ibid., doc. 214.
8. Suvich's record of the conversation, 16.5.35: *ASD*, URSS (1935), b. 16, f. 1.1; also his record of a conversation with Shtein, 26.6.35: ibid.
9. S.T., "Graves difficultés intérieurs de l'Italie – situation désastreuse de l'économie nationale", *Le Journal de Moscou*, 5.1.35.
10. Litvinov (Moscow) to Girshfel'd (Paris), 4.3.35: *DVP SSSR*, doc. 96.
11. Affari politici, ufficio 10 (Rome) to embassies in London, Paris, Berlin, Moscow, Warsaw, Brussels and Madrid, 29.7.35: *ASD*, URSS (1935), b. 16, f. 1.2.
12. Edmond (Geneva) to Hoare (London), 1.8.35: *DBFP*, vol. 14 (London, 1976), doc. 413.
13. Ibid.
14. Editorial, *Le Journal de Moscou*, 8.8.35.
15. Ibid., 23.8.35.
16. Clerk (Paris) to Hoare (London), 18.8.35: *DBFP*, doc. 465.
17. Appeal by the Central Committee of the Italian Communist Party and the Italian youth organisation, 12.2.35: *The Daily Worker* (New York), 12.2.35, translated and reprinted in *Iz Istorii Mezhdunarodnoi Proletarskoi Solidarnosti: Dokumenty i Materialy*, vol. 5: *Mezhdunarodnaya Solidarnost' Trudyashchikhsya v Bor'be s Fashizmom, Protiv Razvyazyvaniya Vtoroi Mirovoi Voiny (1933–1937)*, ed. G. Belov *et al.* (Moscow, 1961), doc. 163.
18. Quoted from the Italian Communist Party archive: G. Procacci, *Il socialismo internazionale e la guerra d'Etiopia* (Rome, 1978) p. 30.
19. Attolico (Moscow) to Rome, 17.4.35: quoted in Procacci, *Il socialismo*, p. 34.
20. P. Togliatti, *Opere*, ed. E. Ragionieri, vol. III, 2 (Rome, 1973), p. 762.
21. Procacci, *Il socialismo*, p. 99.
22. *L'Humanité*; 1.9.35; *Iz Istorii*, doc. 186.
23. *Pravda*, 5.9.35.
24. Editorial, *Le Journal de Moscou*, 6.9.35.
25. *DVP SSSR*, doc. 357; *Izvestiya*, 6.9.35.
26. Editorial, "Italo-abissiniskii konflikt i SSSR", ibid.
27. Editorial, *Le Journal de Moscou*, 30.8.35; and for British complaints – Chilston (Moscow) to Hoare (London), 2.9.35: *DBFP*, doc. 518.
28. *Kommunisticheskii Internatsional*, no. 27, 20.9.35; the date of issue was 16.10.35. It was later reprinted in *Rundschau*, 21.11.35, and *Report of the Seventh Congress of the Communist International* (London, 1936).
29. Editorial, *Le Journal de Moscou*, 21.11.35.
30. *Documents on International Affairs 1935*, vol. 2 (London, 1937) pp. 100–3.
31. *Izvestiya*, 12.9.35 and 14.9.35.
32. Hoare told Litvinov that "if Russia and France were anxious as to our attitude in the future, [to unprovoked aggression in Europe], they ought to mark with great satisfaction the recent outburst of British public opinion in support of the League . . . where the British public were convinced that a flagrant act of unprovoked aggression was being threatened or committed,

it would express itself with overwhelming force in support of the obligations of the Covenant" – Hoare (Geneva) to London, 13.9.35: *FO* 371/19452.

33. Quoted in V. Sipols, *Sovetskii Soyuz v Bor'be za Mir i Bezopasnost' 1933–1939* (Moscow, 1974) p. 100.
34. *Izvestiya*, 12.9.35.
35. K. Radek, "Nuremberg et Moscou", *Le Journal de Moscou*, 27.9.35.
36. This was opinion expressed in January 1936, but evidently one of longstanding, as the manner in which it was formulated suggests; in this the Russians were prone to see Hitler's Austrian origins as decisive in affecting his attitude towards Italy and to see Italian determination to ensure the independence of Austria as a constant – Surits (Berlin) to Krestinsky (Moscow), 27.1.36: *DVP SSSR*, vol. XIX (Moscow, 1974), doc. 29.
37. Krestinsky (Moscow) to Shtein (Rome), 17.7.36: ibid., doc. 223.
38. Editorial, "Sovetskii Soyuz ne prekratit bor'by za mir", *Izvestiya*, 15.9.35.
39. *DVP SSSR*, vol. XVIII, doc. 362.
40. Editorial, "Za politiku mira, protiv kolonial'nykh zakhvatov!", *Pravda*, 15.9.35.
41. Source cited in note 38.
42. The conversation took place on the 10 and 11 September – Edmond (Geneva) to Vansittart (London), 11.9.35: *DBFP*, doc. 554 (enclosure); and Edmond (Geneva) to Vansittart (London), 13.9.35: ibid., doc. 564 (enclosure); also Duroselle, *La Décadence*, pp. 148–9; and R. Parker, "Great Britain, France and the Ethiopian Crisis", *The English Historical Review*, vol. LXXXIX, 1974, pp. 306–7.
43. *Iz Istorii*, doc. 188.
44. Published in *Kommunist*, no. 5, 1969, pp. 33–5; reprinted in *VII Kongress Kommunisticheskogo Internatsionala i Bor'ba Protiv Fashizma i Voiny (Sbornik Dokumentov)*, ed. K. Shirinya *et al.* (Moscow, 1975) pp. 401–3.
45. *Istoriya Kommunisticheskoi Partii Sovetskogo Soyuza*, vol. 4, 2 (Moscow, 1971) p. 299.
46. Litvinov (Moscow) to Potemkin (Geneva), 4.10.35: *DVP SSSR*, doc. 372.
47. Editorial, "Voina v vostochnoi Afrike", *Pravda*, 5.10.35.
48. Source cited in note 46.
49. Edmond (Geneva) to Hoare (London), 4.10.35: *DBFP*, vol. 15, doc. 11.
50. Source cited in note 46.
51. *Documents on International Affairs*, p. 192.
52. Ibid., pp. 193 and 203–5.
53. Surits (Berlin) to Moscow, 9.10.35: *DVP SSSR*, doc. 373.
54. *Kommunisticheskii Internatsional*, no. 28–9, 10.10.35, pp. 59–60.
55. At a meeting of the Comintern executive committee on the 23 March 1936 Dimitrov pointed to the failure to develop "a serious campaign against the imperialist war in Abyssinia" – *Voprosy Istorii KPSS*, no. 3, 1969, p. 10.
56. N. Maiorskii, "Angliya i italo-abissinskaya voina", *Pravda*, 7.10.35; K. Radek, "Imperialisticheskie derzhavy i voina v Abissinii", *Izvestiya*, 8.10.35; and Radek, "Angliya, SSSR i mezhdunarodnoe polozhenie", ibid., 12.10.35.
57. Hoare (London) to Charles (Moscow), 16.10.35: *DBFP*, doc. 89.
58. Ibid., note 3.
59. Krestinsky (Moscow) to Litvinov (Geneva), 15.10.35: *DVP SSSR*, doc. 382.

60. Sipols, *Vneshnyaya Politika Sovetskogo Soyuza 1933–1939gg* (Moscow, 1980) p. 370.
61. *Documents on International Affairs*, pp. 206–7.
62. *DVP SSSR*, doc. 384; *Izvestiya*, 21.10.35.
63. See Chilston's record of a conversation with Litvinov on the train from Geneva – Chilston (Moscow) to Hoare (London), 25.10.35: *DBFP*, doc. 143.
64. Schulenburg (Moscow) to Köpke (Berlin), 5.11.35: *DGFP*, vol. 4 (London, 1962), doc. 407; also Bullitt (Moscow) to Hull (Washington), 9.11.35: *FRUS*, p. 264.
65. K. Radek, "Na polyakh srazhenii v diplomaticheskom fronte", *Izvestiya*, 6.12.35.
66. P. Lisovskii, "Italo-abissinskaya voina", *Mirovoe Khozyaistvo i Mirovaya Politika*, no. 10, October 1935, p. 20. The journal appeared on the 17 November.
67. Hoare (London) to Chilston (Moscow), 11.11.35: *DBFP*, doc. 207.
68. K. Radek, "Liga Natsii i razdel Abissinii", *Izvestiya*, 15.12.35. The term "surprise" was used in the editorial in *Le Journal de Moscou*, 24.12.35.
69. K. Radek, "Otstavka sera Samyuelya Khora", *Izvestiya*, 20.12.35.
70. Litvinov (Moscow) to Potemkin (Geneva), 15.12.35: *DVP SSSR*, doc. 447.
71. Litvinov (Moscow) to Potemkin (Geneva), 16.12.35: ibid., doc. 448.
72. Potemkin (Geneva) to Moscow, 19.12.35: ibid., doc. 452.
73. Edmond (Geneva) to London, 19.12.35: *DBFP*, doc. 403 (enclosure).
74. Source cited in note 81.
75. Shtein (Rome) to Moscow, 24.12.35: *DVP SSSR*, doc. 454.
76. Edmond (Geneva) to London, 19.12.35: *DBFP*, doc. 403 (enclosure).
77. L. Tillett, "The Soviet Role in League Sanctions Against Italy, 1935–6", *The American Slavic and East European Review*, 1956, vol. xv, pp. 11–16; also *Vneshnyaya Torgovlya SSSR v Gody Dovoennykh Pyatiletok (1929–1940): Statisticheskii Sbornik* (Moscow, 1968).
78. Eden (London) to Chilston (Moscow), 30.1.36: *DBFP*, doc. 488.
79. Surits (Berlin) to Krestinsky (Moscow), 27.1.36: *DVP SSSR*, vol. XXI, doc. 29.
80. Eden's conversation with Potemkin, 2.3.36 – Edmond (Geneva) to London, 3.3.36: *DBFP*, vol. 16, doc. 7.
81. E. Varga, "Italiya i Angliya v bor'be za Abissiniyu", *Mirovoe Khozyaistvo i Mirovaya Politika*, no. 2, 17.2.36, pp. 5–30.
82. Shtein (Rome) to Moscow, 30.3.36: *DVP SSSR*, p. 736.
83. The substance of a message delivered by a special envoy from Abyssinia – Eden (London) to Barton (Addis Ababa), 3.4.36: *DBFP*, doc. 243.
84. Litvinov (Moscow) to Potemkin (Geneva), 5.4.36: *DVP SSSR*, loc. cit.
85. Litvinov (Moscow) to Shtein (Rome), 5.4.36: ibid., doc. 118.
86. Editorial, "DEUX FRONTS", *Le Journal de Moscou*, 14.4.36.
87. Eden (London) to MacKillop (Moscow), 28.4.36: *DBFP*, doc. 278.
88. Editorial, "La prochaine session du conseil de la SDN", *Le Journal de Moscou*, 5.5.36.
89. Litvinov (Geneva) to Moscow, 13.5.36: *DVP SSSR*, p. 749.
90. Parker, "Great Britain . . .", p. 330.
91. *Documents on International Affairs*, pp. 542–3.

92. Krestinsky (Moscow) to Shtein (Rome), 17.7.36: *DVP SSSR*, doc. 223.

CHAPTER 6 THE LIMITS TO CO-OPERATION WITH FRANCE, 1935–36

1. E. Varga, "Kon'yunktura germanskogo narodnogo khozyaistva i podgotovka k voine", *Mirovoe Khozyaistvo i Mirovaya Politika*, no. 6, 1934, pp. 118–28; also the same author's "Germaniya na povorote", ibid., no. 8–9, 1934, pp. 159–75; and "Germaniya pri 'novom plane'", ibid., no. 11, 1934, pp. 16–33.
2. Prof. M. Bogolepov, "Finansovoe pokhmel'e tret'ei imperii", *Izvestiya*, 27.10.35.
3. *The Economist*, 5.10.35.
4. Dm. Bukhartsev, "Gosudarstvennaya kon'yunktura tret'ei imperii na ushcherbe", *Izvestiya*, 27.11.35.
5. Stomonyakov's record of the conversation, 17.3.34: *DVP SSSR*, vol. XVII, doc. 82.
6. The trade agreement was signed on the 20th March: ibid., doc. 85.
7. Ibid., pp. 785–6.
8. Litvinov's record of a conversation with Nadolny, 28.3.34: ibid., doc. 94.
9. Schulenburg's record of the conversation, 8.5.35: *DGFP*, Series C, vol. 3, (London, 1950) doc. 78.
10. Editorial, *Le Journal de Moscou*, 25.5.35.
11. Ibid., 1.6.35.
12. *Cmd.* 4930.
13. "Anglo-germanskoe soglashenie o rasshirenii morskikh vooruzhenii", *Pravda*, 19.6.35.
14. Editorial, *Le Journal de Moscou*, 22.6.35.
15. Clerk (Paris) to Hoare (London), 17.6.35: *DBFP*, vol. 13, doc. 343; and Clerk (Paris) to Hoare (London), 18.6.35: ibid., doc. 345.
16. Hoare (London) to Drummond (Rome), 19.6.35: ibid., doc. 352.
17. Clerk (Paris) to Hoare (London), 19.6.35: *DBFP*, doc. 355.
18. Interim, "Frantsuzskaya kritika anglo-germanskogo soglasheniya", *Izvestiya*, 19.6.35.
19. K. Radek, "Anglo-germanskoe morskoe soglashenie i proryv anglo-frantsuzskogo fronta", ibid., 21.6.35.
20. Igor Bogolepov, "Une Menace dans la Mer Baltique", *Le Journal de Moscou*, 20.7.35: and editorial, ibid., 27.7.35.
21. Clerk (Paris) to Hoare (London), 19.6.35: *DBFP*, doc. 353.
22. Potemkin (Paris) to Litvinov (Moscow), 26.6.35: *DVP SSSR*, vol. XVIII, doc. 289.
23. *Inprecorr*, 18.5.35.
24. Ibid., 11.1.36.
25. Litvinov (Moscow) to Potemkin (Paris), 26.6.35: ibid., pp. 646–7.
26. Litvinov (Moscow) to Surits (Berlin), 27.6.35: ibid., p. 647.
27. Schacht's minute of a conversation with Kandelaki and Friedrichson, 15.7.35: *DGFP*, doc. 211; the Soviet documents omit any reference to this episode.

28. K. Radek, "Ce qui se passe en Allemagne", *Le Journal de Moscou*, 16.8.35.
29. A.S. Blank, *V Serdtse' Tret'ego Reikha'* (Moscow, 1974), p. 73; also, K.H. Biernat and L. Krashaar, *Organizatsiya Shul'tse-Boizena-Kharnaka v Antifashistskoi Bor'be* (Moscow, 1974) p. 38. It appears that Schulze-Boysen in the Aviation Ministry was also supplying information to the Russians, though the evidence indicates that he began doing so only from 1938: ibid., pp. 38 and 48.
30. Potemkin (Paris) to Moscow, 11.9.35: *DVP SSSR*, doc. 361.
31. Source cited in chapter 5, note 28.
32. S. Yu. Prunitsa, "Za edinstvo demokraticheskikh sil Chekhoslovakii v bor'be protiv reaktsii i fashistskoi agressii", *VII Kongress Kominterna i Bor'ba za Sozdanie Narodnogo Fronta v Stranakh Tsentral'noi i Yugo-Vostochnoi Evropy*, ed. A. Kh. Klevanskii *et al.* (Moscow, 1977) pp. 312–13.
33. K. Gotval'd, "Za pravil'noe provedenie linii VII kongressa Kominterna (k s" ezdu KP Chekhoslovakii)", *Kommunisticheskii Internatsional*, no. 2, 25.1.36, pp. 15–32.
34. Surits (Berlin) to Moscow, 27.10.35: *DVP SSSR*, p. 663.
35. Litvinov (Moscow) to Potemkin (Paris), 28.10.35: ibid., doc. 394.
36. Litvinov (Moscow) to Potemkin (Paris), 29.10.35: ibid., doc. 395.
37. Schulenburg (Moscow) to Bülow (Berlin), 28.10.35: *DGFP*, doc. 383.
38. Litvinov (Moscow) to Potemkin (Paris), 4.11.35: *DVP SSSR*, p. 667.
39. Schulenburg (Moscow) to Köpke (Berlin), 11.11.35: *DGFP*, doc. 407.
40. Surits refers to these instructions in a letter to Litvinov, 28.11.35: *DVP SSSR*, doc. 424.
41. Surits (Berlin) to Moscow, 22.11.25: ibid., p. 666.
42. Potemkin (Paris) to Moscow, 22.11.35: ibid., doc. 414.
43. Source cited in note 40.
44. *DGFP*, doc. 439 and 453; see also *Survey*, no. 49, October 1963, pp. 128–31.
45. Surits (Berlin) to Litvinov (Moscow), 13.12.35: *DVP SSSR*, p. 671.
46. Surits (Berlin) to Krestinsky (Moscow), 17.12.35: ibid.
47. Litvinov (Moscow) to Surits (Berlin), 19.12.35: ibid., doc. 450.
48. Radek, "Penelope", *Izvestiya*, 1.1.36.
49. Editorial, "La diplomatie européenne réfléchit", *Le Journal de Moscou*, 7.1.36.
50. *DVP SSSR*, vol. XIX, appendix 1.
51. Schulenburg (Moscow) to Berlin, 11.1.36: *DGFP*, vol. 4, doc. 489.
52. "Bor'ba za mir i oborona Sovetskogo Soyuza", *Pravda*, 12.1.36.
53. Editorial, "La politique des bluffs et la politique de la paix", *Le Journal de Moscou*, 13.1.36.
54. *Pravda*, 16.1.36.
55. "Granitsy nashei rodiny nepristupny!", ibid.
56. Radek, "Mezhdunarodnoe polozhenie i politika SSSR", *Izvestiya*, 12.1.36.
57. Source cited in note 50.
58. Alphand (Moscow) to Laval (Paris), 14.1.36: *DDF*, 2nd Series, vol.1, (Paris, 1963), doc. 46.
59. Source cited in note 51.
60. Krestinsky (Moscow) to Surits (Berlin), 11.1.36: *DVP SSSR*, vol. XIX, doc. 12.
61. Ibid.

62. Source cited in note 50.
63. Source cited in note 60.
64. Memorandum by an official in department 2, 18.1.36: *DGFP*, doc. 502.
65. *Izvestiya*, 17.1.36.
66. Surits (Berlin) to Krestinsky (Moscow), 27.1.36: *DVP SSSR*, doc. 29.
67. Source cited in chapter 5, note 78.
68. "Notes sur les conversations de Paris", 30 January–8 February, 1936: *DDF*, doc. 156.
69. Editorial, "La lutte pour la sécurité", *Le Journal de Moscou*, 18.2.36.
70. Litvinov (Moscow) to Potemkin (Paris), 23.2.36: *DVP SSSR*, doc. 51.
71. Ibid., doc. 59.
72. Potemkin (Geneva) to Moscow, 3.3.36: ibid., p. 733.
73. Potemkin's record of the conversation, 7.3.36: ibid., doc. 68.
74. Litvinov (Moscow) to Potemkin (Paris), 9.3.36: ibid., doc. 70.
75. François-Poncet (Berlin) to Flandin (Paris), 10.3.36: *DDF*, doc. 364.
76. Editorial, "Ratifikatsiya franko-sovetskogo dogovora frantsuzskim senatom", *Pravda*, 14.3.36.
77. Editorial, "Ratifikatsiya franko-sovetskogo pakta frantsuzskim senatom", *Izvestiya*, 14.3.36.
78. Duroselle, *La Décadence*, pp. 173–7.
79. *Izvestiya*, 20.3.36; also, *DVP SSSR*, doc. 87.
80. Eden (London) to Chilston (Moscow), 12.3.36: *DBFP*, vol. 16, doc. 71.
81. See E. H. Carr, *Socialism in One Country*, vol. 3, 1 (London, 1964) ch. 29.
82. Minute by Lord Cranborne on British commitments in Europe, 17.3.36: *DBFP*, doc. 122; for Sargent's views: ibid., doc. 122, note p. 156.
83. Memorandum by the XI Marquis of Lothian, 4.6.36: *Neville Chamberlain Papers (NC)* 7/7/4.
84. *DVP SSSR*, doc. 90; also *Izvestiya*, 24.3.36.
85. Krestinsky (Moscow) to Litvinov (London), 22.3.36: ibid., doc. 97.
86. Potemkin's record of a conversation with Mandel, Minister of Posts and Telegraphs, 18.3.36: *DVP SSSR*, doc. 89.
87. Potemkin (Paris) to Krestinsky (Moscow), 26.3.36: ibid., doc. 104.
88. Krestinsky (Moscow) to Surits (Berlin), 26.3.36: ibid., doc.
89. *VII Kongress Kommunisticheskogo Internatsionala i Bor'ba Protiv Fashizma i Voiny (Sbornik Dokumentov)* (Moscow, 1975) pp. 421–32.
90. "Bor'ba za sokhranenie mira", *Kommunisticheskii Internatsional*, no. 7, 10.4.36, pp. 7–15.
91. Litvinov (Moscow) to Maisky (London), 5.4.36: *DVP SSSR*, doc. 117.
92. Ibid., doc. 143; also *DGFP*, vol. 5, doc. 302 and enclosure.
93. Memorandum by Hencke of Department 2, 6.5.36: ibid., doc. 312.
94. Minute by Herbert Göring, 13.5.36: ibid., doc. 341 (enclosure).
95. J. Duclos, "Réponses aux questions posées par les journalistes à la Mutualité", *Cahiers du Bolchévisme*, no. 8–9, 15.5.36, p. 496.
96. Ibid., p. 500.
97. *Inprecorr*, 6.6.36.
98. André Marty, "Obshchee polozhenie vo Frantsii", *Kommunisticheskii Internatsional*, no. 11–12, 25.6.36, pp. 37–48; similar sentiments were expressed by G. Monmousseau in "Une étape historique du mouvement ouvrier français", *Cahiers du Bolchévisme*, no. 10–11, 15.6.36, pp. 625–30.

99. *Inprecorr*, 20.6.36; also, see the summary of Politburo proceedings of the PCF, 4.6.36: *Cahiers du Bolchévisme*, nos 10–11, 15.6.36, pp. 753–6.
100. G. Luciani, *Six Ans à Moscou* (Paris, 1937) pp. 417–18.
101. Procès-verbal, 6.2.36: *Cahiers du Bolchévisme*, no. 3–4, 15.2.36, p. 228.
102. K. Shirinya, *Strategiya i Taktika Kominterna v Bor'be Protiv Fashizma i Voiny (1934–1939gg)* (Moscow, 1979) p. 157.
103. G. Dimitrov, "Le problème français", translated and reprinted in *Cahiers d'Histoire de l'Institut Maurice Thorez*, no. 34, 1980, pp. 107–11.
104. Krestinsky (Moscow) to Surits (Berlin), 4.8.36: *DVP SSSR*, doc. 239.
105. See *Pravda* and *Izvestiya*, 17.7.36.

CHAPTER 7 THE OUTBREAK OF THE SPANISH CIVIL WAR, 1936–37

1. There is a superabundance of literature on the Spanish civil war. The most balanced account is still that of H. Thomas, *The Spanish Civil War* (3rd edn., London, 1977), though even this work relies too much on dubious memoirs. On Soviet involvement, the pioneering works of D. Cattell, *Communism and the Spanish Civil War* (California, 1955) and *Soviet Diplomacy and the Spanish Civil War* (California, 1957), are still sound reading, though E. H. Carr's posthumous work on the Comintern and the Spanish civil war has to a significant extent further deepened our knowledge of the subject.
2. Duroselle, *La Décadence*, pp. 301–2.
3. J. Coverdale, *Italian Intervention in the Spanish Civil War* (Princeton, 1975) and A. Viñas, *La Alemania nazi y el 18 julio* (2nd edn., Madrid, 1977) are the most up-to-date and reliable accounts available.
4. J. Modesto, *Soy del Quinto Regimiento* (Paris, 1969) p. 45.
5. A. Carabantes and E. Cimorra, *Un mito llamado Pasionaria* (Barcelona, 1982) p. 119. An unnamed representative of the Comintern reported to Moscow that after the first successes "a feeling of complacent optimism . . . spread among the workers. . . . The Party has not only taken a position against such a tendency, but has itself encouraged it, daily announcing complete and final victory for the following day and thus creating the illusion that the enemy has no strength whatsoever and that he is demoralised for good". This was also the opinion of Vittorio Codovilla – nom de guerre Medina – the Italian-born Argentinian, heading the Comintern delegation, the PCE's "nanny" in Spain: M. Meshcheryakov, *Vsya Zhizn' – Bor'ba (O Khose Diase)* (Moscow, 1971) pp. 109–10.
6. M. Kol'tsov, "Ispanskii dnevnik", *Novyi Mir*, April 1938, p. 6. Although the claim is frequently made that Kol'tsov was some sort of special agent for Stalin in Spain, this is doubtful. "Kol'tsov would not have been Kol'tsov, if he had remained within the limitations of purely newspaper, journalistic work", his younger brother has recalled. Kol'tsov's assumption of the role of military-political adviser to the Republican forces appears to have been merely a logical extension of his Moscow moonlighting as taxi-driver, pilot, parachute-jumper etc., which gave his writing on such subjects that touch of realism lost to others. "As far as I know", his brother

has written, "no one especially delegated such work to Kol'tsov. He went to Spain merely as a writer, *Pravda* correspondent": "Rasskazyvaet mladshii brat Mikhail Kol'tsova, Boris Efimov, narodnyi khudozhnik respubliki", *Mikhail Kol'tsov, Kakim On Byl: Vospominaniya* (Moscow, 1965) p. 65. Other journalists also became caught up in events: B. Makaseev, "Iz khroniki geroicheskei respubliki", *My – Internatsionalisty: Vospominaniya Sovetskikh Dobrovol'tsev-uchastnikov Natsional'no-Revolyutsionnoi Voiny v Ispanii* (Moscow, 1975) p. 131.

7. I. Erenburg, *Sobranie Sochinenii v Devyati Tomakh*, vol. 9, *Lyudi, Gody, Zhizn'* (Moscow, 1967) p. 100.
8. *Izvestiya*, 29.7.33: *DVP SSSR*, vol. XVI, doc. 258.
9. N. Lunacharskaya-Rozenel', "Poslednii god", *Prometei*, 1966, pp. 216–33; also N. Lunacharskaya-Rozenel', *Pamyat' Serdtsa: Vospominaniya* (3rd, enlarged edn, Moscow, 1975) pp. 430–52.
10. *DVP SSSR*, vol. XIX, pp. 237–8.
11. Ibid., p. 738.
12. *Izvestiya*, 29.8.36.
13. Ibid., 1.9.36.
14. N. Kuznetsov, *Na Dalekom Meridiane* (Moscow, 1971) pp. 9, 16, 26–7.
15. "La URSS y la guerra de España", M. Azaña, *Obras Completas*, III (Mexico, 1967) pp. 475–9.
16. Editorial, "Un rideau de fummie qui ne cache rien", *Le Journal de Moscou*, 27.7.36.
17. Carabantes, Cimorra, *Un mito*, p. 125.
18. *Rundschau*, 23.7.36.
19. *Mezhdunarodnaya Solidarnost' Trudyashchikhsya v Bor'be s Fashizmom, Protiv Razvyazyvaniya Vtoroi Mirovoi Voiny (1933–1937)*, ed. A. Longinov *et al.* (Moscow, 1961), doc. 251.
20. *Inprecorr*, 1.8.36.
21. *Mezhdunarodnaya*, doc. 252.
22. Ibid., doc. 255.
23. Ibid., doc. 256.
24. Ibid., doc. 253.
25. *l'Humanité*, 27.7.36.
26. Mendes (Warsaw) to Monteiro (Lisbon), 6.8.36: *Dez Anos de Politica Externa (1936–1947)*, vol. 3 (Lisbon, 1964), doc. 110.
27. Kol'tsov, "Ispanskii dnevnik", p. 5.
28. Henderson (Moscow) to Hull (Washington), 4.8.36: *FRUS*, 1936, vol. 2 (Washington, 1954) p. 461.
29. Record of the conversation by Veinberg, head of the third Western Department, 5.8.36: *DVP SSSR*, vol. XIX, doc. 242.
30. Quoted in Coverdale, *Italian Intervention*, p. 94.
31. Payart (Moscow) to Delbos (Paris), 6.8.36: *DDF*, vol. 3 (Paris, 1966), doc. 89.
32. Krestinsky (Moscow) to Shtein (Rome) 7.8.36: *DVP SSSR*, doc. 244.
33. Kol'tsov, "Ispanskii dnevnik", p. 6. By the end of October the sum amounted to 47 595 000 roubles: *Trud*, 27.10.36. In the period from 1936 to 1939 more than 274 million roubles were so collected: M. Meshcheryakov, *Ispanskaya Respublika i Komintern (Natsional'no-revolyutsionnaya voina ispanskogo*

naroda i politika Kommunisticheskogo Internatsionala 1936–1939gg). (Moscow, 1981) p. 49.

34. Krestinsky (Moscow) to Maisky (London), 7.8.36: *DVP SSSR*, doc. 243.
35. Editorial, "Pour une neutralité effective", *Le Journal de Moscou*, 18.8.36.
36. Henderson (Moscow) to Hull (Washington), 29.8.36: *FRUS*, p. 515.
37. *DVP SSSR*, doc. 249.
38. *Izvestiya*, 30.8.36.
39. Editorial, "Pour conjurer la guerre", *Le Journal de Moscou*, 25.8.36.
40. "Nevmeshatel'stvo v ispanskie dela i manevry germanskogo fashizma", *Izvestiya*, 26.8.36.
41. Kuznetsov, *Na Dalekom Meridiane*, pp. 14–16.
42. Shtein (Rome) to Moscow, 9.9.36: *DVP SSSR*, doc. 262.
43. A. Rodimtsev, *Pod Nebom Ispanii* (Moscow, 1968) pp. 13–19.
44. Conversation between Litvinov and the French ambassador on the 13 November 1936 – Coulondre (Moscow) to Delbos (Paris), 16.11.36: *DDF*, doc. 497.
45. Schulenburg (Moscow) to Berlin, 12.10.36: *DGFP*, Series D, vol. 3 (London, 1951), doc. 97.
46. Payart (Moscow) to Delbos (Paris), 2.10.36: *DDF*, vol. 4, (Paris, 1967) doc. 153.
47. *Pravda*, 23.8.36 and 24.8.36.
48. Coulondre (Moscow) to Delbos (Paris), 15.12.36: *DDF*, doc. 153.
49. K. Shirinya, I. Ksenofontov, "G. Dimitrov i natsional' no-revolyutsionnaya voina v Ispanii", *Georgii Dimitrov – Vydayushchiisya Deyatel' Kommunisticheskoi Dvizheniya* (Moscow, 1972), p. 356. The Comintern executive met from the 16 to the 19 September 1936: K. Shirinya, *Strategiya i Taktika Kominterna v Bor'be Protiv Fashizma i Voiny (1934–1939gg)* (Moscow, 1979) p. 148.
50. Voelckers (Alicante) to Berlin, 29.9.36: *DGFP*, doc. 89; Kol'tsov arrived in Alicante the day after its arrival: Kol'tsov, "Ispanskii dnevnik", pp. 71–2. Care should, however, be taken with respect to other German reports of Soviet arms shipments – notably those from Turkey. As British Military Intelligence officers noted, the "source in Istanbul" who supplied the information to Germans and Italians was "most unreliable" in respect to detailing Soviet cargo bound for Spain; "on two or three occasions suspect ships have been taken into Palma or Ceuta and searched without result" – Napier (War Office) to Howard (Foreign Office), 2.7.37: *DBFP*, 2nd Series, vol. 19 (London, 1982), doc. 11.
51. V. Sipols, "SSSR i problema mira i bezopasnost' v vostochnoi Evrope (1933–1938gg)", *SSSR v Bor'be Protiv Fashistskoi Agressii 1933–1945*, ed. A. Narochnitskii et al. (Moscow, 1976) p. 51; *Istoriya Kommunisticheskoi Partii Sovetskogo Soyuza*, vol. 4, 2 (Moscow, 1971) p. 301.
52. *The Crimes of the Stalin Era: Special Report to the 20th Congress of the CPSU by Nikita S. Khrushchev* (New York, 1956) p. 23.
53. *VII Kongress*, pp. 452–3.
54. "The Treachery of the POUM", 23.1.36: L. Trotsky, *The Spanish Revolution (1931–39)* (New York, 1973), doc. 48.
55. See, B. Bolloten, *LA REVOLUCIÓN ESPAÑOLA: SUS orígenes, la izquierda y la lucha por el poder durante la guerra civil 1936–1939* (revised and enlarged edition, Barcelona, 1980) p. 534.
56. See Ibid., ch. 27.

57. Erenburg, *Sobranie*, p. 114.
58. Ibid., p. 115.
59. Ibid., p. 118.
60. *Izvestiya*, 3.10.36.
61. Ibid., 4.10.36.
62. The British consul-general's conversation with Antonov-Ovseenko, 12.10.36 – King (Barcelona) to London, 13.10.36: *FO* 371/20543.
63. K. Meretskov, *Na Sluzhbe Narodu* (Moscow, 1968), p. 129.
64. M. Meshcheryakov, *Ispanskaya Respublika*, pp. 16–17.
65. Meretskov, *Na Sluzhbe*, p. 150.
66. Krestinsky (Moscow) to Kagan (London), 4.10.36: *DVP SSSR*, doc. 292.
67. Litvinov (Geneva) to Moscow, 5.10.36: ibid., doc. 294.
68. *DVP SSSR*, doc. 296; I. Maisky, *Spanish Notebooks* (London, 1966) p. 47.
69. *Izvestiya*, 23.9.36.
70. Ibid., 8.10.36.
71. A Viñas, *El Oro de Moscú: Alfa y omega de un mito franquista* (Barcelona, 1979), p. 157.
72. Kuznetsov, *Na Dalekom*, p. 127.
73. Surits (Berlin) to Krestinsky (Moscow), 12.10.36: *DVP SSSR*, doc. 305.
74. Source cited in note 72.
75. Kol'tsov, "Ispanskii dnevnik", pp. 96–7.
76. *Izvestiya*, 16.10.36; *DVP SSSR*, doc. 305.
77. Largo Caballero to Rozenberg, 15.10.36: M. Pascua, "Oro español en Moscú", *Cuadernos Para el Diálogo* (Madrid), vol. 81–2, July 1970, p. 17.
78. See Litvinov's speech to the congress of soviets, 28.11.36: *DVP SSSR*, appendix 2; buttressed later by an editorial, "Vneshnyaya politika SSSR neizmenna!", *Pravda*, 29.11.36.
79. Surits (Berlin) to Moscow, 27.11.36: *DVP SSSR*, p. 779. The Soviet volume of diplomatic correspondence for 1936 stresses that this information on the contents of the pact came from foreign diplomatic sources. The British ambassador Phipps certainly kept Surits informed of these developments. However, a TASS communiqué published in *Pravda* on the 18 November, immediately prior to the signature of the pact, suggests that Moscow already knew of the pact's secret protocol aimed against the USSR. That the Russians were so informed by their agent in Tokyo, Sorge, who had access to German embassy materials, is asserted by Yu. Korol'kov, *Chelovek, Dlya Kotorogo Ne Bylo Tain (Rikhard Zorge)* (Moscow, 1965), p. 108. One must, however, be wary of some of the Soviet literature on spies – it can be as fictitious as its Western counterpart; though this particular piece of information on Sorge is confirmed by the more authoritative F. Volkov, who has had access to the archives: "Legendy i deistvitel'nost' o Rikharde Zorge", *Voenno-Istoricheskii Zhurnal*, no. 12, 1966, p. 100.
80. Dirksen (Tokyo) to Berlin, 23.12.36: *DGFP*, Series C, vol. 6 (London, 1983), doc. 105.
81. Payart (Moscow) to Delbos (Paris), 31.10.36: *DDF*, vol. 3 doc. 429; also Henderson (Moscow) to Hull (Washington) , 24.10.36: *FRUS*, p. 542.
82. For the briefing Coulondre received from Delbos on this theme, prior to taking up the post of ambassador to Moscow in early November 1936: R. Coulondre, *De Staline à Hitler: Souvenirs de Deux Ambassades 1936–1939* (Paris, 1950) p. 13.

83. Coulondre (Moscow) to Delbos (Paris), 12.11.36: *DDF*, doc. 472; Coulondre (Moscow) to Delbos (Paris), 16.11.36: ibid., doc. 497.
84. See, for example, Delbos' record of a conversation with the Italian ambassador, Cerruti, 31.10.36 – Delbos (Paris) to Corbin (London), 4.11.36: *DDF*, doc. 440 (enclosure iii).
85. Alexandrovsky (Prague) to Moscow, 23.10.36: *DVP SSSR*, doc. 328.
86. Litvinov (Moscow) to Alexandrovsky (Prague), 25.10.36: ibid., doc. 331.
87. *Pravda*, 29.11.36.
88. Editorial, "Vneshnyaya politika SSSR neizmenna!", ibid.
89. Editorial, "Obvinitel'nyi akt protiv fashizma", ibid., 3.12.36.
90. Ibid., 1.12.36.
91. Surits (Berlin) to Moscow, 11.9.36: *DVP SSSR*, doc. 762.
92. Ibid.
93. "It has been decided not to send a note", Krestinsky informed Surits brusquely on the 19 September; the phrasing, perhaps deliberately, left it uncertain whether this was a decision taken within the Narkomindel or by Stalin alone or by Stalin and the Politburo (or its foreign affairs committee) – ibid., p. 762.
94. A. Noritskii, "Posrednichestvo v Ispanii?", *Izvestiya*, 11.12.36; such sentiments were similarly expressed in the editorial, "Yasnaya pozitsiya sovetskogo pravitel'stva", *Pravda*, 11.12.36.
95. The words of the French ambassador to Germany, in conversation with Gaus at the Ausamt – François-Poncet (Berlin) to Delbos (Paris), 26.12.36: *DDF*, vol. 4, doc. 211.
96. *Pravda*, 13.1.37.
97. Phipps' annual report on heads of foreign missions in Berlin, 15.1.37: *FO* 371/20732.
98. For the text: *DBFP*, vol. XVII (London, 1979), doc. 530.
99. "Agentstvo Uik o mezhdunarodnom polozhenii", *Pravda*, 16.1.37.
100. This was quoted in an editorial, "Podleishie iz podlykh", ibid., 24.1.37.
101. Editorial, "Vragi chelovechestva, podzhigateli voiny", ibid., 1.2.37.
102. I. Yermashev, "Angliya mezhdu Zapadom i Vostokom", ibid., 4.2.37.
103. D. Borissov, "L'Aide Économique à l'Allemagne", *Le Journal de Moscou*, 2.2.37.
104. Davies (Moscow) to Hull (Washington), 6.2.37: J. Davies, *Mission to Moscow* (London, 1942) p. 49.
105. The quotation comes from Yurenev (Berlin) to Litvinov (Moscow), 31.7.37: *DVP SSSR*, doc. 276. It has been used in this context because the Russians have chosen not to publish the documents relevant to the Kandelaki soundings earlier that year.
106. Memorandum by the head of the Economic Policy Division 4, Schnurre, 19.10.36: *DGFP*, doc. 615.
107. Contained in Berlin to Schulenburg (Moscow), 17.2.37: *AA* 1907H/429293, 429299-30.
108. Neurath to Schacht, 11.2.37: ibid., 429296-7.
109. Schulenburg (Moscow) to Berlin, 18.2.37: *DGFP*, doc. 213.
110. Neurath (Berlin) to Schulenburg (Moscow), 19.2.37: ibid., doc. 218; Schulenburg (Moscow) to Berlin, 22.2.37: ibid., doc. 221; and memorandum by Schulenburg, 6.3.37: ibid., doc. 253.

111. Bullitt (Paris) to Hull (Washington), 20.2.37: *FRUS*, 1937, vol. I (Washington, 1954), p. 53.
112. The evidence is only in the form of extracts from letters written to Ivy, in 1938–9, quoted by Z. Sheinis in his " 'Moemu dal'neishemu potomstvu . . . '. K 90-letiyu so dnya rozhdeniya M.M. Litvinova", *Yunost'*, no. 7, 1966, pp. 88–9. A biography of Ivy has now appeared, based on her papers: J. Carswell, *The Exile: A Life of Ivy Litvinov* (London, 1983).
113. I. Erenburg, *Sobranie*, pp. 708–9.
114. Ibid.

CHAPTER 8 THE YEAR OF THE TERROR, 1937

1. "O nedostatkakh partiinoi raboty i merakh likvidatsii trotskistskikh i inykh dvurushnikov", 3.3.37: *Pravda*, 29.3.37.
2. Coulondre (Moscow) to Delbos (Paris), 15.11.36: *DDF*, doc. 486.
3. Published in its French translation by Spain's former ambassador to Paris, Luis Araquistain: "Moscow 'Counsel' to Spain Revealed", *New York Times*, 4.6.39; a photoprint appears in *Guerra y Revolución en España 1936–1939*, vol. 2, ed. D. Ibárruri *et al.* (Moscow, 1966); illustration between pp. 96 and 97.
4. F. Largo Caballero, *Mis Recuerdos: Cartas a un amigo* (Mexico, 1976 edn) p. 181.
5. See the memoirs of his daughter: N. Murray, *I Spied for Stalin* (London, 1950) pp. 82–3.
6. *Sobranie Zakonov i Rasporyazhenii*, ii no. 11, 10.3.37, 53.
7. Ibid.
8. For evidence: M. Rozenberg, "La lutte de l'Espagne democratique", *Le Journal de Moscou*, 10.4.37; Louis Fischer met him in the Metropol Café in August 1937 – he perished sometime shortly thereafter: L. Fischer, *Men and Politics*, p. 413.
9. *S.Z.*, no. 15, 27.4.37, 75.
10. Ibid., p. 231.
11. Unfortunately Soviet appointments were only intermittently reported during the years of the terror; my evidence for this comes only from the source cited below in note 12.
12. Murray, *I Spied*, p.113.
13. "V Narkomindele. 1922–1939: Interv'yu s E.A. Gnedinym", *Pamyat'*, no. 5, (Paris, 1982), p. 379.
14. *Izvestiya*, 21.3.37.
15. Ibid., 1.4.37.
16. "Vopros Komissaru Inostrannykh Del tov.Litvinov", ibid., 23.4.37.
17. "Otvet Narodnogo Komissara Inostrannykh Del tov. M.M. Litvinova na vopros inzhinera A. Khvatkova", ibid., 24.4.37.
18. Yu. Denike, "Litvinov i Stalinskaya vneshnyaya politika", *Sotsialisticheskii Vestnik*, no. 5, May 1952, pp. 86–7; the only qualification one might add is that Potemkin had a reputation for indulging in intrigue.
19. "V Narkomindele . . .", p. 381.
20. Mackillop (Moscow) to Vereker (London), 3.5.37: *FO* 371/21100.
21. *Sobranie*, no. 21, 5.6.37, p. 630.

22. Fischer, *Men and Politics*, p. 414.
23. Diary entry, 20.5.37: M. Azaña, *Memorias Politicas y de Guerra*, vol. IV (Madrid, 1981) p. 9.
24. P. Malerbe, Tuñon de Lara et al., *Historia de España, IX – La Crisis del Estado: Dictadura, República, Guerra (1923–1939)* (Barcelona, 1981) p. 359; for a more detailed analysis, turn to H. Thomas, *The Spanish Civil War*, pp. 654–5.
25. Azaña, *Memorias*, p. 13.
26. Thomas, *The Spanish Civil War*, pp. 656–61.
27. Ibid., p. 662.
28. Azaña, *Memorias*, pp. 38–9.
29. Meshcheryakov, *Vsya Zhizn'*, pp. 144–5.
30. "Their policy", complained Prieto to Azaña on the 29 June 1937, "consists of taking control over all the levers of power [*resortes del Estado*]. . . . The Commissariat of War is an organ almost entirely Communist, where Alvarez del Vayo acts as a puppet. They have won over large numbers in the army, inviting them to enter the Party, with promises, or forcing them to with threats": Azaña, *Memorias*, p. 105. Similarly, in Catalonia, the head of the PSUC, Comorera, raised such fears among other party leaders by his heavy-handedness: ibid., pp. 292–3.
31. Meshcheryakov, *Vsya Zhizn'*, pp. 144–5.
32. Paolo Spriano, after a careful scrutiny of the PCI archives, which detail Togliatti's activities throughout the period, has refuted claims that Togliatti was involved. Togliatti did not arrive in Spain until early July 1937: P. Togliatti, *Opere*, IV, I (Rome, 1979) pp. xcii–xcv. Uncritical reliance on the recollections of former PCE notable Jesús Hernández has led many astray on this and other issues. One of the accused, Vittorio Vidali (nom de guerre Carlos Contreras) demolishes his accusations concerning involvement in the disappearance of Nin in his *La caduta della republica* (Milan, 1979) pp. 62–71.
33. The story can be followed in Azaña's record of events: entry, 22.7.37, *Memorias*, pp. 271–2; entry, 28.7.37: ibid., pp. 282–3; entry, 6.8.37: ibid., p. 300; entry, 18.10.37: ibid., pp. 488–9; and entry, 20.10.37: ibid., p. 493. Certainly 'Ignace Reiss', a leading Soviet Intelligence operative in Western Europe, who broke with the USSR in July 1937, held the NKVD responsible for the fate of Nin – see his letter to the Central Committee of the CPSU, 17.7.37: E. Poretsky, *Our Own People* (London, 1969) p. 2.
34. Mackillop (Moscow) to Eden (London), 15.6.37: *FO* 371/21104. For their role in the Opposition: *Trotsky Archives*, T 2990, cited in E. H. Carr, *Foundations of a Planned Economy 1926–1929*, vol. 2 (London, 1971) p. 5.
35. People's Commissariat of Justice of the USSR, *Report of Court Proceedings in the Case of the Anti-Soviet Trotskyite Centre* (Moscow, 1937) p. 105.
36. *Report*, p. 146.
37. Haslam, *Soviet Foreign Policy*, pp. 25–6, 72, 121–2.
38. M. Tukhachevsky, *Izbrannye Proizvedeniya*, ed. Biryuzov *et al.*, vol. 1 (Moscow, 1964) pp. 12–13.
39. Haslam, *Soviet Foreign Policy*, pp. 25–6 and 121–2.
40. The Soviet history of the Second World War, based on the Soviet Defence Ministry archives gives the figure of 1 100 000 for the end of 1936, rising to

more than 2 million by the end of August 1939: *Istoriya Vtoroi Mirovoi Voiny 1939–1945*, vol. 2, ed. G. Deborin et al. (Moscow, 1974) p. 199; the British military attaché in Moscow gave the figure of 1 300 000, evidently obtained from Soviet counterparts at the time, in his report of 18 April 1938: *FO* 371/22298.

41. Yu. Petrov, *Stroitel'stvo Politorganov, Partiinykh i Komsomol'skikh Organizatsii Armii i Flota* (Moscow, 1968) p. 235.
42. See T. Rigby, *Communist Party Membership in the USSR 1917–1967* (Princeton, 1968) pp. 200–20.
43. Petrov, *Stroitel'stvo*, p. 237; for the figure of 4.2 million, see his *Partiinoe Stroitel'stvo v Sovetskoi Armii i Flote* (Moscow, 1964) p. 298.
44. Petrov, *Stroitel'stvo*, p. 224.
45. Chilston (Moscow) to Eden (London), 19.4.37: *FO* 371/21100.
46. Hayes (MI 2, War Office) to Collier (Foreign Office), 1.10.37: *FO* 371/21104. This was a view shared by the Germans: J. von Herwarth, *Against Two Evils* (London, 1981) p. 57. The author was a junior diplomat at the German embassy in Moscow.
47. 3.3.37: *Pravda*, 29.3.37.
48. Petrov, *Partiinoe*, p. 299; this quotation does not appear in the published account of the speech which appeared in the Party journal, *Bol'shevik*, no. 8, 15.4.37, pp. 12–45 (published on the 16 April). At the foot of the first page of the article Molotov tells us that the article reproduced his speech "with small changes".
49. I. Lamkin, "Partiinoe sobranie voennoi akademii im. Frunze", *Krasnaya Zvezda*, 27.3.37.
50. Editorial, "Aktiv partiinykh i nepartiinykh bol'shevikov", ibid., 4.9.37.
51. Petrov, *Partiinoe*, p. 299.
52. Editorial, "Krasnoarmeiskaya prisyaga", *Pravda*, 28.4.37.
53. Petrov, *Partiinoe*, p. 303.
54. *S.Z.*, no. 31, 25.5.37, 126.
55. *Marshal Tukhachevskii: Vospominaniya Druzei i Soratnikov* (Moscow, 1965) p. 234.
56. Detailed in *Izvestiya*, 14.6.37.
57. Petrov, *Partiinoe*, pp. 299–300.
58. *Izvestiya*, 14.6.37.
59. *Marshal*, p. 234.
60. *Izvestiya*, 14.6.37.
61. *The Memoirs of Dr Eduard Beneš* (London, 1954) p. 47; an elaborate account appears in the recollections of Walter Schellenberg, formerly a German Intelligence officer. But there are problems with his account. As published it is not a complete translation of the original manuscript. Secondly, the author makes some elementary errors in describing these events; Tukhachevsky's arrest is mis-dated as the 4 June 1937: W. Schellenberg, *The Schellenberg Memoirs*, ed. L. Hagen (London, 1956) pp. 47–9.
62. Firebrace to Mackillop, 14.6.37: *FO* 371/21104.
63. Simon (military attaché, Moscow) to Daladier (Paris), 30.6.37: *DDF*, vol. 6 (Paris, 1970) doc. 162.
64. Schulenburg (Moscow) to Berlin, 14.6.37: *DGFP*, doc. 427.
65. 17.7.37: *FO* 371/21100.

66. Walker, 15.7.37: ibid.
67. Wavell's report, 10.9.36: *FO* 371/20352.
68. Mackillop (Moscow) to Eden (London), 15.6.37: *FO* 371/21104.
69. von Herwarth, *Against Two Evils*, p. 58.
70. To be discussed in a subsequent volume.
71. Simon (Moscow) to Daladier (Paris), 30.6.37: *DDF*, doc. 162.
72. Petrov, *Patiinoe*, p. 303 (note).
73. See pp. 168–9.
74. Report, 10.9.36: *FO* 371/20352.
75. Report, 18.4.38, enclosed in Chilston (Moscow) to Halifax (London) 19.4.38: *FO* 371/22298; also, "Report by the Chiefs of Staff Sub-committee of the CID on the comparison of the strength of Great Britain with that of certain other nations as at January 1938", 12.11.37: *DBFP*, vol. 19, doc. 316.
76. Report, 5.10.36: *DDF*, vol. 7 (Paris, 1972) doc. 343 (annexe).
77. "Note de l'Etat-Major de l'Armée", May 1937: *DDF*, vol. 5, doc. 480.
78. Report, 18.4.38: *FO* 371/22298.
79. von Herwarth, *Against Two Evils*, p. 115.
80. Henderson (Moscow) to Hull (Washington), 13.6.37: *FRUS*, p. 382.
81. Mackillop (Moscow) to Eden (London), 3.7.37: *FO* 371/21100.
82. Memorandum by Kennan, Washington, 24.11.37: *FRUS*, p. 447.
83. Chilston (Moscow) to London, 14.5.37: *FO* 371/21102.
84. Bogomolov's record of the conversation, Shanghai, 13.7.37: *DVP SSSR*, doc. 240.
85. Litvinov (Moscow) to Bogomolov (Shanghai?), 19.7.37: ibid., pp. 737–8.
86. Litvinov (Moscow) to Bogomolov (Shanghai?), 22.7.37: ibid.
87. Chilston (Moscow) to London, 14.5.37: *FO* 371/21102.
88. Entry, 22.7.37: Azaña, *Memorias*, p. 266.
89. Viñas, *El oro*, p. 341.
90. Entry, 6.8.37: Azaña, *Memorias*, p. 301.
91. Stomonyakov (Moscow) to Bogomolov (Nanking), 29.7.37: *DVP SSSR*, doc. 268; Litvinov (Moscow) to Bogomolov (Nanking), 31.7.37: ibid., doc. 274.
92. *Izvestiya*, 27–8 July 1937.
93. Editorial, "Les agresseurs s'entr'appellent", *Le Journal de Moscou*, 17.8.37.
94. The decision was recorded on the 7 April 1937: *S.Z.*, no. 15, 27.4.37, 75. By the 17 April Surits had received instructions to remain in Berlin until his successor, Yurenev, had arrived from Tokyo – Memorandum by Neurath, 17.4.37: *DGFP*, doc. 323.
95. Decision formally taken on the 16 June 1937: *S.Z.*, no. 26, 27.6.37, 176.
96. The decision with respect to Kandelaki was recorded on the 2 April: *Sobranie*, no. 16, 28.4.37, pp. 232–3; and with respect to Friedrichson, on the 16 April: ibid., no. 19, 17.5.37, pp. 618–19.
97. For Astakhov's activities as head of the Narkomindel press department: N. Basseches, *Stalin* (London, 1952) pp. 332–3; for his role in later developments and his character, see p. 24.
98. Nepomnyashchy was appointed on the 23 April: *S.Z.*, no. 19, 17.5.37, 118.
99. Surits (Berlin) to Moscow, 3.6.37: *DVP SSSR*, doc. 188.

100. Yurenev's record of the conversation, 7.7.37: *DVP SSSR*, doc. 231.
101. *Izvestiya*, 23.7.37.
102. Yurenev (Berlin) to Litvinov (Moscow), 31.7.37: *DVP SSSR*, doc. 276.
103. François-Poncet (Berlin) to Delbos (Paris), 22.7.37: *DDF*, vol. 6, doc. 259.
104. Entry, 13.8.37: Azaña, *Memorias*, p. 335.
105. From the Soviet Ministry of Defence archive: *Istoriya Vtoroi Mirovoi Voiny 1939–1945*, vol. 2 (Moscow, 1974) pp. 53–4.
106. P. de Azcárate, *Mi embajada en Londres durante la guerra civil española* (Barcelona, 1976) p. 187.
107. *Istoriya Vtoroi*, p. 54.
108. *DBFP*, doc. 94.
109. Delbos (Paris) to Cambon (London), 29.8.37: *DDF*, doc. 364.
110. "The Secretary of State had two conversations with Delbos on the telephone on Saturday afternoon [the 4 September], and what finally decided him to yield to Delbos' demand for Russian inclusion was the usual plea which French Ministers always put forward when hard pressed, namely that if we insisted on excluding Russia, he, Delbos, would have to resign and we should be responsible for a Ministerial crisis in France! Eventually, when the Secretary of State did agree to Russia's inclusion, he impressed upon Delbos that if things went wrong and Russia tried to torpedo the Conference, it would be the French Government's responsibility" – Mounsey (London) to Lloyd Thomas (Paris), 8.9.37: *DBFP*, doc. 14.
111. Eden (London) to Ingram (Rome), 7.9.37: ibid., doc. 133.
112. Delbos (Paris) to diplomatic representatives in Istanbul [this should read Ankara] Moscow, Berlin, Rome, Belgrade, Tirana, Bucharest, Athens, Cairo, Sofia, 6.9.37: *DDF*, doc. 396.
113. Potemkin (Moscow) to Helfand (Rome), 5.9.37: *DVP SSSR*, doc. 321 (enclosure); *Izvestiya*, 8.9.37.
114. Entry, 6.9.37: G. Ciano, *Diario 1937–1943*, ed. R. de Felice (Milan, 1980 edition), p. 34.
115. Entry, 7.9.37 and 8.9.37: ibid.
116. *DVP SSSR*, doc. 322; *Izvestiya*, 8.9.37.
117. See Zalkind (Ankara) to Moscow, 7.9.37: *DVP SSSR*, doc. 323.
118. Further underlined in conversation with the French ambassador – Eden (London) to Lloyd Thomas (Paris), 7.9.37: *DBFP*, doc. 135; also Corbin (London) to Delbos (Paris), 7.9.37: *DDF*, doc. 403.
119. *The Times*, 15.9.37.
120. Litvinov (Geneva) to Moscow, 11.9.37: *DVP SSSR*, p. 751. For the decision to accept – Potemkin (Moscow) to Litvinov (Geneva), 13.9.37: ibid., doc. 331.
121. Litvinov (Geneva) to Moscow, 13.9.37: ibid., doc. 330.
122. Corbin (London) to Delbos (Paris), 1.10.37: *DDF*, vol. 7 (Paris, 1972), doc. 10 (enclosure).
123. *Istoriya Vtoroi*, p. 54.
124. His son's recollections – A. Antonov-Ovseenko, *Portet Tirana* (New York, 1980) p. 193; the tyrant referred to in the title is Stalin.
125. Journal, 11.11.37: J. Davies, *Mission to Moscow* (London, 1942) p. 166.
126. Coulondre (Moscow) to Delbos (Paris), 31.10.37: *DDF*, doc. 170.

127. Footnote to Monicault (Prague) to Delbos (Paris), 23.11.37: *DDF*, vol. 7, doc. 263.
128. Dateline Riga, 12.11.37: *The Times*, 13.11.37.
129. Ibid., 15.11.37: ibid., 16.11.37.
130. Gurney (Helsinki) to Eden (London), 20.11.37: *FO* 371/21102.
131. Reuter, 19.12.37: *The Times*, 20.12.37.
132. Reported from Paris, 5.12.37: ibid., 6.12.37. For his address to the League for the Defence of the Rights of Man: ibid., 8.12.37. Krivitsky's defection was announced in the same issue. For Barmine's recollections, see his *One Who Survived* (New York, 1945).
133. *Pravda*, 12.11.37.
134. *Le Journal de Moscou*, 16.11.37.
135. Captain King, a cipher clerk, began work for the Russians sometime between 1935 and 1937: R. Deacon, *With My Little Eye: Memoirs of a Spy Hunter* (London, 1982) pp. 164–5, he was arrested, tried and imprisoned in October 1939.
136. Maisky's record of the conversation, 29.7.37: *DVP SSSR*, doc. 269.
137. *Pravda*, 28.11.37.
138. For Halifax's own account of the visit: *DBFP*, doc. 336.
139. See editorial, "Les pourparlers anglo-allemands et la visite de MM. Chautemps et Delbos à Londres", *Le Journal de Moscou*, 1.12.37; "Le Communiqué de Londres", ibid., 4.12.37.
140. François-Poncet (Berlin) to Chautemps (Paris), 8.12.37: *DDF*, doc. 324.
141. Potemkin (Moscow) to Surits (Paris), 19.12.37: *DVP SSSR*, doc. 446; for continuing suspicions as to what went on in Warsaw – Litvinov (Moscow) to Surits (Paris), 22.12.37: ibid., doc. 455.
142. An unsigned article, "Activité diplomatique", *Le Journal de Moscou*, 14.12.37.
143. Coulondre (Moscow) to Delbos (Paris), 27.12.37 (enclosure): *DDF*, doc. 390. Coulondre rightly saw this as "a kind of warning". He did not believe there was any immediate danger, but nevertheless pointed out that for future reference that "if the USSR is not with us, she will be against us": ibid. Also see Luciani, "M. Payart et le rapprochement Germano-Soviétique", *Le Monde*, 19.2.69.
144. *DVP SSSR*, p. 718.
145. Note 2: *DGFP*, doc. 489; memorandum by Schliep, 22.7.37: ibid., doc. 489.
146. Stomonyakov's record of a conversation with Shigemitsu, the Japanese ambassador, 21.6.37: *DVP SSSR*, doc. 208.
147. Potemkin's record of a conversation with Schulenburg, 4.10.37: ibid., doc. 353; also Schulenburg (Moscow) to Berlin, 4.10.37: *DGFP*, doc. 564.
148. Potemkin (Moscow) to Astakhov (Berlin), 27.10.37: ibid., doc. 383.
149. Made clear to Schulenburg by Litvinov, 15.11.37: ibid., doc. 410.
150. Mackensen (Berlin) to Schulenburg (Moscow), 9.11.37: *DGFP*, doc. 579.
151. Source cited in note 148.
152. *FO* 371/21092.
153. Schulenburg (Moscow) to Berlin, 17.1.38: *DGFP*, doc. 615.
154. *Pravda*, 18.1.38.
155. Molotov, 19.1.38: ibid., 20.1.38.

CHAPTER 9 THE CZECHOSLOVAKIAN CRISIS, 1938

1. Letter, 12.2.38: *Pravda*, 14.2.38.
2. "Brestskii mi i bor'ba partii Bol'shevikov protiv trotskistsko-bukharinskikh provokatorov voiny", *Bol'shevik*, no. 5, 5.3.38 (the actual date of publication), pp. 60–7.
3. Editorial, "Prigovor suda – prigovor naroda", *Pravda*, 13.3.38.
4. I. Ermashev, "Zakhvat Avstrii", ibid., 14.3.38.
5. E. Alexandrov, "Anneksiya Avstrii", *Izvestiya*, 14.3.38.
6. Unsigned, "L'annexation de l'Autriche", *Le Journal de Moscou*, 15.3.38.
7. Grzybowski (Moscow) to Beck (Warsaw), 15.3.38: *Dokumenty i Materialy po Istorii Sovetsko-Pol'skikh Otnoshenii*, vol. 6, ed. E. Basin'sky *et al.* (Moscow, 1969), doc. 239.
8. Quoted in *Istoriya Vneshnei Politiki SSSR*, vol. 1, ed. A. Berezkin *et al.* (Moscow, 1980) p. 335.
9. *DDF*, vol. 8 (Paris, 1973) p. 810, note 1.
10. The semi-official *Gazeta Polska*, 11.3.38 – quoted in Noel (Warsaw) to Paul-Boncour (Paris), 16.3.38: *DDF*, doc. 465.
11. *DDF*, loc. cit.
12. S. Stanislawska, *Wielka i Mala Polityka Józefa Becka* (marzec-maj 1938) (Warsaw, 1962) p. 40.
13. Potemkin (Moscow) to Krapivintsev (Kovno), Zotov (Riga), Nikitin (Tallinn) and Listopad (Warsaw) 26.3.38: *DVP SSSR*, vol. XXI, doc. 104.
14. V. Gal'yanov (Potemkin), "Kuda idet Pol'sha", *Bol'shevik*, no. 8, 15.4.38, pp. 60–8; for Potemkin's use of this pseudonym, see note 32, p. 277.
15. See p. 21.
16. "Po stolbtsam inostrannoi pechati", *Izvestiya*, 21.3.38.
17. Litvinov (Moscow) to Maisky (London), Alexandrovsky (Prague) and Listopad (Warsaw), 17.3.38: *Dokumenty i Materialy*, doc. 83.
18. *Izvestiya*, 17.3.38.
19. *Dokumenty i Materialy*, p. 344; this was also the impression conveyed to the German military attaché by his Polish counterpart – Köstring (Moscow) to Tippelskirch (Berlin), 21.3.38: *Profile bedeutender Soldaten, Herausgegeben vom Bundesarchiv/Militararchiv*. Vol. 1: *General Köstring: Der militärische Mittler zwischen dem Deutschen Reich und der Sowjetunion 1921–1941*, ed. H. Teske (Frankfurt/M, 1966) p. 193.
20. Lévi (Moscow) to Paul-Boncour (Paris), 20.3.38: *DDF*, doc. 521; the appropriate Soviet volume of documents omits these and related items.
21. Litvinov's record of the conversation, 18.3.38: *Dokumenty i Materialy*, doc. 242; *DVP SSSR*, doc. 87.
22. *Pravda*, 21.2.56; for the history of the affair, based on the Polish Party archive: J. Kowalski, *Komunistyczna Partia Polski 1935–1938: Studium Historyczne* (Warsaw, 1975) pp. 424–37.
23. *Dokumenty Komunistycznej Partii Polski 1935–1938* (Warsaw, 1968), doc. 61; also *Mezhdunarodnaya Solidarnost' Trudyashchikhsya v Bor'be za Mir i Natsional'noe Osvobozhdenie protiv Fashistskoi Agressii, za Polnoe Unichtozhenie Fashizma v Evrope i Azii (1938–1945)* (Moscow, 1962), doc. 16; Kowalski, *Komunistyczna*, p. 409.
24. Source cited in note 13.

25. "Note du département", 22.3.38: *DDF*, vol. 9, (Paris, 1974) doc. 17; also Chilston (Moscow) to Halifax (London), 17.3.38: *DBFP*, 3rd Series, vol. I (London, 1949), doc. 92.
26. Litvinov (Moscow) to Ostrovsky (Bucharest), 13.11.36: *DVP SSSR*, vol. XIX, doc. 357; for the background to this affair, there is a Soviet account based in part on Romanian archival material: A. Shevyakov, *Sovetsko-Rumyanskie Otnosheniya i Problema Evropeiskoi Bezopasnosti 1932–1939* (Moscow, 1977) pp. 194–9; the anti-Romanian tone of the work does not obscure its value.
27. Ibid., pp. 189–90.
28. International Labour Office, *Annuaire des Statistiques du Travail/Year-book of Labour Statistics* (Geneva, 1938) p. 236.
29. Quoted in Shirinya, *Strategiya*, p. 304; also V. Chugaev, *V Bor'be Protiv Fashizma i Ugroz Voiny: Iz Istorii Internatsional'noi Solidarnosti Trudyashchikhsya Pol'shi i Zapadnoi Ukrainy v Bor'be Protiv Nastupleniya Fashizma i Rosta Voennoi Opasnosti 1933–1939* (Kiev, 1980) p. 301.
30. Fifth plenum of the Party's Central Committee, February 1937: quoted in *Istoriya Vtoroi Mirovoi Voiny*, p. 347.
31. Editorial, "Le problème des minorités nationales comme prétexte à l'agression", *Le Journal de Moscou*, 5.4.38.
32. Ya. Kopansky, *Internatsional'naya Solidarnost' s Bor'boi Trudyashchikhsya Bessarabii za Vossoedinenie s Sovetskoi Rodinoi (1918–1940)* (Kishinev, 1975) pp. 278–98.
33. In the original this reads "not the only" – a revealing slip – but it was corrected subsequently in *Le Journal de Moscou*, 11.1.38.
34. Editorial, "Prémesses et suites des évenements de Roumanie", ibid., 4.1.38; for documentary evidence of Soviet reactions to events in Romania: Ostrovsky (Bucharest) to Moscow, 5.1.38: *DVP SSSR*, vol. XXI, doc. 6.
35. Potemkin's record of the conversation, 15.3.38: *DVP SSSR*, doc. 79; also *Dokumenty po Istorii Myunkhenskogo Sgovora 1937–1939*, ed. V. Mal'tsev et al. (Moscow, 1979), doc. 19; for Fierlinger's record – Fierlinger (Moscow) to Prague, 15.3.38: *Dokumenty i Materialy po Istorii Sovetsko-Chekhoslovatskikh Otnoshenii*, doc. 252.
36. Alexandrovsky's record of the conversation, 21.3.38: *DVP SSSR*, doc. 98; *Dokumenty po Istorii Myunkhenskogo*, doc.30.
37. *Izvestiya*, 18.3.38: *DVP SSSR*, doc. 82.
38. On the 17 March Litvinov instructed polpreds in London, Paris, Prague and Washington, to deliver a translation of the interview to the host Foreign Ministry: *DVP SSSR*, doc. 81. "In present circumstances . . . it would not appear that such a meeting could be arranged. A conference only attended by some of the European Powers, and designed less to secure the settlement of outstanding problems than to organise concerted action against aggression, would not necessarily, in the view of His Majesty's Government, have such a favourable effect upon the prospects of European peace", Lord Halifax, Eden's successor at the Foreign Office, wrote to Maisky on the 24 March, adding with typical understatement: "there may be a difference of opinion regarding the methods to be adopted" in strengthening peace: *DBFP*, doc. 116. The French were scarcely more responsive. Massigli, *directeur des Affaires politiques et commerciales*,

wrote on the copy he received: "There is no question of this being a diplomatic note. There is therefore no formal proposal"; nonetheless he was ultimately obliged to draft a reply, along the lines of "sympathy – but practical difficulties". Various excuses were then invented: *DDF*, vol. 8, p. 890, footnote 3; the text of the response has not been reprinted.

39. Stomonyakov (Moscow) to Luganets-Orel'sky (Nanking), 17.4.38: *DVP SSSR*, doc. 135.
40. Neville to Hilda, 27.2.38: *NC* 18/1/1040.
41. *Cmd.* 5726; for Soviet comment: Editorial, "L'accord anglo-italien et le danger de guerre", *Le Journal de Moscou*, 19.4.38.
42. Source cited in note 38.
43. Neville to Hilda and Ida, 26.11.37: *NC* 18/1/1630.
44. Entry, 14.2.38: *The Diplomatic Diaries of Oliver Harvey 1937–1940*, ed. J. Harvey (London, 1970), p. 89; N. Gibbs, *Grand Strategy*, vol. 1 (London, 1976) pp. 642–3.
45. Neville to Ida, 11.9.38: *NC* 18/1/1068.
46. Neville to Ida, 20.3.38: *NC* 18/1/1042.
47. Davies, *Mission to Moscow*, p. 223.
48. See Haslam, *Soviet Foreign Policy*, p. 152, note 1.
49. Maisky (London) to Moscow, 24.3.38: *DVP SSSR*, doc. 103.
50. Maisky (London) to Moscow, 8.4.38: ibid., doc. 121. The Russians were confused by Churchill's visit to Paris, reportedly on a mission for Chamberlain: Maisky (London) to Moscow and Surits (Paris), 31.3.38: ibid., doc. 111.
51. Stomonyakov (Moscow) to Luganets-Orel'sky (Nanking), 17.4.38: ibid., doc. 135.
52. From Calinescu's diary: quoted in A. Shevyakov, *Sovetsko-Rumyanskie Otnosheniya*, p. 267.
53. Litvinov (Moscow) to Alexandrovsky (Prague), 27.3.38: *DVP SSSR*, doc. 106; for Alexandrovsky's subsequent conversation with Krofta, 30.3.38: ibid., doc. 110.
54. Alexandrovsky (Bucharest) to Moscow, 14.4.38: ibid., doc. 132.
55. Fierlinger (Moscow) to Krofta (Prague), 23.4.38: *Dokumenty i Materialy po Istorii Sovetsko-Chekhoslovatskikh Otnoshenii*, doc. 271; also the source cited below in note 56.
56. Coulondre (Moscow) to Bonnet (Paris), 24.4.38: *DDF*, vol. 9, doc. 225.
57. Speech delivered in Moscow: *Dokumenty i Materialy po Istorii Sovetsko-Chekhoslovaktskikh Otnoshenii* doc. 272.
58. Coulondre (Moscow) to Bonnet (Paris), 8.6.38: *DDF*, doc. 521.
59. Coulondre (Moscow) to Bonnet (Paris), 10.6.38: *DDF*, vol. 10, (Paris, 1976) doc. 5.
60. Fierlinger (Moscow) to Prague, 18.6.38: *Dokumenty i Materialy po Istorii Sovetsko-Chekhoslovatskikh Otnoshenii*, doc. 305.
61. Thierry (Bucharest) to Bonnet (Paris), 22.5.38: *DDF*, vol. 9, doc. 416.
62. *Iz Istorii*, doc. 27.
63. *Kommunisticheskii Internatsional*, no. 5, May 1938, pp. 5–9.
64. Litvinov's speeches to the League assembly on the 12 May and 14 May 1938: *DVP SSSR*, docs. 173 and 181.
65. Litvinov (Moscow) to Alexandrovsky (Prague), 25.5.38: ibid., doc. 197.
66. Surits (Paris) to Moscow, 25.5.38: ibid., doc. 198.

67. For an account by the chief of Czechoslovakia's Military Intelligence: F. Moravec̆, *Master of Spies* (London, 1981) pp. 107–9; but this assertion that Germany intended to take over Czechoslovakia at this stage appears unfounded.
68. Dated 21.5.38: reprinted in *Dokumenty po Istorii Myunkhenskogo*, doc. 64.
69. The wording used was evasive: "His Majesty's Government could not guarantee that they would not be forced by circumstances to become involved also" – Halifax (London) to Henderson (Berlin), 21.5.38: *DBFP*, doc. 250.
70. "If . . . the French Government were to assume that His Majesty's Government would at once take joint military action with them to preserve Czechoslovakia against German aggression, it is only fair to warn them that our statements do not warrant such an assumption" – Halifax (London) to Phipps (Paris), 22.5.38: ibid., doc. 271; *DDF*, doc. 419.
71. Editorial, "La tension en Europe", *Le Journal de Moscou*, 24.5.38.
72. Symptomatic was the absence of any editorial on the subject in *Pravda* or *Izvestiya*.
73. E. Gnedin, "Ne mech, no mir (Zametki o stanovlenii sovetskoi diplomatii)", *Novyi Mir*, no. 7, July 1967, p. 172.
74. Published in *Le Journal de Moscou*, 5.7.38, under the title "La lutte pour la paix et la situation internationale"; it did not appear elsewhere in the Soviet press.
75. Coulondre (Moscow) to Bonnet (Paris), 12.7.38: *DDF*, vol. 10, doc. 197.
76. "General Strategic Directive", 18.6.38: *DGFP*, Series D, vol. 2, (London, 1950), doc. 282.
77. *Istoriya Vtoroi*, p. 104.
78. Report by Col. Fedotov of the Far Eastern Border Forces headquarters, 14.7.38: *Pogranichnye Voiska SSSR 1929–1938: Sbornik Dokumentov i Materialov*, ed. P. Zyryanov *et al.* (Moscow, 1972), doc. 623.
79. The first exchange took place between Stomonyakov and Nisi, the Japanese chargé d'affaires, on the 15 July: *DVP SSSR*, doc. 260; in his meeting with Shigemitsu on the 20 July Litvinov could scarcely restrain himself and suggested that "the ambassador evidently considers the tactic of threats a good method of diplomacy. Unfortunately", he continued, "there are now a number of countries which give in to bullying and threats, but the ambassador should know that this method will not be successfully applied in Moscow" – ibid., doc. 264.
80. Litvinov (Moscow) to polpreds in Germany, France, the USA, Czechoslovakia, Italy, China, Japan, Turkey, Afghanistan, Iran, Greece, Finland, Estonia, Latvia and Lithuania, 11.8.38: ibid., doc. 298.
81. At the time of the confrontation the Soviet agent Sorge in Tokyo reported that "this incident will not lead to war between the Soviet Union and Japan": quoted in F. Volkov, "Legendy i deistvitel'nost' o Rikharde Zorge", *Voenno-Istoricheskii Zhurnal*, no. 12, 1966, p. 100.
82. "Our performance was inadequate", noted Voroshilov: V. Akshinskii, *Kliment Efremovich Voroshilov: Biograficheskii Ocherk* (Moscow, 1974) p. 198.
83. Maisky (London) to Moscow, 10.8.38: *DVP SSSR*, doc. 295; and Maisky (London) to Moscow, 17.8.38: ibid., doc. 300.
84. Litvinov saw Schulenburg on the 22 August – Litvinov (Moscow) to

Alexandrovsky (Prague) and Merekalov (Berlin), 22.8.38: ibid., doc. 305; and Litvinov (Moscow) to Merekalov (Berlin) 27.8.38: ibid., doc. 312.

85. Editorial, "La Tchécoslovaquie sous la menace allemande", *Le Journal de Moscou*, 23.8.38.
86. Editorial, "Le chantage et le danger de guerre s'aggravent", ibid., 30.8.38.
87. *Papers and Memoirs of Juliusz Lukasiewicz, Ambassador of Poland, Diplomat in Paris 1936–1939*, ed. W. Jedzejewicz (London, 1970) p. 120.
88. Bonnet (Paris) to Payart (Moscow), 31.8.38: *DDF*, vol. 10, doc. 511; Payart (Moscow) to Bonnet (Paris).
89. Litvinov (Moscow) to Alexandrovsky (Prague), 2.9.38: *DVP SSSR*, doc. 324.
90. N. Comnène, *Preludi del Grande Dramma (Ricordi e documenti di un diplomatico)* (Rome, 1947), p. 90.
91. Payart (Moscow) to Bonnet (Paris), 2.9.38: *DDF*, doc. 534.
92. Source cited in note 89.
93. This appears in I. Maisky, *The Munich Drama* (Moscow, 1972), p. 38; but it was excised from the latest edition of his *Vospominaniya Sovetskogo Diplomata 1925–1945gg* (Tashkent, 1980), p. 300, published posthumously, probably because it weakens the argument that there were no doubts about the wisdom of collective security amongst the Russians. Maisky related the contents of the Payart-Litvinov exchange to Churchill on the 2 September, and Churchill duly passed them on to Halifax, but to no result: M. Gilbert, *Winston S. Churchill*, vol. v, 1922–1939 (London, 1976) p. 968.
94. "Note de la Direction politique: Mise en oeuvre éventuelle du pacte soviéto-tchécoslovaque 6.9.38": *DDF*, vol. 11, (Paris, 1977) doc. 29.
95. Litvinov (Moscow) to Surits (Paris), 2.9.38: *DVP SSSR*, doc. 325.
96. He later explained this to the Czech ambassador: Fierlinger (Moscow) to Prague, 17.9.38: *Dokumenty i Materialy po Istorii Sovetsko-Chekhoslovatskikh Otnoshenii*, doc. 339.
97. Surits (Paris) to Moscow, 3.9.38: *DVP SSSR*, doc. 330.
98. Coulondre (Moscow) to Bonnet (Paris), 11.9.38: *DDF*, doc. 93.
99. Maisky (London) to Potemkin (Moscow), 5.9.38: *Dokumenty i Materialy po Istorii Sovetsko – Chekhoslovatskikh Otnoshenii*, doc. 327.
100. "Notes du Ministre: Conversation avec M. Litvinov", 11.9.38: *DDF*, doc. 95.
101. Litvinov (Geneva) to Moscow, 11.9.38: *DVP SSSR*, doc. 343.
102. Source cited in note 100.
103. Source cited in note 101.
104. A declaration to members of the press, 11.9.38: *DBFP*, vol. 2, appendix III.
105. "Note du Ministre", 13.9.38: *DDF*, doc. 125.
106. I. Colvin, *Vansittart in Office* (London, 1965) p. 243.
107. Source cited in note 101.
108. Litvinov (Geneva) to Moscow, 15.9.38: *DVP SSSR*, doc. 348.
109. Fierlinger (Moscow) to Prague, 15.9.38: *Dokumenty i Materialy po Istorii Chekhoslovatskikh Otnoshenii*, doc. 335; for the Soviet record: *DVP SSSR*, doc. 349.
110. Potemkin (Moscow) to Litvinov (Geneva), 15.9.38: *DVP SSSR*, doc. 350.
111. Astakhov (Berlin) to Moscow, 15.9.38: ibid., doc. 352.
112. K. Shirinya, "Georgi Dimitrov and the Struggle for the Implementation

and Development of the Comintern's New Orientation in 1935–1939", *Georgi Dimitrov: an Outstanding Militant of the Comintern* (Sofia, 1972) p. 193.

113. Dated 2.8.38: *Dokumenty i Materialy po Istorii Sovetsko-Chekhoslovatskikh Otnoshenii*, doc. 315.
114. *Dokumenty Komunistycznej*, doc. 63; *Iz Istorii*, doc. 45.
115. *World News and Views*, 3.9.38.
116. *Iz Istorii*, doc. 52.
117. Ibid., doc. 54; *World News and Views*, 10.9.38.
118. 6.9.38: ibid.
119. Ibid., 17.9.38.
120. Editorial, "Chamberlain's Visit to Hitler", ibid.
121. Ibid., 17.9.38.
122. Ibid.
123. Neville to Ida, 19.9.38: *NC* 18/1/1069.
124. Arnal (Geneva) to Bonnet (Paris), 18.9.38: *DDF*, doc. 201.
125. Beneš saw Alexandrovsky on the 19 September – Alexandrovsky (Prague) to Moscow, 19.9.38: *DVP SSSR*, doc. 354; for Moscow's positive response – Potemkin (Moscow) to Alexandrovsky (Prague), 20.9.38: ibid., doc. 356.
126. Fierlinger (Moscow) to Krofta (Prague), 20.9.38: *Dokumenty i Materialy po Istorii Sovetsko-Chekhoslovatskikh Otnoshenii*, doc. 345.
127. *DVP SSSR*, doc. 357.
128. Editorial, "Igra s Ognem", *Pravda*, 21.9.38.
129. *Dokumenty i Materialy po Istorii Sovetsko-Chekhoslovatskikh Otnoshenii*, doc. 352.
130. Comnène, *Preludi*, pp. 96–7.
131. Litvinov (Geneva) to Moscow, 23.9.38: *DVP SSSR*, doc. 369.
132. "Immediately deliver and send to the Kremlin" – Litvinov (Geneva) to Moscow, 23.9.38: *DVP SSSR*, doc. 370. In the Soviet volume the document is placed after document 369, though the true order might be the reverse.
133. Not printed in *DVP SSSR*, but cited in V. Sipols, *Sovetskii Soyuz v Bor'be za Mir i Bezopasnost' 1933–1939* (Moscow, 1974) p. 245.
134. "Resumé der letzten di ČSR betreffenden Ereignisse vom Gesichtspunkt der englischen Regierung und der englischen Konservativen", gez. F. Dvornik – *Kabinett* Nr. 3469/38: reprinted in *Das Abkommen von München 1938*, ed. V. Král (Prague, 1968), doc. 270 (2).
135. Entry, 24.9.38: *The Diaries*, p. 103.
136. Statement in Cabinet, cited in ibid., p. 104.
137. *Dokumenty po Istorii Myunkhenskogo*, p. 256; *Istoriya Vtoroi*, pp. 104–6.
138. Alexandrovsky (Prague) to Moscow, 22.9.38: *Dokumenty i Materialy po Istorii Sovetsko-Chekhoslovatskikh Otnoshenii*, doc. 364.
139. Information from "a very good source" – Coulondre (Moscow) to Bonnet (Paris), 21.9.38: *DDF*, doc. 267.
140. Information relayed by Fierlinger to his French counterpart – Coulondre (Moscow) to Bonnet (Paris), 22.9.38: *DDF*, doc. 292.
141. *Izvestiya*, 26.9.38; *Dokumenty i Materialy po Istorii Sovetsko-Chekhoslovatskikh Otnoshenii*, docs. 257 and 258.
142. Potemkin's record of the conversation with chargé d'affaires Janowski, held at 7.00am, 23.9.38: ibid., doc. 259.
143. Gilbert, *Winston S. Churchill*, pp. 982–4.
144. *The Diaries*, pp. 107–9; Gilbert, *Winston S. Churchill*, pp. 985–6.

145. In an autobiographical short-story, entitled "Call it Love", Litvinov's widow describes the beginnings of her love affair with Maxim Maximovich, who is given the name "Belkin" – Ivy Litvinov, *She Knew She Was Right* (London, 1971).
146. *Iz Istorii*, doc. 58.
147. *DVP SSSR*, doc. 382.
148. *Dokumenty po Istorii Myunkhenskogo*, doc. 204.
149. Directive from the General Staff to military districts, 28.9.38: ibid., doc. 205.
150. Directive to the Byelorussian military district, 29.9.38: ibid., doc. 206 (and enclosure).
151. Maisky (London) to Moscow, 29.9.38: *DVP SSSR*, doc. 390.
152. This was after a meeting with Churchill on the same day – Maisky (London) to Moscow, 29.9.38: ibid., doc. 391.
153. *Pravda*, 29.9.38.
154. Alexandrovsky (Prague) to Moscow, 30.9.38: *DVP SSSR*, doc. 393.
155. Alexandrovsky (Prague) to Moscow, 30.9.38: ibid., doc. 394.
156. Potemkin (Moscow) to Alexandrovsky (Prague), 30.9.38: ibid., doc. 395.
157. Alexandrovsky (Prague) to Moscow, 1.10.38: ibid., doc. 399.
158. Litvinov (Paris) to Moscow, 2.10.38: ibid., doc. 402.

CHAPTER 10 THE COLLAPSE OF COLLECTIVE SECURITY, 1938–39

1. Editorial, "Politika premirovaniya agressora", *Izvestiya*, 4.10.38.
2. Recorded by Ernst Fischer, Austrian representative on the Comintern executive committee: E. Fischer, *An Opposing Man* (London, 1974) pp. 335–6.
3. Coulondre (Moscow) to Bonnet (Paris), 4.10.38: *DDF*, vol. 12 (Paris, 1978) doc. 17.
4. BALTICUS, "Ce qui attend les agresseurs polonais", *Le Journal de Moscou*, 11.10.38.
5. Editorial, "LE PROBLÈME DES MINORITÉS NATIONALES APRÈS MUNICH", ibid., 1.11.38.
6. Grzybowski (Moscow) to Warsaw, 9.10.38: *Dokumenty i Materialy po Istorii Sovetsko–Pol'skikh Otnoshenii*, vol. VI (Moscow, 1969) doc. 262.
7. *Izvestiya*, 28.11.38; *Dokumenty i Materialy*, doc. 267.
8. *Georgi Dimitrov: an Outstanding Militant of the Comintern*, p. 193.
9. Source as cited in note 3.
10. *Iz Istorii*, doc. 61; the declaration was originally published in l'*Humanité*, 30.9.38.
11. *Iz Istorii*, doc. 63.
12. Reprinted in the Comintern journal, *Kommunisticheskii Internatsional*, no. 10, October 1938, pp. 125–8.
13. "SSSR – oplot bor'by narodov protiv fashistskoi agressii", ibid.; the article went to press on the 21 October and was passed for publication on the 2 November.

14. Reprinted in *Dokumente der Deutschen Politik und Geschichte von 1848 bis zur Gegenwart*, vol. 4: *Die Zeit der nationalsozialistischen Diktatur 1933–1945, Aufbau und Entwicklung 1933–1938*, ed. K. Hohlfeld (Berlin, ?), doc. 201.
15. The author, an emigré in the USA, has since identified himself: E. Gnedin, *Iz Istorii Otnoshenii Mezhdu SSSR i Fashistskoi Germaniei: Dokumenty i Sovremennye Kommentarii* (New York, 1977) p. 46.
16. Evg. ALEXANDROV, "Myunkhenskii Balans", *Izvestiya*, 23.10.38.
17. Evg. ALEXANDROV, "Mezhdunarodnaya politika SSSR", *Kommunisticheskii Internatsional*, no. 10, October 1938, pp. 21–8.
18. Editorial, "L'HEURE DE L'ÉCHEANCE SONNE", ibid., 25.10.38. 15.11.38.
19. Editorial, "L'HEURE DE L'ÉCHEANCE SONNE", ibid., 25.10.38.
20. Evg. ALEXANDROV, "Fashistskaya reaktsiya i sily mira", *Izvestiya*, 7.11.38.
21. The speech was delivered in the Bol'shoi theatre Moscow, on the 29 October: *Izvestiya*, 7.11.38.
22. *Pravda*, 1.9.39.
23. Litvinov (Moscow) to Surits (Paris), 31.12.38: *Soviet Peace Efforts on the Eve of World War II (September 1938–August 1939)*, Pt. 1, ed. V. Falin *et al.* (Moscow, 1973), doc. 85.
24. Maisky (London) to Litvinov (Moscow), 10.1.39: ibid., doc. 90.
25. Neville to Ida, 20.3.38: *NC* 18/1/1042.
26. Editorial, "UNE TENTATIVE VOUÉE À L'ÉCHEC", *Le Journal de Moscou*, 27.12.38.
27. Signs that the Germans – or at least some of them – were interested in reviving trade with the USSR first appeared in late October, but nothing came of them until December 1938, under pressure from Göring, when a preliminary sounding of the Russians at the end of the month laid the basis for future talks: *DGFP*, vol. 4 (London, 1951), docs. 478 and 483.
28. Memorandum by Wiehl, director of the economic policy department, 12.1.39: ibid., doc. 484.
29. Schulenburg (Moscow) to Wiehl (Berlin), 1.3.39: ibid., doc. 493.
30. Memorandum by Wiehl, 20.1.39: ibid., doc. 485.
31. *The Diaries of Sir Alexander Cadogan 1938–1945*, ed. D. Dilks (London, 1971) p. 146.
32. Potemkin's identity is revealed by biographer N. Zhukovskii, *Na Diplomaticheskom Postu* (Moscow, 1973), p. 308; V. Gal'yanov, "Mezhdnarodnaya obstanovka vtoroi imperialisticheskoi voiny", *Bol'shevik*, no. 4, February 1939, pp. 46–65.
33. Litvinov (Moscow) to Maisky (London), 19.2.39: *Soviet Peace Efforts*, doc. 128.
34. Naggiar (Moscow) to Bonnet (Paris), 24.2.39: *DDF*, vol. 14 (Paris, 1980), doc. 195.
35. A. ALEXANDROVA, "La faiblesse militaire de la Grand-Bretagne et sa politique de capitulation", *Le Journal de Moscou*, 28.2.39.
36. *Pravda*, 11.3.39.
37. D. Kraminov, *V Orbite Voiny: Zapiski Sovetskogo Korrespondenta za Rubezhom 1939–1945 Gody* (Moscow, 1980) pp. 17–18.
38. Editorial, "Vneshnyaya politika strany pobedivshego sotsializma", *Izves-*

tiya, 13.3.39; editorial, "Mudry stalinskii analiz mezhdunarodnogo polozheniya", *Pravda*, 13.3.39.

39. Schulenburg (Moscow) to Berlin, 13.3.39: *DGFP*, vol. 6 (London, 1956), doc. 1.
40. For the note: *Soviet Peace Efforts*, doc. 157; for Litvinov's unenthusiastic attitude towards it – Schulenburg (Moscow) to Berlin, 19.3.39: *DGFP*, doc. 43.
41. Litvinov (Moscow) to Maisky (London), and Surits (Paris), 18.3.39: *Soviet Peace Efforts*, doc. 162.
42. S. Aster, *1939: The Making*, pp. 81–2.
43. Litvinov (Moscow) to Maisky (London), 19.3.39: *Soviet Peace Efforts*, doc. 167.
44. Litvinov (Moscow) to Maisky (London) and Surits (Paris), 22.3.39: ibid., doc. 178.
45. N. Gibbs, *Grand Strategy*, vol. I: *Rearmament Policy* (London, 1976) p. 696.
46. Neville to Ida, 26.3.39: *NC* 18/1/1091.
47. Obozrevatel', "Posle Chekho-Slovakii – Klaipeda", *Izvestiya*, 23.3.39.
48. Speech to a congress of soviets, 30.11.36: *Pravda*, 1.12.36.
49. M. Jakobsen, *The Diplomacy of the Winter War: An Account of the Russo-Finnish War 1939–1940* (Camb., Mass., 1961) pp. 7–8. For a more detailed discussion of the issue, turn to Appendix 2, below.
50. Ibid.
51. Ibid.; also "Report by General Sir Walter Kirke", 26.6.39: *FO* 371/23648.
52. P. Egorov, *Marshal Meretskov* (Moscow, 1974) p. 53.
53. K. Meretskov, *Na Sluzhbe Narodu: Stranitsy Vospominanii* (Moscow, 1968) p. 171.
54. *Soviet Peace Efforts*, doc. 192.
55. Gibbs, *Grand Strategy*, pp. 703–4.
56. Maisky (London) to Moscow, 31.3.39: *Soviet Peace Efforts*, doc. 200; and Litvinov's record of the conversation with Seeds, 1.4.39: ibid., doc. 203.
57. Litvinov (Moscow) to Surits (Paris), 11.4.39: ibid., doc. 223.
58. Litvinov (Moscow) to Maisky (London), 4.4.39: *Soviet Peace Efforts*, doc. 210.
59. J-B. Duroselle, *La Décadence 1932–1939*, p. 419.
60. For Bonnet's previous rejection of commitments in Eastern Europe: ibid., pp. 387–8; for the transformation in French policy: ibid., pp. 417–18.
61. Surits (Paris) to Moscow, 14.4.39: *Soviet Peace Efforts*, doc. 232; and Duroselle, *La Décadence*, p. 420.
62. Sorge (Tokyo) to Moscow, 15.4.39: *Soviet Peace Efforts*, doc. 236.
63. Proposals presented to Seeds, 17.4.39: ibid., doc. 239.
64. Memorandum by Weiszäcker, 17.4.39: *DGFP*, doc. 215.
65. "Our proposal made a tremendous impression on Bonnet", Surits wrote to Moscow on the 18 April: *Soviet Peace Efforts*, doc. 240.
66. For the text – Surits (Paris) to Moscow, 25.4.39: ibid., doc. 253; and Surits' remarks appear in a further telegram to Moscow, 26.4.39: ibid., doc. 256.
67. Litvinov (Moscow) to Surits (Paris), 26.4.39: ibid., doc. 255.
68. Ibid., doc. 262.
69. Surits (Paris) to Moscow, 29.4.39: ibid., doc. 263.
70. Quoted in Aster, *1939: The Making*, pp. 165–6.

71. Chamberlain in Cabinet, 26.7.39: quoted in I. Colvin, *The Chamberlain Cabinet* (London, 1971) p. 228.
72. Neville to Hilda, 29.4.39: *NC* 18/1/1096.
73. I. Erenburg, *Sob. Soch.*, p. 228.
74. Ibid. His articles had been criticised for "excessive emotionalism" – Kraminov, *V Orbite*, p. 11; the fact that they had been published regularly hitherto indicates that their disappearance reflected a softening of hostility towards Germany.
75. Litvinov's record of the conversation, 3.5.39: *Soviet Peace Efforts*, vol. 2, doc. 267.
76. Gnedin and his assistant were removed from the Press Department; others removed included Kelyavin, assistant of the Chef du Protocole, Dobrov (head of Burobin) and two minor officials in the Third Western Department, Vinogradov and Gochman – Seeds (Moscow) to Collier (London), 29.5.39: *FO*371/23685. Lozovsky (formerly head of the now dissolved Profintern) and Dekanozov were then appointed Deputy Commissars, on the 4 and the 14 May respectively: *Sobranie Postanovlenii i Rasporyazhenii Pravitel'stva Soyuza Sovetskikh Sotsialisticheskikh Respublik*, no. 37, 1939, 257 and 258. For Gnedin's account of the Star Chamber treatment they received, see his *Katastrofa i Vtoroe Rozhdenie: Memuarnye Zapiski* (Amsterdam, 1977), p. 108.
77. I. Pal'gunov, *Tridtsat' Let (Vospominaniya Zhurnalista i Diplomata)* (Moscow, 1964) p. 174.
78. Entry, 4.5.39: *Diariusz i Teki Jana Szembeka (1935–1945)*, vol. IV, ed. J. Zarański (London, 1972) p. 587; the British were less given to delusions, but were nonetheless hopelessly complacent. When Sir Percy Loraine reported the fears of his French counterpart in Rome, Cadogan commented: "That Monsieur Stalin contemplates arrangement with Germany is not obvious"; the worst he expected was a retreat into isolation and neutrality – Cadogan (London) to Loraine (Rome), 6.5.39: *FO* 371/23685.
79. Memorandum by Schnurre, 5.5.39: *DGFP*, doc. 332.
80. J. von Herwarth, *Against Two Evils*, p. 144; for confirmation – Lubomirski (Berlin) to Warsaw, 8.6.39: *Dokumenty i Materialy po Istorii Sovetsko-Pol'skikh Otnoshenii*, vol. 7, doc. 74.
81. Minute by von Stumm of the Press and Information Department, 9.5.39: *DGFP*, doc. 351. This was also the message relayed to Paris and London; see, for example, Phipps (Paris) to London, 5.5.39: *FO* 371/23685.
82. Quoted at length by Kraminov, *V Orbite*, pp. 28–9; later, in the same work, Kraminov refers to German use of the Swiss press to circulate rumours that trade talks with the USSR had led to the establishment of political contacts. It seems that the Russians also made use of the Swiss press for their own purposes; the Comintern's *Rundschau* was printed in Basel, so contact would not have been difficult. For the reference to German use of the Swiss press: ibid., p. 50.
83. F. Roberts, "Maxim Litvinov and Soviet Diplomacy", a despatch written at the Moscow embassy, 6.9.46: *FO* 371/56731.
84. von Herwarth, *Against Two Evils*, p. 143.
85. This was an opinion common to most, if not all, the diplomatic community in Moscow. The British, who bore the brunt of Molotov's stubbornness,

naturally disliked him considerably: "it is my fate to deal with a man totally ignorant of foreign affairs and to whom the idea of negotiation . . . is utterly alien", wrote the despairing Seeds towards the end of May 1939: quoted in Aster, *1939*, p. 261. But the Italians were also taken aback by his indifference to diplomatic courtesies, his "closed and cold personality", his ignorance of foreign languages and his legalistic approach to everything – Rosso (Moscow) to Ciano (Rome), 10.6.39: *DDI*, 8 Serie, 1935–1939, vol. XII (Rome, 1952) doc. 183.

86. Reprinted in *Soviet Peace Efforts*, doc. 279.
87. Molotov (Moscow) to Surits (Paris), 8.5.39: ibid., doc. 280.
88. Seeds' words, quoted in Aster, *1939*, p. 174.
89. *Izvestiya*, 10.5.39; a translation is reprinted in *Soviet Peace Efforts*, doc. 282.
90. Surits (Paris) to Moscow, 10.5.39: ibid., doc. 283.
91. Editorial, "Kmezhdunarodnomu polozheniyu", *Izvestiya*, 11.5.39; for Molotov's authorship – Kraminov, *V Orbite*, p. 29.
92. Neville to Hilda, 14.5.39: *NC* 18/1/1099.
93. *Soviet Peace Efforts*, doc. 291.
94. Memorandum by Schnurre, 17.5.39: *DGFP*, doc. 406.
95. Memorandum by Schulenburg, 20.5.39: ibid., doc. 424 (enclosure).
96. Schulenburg (Moscow) to Berlin, 20.5.39: ibid., doc. 414, note 2.
97. K. Gofman, "Ekonomicheskoe polizhenie fashistskoi Germanii", *Krasnaya Zvezda*, 22.5.39.
98. Aster, *1939*, p. 176.
99. Neville to Hilda, 28.5.39: *NC* 18/1/1101.
100. Molotov (Moscow) to Surits (Paris), 26.5.39: *Soviet Peace Efforts*, doc. 309.
101. Molotov's comment to Seeds and Payart, 27.5.39: ibid., doc. 311.
102. *Pravda*, 1.6.39: a translation of the speech is reprinted in *Soviet Peace Efforts*, doc. 314.
103. Molotov concluded his speech with the statement that "the Soviet Union belongs in the vanguard of the united front of peace-loving states genuinely combatting aggression"; as usual the motion to approve the government's foreign policy was accepted without demur – *Tret'ya Sessiya Verkhovnogo Soveta 25–31 maya 1939: Stenograficheskii Otchet* (Moscow, 1939) p. 476.
104. *Soviet Peace Efforts*, doc. 315.
105. Aster, *1939*, p. 264.
106. Molotov (Moscow) to Maisky (London), 10.6.39: *Soviet Peace Efforts*, doc. 323.
107. Editorial, "Vopros o zashchite trekh baltiskikh stran ot agressii", *Pravda*, 13.6.39.
108. Memorandum by Woermann, 15.6.39: *DGFP*, doc. 529.
109. Quoted in Aster, *1939*, p. 268.
110. *Soviet Peace Efforts*, doc. 329.
111. Molotov (Moscow) to Maisky (London) and Surits (Paris), 16.6.39: ibid., doc. 331.
112. Source cited in note 109. The claim, made retrospectively, by former Soviet counsellor at the Rome embassy, Guelfand, that "up until the middle of June, 1939" it would have been possible for Britain to obtain an agreement with Stalin is undoubtedly true, but the implication that thereafter this was impossible is probably false. Guelfand links his claim with British refusal to

grant guarantees concerning indirect aggression, which in fact does not occur till later (see pp. 223–4). Other information Guelfand gave the British proved inaccurate – Butler (Washington) to Sargent (London), 13.9.40, and Postan (Ministry of Economic Warfare) to Maclean (Foreign Office), 24.10.40: *FO* 371/24845.

113. Soviet aide-memoire handed to British and French representatives, 16.6.39: *Soviet Peace Efforts*, doc. 330.
114. Reprinted in ibid., doc. 338.
115. Ibid., note 127, p. 315.
116. *Diariusz*, p. 641.
117. Nikitin (Tallinn) to Moscow, 21.6.39: ibid., doc. 337.
118. Derevyansky (Helsinki) to Moscow, 28.6.39: ibid., doc. 352. The British Minister in Finland reported: "I have been informed from a source which is not altogether reliable that on the occasion of General Halder's visit conversations took place in regard to the protection of Finland by German air forces in the event of Russia's opening hostilities with Finland, and that it was agreed that air bases should be provided in the Karelian district, at Helsingfors [Helsinki] and at Petsamo in Finnish Lapland" – Snow (Helsinki) to Halifax (London), 3.7.39: *FO* 371/23648. One can only guess what the Russians made of such rumours. In a minute on this episode, Collier at the Northern Department in London pointed out (15.7.39): "The Finnish Government have never had the courage to forbid the General Staff from conducting talks and [sic] negotiations of this sort without their knowledge or approval. . . . This situation long antedates the anglo-soviet negotiations, and is, indeed, one of the causes of the Soviet attitude in these: that, in turn, encourages the General Staff to proceed with their pro-German policy; and so matters move in a vicious circle": ibid.
119. Meretskov, *Na Sluzhbe*, pp. 177–8.
120. A. Zhdanov, "Angliiskoe i frantsuzskoe pravitel'stva ne khotyat ravnogo dogovora s SSSR", *Pravda*, 29.6.39.
121. *Soviet Peace Efforts*, doc. 357.
122. Molotov (Moscow) to Maisky (London) and Surits (Paris), 3.7.39: ibid., doc. 361.
123. Neville to Hilda, 2.7.39: *NC* 18/1/1105.
124. Quoted in Aster, *1939*, p. 272.
125. Ibid., pp. 278–9.
126. See, for example, Nikitin (Tallinn) to Moscow, 13.7.39: *Soviet Peace Efforts*, doc. 369.
127. Molotov (Moscow) to Maisky (London) and Surits (Paris), 17.7.39: ibid., doc. 376.
128. Memorandum by Schnurre, 18.7.39: *DGFP*, doc. 685.
129. "V Narkomate Vneshnei Torgovli", *Pravda*, 22.7.39.
130. Quoted in Aster, *1939*, p. 282.
131. Meretskov, *Na Sluzhbe*, pp. 178–9.
132. Memorandum by Schnurre, 27.7.39: *DGFP*, doc. 729.
133. Weizsäcker (Berlin) to Schulenburg (Moscow), 29.7.39: ibid., doc. 736.
134. Schulenburg (Moscow) to Berlin, 4.8.39: ibid., doc. 766.
135. C. Bohlen, *Witness to History* (New York, 1973) p. 76; Molotov also later

commented on the absence of top-level figures, in his speech to the Supreme Soviet, 31.8.39: *Pravda*, 1.9.39.

136. The German ambassador noted, after his conversation with Molotov on the 4 August, that, despite the progress made, "the old mistrust of Germany persists" – Schulenburg (Moscow) to Berlin, 4.8.39: *DGFP*, doc. 766.
137. Astakhov (Berlin) to Moscow, 8.8.39, quoted in *Istoriya Vtoroi Mirovoi Voiny*, vol. 2, p. 280.
138. *Soviet Peace Efforts*, doc. 411.
139. L. Bezymenskii, "Osobaya papka 'barbarosa' – glavy iz dokumental'noi povesti", *Moskva*, no. 9, 1969, p. 192.
140. *Soviet Peace Efforts*, doc. 415.
141. Ribbentrop (Berlin) to Schulenburg (Moscow), 14.8.39: *DGFP*, vol. 8 (London, 1956), doc. 56.
142. Schulenburg (Moscow) to Berlin, 16.8.39: ibid., doc. 70.
143. Ribbentrop (Berlin) to Schulenburg (Moscow), 16.8.39: ibid., doc. 75.
144. Ribbentrop (Berlin) to Schulenburg (Moscow), 20.8.39: ibid., doc. 142.
145. Neville to Ida, 10.9.39: *NC* 18/1/1116.
146. Halifax, "A Record of Events Before the War, 1939", 21.8.39: *FO* 800/317.
147. *DGFP*, doc. 284.
148. Quoted in Aster, *1939*, p. 318.

APPENDIX 1: THE SOVIET PRESS AND SOVIET FOREIGN POLICY, 1933–39

1. "Pervonachal'nyi variant stat'i 'Ocherednye zadachi sovetskoi vlasti' (23–28 marta 1918)", V. Lenin, *Polnoe Sobranie Sochineniya*, vol. 36 (5 edn, Moscow, 1962) p. 146.
2. "Ocherednye zadachi sovetskoi vlasti" (written between the 13 and 26 April 1918 and first published in *Pravda*, 28.4.18): ibid., p. 192.
3. "V Narkomindele", p. 381; in her memoirs, Otto Kuusinen's widow talks of "grey" and "pink": A. Kuusinen, *Before and After Stalin* (London, 1974) p. 48.
4. "V Narkomindele", loc. cit.
5. V. Kraminov, *V Orbite*, pp. 6–8.
6. Ibid., p. 26.
7. For the muddle after Stalin's speech, see p. 205; for the confusion after the non-aggression pact: Kraminov, *V Orbite*, pp. 54–5.
8. "V Narkomindele", p. 383.
9. Kraminov, *V Orbite*, pp. 75–6.

APPENDIX 2: THE SOVIET UNION AND THE DEFENCE OF LENINGRAD, 1936–39

1. E. Henri, *Hitler Over Europe?* (London, 1936) p. 265.
2. Ibid., p. 255.
3. Editorials, "Ålandskonventionen inför revision", and "Finland – Åland.

Ett Nytt inlägg med vädjan till Sverige", *Dagens Nyheter*, 27 and 29 March 1938.

4. K. Wählbäck, *Finlandsfrågan i svensk politik 1937–1940* (Stockholm, 1964) p. 144.
5. Kollontai (Stockholm) to Moscow, 10.4.38: *DVP SSSR*, vol. xxi, doc. 125.
6. See p. 208, above; and V. Tanner, *The Winter War: Finland Against Russia 1939–1940* (Stanford, 1957) pp. 3–5.
7. Wählbäck, *Finlandsfrågan*, pp. 144–5.
8. Kollontai (Stockholm) to Potemkin (Moscow), 10.7.38: *DVP SSSR*, doc. 254.
9. Wählbäck, *Finlandsfrågan*, p. 145.
10. Tanner, *The Winter War*, p. 6.
11. See Kollontai (Stockholm) to Potemkin (Moscow), 10.8.38: *DVP SSSR*, doc. 297.
12. The offer was read out in imperfect German and noted by Tanner in his own hand: Tanner, *The Winter War*, pp. 8–9.
13. Ibid., p. 10.
14. The full record of these conversations does not appear in the Soviet volume of diplomatic correspondence, but extracts from two of Litvinov's telegrams on the subject, dated the 14 and 15 September, appear in the notes to the volume: *DVP SSSR*, p. 734.
15. Tanner, *The Winter War*, pp. 13–15.

Bibliography

PRIMARY SOURCES

1 The USSR

Vneshnyaya Torgovlya SSSR v Gody Dovoennykh Pyatiletok (1929–1940): Statisticheskii Sbornik (Moscow, 1968).

Dokumenty Vneshnei Politiki SSSR, vol. XVI, ed. F. Dolya *et al.* (Moscow, 1970).
XVII, ed. G. Deev *et al.* (Moscow, 1971).
XVIII, ed. Yu. Borisov *et al.* (Moscow, 1973).
XIX, ed. G. Deev *et al.* (Moscow, 1974).
XX, ed. F. Dolya *et al.* (Moscow, 1976).
XXI, ed. G. Deev *et al.* (Moscow, 1977).

Dokumenty i Materialy po Istorii Sovetsko-Pol'skikh Otnoshenii, vol. VI, ed. E. Basin'sky *et al.* (Moscow, 1969); vol. 7, ed. E. Basin'sky *et al.* (Moscow, 1973).

Dokumenty i Materialy po Istorii Sovetsko-Chekhoslovatskikh Otnoshenii, vol. 2, ed. Ch. Amort *et al.* (Moscow, 1977).

Dokumenty po Istorii Myunkhenskogo Sgovora 1937–1939, ed. V. Mal'tsev *et al.* (Moscow, 1979).

Iz Istorii Mezhdunarodnoi Proletarskoi Solidarnosti: Dokumenty i Materialy.
Vol. V: *Mezhdunarodnaya Solidarnost' Trudyashchikhsya v Bor'be s Fashizmom, Protiv Razvyazyvaniya Vtoroi Mirovoi Voiny (1933–1937)*, ed. G. Belov *et al.* (Moscow, 1961).
VI: *Mezhdunarodnaya Solidarnost' Trudyashchikhsya v Bor'be za Mir i Natsional'noe Osvobozhdenie Protiv Fashistskoi Agressii, za Polnoe Unichtozhenie Fashizma v Evrope i Azii (1938–1945)* (Moscow, 1962).

Kirov, S., *Izbrannye Stat'i i Rechi* (Moscow?, 1937).

Lenin, V., *Polnoe Sobranie Sochinenii*, vol. 54 (5th edn, Moscow, 1965).

Litvinov, M., *Vneshnyaya Politika SSSR: Rechi i Zayavleniya 1927–1935* (Moscow, 1935).

Pogranichnye Voiska SSSR 1929–1938: Sbornik Dokumentov i Materialov, ed. P. Zyryanov *et al.* (Moscow, 1972).

Report of Court Proceedings in the Case of the Anti-Soviet Trotskyite Centre (Moscow, 1937).

Report of the Seventh Congress of the Communist International (London, 1936).

VII Kongress Kommunisticheskogo Internatsionala i Bor'ba Protiv Fashizma i Voiny (Sbornik Dokumentov), ed. K. Shirinya *et al.* (Moscow, 1975).

Sobranie Zakonov i Rasporyazhenii Soyuza Sovetskikh Sotsialisticheskikh Respublik (continued as *Sobranie Postanovlenii i . . .*).

Soviet Peace Efforts on the Eve of World War II (September 1938–August 1939) Parts I and II, ed. V. Falin *et al.* (Moscow, 1973).

Stalin, J., *Works*, vol. 13 (Moscow, 1955).
The Crimes of the Stalin Era: Special Report to the 20th Congress of the CPSU by Nikita S. Khrushchev (New York, 1956).
Tret'ya Sessiya Verkhovnogo Soveta, 25–31 maya 1939: Stenograficheskii Otchet (Moscow, 1939)

2 Britain

Winston S. Churchill. vol. v. *Companion. Part 3: Documents (1936–1939)*, ed. M. Gilbert (London, 1982).
Cmd 4286, 4798, and 5726.
The Diaries of Sir Alexander Cadogan 1938–1945, ed. D. Dilks (London, 1971).
The Diplomatic Diaries of Oliver Harvey 1937–1940, ed. J. Harvey (London, 1970).
Documents on British Foreign Policy 1919–1939, 3rd Series, vol. I, ed. L. Woodward and R. Butler (London, 1949)
2nd Series, vol. 14, ed. W. Medlicott *et al.* (London, 1976)
15, ibid. (London, 1976)
16, ibid. (London, 1977)
17, ibid. (London, 1979)
18, ibid. (London, 1980)
19, ibid. (London, 1982)
Foreign Office Correspondence (Public Record Office, London).
Halifax Papers (ibid.).
Neville Chamberlain Papers (Birmingham University Library).
Parliamentary Debates: the House of Commons.
Beatrice Webb: Diary (British Library of Political and Economic Sciences).

3 Czechoslovakia

Das Abkommen von München 1938, ed. V. Král (Prague, 1968).

4 France

Documents Diplomatiques Français 1932–1939, 1st Series, vol. 2, ed. M. Baumont *et al.* (Paris, 1966).
vol. 3, ibid., (Paris, 1967).
4, ibid., (Paris, 1968).
5, ibid., (Paris, 1970).
6, ibid., (Paris, 1972).
7, ibid., (Paris, 1979).
8, ibid., (Paris, 1979).

9, ibid., (Paris, 1980).
10, ibid., (Paris, 1981).
2nd Series, Vol. 1, ed. M. Baumont *et al.* (Paris, 1963).
2, ibid., (Paris, 1964).
3, ibid., (Paris, 1966).
4, ibid., (Paris, 1967).
5, ibid., (Paris, 1968).
6, ibid., (Paris, 1970).
7, ibid., (Paris, 1972).
8, ibid., (Paris, 1973).
9, ibid., (Paris, 1974).
10, ibid., (Paris, 1976).
11, ibid., (Paris, 1977).
12, ibid., (Paris, 1978).
13, ibid., (Paris, 1979).
14, ibid., (Paris, 1980).
15, ibid., (Paris, 1981).

5 Germany

Diplomatic Correspondence (Photostats, FCO Library and Records, London).
Documents on German Foreign Policy 1918–1945, Series C, vol. I, ed. P. Sweet *et al.* (London, 1957).
vol. 2, ibid., (London, 1959).
3, ibid., (London, 1959).
4, ibid., (London, 1962).
5, ibid., (London, 1966).
6, ed. M. Lambert *et al.* (London, 1983).
Series D, vol. 1, ed. J. Sontag *et al.* (London, 1949).
2, ibid., (London, 1950).
3, ed. B. Schmitt *et al.* (London, 1951).
4, ibid., (London, 1951).
Dokumente der Deutschen Politik und Geschichte von 1848 bis zur Gegenwart. vol. 4: Die Zeit der nationalsozialistischen Diktatur 1933–1945, Aufbau und Entwicklung 1933–1938, ed. K. Hohfeld (Berlin,?).
Hitler, A., *Mein Kampf*, ed. D. Watt (London, 1969).
Protsess o Podzhoge Reikhstaga i Georgii Dimitrov: Dokumenty, ed. G. Berngard et al., vol. I (Moscow, 1981).

6 Italy

Ciano, G., *Diario 1937–1943*, ed. R. de Felice (Milan, 1980).
Diplomatic Correspondence (Farnesina, Rome).
Documenti Diplomatici Italiani, 8th Series, vol. XII, ed. M. Toscano *et al.* (Rome, 1952).
Togliatti, P., *Opere*, III, 2, ed. E. Ragionieri (Rome, 1973).
Togliatti, P., *Opere*, IV, 1, ed. F. Andreucci, P. Spiano (Rome, 1979).

7 Poland

Diariusz i Teki Jana Szembeka (1935–1945), vol. IV, ed. J. Zarański (London, 1972).
Dokumenty Komunistycznej Partii Polski 1935–1938 (Warsaw, 1968).
J. Lipski, Diplomat in Berlin 1933–1939, ed. W. Jedrzejewicz (London, 1968).
Papers and Memoirs of Juliusz Lukasiewicz, Ambassador of Poland, Diplomat in Paris 1936–1939, ed. W. Jedrzejewicz (London, 1970).

8 Portugal

Dez Anos de Politica Externa (1936–1947), vol. 3 (Lisbon, 1964).

9 Spain

Azaña, M., *Obras Completas*, 3 (Mexico, 1967).

10 The USA

J. Davies, *Mission to Moscow* (London, 1942).
Foreign Relations of the United States, The Soviet Union 1933–1939 (Washington, 1952).
For the President, Personal and Secret: Correspondence Between Franklin D. Roosevelt and William C. Bullitt, ed. O. Bullitt (London, 1973).

Periodicals

Bol'shevik
Cahiers du Bolchévisme
Cahiers d'Histoire de l'Institut Maurice Thorez
Cuadernos Para el Diálogo (Madrid)
Dageus Nyheter
The Economist
l'Humanité
International Press Correspondence
Izvestiya
Le Journal de Moscou
Keesing's Contemporary Archives
Kommunist
Kommunisticheskaya Revolyutsiya
Kommunisticheskii Internatsional
Krasnaya Zvezda
Kultura (Paris)
Mirovoe Khozyaistvo i Mirovaya Politika
Le Monde
Moskauer Rundschau
Moskva
The New Leader
Novy Mir
Pamyat' (Paris)
Posev (Munich)
Pravda
Prometei
Rundschau (Basel)
The Saturday Evening Post
Sotsialisticheskii Vestnik (Paris)
Survey (London)
Le Temps
The Times
Trud
Voenno-Istoricheskii Zhurnal
Voprosy Istorii KPSS
World News and Views (London)
Yunost'

Memoirs

Antonov-Ovseenko, A., *Portret Tirana* (New York, 1980).
Azaña, M., *Memorias Politicas y de Guerra*, vol. 4 (Madrid, 1981).
de Azcárate, P. *Mi embjada en Londres durante la guerra civil española* (Barcelona, 1976).
Barmine, A., *One Who Survived* (New York, 1945).
Basseches, N., *Stalin* (London, 1952).
Beck, J., *Dernier Rapport: Politique Polonaise. 1926–1939* (Paris, 1951).
Bohlen, C., *Witness to History* (New York, 1973).
Comnène, P., *Preludi del Grande Dramma (Ricordi e documenti di un diplomatico)* (Rome, 1947).
Coulondre, R., *De Staline à Hitler: Souvenirs de Deux Ambassades 1936–1939* (Paris, 1950).
Eden, Sir A., *The Memoirs of Anthony Eden. Facing the Dictators* (London, 1962).
Erenburg, I., *Sobranie Sochinenii v Devyati Tomakh, Vol. 9: Lyudi, Gody, Zhizn'* (Moscow, 1967).
Fischer, E., *An Opposing Man* (London, 1974).
Fischer, L., *Men and Politics: An Autobiography* (London, 1941).
——, *The Life and Death of Stalin* (London, 1953.
Gnedin, E., *Iz Istorii Otnoshenii Mezhdu SSSR i Fashistskoi Germaniei: Dokumenty i Sovremennye Kommentarii* (New York, 1977).
——, *Katastrofa i Vtoroe Rozhdenie: Memuarnye Zapiski* (Amsterdam, 1977).
von Herwarth, J., *Against Two Evils* (London, 1981).
Hilger, G. (with A. Meyer), *The Incompatible Allies: A Memoir-History of German–Soviet Relations 1918–1941* (New York, 1953).
Kraminov, D., *V Orbite Voiny: Zapiski Sovetskogo Korrespondenta za Rubezhom 1939–1945 Gody* (Moscow, 1980).
Kuusinen, A., *Before and After Stalin* (London, 1974).
Kuznetsov, N., *Na Dalekom Meridiane* (Moscow, 1971).
Largo Caballero, F., *Mis Recuerdos: Cartas a un amigo* (Mexico, 1976).
Litvinov, I., *She Knew She Was Right* (London, 1971).
Luciani, G., *Six Ans à Moscou* (Paris, 1937).
Lyons, E., *Assignment in Utopia* (London, 1938).
Maisky, I., *The Munich Drama* (Moscow, 1972).
——, *Spanish Notebooks* (London, 1966).
——, *Vospominaniya Sovetskogo Diplomata 1925–1945gg* (Moscow, 1971. 2nd edn, Tashkent, 1980).
Marshal Tukhachevskii: Vospominaniya Druzei i Soratnikov (Moscow, 1965).
The Memoirs of Dr Eduard Beneš (London, 1954).
The Memoirs of Lord Gladwyn (London 1972)
Meretskov, K., *Na Sluzhbe Narodu: Stranitsy Vospominanii* (Moscow, 1968).
Mikhail Kol'tsov, Kakim On Byl: Vospominaniya (Moscow, 1965).
Modesto, J., *Soy del Quinto Regimiento* (Paris, 1969).
Moravec, F., *Master of Spies* (London, 1981).
Murray, N., *I Spied for Stalin* (London, 1956).
My – Internatsionalisty: Vospominaniya Sovetskikh Dobrovol'tsev-Uchastnikov Natsional'no-Revolyutsionnoi Voiny v Ispanii (Moscow, 1975).
Orlov, A., *A Secret History of Stalin's Crimes* (London, 1954).

Pal'gunov, I., *Tridtsat' Let (Vospominaniya Zhurnalista i Diplomata)* (Moscow, 1964).
Poretsky, E., *Our Own People: A Memoirs of "Ignace Reiss" and His Friends* (London, 1969).
Rodimtsev, A., *Pod Nebom Ispanii* (Moscow, 1968).
Tabouis, G., *Vingt ans de 'suspense' diplomatique* (Paris, 1958).
Vidali, V., *La caduta della republica* (Milan, 1979).

SECONDARY WORKS

Akshinskii, V., *Kliment Efremovich Voroshilov: Biograficheskii Ocherk* (Moscow, 1974).
Aster, S., *1939: The Making of the Second World War* (London, 1973).
Beloff, M., *The Foreign Policy of Soviet Russia 1929–1941*, vol. 1 (London, 1947), vol. 2 (London, 1949).
Benvenuti, F., "Kirov nella politica sovietica", *Annali dell'Istituto Italiano per gli Studi Storici*, IV, 1973/1975 (Naples, 1979).
Berstein, S., *Le 6 février 1934* (Paris, 1975).
Biernat, K., Krashaar, L., *Organizatsiya Shul'tse-Boizena-Kharnaka v Antifashistskoi Bor'be* (Moscow, 1974).
Blank, A., *V Serdtse 'Tret'ego Reikha'* (Moscow, 1974).
B. Bolloten, *LA REVOLUCIÓN ESPAÑOLA: Sus orígenes, la izquierda y la lucha por el poder durante la guerra civil 1936–1939* (revised and enlarged edition, Barcelona 1980).
Brower, D., *The New Jacobins: The French Communist Party and the Popular Front* (New York, 1966).
Carabantes, A., Cimorra, E., *Un mito llamado Pasionaria* (Barcelona, 1982).
Carr, E., *Foundations of a Planned Economy*, vol. 2 (London, 1971).
——, *Socialism in One Country*, vol. 3 (London, 1964).
——, *The Twilight of Comintern, 1930–35* (London, 1982).
Carr, E., Davies, R., *Foundations of a Planned Economy 1926–1929*, 1, 2 (London, 1969).
Carswell, J., *The Exile: A Life of Ivy Litvinov* (London, 1983).
Cattell, D., *Communism and the Spanish Civil War* (California, 1956).
——, *Soviet Diplomacy and the Spanish Civil War* (California, 1956).
Chugaev, V., *V Bor'be Protiv Fashizma i Ugroz Voiny: Iz Istorii Internatsional'noi Solidarnosti Trudyashchikhsya Pol'shi i Zapadnoi Ukrainy v Bor'be Protiv Nastupleniya Fashizma i Rosta Voennoi Opasnosti 1933–1939* (Kiev, 1980).
Coates, W. and Z., *A History of Anglo-Soviet Relations* (London, 1943).
Colvin, I., *The Chamberlain Cabinet* (London, 1971).
——, *Vansittart in Office* (London, 1965).
Coverdale, J., *Italian Intervention in the Spanish Civil War* (Princeton, 1975).
Deacon, R. (pseud.), *With My Little Eye: Memoirs of a Spy Hunter* (London, 1982).
Duroselle, J-B., *La Décadence 1932–1939* (Paris, 1979).
Egorov, P., *Marshal Meretskov* (Moscow, 1974).
Erickson, J., *The Soviet High Command 1918–1941* (London, 1962).
de Felice, R., *Mussolini il duce. I. Gli anni del consenso 1929–1936* (Turin, 1974).
Georgii Dimitrov: an Outstanding Militant of the Comintern (Sofia, 1972).

Gibbs, N., *Grand Strategy*, vol. I (London, 1976).
Gilbert, M., *Winston S. Churchill*, vol. v, 1922–1939 (London, 1976).
Gladkov, T., Smirnov, M., *Menzhinskii* (Moscow, 1969).
Guerra y Revolución en España 1936–1939, vol. 2, ed. D. Ibárruri *et al.* (Moscow, 1966).
Hajek, M., *Storia dell'internazionale comunista (1921–1935): la politica del fronte unico* (Rome, 1969).
Haslam, J., *Soviet Foreign Policy, 1930–33: the Impact of the Depression* (London, 1983).
——, "The Comintern and the Origins of the Popular Front 1934–1935", *The Historical Journal*, 22, 3 (1979).
Henri, E., *Hitler Over Europe?* (London, 1936).
Hinsley, F., *British Intelligence in the Second World War*, vol. I (London, 1979).
Istoriya Vneshnei Politiki SSSR 1917–1945, ed., A. Berezkin *et al.* (Moscow, 1980).
Istoriya Vtoroi Mirovoi Voiny, vol. I (Moscow, 1973).
Jakobson, M., *The Diplomacy of the Winter War: an Account of the Russo-Finnish War 1939–1940* (Camb., Mass., 1961).
Kommunisticheskii Internatsional: Kratkii Istoricheskii Ocherk (Moscow, 1969).
Kopansky, Ya., *Internatsional'naya Solidarnost' s Bor'boi Trudyashchikhsya Bessarabii za Vossoedinenie s Sovetskoi Rodinoi (1918–1940)* (Kishinev, 1975).
Korol'kov, Yu., *Chelovek, Dlya Kotorogo Ne Bylo Tain (Rikhard Zorge)* (Moscow, 1965).
Kowalski, J., *Kommunistyczna Partia Polski 1935–1938: Studium Historyczne* (Warsaw, 1975).
Leibzon, B., Shirinya, K., *Povorot v Politike Kominterna* (2nd ed, Moscow, 1975).
Malerbe, P., Tuñon de Lara, *et al.*, *Historia de España*, IX – *La Crisis del Estado: Dictadura, República, Guerra (1923–1939)* (Barcelona, 1981).
Meshcheryakov, M., *Vsya Zhizn' – Bor'ba (O Khose Diase)* (Moscow, 1971).
Niclauss, K., *Die Sowjetunion und Hitlers Machtergriefung. Eine Studie über die deutsch-russischen Beziehungen der Jahre 1929–1935* (Bonn, 1966).
Parker, R., "Great Britain, France and the Ethiopian Crisis", *The English Historical Review*, vol. LXXXIX, 1974.
Petrov, Yu., *Stroitel'stvo Politorganov, Partiinykh i Komsomol'skikh Organizatsii Armii i Flota* (Moscow, 1968).
Procacci, G., *Il socialismo internazionale e la guerra d'Etiopia* (Rome, 1978).
Rigby, T., *Communist Party Membership in the USSR 1917–1967* (Princeton, 1968).
VII Kongress Kominterna i Bor'ba za Sozdanie Narodnogo Fronta v Stranakh Tsentral'noi i Yugo-Vostochnoi Evropy, ed. A. Klevanskii *et al.* (Moscow, 1977).
Shevyakov, A., *Sovetsko-Rumyanskie Otnosheniya i Problema Evropeiskei Bezopasnosti 1932–1939* (Moscow, 1977).
Shirinya, K., *Strategiya i Taktika Kominterna v Bor'be Protiv Fashizma i Voiny (1934–1939gg)* (Moscow, 1979).
Sipols, V., *Sovetskii Soyuz v Bor'be za Mir i Bezopasnost' 1933–1939* (Moscow, 1974).
Vneshnyaya Politika Sovetskogo Soyuza 1933–1939gg (Moscow, 1980).
SSSR v Bor'be Protiv Fashistskoi Agressii 1933–1945, ed. A. Narochnitskii *et al.* (Moscow, 1979).
Stanislawska, S., *Wielka i Mala Polytika Józefa Becka (marzec–maj 1938)* (Warsaw, 1962).
Tanner, V., *The Winter War: Finland Against Russia 1939–1940* (Stanford, 1957).

Thomas, H., *The Spanish Civil War* (3rd edn, London, 1977).
Tillett, L., "The Soviet Role in League Sanctions Against Italy, 1935–6", *The American Slavic and East European Review*, 1956, vol. xv.
Trotsky, L., *The Spanish Revolution (1931–39)* (New York, 1973).
Viñas, A., *La Alemania nazi y el 18 julio* (2nd edn, Madrid, 1977).
El Oro de Moscú: Alfa y omega de un mito franquista (Barcelona, 1979).
Wählbäck, K., *Finlandsfrågan i svensk politik 1937–1940* (Stockholm, 1964).
Weinberg, G., *The Foreign Policy of Hitler's Germany: Diplomatic Revolution in Europe 1933–1936* (Chicago, 1970).
W Kregu Historii (Warsaw, 1970).
Zhukovski, N., *Na Diplomaticheskom Postu* (Moscow, 1973).

Index